66-22284 (12-1-66)

George the Magnificent

George IV

From the unfinished portrait by Sir Thomas Lawrence
in the National Portrait Gallery, London

Joanna Richardson

GEORGE
THE MAGNIFICENT

A Portrait of King George IV

HARCOURT, BRACE & WORLD, INC.

New York

For

ENID

with love

Preface

George the Fourth lived through a time of immense political upheaval. The American War of Independence broke out in the year of his thirteenth birthday; the Declaration of Independence was made before he reached the age of fourteen. When he was a young man, at the end of the eighteenth century, the Ottoman Empire seemed to be on the point of falling apart; when he was middle-aged, South America was shaken by revolution.

As for Europe, it remained in almost perpetual ferment. In 1789, at Brighton, he could see the *émigrés* land from France, driven ashore in England by the French Revolution. There followed the execution of Louis XVI and Marie-Antoinette; and those in England who condemned the extravagance of the Prince of Wales were very ready to draw the implicit moral. As a pamphleteer observed, in a public letter to him:

It was owing to the scandalous waste, profligacy and profusion of the Court of Versailles, and of its worthless Princes, that the former has been deservedly annihilated, and the latter become despicable, and degraded mendicants! . . . The sad reverse which the French Princes have experienced, ought not to be an unprofitable lesson to your Royal Highness.

Long before he ascended the throne, the Prince of Wales was reminded that absolute monarchy had had its day, that the divine right and rightness of kings was a debatable dogma. He learned that republicanism might raise its head even in those countries where the monarchy seemed to be most revered.

The French Revolution was followed by the Consulate and the Directory, the First Empire, and the protracted Napoleonic Wars. Throughout his manhood, the Prince of Wales was constantly

vii

reminded of France. He pleaded, in vain, with his father to be given a military command when there was a threat of French invasion. In 1805 he mourned the death of Nelson, his friend, "the greatest character England could ever boast of," at Trafalgar; and in 1815, as Regent, he received the imperial trophies which Wellington, "my friend Arthur," had captured at Waterloo. It was the Regent who rightly refused Napoleon asylum in England (though he issued orders to provide for his "gratification and comfort" at St. Helena). The Regent may have been partly responsible for the Bourbon Restoration in 1814; he saw not only the reign of Louis XVIII, *le Préfet d'Angleterre*, as they called him in France, but nearly all the reign of Charles X. Had he lived a few months longer, he would have witnessed the July Revolution of 1830, and the accession of Louis-Philippe, the Citizen King.

George IV did not only watch the old order changing, the move from absolute sovereignty to bourgeois monarchy. During his lifetime—and his life was not so long, by modern measures—almost every country in Europe learned the meaning of war. The Napoleonic campaigns swept from Portugal to Russia, from Denmark to Italy, and, further south, to the continent of Africa. The Napoleonic adventure dominated the age. The French Revolution had made it possible; French history, after Waterloo, was determined by it. And so, for a number of years, was the Georgian Age. When George, Prince of Wales, was seven years old, Napoleon was born. When George IV, aged fifty-eight, prepared for his Coronation, Napoleon died in exile. In the interval, Napoleon had given superlative prestige to British arms. He had enabled the regency, in particular, to be claimed as "the brightest portion of British history."

The age of George IV was an age of political upheaval, of protracted war and artistic achievement; it was also an age of far-reaching social change. It saw not only the French Revolution, but the birth of the English Industrial Revolution. It saw the beginning of the railways, and faster transport by sea; it saw the increasing use of gas-light, the increasing use of machines. It saw new discoveries in science and in medicine; and Captain Parry, proposing an expedition to the North Pole, enquired ardently: "Might it not tend to raise Great Britain in the eyes of every civilised Nation, that, while a spot upon the earth remains untrodden by the foot of man, her Subjects should be employed in exploring it?" The age of George IV saw, most significant of all, the broadening of education, the rise of the middle classes, the first signs of the adjustment of the whole social structure. It might be called the age when the modern world began.

No-one was more fitted to be King of England at this brilliant, significant moment in history than King George IV. He had extraordinary natural royalty, he had some of the happiest virtues of the aristocracy (a cultivated aesthetic sense, a versatile, well-trained mind, a proper understanding of patronage). He also possessed—and few of his forebears had known it to such a degree—a real love of his country and his people. He was a patriot, in the best sense of that excellent word. He had a true feeling for distinction, a noble and a fertile creative instinct. He left an unequalled legacy of achievement. He could charm Byron and entertain Wellington; he could also talk, as an equal, to a valet or an Irish peasant. He was magnificently royal, and he had a common touch. He united, and understood, the old order and the new.

Contents

List of Illustrations

LIST OF ILLUSTRATIONS

Introduction

'He was admitted by all to be the most accomplished man of his age.' So the Duke of Wellington reminded the House of Lords, three days after George IV had died.

Such eulogies may be habitual on the death of kings, but on this occasion they rang true. George IV was the most accomplished King of England since Charles I; and as Prince of Wales, as Regent, and as King, he had fostered the arts and sciences, he had encouraged scholarship and taste as only the truly civilised could do. He had been deeply involved, all his life, in the art of living. He had made friends of men whose achievements had adorned the age. He had been a superbly creative King, and left his generous mark on the life of his epoch. As Sir Max Beerbohm would write, one day, in his essay, *King George the Fourth*: 'George was a splendid patron . . . Indeed, he inspired Society with a love of something more than mere pleasures, a love of the "humaner delights". He was a giver of tone . . .' As Mr. Roger Fulford would observe, years later, 'He did more than any other man before him, or after, to develop the art of living in England.'

This aspect of King George the Fourth has always been neglected. The splendid patron has been dismissed as a squandering dilettante; the lover of humaner delights has been dismissed as the faithless husband and philanderer, the artificial figure whom Thackeray condemned. I have tried to focus the sights more correctly: to assess the creative achievement of King George the Fourth, and to re-assess his simple, complex, vexing and quite fascinating nature. This is not a political study, or a simple repetition of the vagaries of his

xv

private life. It is, I hope, a more just appreciation of his character and achievement.

I must acknowledge the gracious permission of Her Majesty the Queen to republish extracts from *The Correspondence of George, Prince of Wales* (published by Cassell & Co.), and *The Letters of George IV* (published by the Cambridge University Press). Both these works were edited by Professor A. Aspinall.

I am grateful to the Librarian of the Royal Society for permission to use the Society's archives, and to the Librarian of the Royal Academy of Arts, who allowed me to consult the papers of Sir Thomas Lawrence and the Council Minutes of the Academy. I gladly record my gratitude to Mrs. L. M. Patterson, the Secretary of the Royal Society of Literature, for giving me the freedom of the Society's papers. I am indebted to Mr. J. G. Broadbent, the Secretary of the Royal Literary Fund, who let me examine the documents in his care; and to Mrs. Gleed, of the Royal Society of Musicians. I owe my thanks to Mr. D. G. C. Allan, Curator-Librarian of the Royal Society of Arts, who allowed me to consult the Society Minutes; and to Mr. L. M. Payne, Librarian of the Royal College of Physicians, who let me use books and manuscripts at the College. I am grateful to Mr. W. R. LeFanu, Librarian of of the Royal College of Surgeons, who showed me the Baillie-Hunter letters in his archives; and I am glad to acknowledge the help of Dr. R. W. Hunt, Keeper of Western Manuscripts, who let me quote from papers in the Bodleian Library, Oxford.

The following kindly answered enquiries: Mr. Martin Davies (the National Gallery); Sir Mortimer Wheeler (the British Academy); Mr. John Harris (the Royal Institute of British Architects); Mr. K. D. C. Vernon (the Royal Institution); Mr. D. S. Porter (Department of Western Manuscripts, the Bodleian Library). I am most grateful to the Bishop of Worcester and Mrs. Charles-Edwards for their kind hospitality, and for letting me use the papers of Bishop Hurd. I gladly express my thanks to Lord Croft, who told me about his ancestor, Sir Richard Croft, and about the Conyngham family; I am grateful to Mr. Robert Speaight, who helped me to discuss the King and Rossini; and to my father, for translating the letters of Canova. I must thank the staff of the North Library at the

British Museum, who supplied me with so many books, and the staff of the Bodleian Library, who helped me with my work on the Finch Papers.

I am most grateful to Winifreda, Countess Portarlington, who has generously allowed me to reproduce two Cosway miniatures, and a painting of George IV, as Prince of Wales, by Reynolds; the latter is reproduced here for the first time. I should like to thank the Earl of Jersey for letting me use the portrait of Frances, Lady Jersey, by Hoppner. I am also indebted to Mr. Clifford Musgrave, Director of the Royal Pavilion Estate, who helped to obtain the illustrations of the Royal Pavilion and Chantrey's statue of George IV at Brighton.

J. R.

Hampstead
1966

George the Magnificent

PART ONE

Prince of Wales

I

ON 12 August 1762, within a year of her marriage to
George III, Charlotte of Mecklenburg-Strelitz gave
birth to his heir. The new prince entered his father's kingdom at twenty-four minutes past seven in the evening, and
when a messenger gave the King the news, the delighted
monarch presented him with £500. It was a time for
munificence: earlier that day the immense riches taken in a
Spanish galleon had passed St. James's Palace on their way
to the Bank of England. 'All was joy, merriment and gladness
in London.'(1) The infant had had a splendid, appropriate
coming.

Prayers of thanksgiving were duly said, and loyal
addresses were suitably presented. On the fifth day after his
birth, the child was created twenty-first Prince of Wales.
On 18 September he was christened George Augustus
Frederick. He had his own infantine establishment: Lady
Charlotte Finch, somewhat prematurely. became his governess; Mrs. Henrietta Coultworth became her deputy. There
were also a wet-nurse and a dry-nurse, a necessary woman,
and two rockers for the cradle. Fraulein Albert (later Mrs.
Papendiek), the Queen's assistant keeper of the wardrobe,
recalled that the dominant figure was the dry-nurse, Mrs.
Chapman:

> She was a fine, active woman, and it may be truly said

1

that while she lived, about twelve years, everything was
well done, with an affection supported by truth and sincerity. Her daughter, Miss Chapman, was appointed
sempstress to the young Prince, which appointment was
continued to the succeeding eight children. Their frocks
were of cambric, the tucks and hems being hem-stitched
with Valenciennes lace tuckers and cuffs for the evening;
plain for the morning. This place was no sinecure.(2)

As for the Prince of Wales himself, he had entered public
life before he was twelve days old. He was put on show at
St. James's Palace, from one o'clock till three, on drawing-
room days. So many of the nobility accepted Queen Charlotte's invitation to see him, and the caudle and cake that
she provided, that the daily expense for cake was £40. Part
of the apartment was latticed off, in the Chinese style, to
prevent the visitors from touching their future King. It was
an unhygienic exhibition.

On St. David's Day, 1765, when the Prince was two and
seven months, he received his first public address. The
Governors of the Society of Ancient Britons came to beg
his patronage for a Welsh charitable institution. The Prince
had been taught by his parents to deliver a formal answer,
and pronounced his single sentence of thanks 'with great
propriety and suitableness of action'.(3) He presented the
treasurer with £100.

That year he was elected a Knight Companion of the
Most Noble Order of the Garter.

And yet his childhood was not merely a series of premature public appearances: it was not just a record of enforced
precocity, of pomp and circumstance imposed on a bewildered little boy. The Prince was looked after with 'unexampled care'. King George III and Queen Charlotte were
remarkably domestic, and the life at the palace at Kew, as
Mrs. Papendiek recorded it in her journal, had an idyllic
quality about it.

The royal establishment at Kew, in the 1770s, was a com-
munity of friends and dependents. The royal governess,

Lady Charlotte Finch, had her separate house; so did the clerk of the works, Mr. Kirby (the father of Mrs. Trimmer, the writer on education); and the two fenced-off houses had gates which led into the royal gardens. In the Queen's house lived the sub-governess, Mrs. Coultworth, and the English teacher, Miss Margaret Planta, who was 'quiet, patient, plodding, persevering'.(4) Mr. Montagu, the riding master, was also riding attendant to the King; and such was His Majesty's addiction to early rising that Mr. and Mrs. Montagu had to breakfast every morning at half-past four.

If the King believed in early rising, the Queen believed in health; she not only had the Prince of Wales inoculated for smallpox, she had two doctors 'always on the spot to watch the constitutions of the royal children, to eradicate, if possible, or at least to keep under, the dreadful disease, scrofula, inherited from the King. She herself saw them bathed at six every morning, attended the schoolroom of her daughters, was present at their dinner, and directed their attire, whenever these arrangements did not interfere with public duties.'(5)

It was a gentle, Morland world. Mrs. Clewly at the farm-house supplied the milk and butter, the eggs, pork and bacon. In the timber yard worked Warren, the King's carpenter. In the Queen's bijou flower-garden, up Richmond Lane, her gardener, Mr. Green, grew orange trees. Since the King and Queen believed in economy, poor Green was not allowed the extravagance of enlarging his hothouses; and the thought that his cherished trees were dwarfed, and would never yield fruit 'as fine as our ripened China orange', nearly broke his heart. The Prince of Wales and his younger brother, Frederick, Duke of York, had their personal experience of agricultural economy: they dug their own piece of ground at Kew, sowed it with wheat, reaped and harvested the crop, winnowed it and baked their own loaves of bread. The King and Queen, wrote Robert Huish, the Prince's biographer, 'partook of the philosophical repast, and beheld with pleasure the very amusements of their children rendered the source of useful knowledge.'(6)

By 1773 the Prince and the Duke had moved to a separate

3

house, with their governor, the Earl of Holderness, and their sub-governors, while the three Miss Ducks were appointed housekeepers for their joint lives. The three Miss Ducks 'were by no means prepossessing, but clever, sensible women, and in the absence of the Royal Family entered into society with a friendly though rather constrained politeness'.(7) The Kew establishment also included Johann Christian Bach, the composer's youngest son. The most elegant and worldly of Bach's children, he was music master in the Queen's household; he taught the princesses and the Queen, and gave evening concerts for the King. Mrs. Delany, the widow of Swift's friend, often visited the Queen's Lodge when the royal children were young, and she usually found the King on the floor romping with his family, while the royal band in the next room received his directions as to what they should play, Handel being the favourite. The Prince of Wales was probably introduced to Handel's music before he was two years old, for early in 1764, 'the little Wizard', Wolfgang Amadeus Mozart (who was not past his ninth year himself), had been summoned to play at Buckingham House; the King had listened astounded as the child sat down at the organ, and improvised on the continuo of one of Handel's airs.

In 1776, Mrs. Papendiek remembered, the public were admitted to Richmond Gardens on Sundays, and to Kew Gardens on Thursdays. 'The Green on these days was covered with carriages, more than 300 being often taken at the bridge on Sundays. Their Majesties were often to be seen at the windows speaking to their friends, and the royal children amusing themselves in their own gardens. Parties came up by water, too, with bands of music, to the aït opposite the Prince of Wales's house. The whole was a scene of enchantment and delight; Royalty living amongst their subjects to give pleasure and to do good.'(8)

The days passed at Kew with charming domestic regularity. After an early dinner at four o'clock, the King and Queen would gather their children round them, and visitors according to their ages. There were birthday enter-tainments, dances, firework displays, 'and amusements adapted to their several tastes'.(9) The elder princes and princesses attended the Queen's small evening parties at Kew, just as they attended those at St. James's Palace, or at Buckingham House, the handsome, red brick Queen's House at the end of the Mall.

In London, from his infancy, the Prince of Wales had always gone to the Thursday Drawing-Rooms; and from the age of ten he and the Duke of York had always attended the evening parties from eight till ten o'clock. These parties were held on Tuesdays and Thursdays, when two or three hundred people would be invited to cards or to music. The concert was given by the King's private band and two or three other performers, and among these were Stanley, the organist, and John Crosdill, the violoncellist. Once a week, the King and Queen went to the theatre. The Prince of Wales himself went to Covent Garden before he was five, to see *The Fairy Favour*, a children's operetta with music by J. C. Bach, which was specially given for him; and, since Bach was in royal favour, the Prince later attended his opera *Caratacco*.(10) The Prince was also made aware of the world of art; for the first royal commission given to that elegant artist, John Zoffany, was to paint the Prince of Wales and the Duke of York as cupids. The picture has unaccountably vanished, but two other pictures by Zoffany still record the Prince's childhood: one shows him in the park at Windsor, with his mother and her two brothers from Mecklenburg-Strelitz; the other shows him, with his sister, the Princess Royal, in Queen Charlotte's dressing-room in old Buckingham House. The Prince is wearing Roman military costume, and the Princess is dressed in Oriental style.(11) Thomas Gainsborough, commissioned to paint the royal children, 'was all but raving mad with ecstasy in beholding such a constellation of youthful beauty'.(12)

2

On 12 April 1771, when the Prince was nine, and the Duke of York was eight, Dr. William Markham was appointed their preceptor. He was eminently qualified for the post. Educated at Westminster and Christ Church, Oxford, he had been a much loved and much respected headmaster of his old school. 'As an instructor he had no equal', wrote a later Westminster.

> It is difficult to say whether he most excelled in the manner of conveying knowledge, or in exciting youth to laudable pursuits. His knowledge of Greek and Roman literature was universal; his taste pure. ... He was at the same time so perfectly master of different incentives for different dispositions, that the studious were ever ambitious of his praise, and the idle feared his rebuke.(*13*)

In 1767 Dr. Markham had left Westminster to become Dean of his college at Oxford. In January 1771, three months before his royal appointment, he had been made Bishop of Chester; he now divided his time between his college, his cathedral, and a house near Kew, called Sion End, where, for a short time every year, he could supervise the two eldest princes at Kew Palace.

He earned their attention and their devotion. At the age of twelve, the Prince of Wales wrote: 'The time since you went seems to have passed very slow, for I always must think so when you are not with us. Your good instruction, your kindness, your good nature will never be effaced from my heart.'(*14*) No doubt the Prince of Wales owed much of his taste for the classics to his 'dear and much-loved Friend', Dr. Markham; years later, when he had grown to manhood, he still assured him that he remained his 'old and most gratefully attached pupil'.(*15*) Dr. Markham fostered the best traits of the Prince of Wales; his natural taste, and his natural warmth of heart.

However, on 26 May 1776, the King undertook what he
called a 'painful task'; he sent for Dr. Markham and told
him that, as Lord Holderness, the Princes' governor, meant
to retire, he must also appoint a new preceptor. The
Princes, so His Majesty explained to Lord North, the Prime
Minister, 'would secretly feel a kind of victory if the Bishop
remained.'(*16*) Since Lord Holderness was retiring on
grounds of ill-health, there was no valid reason to dismiss
the Bishop whose wise, firm supervision was precisely what
the Princes needed. But George III showed little understanding of education. He presented Dr. Markham with a
handsome copy of the *Odes of Pindar*, and in December he
made him Archbishop of York. He was determined to sub-
due and control his eldest son.

Indeed, he seemed, even now, to be jealous of his heir,
and to be apprehensive of the day when he would come of
age. It was said that the Prince of Wales, at ten, had known
less of the world than any boy in the country; and Horace
Walpole wrote, in his *Journal,* that 'nothing could equal
the King's attention to seclude his son and protract his
nonage. It went so absurdly far, that he was made to wear
a shirt with a frilled collar like that of babies. He one day
took hold of his collar, and said to a domestic, *"See how I
am treated!"* '(*17*) The King was cold and unjust to the
Prince of Wales in his childhood; distant and suspicious
ever afterwards. His behaviour was to have disastrous re-
sults.

However, in May 1776, Dr. Markham was succeeded by
Dr. Richard Hurd, the Bishop of Lichfield and Coventry.
Dr. Hurd drew up his exacting *Plans of Study for the
Princes*,(*18*) which embraced religion and morals, history,
government and laws, mathematics, natural philosophy and
polite literature. In his history lessons, he warned his pupils
against 'the despotic and popish views of the Stewart
family';(*19*) in his lessons on civil government, he taught
them that, as Christians, they must 'give all due honour to
the Magistrates' and ignore 'the language of flattery, which
... degrades subjects to slaves, in order that it may lift

7

princes into the rank of GODS'.(*20*) The classics were regularly instilled into the Prince and his brother. 'My Dear Lord,' wrote the Prince of Wales to his new preceptor, in August,

> I am afraid that the inclosed translation will not prove so delicious a Morsel as yr. Lordship expected to receive, however I have tried to give it as good a relish as possible; but the Author is very difficult and I not at all versed in translation as yr. Lordship knows. Euclid goes on very well for we are in the middle of the third Book; and as to Livy, I have just left Canuleius prating away for marriage at a fine rate though I think he has the best of the Argument. We are in hopes of having a most glorious day at Windsor on Monday next. I have a new Mare, which without boasting, I may say is at least as good as yr. Lordships. We all long to see you again at Kew and [I] am
> > with the truest and sincerest affection
> > > your's
> > > > GEORGE P.(*21*)

Despite the riding at Kew and Windsor, the Princes worked intensively. 'Greek for some time omitted,' noted Dr. Hurd, 'except on Sunday mornings, when the Greek Testament is to be constantly read.'(*22*) It was in keeping with this rigorous education that Dr. Hurd sent the Prince of Wales some prayers as his new year present in 1780. 'If constantly used with seriousness and recollection,' he assured his pupil, 'these few prayers must have the happiest effect upon your virtues in this life, and upon your best hopes in another.'(*23*)

The exhortations were made in the year in which the Prince of Wales came of age. On 21 August, a few days after the Prince's eighteenth birthday, the Bishop had a long conference with the King, in which, he wrote, 'I explained to His Majesty at large what I had done in the education of the Princes, and for what reasons I could do no more.'(*24*) On 29 December, Dr. Hurd attended the King's levée at St. James's, when the lords and gentlemen of the Prince of Wales's establishment kissed hands. He then went to the Queen's House, 'and was introduced to the P.W. by his new Groom of the Stole, Lord Southampton, to take my leave of his R. Highness. ... Thus,' he wrote, 'ended my Preceptorship (of which I had felt the full weight) and, it seemed, to the satisfaction of their Majesties &c.' He added, with some feeling, '*Deo Gratias.*'(25)

It must be asked if this private and exacting education did more service to the Prince than a proper number of years at Eton and Oxford. He had assimilated, as his father wished, every kind of useful knowledge; he had spent eight hours a day learning languages and 'the liberal sciences'. He had become a classical scholar, a fluent speaker of French, Italian and German. He had formed sound literary tastes, he was already an impressive amateur singer, he had cultivated a taste in the fine arts. Crosdill had taught him to play the violoncello with commendable skill. Alexander Cozens, the elder (who later taught at Eton), had given him his lessons in landscape drawing. Henry Angelo, the famous fencing-master, had gone to Buckingham House to initiate him into the art of the *fleuret*. But no one had roused his lasting interest in the art of government; no one had taught him the principles of politics, or shown him the practical lessons of history in a manner he would always remember. No Fénelon had written a *Télémaque* for the prince who would one day rule a vast and growing empire. No one had given him unforgettable moral instruction. He had been left in ignorance of social conditions, and wilfully kept ignorant of the workings of the human mind. Queen Charlotte admired, and presumably practised, the chief principle laid down, in *The Economy of Charity*, by that excellent educationist, Mrs. Trimmer: people must be taught to help themselves. The King insisted that the outside world should be veiled from his son by 'all those who cirrounded you'.(26) To educate the heir to the Throne, with all his potential gifts, on such principles as these, was not merely ridiculous. It was deplorably irresponsible.

Indeed, the Prince's education anticipated that of Edward

VII: it was so restricted, so exacting, it so excluded human understanding, that any sensible observer might have predicted the result. The moment the Prince was allowed his freedom, he would be beyond control. As Huish wrote: 'the moment of his Royal Highness's emancipation was that of a prisoner released from confinement—it was the daring and boundless flight of the eagle, which had been long chained to the earth by some tyrannical power.'(27)

3

On New Year's Day, 1781, when Dr. Hurd had resigned, the Prince of Wales was introduced at Court as having attained his official majority. He had, that is, reached the age when, should he ascend the Throne, no regency would be thought necessary. However, though he was considered capable of governing the country, he was not yet considered old enough to enjoy a separate establishment. 'It is ever better,' wrote his father to Lord North, 'that Persons should feel their situations by degrees improve, and particularly young persons.'(28) He himself had been tied to his mother's apron-strings; he was determined that his son should remain under his roof. In Mrs. Papendiek's words, he wanted 'some little check ... sustained over his actions.'(29)

This was not the only time when George III was guided by the lamentable pattern of his past. But only the stubborn and unthinking would impose such rigid object lessons on their children. George III was docile, domestic, unambitious, conventional. His eldest son was impulsive, adventurous, ambitious and highly original. He was full-blooded and eighteen, and he had for years been repressed. He longed, as he said, to 'dash into the wide world'.

There is no doubt that the King meant well: 'Indeed my good Lord,' he told Bishop Hurd, 'we live in unprincipled days and no change can be expected but by an early attention to the Education of the rising generation.'(30) George III meant his son to be a sober and Godfearing

English gentleman; but he could hardly have found a more unlikely way to achieve his purpose.

However, the Prince of Wales was given a small allowance, and his own horses, while his governor and subgovernor remained, and he still lived with his parents at Buckingham House. 'All was to be gaiety itself in London this year, to attract the attention of the young Prince,' but he was not allowed to be attracted too deeply. Some time before his eighteenth birthday, he had been invited 'by some of the most distinguished nobility' to tour the country during the summer: to make a royal progress from one great country house to another. The Prince accepted eagerly, and preparations began; the King refused to give his consent. His ostensible excuse was that he intended to make a tour himself, in the Prince's company. In August they duly sailed to the Nore, visited the dockyard and fortifications, and returned to Chatham. This tour, says Robert Huish, 'met with the ridicule it deserved.'(31)

However, the musical parties continued at Buckingham House; and the Prince 'accompanied the piano on the violoncello with taste and precision'. He joined in 'the interesting quartett parties', which Giardini conducted, and adapted music for them. He was a director of the King's Concert of Ancient Music, and chose the programme for the first night's performance. He was already 'the great and liberal supporter of all musical concerns'.(32) He had received singing lessons from Sir William Parsons, the Master and Conductor of the King's Band; his voice was said to be good, and his technique very correct. 'He was a very effective member of the Noblemen's and Gentlemen's Catch and Glee Club at the Thatched House Tavern, which he attended very frequently, conversing with the utmost familiarity with all the professors'.(33)

No doubt, when the Court returned to Kew, he was eager to join the river parties, when 'the nobility, on fine afternoons, came up in boats, other boats being filled with bands of music, to take the Prince to the promenade at Richmond'. Mrs. Papendiek remembered how Mr. Zoffany, the portrait painter, had a decked sailing vessel, 'elegantly and conveniently fitted up'.(*34*) It was, more precisely, a shallop, painted green, pink and drab; and the servants' livery was scarlet and gold with blue facings, the heraldic colours of the coat-of-arms that had been granted to Zoffany by the Empress Maria Theresa. Tradition has it that Zoffany also had a summerhouse facing his house at Strand-on-the-Green. This was fixed to a tree, and projected over the river, and a covered way was built, connecting house and summerhouse, because the Prince had promised to attend a concert on Zoffany's shallop, and afterwards drink tea with Mrs. Zoffany.(*35*) One hopes that the overhead passage was used; but, alas, Mrs. Papendiek records that the Prince of Wales, officially of age, 'was always accompanied by his governor and sub-governor, and returned for the Queen's party in the evening'.(*36*)

The Prince of Wales would have been a poor example of manhood had he submitted tamely to the spinsterish domestic round; but, when he reached his sixteenth year, Mrs. Papendiek had already found the eagle stretching its wings. 'Much do I lament,' she wrote, 'that some of those about the young Prince swerved from principle, and introduced improper company when their Majesties supposed them to be at rest, and after the divines had closed their day with prayer.'(*37*) The Prince of Wales was naturally eager for human experience: for the passion, wit, audacity and rebellion that had been denied him. By the time he was eighteen, the world which, in his father's words, had been 'kept under a veil by all those who have cirrounded you', had been delightfully revealed to him.

'Your love of dissipation has for some months been with enough ill nature trumpeted in the public papers,' the King admonished him in a birthday letter.(*38*) The King's ideas of dissipation were puritan. It was said that he himself was amorous by nature, that he was only faithful from a sense of duty. Whatever the reason, he had been notoriously faithful to a plain wife, and he was disturbed to think that his son, on the verge of manhood, should enjoy impulsive love-affairs. However, the Prince, who was expected to give his father notice when he went to plays and operas, the Prince who was told he must always go to the royal box, attended by his equerries, had already found a more private interest in the theatre. He had seen Mary Robinson play Perdita in *A Winter's Tale*; he had contrived to meet her in the grounds of Kew Palace, he had given her his picture in a locket, and she had left her husband to be his mistress. 'The graces of his person,' she would recall in her *Memoirs*, 'the irresistible sweetness of his smile, the tenderness of his melodious yet manly voice, will be remembered by me, till every vision of this changing scene shall be forgotten.'(*39*)

The scene soon changed; and Mrs. Robinson, who had worn the Prince's picture round her neck, and had driven about 'with four nag tailed horses and two servants behind her', fell out of favour in 1781. It cost £5,000 to buy back the letters and written promises which the reckless Prince of Wales had sent her; and by April that year she had become, in his own words, 'ye old infernal cause Robinson.'(*40*) In 1785, her affairs were so hopeless that her possessions were auctioned; her portrait by Gainsborough was knocked down for 32 guineas, and passed into her former lover's hands. In time it passed into those of the Marquis of Hertford.(*41*) The Prince's love had not run deep; and while his pension of £500 may have helped Perdita to keep up her little cottage *orné* near Windsor, she spent the rest of her life embittered, and she died, nineteen years later, sinking under 'acute rheumatic disorders, aggravated by pecuniary distress'.(*42*)

She was only one of several women in whom the Prince took an interest. Nathaniel Wraxall, in his *Memoirs,* declares that even in the days of Mrs. Robinson, the Prince showed his attachment to Lady Augusta Campbell, a daughter of the Duchess of Argyll. He soon transferred his affections to Lady Melbourne, who was 'no longer in her first youth when she became the object of his admiration'.(*43*) Lady Melbourne was the kind of woman whom he would always admire; and even the critical Wraxall

13

described her with partiality. She had, he said, 'a commanding figure, exceeding the middle height, full of grace and
dignity, an animated countenance, intelligent features,
captivating manners and conversation; all these, and many
other attractions, enlivened by coquetry, met in Lady Melbourne.'(44) After a short interval, continues the memoir-
writer, Lady Melbourne was followed by Georgiana,
Duchess of Devonshire, 'but of what nature was that attachment and what limits were affixed to it by the Duchess,
must remain a matter of conjecture.'(45)

It would be unwise to accept all Wraxall's declarations
and innuendoes; but the Prince's correspondence must be
relied on. In January 1781, Colonel Gerard Lake, his First
Equerry, felt obliged to beg him not to write 'any more
letters to a certain sort of ladies, and I should hope that
what you have already suffered will be a sufficient warning'.(46) The Prince was not prepared to hear warnings.
In July, in an energetic letter which reflected the violence
of his feelings, he told his favourite brother, Frederick,
Duke of York, about his affair with Madame Hardenberg.

She was the wife of Karl August von Hardenberg, a
Hanoverian diplomat who hoped, one day, to be Minister at
the Court of St. James's. By some irony, the Prince of Wales
had first noticed her at Court, and first spoken to her at a
concert in the Queen's apartment. 'I perceived,' he told
his brother, 'yt. she was a very sensible, agreeable pleasant
little woman, but devilish severe. I thought no more of
her at yt. time.'(47) But the irony persisted; he met her
again in the Queen's apartment, when she was forced to
play cards with one of his sisters. 'I observed her to be
equally inattentive to her play, as I was,' he told Frederick,
'but I thought I met her eyes too frequently to fancy yt. it
proceeded from inattention or common curiosity only. . . .
From that moment ye. fatal tho' delightful passion arose
in my bosom.'(48)

Circumstances still contrived to intensify his passion. The
King invited the Hardenbergs to Windsor, and there they
spent a fortnight. The Prince 'dropped every other connex-

ion of whatever sort or kind, & devoted myself entirely to this angelick little woman'.(49) After a due display of reticence, Madame Hardenberg surrendered.

The *liaison* might have lasted longer if it had not been for an almost libellous statement in the press. The *Morning Herald* announced, said the Prince, 'yt. ye. German Baroness who had been imported by ye Queen, had taken a house next to Perdita's, in Cork Street, & yt. my carriage was seen constantly at her door.'(50) The statement was based on misunderstanding: it was a Polish Countess who had taken the house next to Perdita's, and it was the Duke of Gloucester's carriage which was seen outside her door nearly every day. However, Hardenberg, warned by a servant, told his wife that unless she wrote to the Prince, saying she would drop all connexion with him, he would suppose that she had been unfaithful.

When the Prince received her letter, he thought he 'should have run distracted'.(51) He told Hardenberg, gallantly, that his wife had always shown him the utmost coolness. To Madame Hardenberg he sent the most passionate letter. And, extremist as ever, he summoned Lord Southampton '& desired he wld. go into ye. King & ask his permission for me to go abroad'.(52) Southampton brought a sober answer: His Majesty could not think of letting the Prince of Wales leave the country in wartime. A few hours later came a note from Mme Hardenberg, 'saying she hoped I had not forgot all my vows, & would run off with her yt. night.'(53) In a moment of melodrama, the Prince saw himself as a penniless exile on the Continent, and his mistress 'perishing for want'.(54)

There was clearly no comfort to be gained from his dour, responsible father; and in a childlike burst of confidence, on the eve of his nineteenth birthday, the Prince of Wales sought advice from his mother. She, at least, would not see his distress without showing sympathy.

Queen Charlotte was soothingly maternal. After her son had fainted, and she had 'cried excessively',(55) she showed the practical side of her nature. As the Prince had no doubt hoped, she made the decision for him. She explained the affair to the King; and, within the week, the Hardenbergs had departed for Brussels.

It was left to the Duke of York to tell his brother of his happy escape. Mme Hardenberg was known for her easy virtue; she had made a determined if vain attempt to seduce the Duke himself. Her affair with the Prince of Wales had forced her husband to leave the Hanoverian service for that of Brunswick; her conduct in Brunswick compelled him to divorce her. It was, finally, in the Prussian service that Hardenberg earned distinction.

It was natural that the young, susceptible, highly emotional Prince should look for pleasures outside the ring of respectable ladies-in-waiting, outside 'our usual circle of old tabbies.'(56) It was perhaps natural that a young man, devoted to his mother, should so often have been drawn to older women. And while the Prince did not seek for mistresses of his mother's age, he usually liked the conventional maternal figure, and he needed a certain domination from a woman. His early, unimportant *liaisons* suggested the pattern that his later, deeper attachments were to follow.

Vital himself, he was also attracted by vitality. His warm and sometimes theatrical nature (and, perhaps, the puritan atmosphere of the Court) caused him to pursue his affairs with violence, and to choose, among his early mistresses, a number of flamboyant, theatrical women.

The youth who played Florizel to Perdita Robinson, and was obviously ensnared by the brash, determined Madame Hardenberg, also enjoyed the favours of Elizabeth Billington, the singer. Mrs. Billington has been dismissed as 'a second-rate public singer, who warbled at Covent Garden Theatre',(57) and she did indeed make her début there, in 1786, as Rosetta, in the opera *Love in a Village*. But she was hardly second-rate: she sang 'with such sweetness, taste and brilliancy' that later in the year she found herself 'at the head of the vocal corps' at a charity concert in Westminster Abbey, when the King and Queen themselves were present. She delighted Covent Garden in Arne's opera *Artaxerxes*, she sang triumphantly at Drury Lane; she sang at the fashionable Sunday concerts, when the Prince of Wales played an overture before more than four hundred of the *haut ton*. William Parke, one of the Prince's band, declared in his *Musical Memoirs* that she was a 'great and fascinating singer ... a true musical genius'. Married early to James Billington, 'a genteel young man, and an excellent double-bass player at Drury Lane Theatre', she must have responded eagerly to the Prince of Wales.(*58*)

4

But the prodigal lover already showed the more refined side of his nature. In August, 1781, the month after he had broken his liaison with Mme Hardenberg, he gave his patronage to Gainsborough, and sat several times at Schomberg House for a portrait of himself in military uniform, 'easily reclining on a massy sabre.' Gainsborough's large portrait of him standing by his horse was also in progress this autumn; it was shown at the Royal Academy the following spring, with the companion portrait of the Prince's friend, Colonel Anthony St. Leger. In the autumn of 1783 the Prince sat again to Gainsborough; in the summer of 1784 he commissioned him to paint a picture of himself in hussar uniform. That June Sir Joshua Reynolds, the President of the Royal Academy, exhibited his full-length portrait of the Prince of Wales with his favourite charger; and on 30 May 1785 a gratified Reynolds told the Duke of Rutland that he had begun a portrait of the Duc de Chartres (Philippe Egalité) for the Prince of Wales, and that the Prince intended to sit for him.

I have sent a head of the Prince to the Exhibition [added Reynolds], which I hear is much approved of. He dined with the Academy at our great dinner before the opening of the Exhibition, as did likewise the Duc de Chartres. The Prince behaved with great propriety; we were all mightily pleased with him.(*59*)

The Prince of Wales, who had shown himself an admirer of handsome women, had already begun to show himself a patron of the arts.

5

One of his most original essays had probably entered his mind soon after his twenty-first birthday. On 7 September, 1783, on a visit to his uncle, the Duke of Cumberland, he had gone, for the first time, to the little town on the coast of Sussex which was still sometimes known as Brighthelmstone.

Brighton (as it has been called since the early years of last century) was already a town to charm society. The tonic air which blew in from the Channel, or over the grand bosom of the Downs, the bracing sea which Dr. Richard Russell had established as the panacea for all ills; the hot and cold sea-water bathing establishment south of the Steine, the mineral-water spring nearby at Wick: these amenities already made it a health resort for the *ton*. And since spas and fashion went hand in hand, and since the Sussex Militia were quartered on the town, life in Brighton had already assumed a little of its zest and vulgarity. There were a circulating library, and bookshops, and even chapels, there were hunting and coursing on the Downs; there were riding and gossiping and sometimes theatrical performances. There were the races at Lewes, when nearly the whole population of Brighton emigrated to the racecourses for a week. And, with it all (and this, perhaps, was its most powerful charm), Brighton remained a fishing-town, where mackerel boats were pulled up on the shingle, and, outside the low-beamed fishermen's cottages, nets were draped up to dry. The air gave an appetite, the fish was delicious; and sometimes the sea mist lay so thick that the ships off shore seemed to be suspended in mid air.

While Marie-Antoinette delighted in milking cows at the Petit Trianon, in a world of pastoral artifice, the Prince of

Wales found escape on the Sussex coast. Newly independent, he revelled in the sudden informality, in the sense of physical escape; and Samuel Rogers, the poet, remembered seeing him 'drinking tea in a public room of what was then the chief inn, just as other people did'. Brighton caught his imagination. He soon decided that he must have a house there. On 13 July the following year, not long before the Lewes and Brighton Races were to be held, Louis Weltje arrived in Brighton to find a house for him.

It might seem strange that the Prince should choose to send, on such an errand, the Comptroller and Clerk of the Kitchen and Cellars; but the Prince's servants were often asked to perform unexpected and confidential functions. (Weltje was also to help him to form his collection of Dutch pictures.) The Prince, who liked original characters, had no more original servant than this dumpy, snub-nosed German, a former gingerbread baker who had once peddled cakes about the streets. Weltje's manners were hardly polished, but his outspokenness, his barbarous Anglo-Westphalian jargon, and his gastronomic gifts endeared him to his master. He had, too, a sharp financial sense. When, at last, by his own folly, he lost his place in the household, he had accumulated a fortune; he had built several houses in Brighton, and, in London, he entertained guests more suited to a palace than to Hammersmith. Painters, poets, artists and musicians 'drank choice wines, ate boar's head, and delicious fruits from Weltje's hothouse'; and, showing his guests round the little estate which he would bequeath to his children, Weltje would say proudly: 'Dish ish moine, dat ish moine; and, what ish more, I can leave it all to my posteriors.'(60)

Meanwhile, in July 1784, Weltje chose the Prince a house on the west side of the Steine, next to the grounds of the Duke of Marlborough. It belonged to a Mr. Thomas Kemp, after whom Kemp Town was named. It was, so Samuel Rogers remembered, 'a respectable farmhouse', with an unbroken view of the sea. The following summer, when the Prince had decided to be a regular visitor, he employed Henry Holland, the architect, to enlarge it. The two-storey house, with its balconies and verandahs, its bow-fronted rooms, was to cast a happy, gentle influence on Brighton architecture for half a century.

It was not the Pavilion that the Prince would leave to posterity. Yet, in a generation trained to admire classical simplicity, even this early Pavilion, built on traditional lines, was condemned as 'a nondescript monster' and a 'mad-house'.(*61*)

It was the Prince's heating arrangements which deserved criticism. The patent stove which he set in the hall to warm the whole Pavilion, heated the ground-floor rooms like Weltje's gingerbread ovens; and the Prince's guests agreed that hell-fire would be no novelty, now.

By the time that Weltje found the house at Brighton, the Prince had already installed himself in the London palace which would be the Nonesuch of the age. When he had reached his twenty-first birthday in 1783, the King could no longer deny him independence, and he had given him Carlton House, which stood on the site of the present Waterloo Place, with handsome gardens stretching down to the Mall.

Carlton House had been the house of the King's late mother; it was an obvious choice to the King. But the choice was also disastrous. Since the death of the Princess Dowager of Wales, eleven years earlier, Carlton House had fallen into dilapidation. It could not be made habitable without substantial expense. The Prince of Wales, as the King must have known, could hardly be content with an economic restoration.

To the impulsive, artistic young man released from the Queen's House, the abandoned mansion gave a breath-taking chance of creating his own new world: a brave new world that would reflect his taste, his dignity, his love of pleasure and splendour. Here, for the first time, the Prince of Wales might present himself as he chose, and create a work of art around him. 'I am hard at work upon my mansion at Carlton House,' he told the Duke of York in November 1783. 'I hope to take possession ye third or fourth of next month, tho the house will then be very far from being finished. I am adding & building considerably to it, & hope on yr. return you will not think me a bad architect.'(*61*)

By 11 November, when he took his seat in the House of Lords, he had eagerly moved into Carlton House, where Henry Holland, Architect to His Royal Highness, was still at work. The alterations were to continue for nearly thirty years. The expenses of building and furnishing were, as the Prince confessed, to be 'enormous'. When he came of age, his natural taste and his love of the arts had already begun to determine his future.

6

On 10 March 1784, when the interior alterations were said to be finished, the Prince of Wales gave a grand ball at Carlton House. The principal nobility and gentry, who attended it, must have seen at once that he had not observed his father's instructions, 'only painting it and putting handsome furniture where necessary'. But 'there is an august simplicity that astonished me', wrote Horace Walpole. 'You can not call it magnificent; it is the taste and propriety that strike. ... In all the fairy tales you have been [*sic*], you never was in so pretty a scene. ... How sick one shall be after this chaste palace, of Mr. Adam's gingerbread and sippets of embroidery!'(*62*) He thought that Carlton House would be the most perfect palace in Europe.

The Prince no doubt intended this. In time there were new kitchens, cellars and larders, a pastry scullery, a silver scullery, a coffee-room pantry, a footman's hall, a maids' kitchen and a confectionary. There was a bow-windowed bedroom for the Prince himself, with a dressing-closet and 'hot bath' room opening out of it. On the first floor three spacious rooms overlooked the gardens with their elms, two hundred years old, their 'beds of the choicest flowers,' their cascade, their temple paved with Italian marble, and their statues of King Alfred and the Black Prince. On the first floor, too, was the state apartment, used for audiences, a small music-room, and a Chinese drawing-room decorated in yellow silk and filled with Chinese furniture and porcelain.

Through this delectable décor moved the Prince of Wales, 'undoubtedly cast by nature in an elegant and pleasing mould'. As Nathaniel Wraxall observed, there was an air of repose, rather than of energy, about him. But despite a general softness of outline, a lack of masculine strength, there was something Apollonian about his handsome face, his animated grey eyes and light brown hair; there was a charm in the moods which passed across his features, in the graceful readiness with which he quoted Homer and Virgil. To William Beckford, the author of *Vathek*, the builder of Fonthill, the Heir Apparent was a radiant figure.

I danced till six this morning [wrote Beckford, in March 1782], in the midst of festoons, glittering lustres, painted Cupids and garlands of roses. All our first butterflies displayed their gayest colours. Jewels, as in duty bound, sparkled on every side. The prince, brighter than sunshine, cast a brilliant gleam wherever he moved. I never saw him in a livelier or kindlier mood, more graceful, more insinuating. To me in particular he was graciousness personified....(*63*)

The graciousness that made Beckford feel the Prince's chosen friend was felt by many others. Women might be expected, perhaps, to praise his deep musical voice, his flair for paying compliments, his kindness, his transparent pleasure in their company; Mrs. Papendiek, watching him dance with his sister, the Princess Royal, declared that he 'showed an elegance indescribable in everything that he did before the public'.(*64*) But distinguished men, accustomed to splendour, fine manners and fine intellects, were also quite exceptionally impressed. Haydn, in time, would declare: 'The Prince of Wales is the most handsome man on God's earth. ... I am more pleased by his kindness than by any financial gain.'(*65*) Richard Rush, the American Minister to St. James's, would record his 'commanding

union' of 'exterior qualities'; he made an audience, added
Rush, 'a pleasurable duty instead of a repulsive ceremony'.(*66*)

The Prince knew more than most of his contemporaries
about the art of living. One imagines him at the breakfast
he gives in the gardens of Carlton House in the early summer
of 1784. One imagines him moving round the marquees,
where two hundred and fifty guests are enjoying 'the finest
fruits of the season, confectionaries [*sic*], ices, creams, and
ornamental designs'. One sees him rise from table, and
lead the Duchess of Devonshire, 'the leading star of the
fashionable hemisphere', on to the 'beautiful level, in the
shade of a group of trees', where the ball is to begin.(*67*)
He dances elegantly through the memoirs of the early
1780s. He commissions Gainsborough to paint a picture of
his three eldest sisters to adorn the state room at Carlton
House.(*68*) He condescendingly comes down from his box
at the Pantheon to assure the great singer Mara of his admiration; he engages her constantly, and goes to hear her
everywhere she sings.(*69*) He attends the charity concert to
commemorate the anniversary of the death of Handel; and,
changing his dark blue Windsor uniform for less formal
dress, he gives small parties at Carlton House, where he
plays the violoncello in quartets. He hunts stags at Windsor,
though sometimes the stag is taken after a run of thirty or
even forty miles, with the same number of miles to return.(*70*) He promises to sit for his portrait to Gainsborough, to please his friend Thomas Coke of Norfolk (the
future Earl of Leicester).(*71*) He goes to Ranelagh and
Vauxhall; and, on 14 April 1784, at his own request, he be-
comes a member of the Sublime Society of Beefsteaks,(*72*)
which meets on Saturdays from November to June, at
Covent Garden Theatre, 'to grill steaks over the original
grate furnished for the purpose' by the founder, and to
drink port, porter, punch and whisky toddy. The member-
ship has loyally been raised from twenty-four to twenty-five,
so that the Prince of Wales may be admitted; and among
his fellow-members, who include 'some of the most classical
and sprightly wits in the kingdom', he is at home. Here, no

doubt, he meets the young actor John Philip Kemble ('he was one of my earliest friends'), and they exchange mimicries and pinches of snuff. More than once, at Covent Garden, Kemble is summoned to the royal box for a chat; and he knows the Heir Apparent and his tastes well enough to go shopping in Madrid 'for choice Spanish snuff to give to the Prince of Wales'.(73)

The Prince was happy with actors and actresses; he understood their romance, their warmth, their adventure and panache. He had always found it hard to tolerate prosaic, unemotional people. He liked originality, even to the point of eccentricity; he liked vitality, even when it turned into rudeness, bawdiness or excess. When Delpini, the comedian, was to have a benefit performance, he admonished the Prince, with astonishing freedom: 'Mistare Prance, you no come to my benefice, by Gar, me go to your papa's banche' (meaning the King's Bench Prison, for debt).(74) The Prince was no doubt entertained, rather than offended, by such freedom of manner. Yet for all his accessibility, his condescension, his manifest kindness, he remained aware of his station. Though actors and managers were often invited to Carlton House, Charles Bannister, the actor and singer, remembered: 'The Prince never assumed familiarity with us, though his demeanour was always most gracious ... At proper moments, with inimitable politeness, he would suggest that he should be pleased with a song, and the individual selected received his highest reward in praises which his royal highness bestowed with an excellent judgment, and expressed with a taste peculiar to himself.'(75)

It must be admitted that Carlton House was not always the scene of artistic gatherings, or superbly elegant behaviour. It was not even, in Wraxall's words, Thomson's *Castle of Indolence*, delay and attendance. It was often the scene of what he euphemistically described as Bacchanalian festivals.

It would have been astonishing if they had not occurred. The men who rode forty miles after a stag, and raced phaetons from London to Brighton, the men who ate massive breakfasts and titanic dinners, the men who were prodigal in love and intense in living, were also men who drank well, drank often and drank deep. The quantities of wine they drank would overflow modern measures: the Prince's brother, Frederick, at his meridian, would drink six bottles of claret before dinner with scarce a change in his countenance;(76) and the Prince's brother William would be considered a model of temperance because at dinner he drank 'only sherry, and that in moderation—never exceeding a pint'.(77) The young Prince of Wales, who had dashed into the wide world from the Queen's House with his uninhibited passion for living, the Prince who entertained the wits and actors, the artists and politicians at Carlton House, drank as hard as any of his contemporaries. Mrs. Papendiek lamented that, at certain music parties, when Giardini, or Crosdill, took the lead, 'or when there were a set of singers with whom the Prince took a part in glees, &c., then much disorder took place'. Mr. Papendiek prudently told the Prince that 'he held himself responsible to the Queen for his character', and must refuse 'to join a set to which he could never bring himself to belong'.(78) Henceforward Papendiek was asked to the more decorous evenings at Carlton House; but the bacchanalia continued. Wraxall, who showed no particular affection for the Prince, declared that while the King was caricatured as Farmer George, riding to market with his milk and butter, the Prince of Wales was shown in the print-shops of Bond Street 'as a voluptuary: his waistcoat unbuttoned, his respiration impeded by repletion, and the board before him covered with bottles of maraschino or cedrate'. These indulgences so affected him that he could not bear the dark; and he later had to sleep in a room 'illuminated by a number of wax candles, the light of which was indispensable to procure him repose'.

More than once, Wraxall continued, the effects of intoxication nearly proved fatal; and very early in life, when his drinking brought on a fever, the Prince had recourse to the lancet. When his principal physician refused (as he frequently did) to authorise bleeding, the Prince often 'opened a vein for himself. I recollect', wrote Wraxall, 'the first time Dr. Warren was called in to him in one of his violent paroxysms of fever, about the year 1786, that physician declared his pulse could not be counted, and resembled a machine completely disorganised'.(79) Wraxall was always inclined to enlarge the Prince's weaknesses. Yet it is clear that the Prince was already taxing his constitution, that his life was already taking a wrong turning.

Alas, as the Bishop of Llandaff would write, years later, to the Duke of Queensberry, the Prince 'was a man occupied in trifles, because he had no opportunity of displaying his talents in the conduct of great concerns'.(80)

7

The fact that the Prince of Wales did not take a more responsible interest in 'the conduct of great concerns' was largely due to his education. Perhaps the King had truly believed in the exclusive pursuit of accomplishments. Perhaps he had really felt that a liberal education and a strict, Germanic régime would between them make an exemplary man. He himself, the first of the Georges to 'glory in the name of Briton', the first of them to speak the King's English, had not enjoyed a conventional education; and since he had not enjoyed it himself, he had seen no reason why his eldest son should do so.

But his attitude to the Prince of Wales was not, it seems, simply dictated by narrowness of mind, or obtuse conservatism. It had been influenced by a deep, ineradicable dislike.

It is not unknown for a man to resent his eldest child, to dislike it for dividing his wife's affection. It is not unknown for a king to resent the heir who will, almost certainly, ascend his throne. But among the kings of the House of Hanover, this hatred of the first-born had become a lamentable tradition. George I (who detested his wife, and had her imprisoned for thirty-two years) showed a violent jealousy of his successor. George II could hardly find words to describe Frederick, Prince of Wales. 'He is the greatest boor and the greatest ass and the greatest beast in the whole world.'

George III did not try to understand the son who was so different from himself; he made it abundantly clear that his second son, Frederick, Duke of York, was his favourite. 'He hates me', the Prince of Wales insisted in 1785. 'He always did, from seven years old.'(*81*)

It was impossible not to be affected by such antipathy; and while the King's system of education left the Prince in ignorance, while his puritan discipline intensified the Prince's love of pleasure, his permanent, open antipathy made him reckless. Since the King was staunchly Tory, it was the most natural thing for the Prince of Wales to dance at a fête at Devonshire House to celebrate Lord North's resignation, and to embrace the cause of the Whigs.

He did so ardently, for, just before he was twenty-one, he came under the spell of Charles James Fox. It is easy to see why Fox, who was thirteen years his senior, found the Prince a boon companion. It is easy to see why the Prince admired this hard-living, eloquent, passionate politician with an almost boyish hero-worship. Fox possessed many qualities which the Prince admired; he also made him feel magnificently adult, and superbly independent of his father.

Horace Walpole, in his *Last Journals*, spoke of Fox with bitterness and fury:

> The Prince of Wales [he wrote on 6 March 1783] had of late thrown himself into the arms of Charles Fox, and this in the most indecent and undisguised manner. Fox lodged in St. James's Street, and as soon as he rose, which was very late, had a levée of his followers, and of the members of the Gaming Club at Brookes's [*sic*], all his disciples. His bristly, black person, and shagged breast quite open, and rarely purified by any ablutions, was wrapped in a foul linen night-gown, and his bushy hair dishevelled. In these cynic weeds, and with epicurean good humour, did he dictate his politics—and in this school did the heir of the Crown attend his lessons and imbibe them. Fox's followers ... were strangely licentious in their conversation about the King. At Brookes's they proposed

wagers on the duration of his reign; and if they moderated their irreverent jests in the presence of the Prince, it was not extraordinary that the orgies at Brookes's might be reported to have passed at Fox's levées, or that the King should suspect that the same disloyal topics should be handled in the morning that he knew had been the themes of each preceding evening . . .

This anguish to a mind that had from the Prince's childhood anticipated jealousy, rendered the already conceived antipathy to Fox a rankling ulcer.(*82*)

The King had never hunted until the Prince of Wales reached manhood; and it was generally thought, said Walpole, that he 'employed the chase to take the Prince, as often as he could, from other diversions and connexions'.(*83*) One of them, no doubt, was his friendship with Fox.

8

The Prince of Wales's devotion to his mother, his brothers and sisters, his wholehearted friendships and his intense *liaisons* had all borne witness to his affectionate nature. The Prince needed love; he needed to feel an all-absorbing love, based on deep respect as well as passion; he needed what must, in his position, have seemed impossible: the constant, strong devotion of a woman who loved him for himself. If he could find and marry such a woman, all the unhappy legacies of his youth would be forgotten; his excesses would be readily abandoned. The Prince could not be led by force; affectionate as he was, he could always be persuaded by his heart.

The very quantity of his mistresses had shown that he soon tired of superficial relationships. It says much for his character that the woman he really chose was a woman of exceptional distinction. She was gentle, maternal, devout, and eminently lovable. She loved the Prince with a profound, disinterested love that lasted until his death, nearly half a century later. He fell in love with her at about the time he came of age; when he died, at sixty-seven, he would be buried with her picture *'placed right upon my Heart'.(84)* The relationship between the Prince and Mrs. Fitzherbert was the supreme event in both their lives.

The Prince first saw Maria Fitzherbert in about 1783. He was twenty-one, and she was twenty-seven. She came of an old Catholic family, and at nineteen she had been married to Edward Weld, of Lulworth Castle in Dorset, a widower twenty-six years older than herself. Within the year, Mr. Weld had died, leaving his will unsigned and his widow dependent on the generosity of his younger brother. Three years later Maria Weld became the wife of Thomas Fitzherbert of Swynnerton in Staffordshire. Mr. Fitzherbert died prematurely of tuberculosis, and since the age of twenty-four Mrs. Fitzherbert had been a widow with a small house at the end of Park Street, near Park Lane.

Mrs. Fitzherbert was not conventionally beautiful: her nose was too long and aquiline. But she had a delicate mouth, dark eyes, a pink-and-white English complexion, a splendid bosom, and a gentle expression true to her gentle nature. It was either in Lady Sefton's box at the opera, or driving in the Park, that the Prince of Wales, with the world at his feet, first saw her, and found himself to be 'really mad for love'.(85)

Mrs. Fitzherbert was immensely flattered by his admiration, but she was not the woman to be his mistress. She was devoutly Catholic, and, besides, she knew the misery and bitterness that beset a royal favourite. Twice widowed, she must have longed all the more for a permanent relationship; and, as she would tell Lady Jerningham, years later, 'She was particularly fond of Children and Should have Liked to have a dozen of her own'.(86) She was above becoming the mistress of the Prince of Wales; as a commoner and a Catholic, she could not aspire to be his wife. She could only resist his attentions.

She seems to have done so for several months; but on 8 July 1784, her resolution was shaken. The royal surgeon arrived at her house 'in the utmost consternation', and told her that the Prince had stabbed himself, and that only her instant presence would save his life.

At first she resisted these wild, disturbing importunities; but at last, being only human, she succumbed. She agreed to go to Carlton House provided that a lady of impeccable character attended her. The Duchess of Devonshire was therefore snatched from her supper, and together they entered the Prince's room, where they found him pale and blood-stained, with brandy at his side. He declared that he did not want to live unless Mrs. Fitzherbert married him. At such a moment, she could only have done as she did. She borrowed a ring from the Duchess, and let the Prince put it on her finger. Then the two women, overwrought, hurried back to Devonshire House.

The melodrama was characteristic of the Prince of Wales; the whole scene sounds unpleasantly contrived. Had the royal surgeon been taken into the Prince's confidence? Was the stab-wound serious, or even genuine? Had the Prince, who sometimes used the lancet to relieve a fever, merely bled himself for effect? The questions arise; and yet it is clear that he felt uncommon love. He had grown desperate, and there had seemed no other way to gain his desire.

He had not yet gained it; for, next day, Mrs. Fitzherbert came suddenly to her senses. She and the Duchess of Devonshire signed a statement of events, declaring that 'promises obtain'd in such a manner are entirely void'. But Mrs. Fitzherbert was still alarmed. The deposition seemed a frail security for her future. That day she left the country. She intended to stay abroad until the Prince of Wales was safely married.

The Prince of Wales could not leave England without the King's permission; and, as he had learned, permission would not conceivably be granted. Three years ago he had been relieved not to follow Mme Hardenberg to the Continent. But Mme Hardenberg had merely been the object of a passing infatuation. Mrs. Fitzherbert had shown him the futility of love-affairs. She was '*my ever beloved Maria, wh. I ... must ever glory in'.(87)* However unorthodox the ceremony, she had in fact agreed to marry him.

On 24 August, from Brighton, he wrote formally to his father: 'I think it my duty to inform your Majesty of a resolution I have been induced to take, from the peculiar and very embarrassed situation of my affairs ... I mean the putting in full practice a system of economy by immediately going abroad.'(88)

> I have found myself [replied the King] under the disagreeable necessity of shewing the Prince of Wales's letter to the Queen, who is as much hurt as me, and coincides in the opinion that if his improper plan was put into execution his character would be forever blasted in this country, and also in all Europe. ... But if he is resolved to ruin his character, at least I will not bear any part of the blame, and my people shall know that this shameful flight is in defiance of my express prohibitions both as King and father.(89)

The correspondence, painfully formal, continued into September. The King refused to see his son. On 2 September he sent him a letter which left little room for compromise. He thought it necessary, he wrote, 'as his father and his Sovereign strictly to charge and command him by this paper not to leave the realm without having obtained my particular leave'.(90)

The Prince still insisted that only financial necessity drove him abroad; the King enquired how much would be needed to pay the Prince's debts, and found that they could not be paid without assistance from Parliament. Queen Charlotte, showing the first sign of affection in the struggle, commanded Lord Southampton, the unfortunate intermediary, to send her son her good wishes for his happiness; and 'she trusts', Lord Southampton told the Prince, 'you will not venture to go abroad at the risque of offending the K- for ever'.(91) Perhaps her kindness helped the Prince to make his decision. On 17 September he agreed to postpone his departure until he had learned the King's intentions.

Colonel Hotham, the Prince's treasurer and secretary,

made out 'as near a state' of his debts as he could; the estimate was intended for the King. Late in October, the Colonel delivered it with alarm and regret. The debts and engagements amounted to £147,293; the Prince's finances were in a 'wretched and disgraceful state'.(92)

The Prince had now not only revealed his financial distress, he had manoeuvred himself into a corner from which he could not escape. All he could do was to write impassioned letters to Mrs. Fitzherbert, and threaten again and again to kill himself unless she returned to England and married him.

While the King and Queen watched Mrs. Siddons as Lady Macbeth, while the King 'often vainly endeavoured' to conceal his tears behind his eye-glass, while the Queen told Mrs. Siddons 'in her gracious broken English that her only refuge from me was actually turning her back upon the stage',(93) the Prince of Wales was engaged in a vital drama. Courier after courier was speeding down the roads of France, bearing his massive vows of love to Mrs. Fitzherbert, 'who ever must be transcendently the dearest to me thro' life'.(94)

On 27 April 1785 an accomplished diplomat called at Carlton House. Sir James Harris, who would one day be Earl of Malmesbury, came to discuss the Prince's financial affairs. He heard a wretched story of dissension. 'What can I do, my dear Harris?' asked the Prince. 'The King hates me ... I have no hopes from him. He won't let even Parliament assist me till I marry ... He hates me; he always did, from seven years old. ... We are too wide asunder ever to meet.'(95)

Sir James recorded the conversation in his diary; but judging, perhaps, that the Prince was inclined to dramatise events, he hesitated to believe him. On 23 May, when he returned to Carlton House, he suggested that the Prince might be mistaken. The answer was vehement. 'Why, my dear Harris, will you force me to repeat to you that *the King hates me*? He will never be reconciled to me ... If you will not credit me, you will, perhaps, credit the King himself.' The Prince took a bundle of letters out of an escritoire, and read them to Sir James. They were the letters which had passed between him and his father, beginning with the one in which he had asked to go abroad last autumn. The Prince's letters

> were full of respect and deference, written with great plainness of style and simplicity. Those of the King [Sir James considered] were also well written, but harsh and severe; constantly refusing every request the Prince made, and reprobating in each of them his extravagance and dissipated manner of living. They were void of every expression of parental kindness or affection; and, after both hearing them read, and perusing them myself, I was compelled to subscribe to the Prince's opinion.

The conversation that followed was poignant. 'Look ye, Harris,' said the Prince, 'the King has used me ill; and I wish the public knew what you now know, and was to pronounce between us.' Sir James replied wisely: 'I should be very sorry indeed, Sir, if this was known beyond these walls; for as long as any part of your conduct is open to censure, the voice of the public ... will always go with the King.' And then, directly, not knowing how sensitive a point he had touched, Sir James continued: 'May I suggest, Sir, the idea of your marrying? It would, I should think, be most agreeable to the King, and, I am certain, most grateful to the nation.'

The Prince replied with vehemence. 'I never will marry! My resolution is taken on that subject. I have settled it with Frederick. No, I never will marry!' 'Till you are married, Sir, and have children,' answered the diplomat, 'you have no solid hold on the affections of the people.'(96)

Sir James had warned the Prince of Wales of the tragedy that would shape his life; and it was indeed a tragedy. From the moment that he met Mrs. Fitzherbert the Prince of Wales was virtually married. She was a woman of different clay; she set her conscience above position, her piety above material gain. As he had told the Duchess of Devonshire, Mrs. Fitzherbert's character 'to all who knew her must be most unblemished and respectable'.(97) He admired her strength of mind, her natural nobility. His respect was equal to his passion. And since he knew that she was not indifferent to him, that she had only escaped because she was afraid of her own emotions, as well as his, he could not let her out of his life. For sixteen months he continued to send her his protestations of love, thirty and even forty pages long. He had not, he wrote on 3 November 1785, 'a wish nor a desire in life yt. does not center in you. ... Come then, oh! come, dearest of wives, best & most adored of women, come & for ever crown with bliss him who will thro' life endeavour to convince you by his love & attention of his wishes to be ye. best of husbands & who will ever remain unto ye. latest moments of his existence, *unalterably Thine*'.(98)

It was this letter, which contained his proposal of marriage, that weakened her at last.

The Prince of Wales put himself into touch with Mrs. Fitzherbert's family; he secretly sought a clergyman who would risk his future by performing the ceremony. The Prince was under twenty-five and had not asked the King's consent, so the marriage was invalid under the Royal Marriage Act; he had chosen to marry a Catholic, and so, by the Act of Settlement, he would forfeit the Crown. But he was in love, and he brushed aside law and rational thinking. It was (recorded Lord Holland) at his 'earnest and repeated solicitations, not at Mrs. Fitzherbert's request, that any ceremony was resorted to'. Mrs. Fitzherbert 'knew it to be invalid in law; she thought it nonsense, and told the Prince so. ...' She knew that it would be almost as unreal as the melodramatic betrothal at Carlton House.

If she had been a saint, she would no doubt have entered a convent rather than endanger her future sovereign; but she was nearing thirty and she was needed by the man she loved. She agreed to keep the marriage secret as long as the Prince should live; but, years later, to a friend of Lord Holland's, 'a man of strict veracity', she showed that she had understood her surrender. She frankly owned 'that she had given herself up to him, exacted no conditions, trusted to his honour, and set no value on the ceremony which he insisted on having solemnised'.(*99*)

On 15 December 1785, secretly, in her drawing-room in Park Street, witnessed by her brother Mr. Smythe, and her uncle Mr. Errington, Mrs. Fitzherbert became the wife, as far as the Church could make her, of George Augustus Frederick, Prince of Wales.

Long before the Reverend Robert Burt of Twickenham declared on his deathbed that for five hundred pounds he had performed the ceremony, the royal marriage was an open secret. Within a few days of the wedding, Sir Gilbert Elliot reported 'that Mrs. Fitzherbert is, or is to be, at Carlton House; that she was married by a Roman Catholic priest; is to have £6,000 a year, and is to be created a Duchess'.(*100*) The rumour raced round Catholic circles and reached Lady Jerningham: 'Mrs. Fitzherbert has, I believe, been married to the Prince. God knows how it will turn out!'(*101*)

There was certainly room for speculation. After the honeymoon (tradition says that it was spent at Richmond), Mrs. Fitzherbert continued to live in Park Street, while the Prince continued to live at Carlton House. The situation was distinctly curious.

But Mrs. Fitzherbert overcame comment. She was 'so thoroughly amiable and good-natured, that every one who came within the circle of her influence, felt inclined to shut his eyes against any cognizance of her true position'. 'Her own manners,' attested Mary Frampton, 'ever remained quiet, civil and unpretending, and in the days of her greatest influence she was never accused of using it improperly.'(*102*)

9

The idyllic first years of the marriage were recorded by Richard Cosway. His miniature of Mrs. Fitzherbert, which gave the Prince 'extreme satisfaction', had started him on his highly successful career; the Prince had gone to his studio in Berkeley Street, followed by all the fashion of the day.(*103*) It was Cosway who painted the eyes of the Prince and Mrs. Fitzherbert, each to be set in a ring (the Prince had sent Maria his eye with his proposal of marriage). Cosway painted twenty pictures of the Heir Apparent; he was honoured 'with more than common patronage', for the Prince not only admired his work, he gave him his friendship. As Allan Cunningham would write, in his *Lives of the Most Eminent British Painters,* Cosway was one of the Prince's train, and 'voyaged with him for a time "Down pleasure's stream with swelling sails".'(*104*) The strutting little miniaturist (even his everyday dress was sometimes embellished with 'strawberry embroidery') was not perhaps an ideal companion; polite society sometimes looked askance at his behaviour, and for some time before his marriage it was said that he had turned his house into a brothel. However, the royal friendship was to last until the Regency, when the Prince grew tired of Cosway's excessive familiarity, and became more select in his company.

While Cosway painted the Prince and Mrs. Fitzherbert in miniature, Gainsborough painted them in large, idyllic style, in a boat with Lord Radnor (a 'simple old Phoebus', said Horace Walpole) and Richard Brinsley Sheridan, the Whig politician and dramatist; the picture had a Fragonard touch about it.(*105*) And, since the Prince appreciated Gainsborough's landscape work when only the most advanced critics had recognised it, he commissioned a pair of pictures in the style of the *Harvest Waggon.* They were almost the only commissioned landscapes which Gainsborough ever painted. He is said to have received two thousand guineas, an extravagant sum for the time, and the Prince gave the pictures to Mrs. Fitzherbert.(*106*)

Had the Prince been simply a peer of the realm, he might have lived the rest of his life in enviable domestic happiness. Given his volatile, passionate nature, he might not have set a pattern of fidelity; but in his fashion he would have been faithful to Mrs. Fitzherbert, he would always have considered her his wife. He was fond of children; he might have been an indulgent father. He would have been content to build and decorate his Chatsworth or his Blenheim, plan its estates, and commission artists to adorn its ceilings with frescoes, and its walls with paintings and sculptures. He would have combined the extravagant romanticism of Beckford with the more refined taste of Horace Walpole; he would have gathered round him an eager, growing circle of poets and novelists, scholars and musicians, scientists and politicians. Had the Prince of Wales not happened to be the eldest son of the King, he might have been happily married. He might have been remembered as a natural impressario, an inspired amateur and patron of the arts.

The misfortune was that his birth forbade him to marry his chosen wife; it ensured that all his actions became public property. And since the larger part of his income was voted by Parliament, the public resented seeing it spent on luxuries. 'The Prince of Wales's profuse expenses,' wrote Wraxall, in his *Memoirs*, 'could neither be imputed to insanity, nor did they bear the impression of beneficence, nor were they productive of national advantage; they were mere gratifications of caprice, luxury and appetite.'(*107*) When the Prince of Wales married Mrs. Fitzherbert, he must have owed between two and three hundred thousand pounds; without Parliament's help, he could not hope to pay his debts before his father's death.

In the first months of 1786 there were attempts to improve relations between him and his father; but the King (who knew his own strong position) refused to help the Prince unless he made a dynastic marriage and ceased to be an active Whig supporter. The Prince was hardly likely to abandon Mrs. Fitzherbert, and he had no intention of dropping Fox; all attempts at reconciliation failed. On 9 July, in desperation, the Prince told the King that he meant to reduce all expenses, 'even those to which my birth and rank entitle me'. Within a few days, Carlton House was shut up, the servants were dismissed, the carriages were all sold and (a somewhat theatrical gesture) the Prince and Mrs. Fitzherbert had hired a chaise and clattered down to Brighton.

'The Prince of Wales's birthday,' noted Fanny Burney on 12 August. 'How I grieve at whatever may be the cause which absents him from his family!—a family of so much love, harmony, and excellence, that to mix with them, even rarely, must have been the first of lessons to his heart.'(*108*) Miss Burney had recently been appointed Second Keeper of the Wardrobe to Her Majesty; she may be forgiven for her effusion. Others were slower to perceive the love and harmony in the Royal Family. For once, the public felt that the King had been unduly harsh, and they sympathised with the Heir Apparent, compelled to lead a life beneath his dignity. Public opinion was strong enough for the Whigs to advise the Prince to appeal to Parliament; and on 27 April 1787, Alderman Newnham, a City merchant, announced in the House of Commons that he would move that an humble address be presented to His Majesty, praying him to consider the present embarrassed state of affairs of the Prince of Wales.

The House of Commons was largely Tory, and it was unlikely to desert the King for his prodigal Whig son. Mr. Rolle, one of the Members for Devonshire, called on Parliament to attend to a question which might affect both Church and State. This was a bold allusion to the Prince's marriage to a Roman Catholic.

The allusion brought Fox to his feet. He not only denied the marriage, he described it as a 'miserable calumny'. He declared that it 'not only could have never happened legally, but never did happen in any way whatsoever'. He added that he spoke from direct authority.

It is commonly thought that Fox had based his denial of
the marriage on the letter of denial which the Prince himself had sent him in 1785; but, whatever his authority, he
could only have said what he did. The interests of the State
were of greater moment than the admission of a drawing-
room ceremony which would have roused the nation, destroyed the Prince's position, and ruined Fox and Sheridan
and their colleagues. However, there seemed some truth in
the comment that the Prince had sacrificed Mrs. Fitzherbert's
reputation for money. Gillray soon published a cartoon of
Mrs. Fitzherbert clasping a crucifix and forlornly sitting on
a rock; the Prince and his Whig friends were sailing away
in a boat called *Honour,* and the Prince was swearing: 'I
never saw her in my life.'

But the subjects that Gillray caricatured were not the
proper subjects for a Parliamentary debate; and, after the exchange between Rolle and Fox, the Cabinet told the Prince
that if he withdrew his motion, everything would be
settled as he wished. The motion was withdrawn. The King
then declared that he would only help his son if he
was given a complete list of his debts, and the Prince would
promise to incur no others. The Prince's debts now amounted
to £160,000; Parliament was asked to pay that sum, and
to give him another £60,000 to finish Carlton House. The
King undertook to pay him a further £10,000 a year. The
Prince was again received at Court; and Miss Burney recorded happiness at Windsor.

For all his emotional and financial troubles, the Prince
of Wales had led a pleasant life since he had come of age.
He had also adorned society as no Prince of Wales had
done before him; and it was notable that he had not merely
attended balls and routs, he had sought the company of
the learned and the civilised. He delighted in the sumptuous dinners, 'with artists and others', at Alexander Davison's,
in St. James's Square; and he admired the fine collection of
modern paintings assembled by this Government contractor,
the friend and prize agent of Nelson.(*110*) He dined with
Samuel Rogers, the poet, at Lord Erskine's house in

39

Hampstead, where Rogers found him 'very agreeable and familiar', and enjoyed his anecdotes of Lord Thurlow.*(111)* At one of the Sunday concerts, he and his uncle the Duke of Gloucester played the violoncello in an overture, while the Duke of Cumberland played the violin. This habit of playing in concert, wrote Parke, in his *Musical Memoirs*, 'made him a good timeist, refined in his taste, and imparted to him scientific knowledge. His music parties were of course assisted by performers of superior talent. ... The Prince had concerts frequently in the morning, which might be considered private parties. ... His music parties in the evening were on a more extended scale. ... They were entirely instrumental and might be termed chamber music'.*(112)*

Meanwhile, at Brighton, Henry Holland's Pavilion was habitable in 1787, and in the grounds rose the elegant house designed by Robert Adam for Mrs. Fitzherbert. The Prince moved in an entertaining, elegant and heartwarming world.

10

In 1788 this happy existence was interrupted. Ever since August, when the King returned from taking the waters at Cheltenham, his health had caused anxiety. That autumn, when Mrs. Siddons was paying one of her frequent visits to Windsor Castle, 'his Majesty handed her a sheet of paper, that was blank all but the signature of his name'. As Campbell, her biographer, wrote: 'She judged too highly both of her Sovereign and herself to believe that, in his right mind, he could shew such extraordinary conduct. ... She immediately took the paper to the Queen.' Campbell says that Mrs. Siddons was the first person to observe the King's mental aberration.*(113)*

Mrs. Siddons was wiser about it than most. Some people described the complaint as 'a flurry of spirits', brought on by remaining in wet stockings. Grenville, the future Prime Minister, wrote simply that the medicines had repelled the illness 'from the bowels to the brain. The physicians', he explained, 'are now endeavouring by warm baths to bring it down to the legs again'. Alas, the royal complaint was immovable. In October, Court functions were postponed, and the King was too unwell to be taken from Kew to Windsor. When, towards the end of the month, he returned to the Castle, the Duke of York was so alarmed that he summoned the Prince of Wales from Brighton. The Prince arrived on 5 November; and that evening, at dinner, the King's instinctive, lifelong dislike of his eldest son burst out. He caught him by the collar and thrust him against the wall. The Prince of Wales wept.

For two nights he and the Duke of York sat up all night, fully dressed and wearing their stars, in a room next to the King's; with them were the doctors and the gentlemen of the household in attendance. For sixteen hours, incessantly, the King continued talking. On the second night he suddenly appeared in the ante-room, and when one of the doctors tried to persuade him to go back to bed, he penned him in a corner, and shouted: 'You are nothing but an old woman.'

The doctors were afraid that, in a paroxysm, he might burst the solid mahogany doors of his rooms; and the doors were strengthened.(*114*) It became impossible to shave him; indeed he was only shaved twice between November and January. His principal barber was too nervous to undertake the task, and when Mr. Papendiek 'succeeded in clearing the two cheeks at one sitting', the King talked so much that it was 'nearly a two hours' job'.(*115*) A pall of silence fell over Windsor. No bells were rung; attendants changed places, noiselessly, at stated intervals, the park gates were locked, and no stranger was allowed to enter. Another equerry was ordered down from London; three gentlemen porters were added at the royal entrance gate, and four sergeant porters at the gate in the Home Park. On 16 November, prayers were offered throughout the country for the King's recovery.(*116*)

In the heart of this silent, nightmare world, while the doctors, in the next room, eavesdropped for clues, the King himself talked sadly on and on. He spoke, said Mrs. Papendiek,

> of the general conduct of the Prince of Wales, fearing that his brothers, with the exception of Adolphus, were following him; of his little Octavius who had been his companion, his comfort, his delight; adding that the Almighty had taken him. He hoped and thought he was resigned to His will, but he must be very sinful to be so sorely chastened; and then the tears rolled down his cheeks in a manner pitiful to behold.(*117*)

The Prince of Wales himself behaved with consideration. When the doctors recommended that the King should take a little wine, he sent a few bottles of superlative madeira, 'and proposed tasting it with the King when the family dined at four o'clock. The King,' wrote Mrs. Papendiek, 'thanked his Royal Highness, but said that he hoped for the credit of his gentleman of the wine cellar ... that the best was always provided'.(*118*) The answer, if apocryphal, was still true to the King's character. His malady had removed any frail pretence of affection for his eldest son.

The Prince himself remained affectionate. When the King's delirium was at its wildest, the Prince went to see him. The King recognised him. 'Yes, I knew him very well, and he cried to see me so ill.'(*119*)

The politicians had no time for tears. When the King's condition was understood, Pitt's unshakeable ministry suddenly seemed less secure. He had derived his strength from the King; if the King was not to reign, if the Prince of Wales was to come to the throne, the Whigs might be in office at last. Pitt himself was so certain that his Government would fall that he arranged to resume his legal practice at Lincoln's Inn. Fox was on holiday abroad; messengers sped across Europe to call him home.

Fox considered that a void in the royal power caused by madness was the same as a void caused by death; he maintained that as the King was incapable of transacting public business, his authority must be assumed by the heir to the throne. Such views were incontrovertible. But Pitt put Tory politics before constitutional rights. He presumed that the moment the Prince became Regent, he would dismiss the Government and send for the Whigs. He therefore introduced a Regency Bill, which was strictly to limit the Regent's powers. This bill was itself unconstitutional, as there was no means of obtaining the royal assent to it.

The debate on the Regency Bill continued throughout December and January. Society was now divided into those who wore regency caps with three feathers in front, and the gold inscription *Ich dien*, and those who sported constitutional coats. The Royal Family was divided; the Queen and her daughters were ranged against the Prince, the Duke of York, and the King's brothers, the Dukes of Gloucester and Cumberland. The Queen apparently felt that the Prince and the Duke of York had fomented Whig opposition, and she refused to let them come to Kew. The Princes were enraged, and the Duke referred to their exclusion in a speech in the House of Lords. The family dissensions became public property. The Princes were cut off from their father, and merely received a slightly fuller bulletin than the one that was posted daily at St. James's; it is said that they retaliated by spreading the wildest stories of his behaviour. ('Hush, hush! Don't talk of stars,' he had said, 'we must not talk of stars; you know I am *mopsimus* and don't like French mottoes.')

Early in 1789, the Prince of Wales sent Pitt a formal letter of protest at the proposed restrictive regency. The letter had been drafted by Burke, and its violent passages had been amended by Sheridan; it emphasised the Prince's grief at his father's illness, and at the horror the King would feel when his sanity returned and he saw his sovereign power so mutilated. These regrets were largely idealistic: the Prince and his friends believed that the King was unlikely to recover. But whatever their hypocrisy, Pitt was more hypocritical: he had (as Burke said) set himself up as one of the Prince's competitors, and his Regency Bill was a public, personal and unconstitutional slight on the Heir Apparent. As the Bill passed through an almost hysterical

House of Commons, the Whigs could only cling to the fact that at least the Prince would have the right to dismiss Pitt and to send for Fox.

And then, quite suddenly, all the ruthless cabals and bitter debates were proved unnecessary; all the dreams of power dissolved. On 26 February, 1789, the King's physicians pronounced that His Majesty was perfectly recovered.

The Whigs' discomfiture was complete. The Queen, with more emotion than tact, told the King about the conduct of his two eldest sons. The King needed no encouragement to widen the breach between himself and his heir apparent; but now a breach was opened between him and the Duke of York. Early in March he refused to see the Prince and the Duke, on the grounds of avoiding agitation; and (though he had discussed their behaviour with some of his ministers) they were given no chance to explain it.

> And thus [wrote the Prince of Wales to the Queen] instead of having the preference, to which we had so just a claim, and which we were induced to expect, we dare not even attempt to counteract the impressions which our enemies, who have daily access to the King, may have given of the part we took in the late important occurrences. Your Majesty must surely be of opinion that this state of things is neither decent not just. ...(*120*)

The Queen remained intransigent. When she gave a concert at Windsor to celebrate the King's recovery, neither of the Princes was invited. When they protested, she answered coldly: 'We have asked those persons who have voted in Parliament for the King and me.' 'The King is recovered,' wrote Lady Louisa Stuart to Lady Portarlington, 'and everybody else, I think, gone mad. Oh, what a winter have we passed!'(*121*)

That summer, when the Bastille fell and the House of Bourbon began to crumble, the House of Hanover was miserably divided. Burke drew up a manifesto from the Prince of Wales to his father, justifying the Prince's behaviour, and setting down the unfeeling conduct of the

Queen. Fortunately the manifesto (which took two hours to read) was never sent; it would have forced the King to separate from the Queen, or to banish his two eldest sons from his presence.

It is easy to criticise the Prince of Wales's conduct during the Regency crisis; he had, at times, been unfilial, cruel, mischievous and disloyal. But in all his twenty-six years he had had few signs of real affection from his father; he had been aware, since he was seven, that the King disliked and despised him. He was human enough to feel excited at the thought of a crown. As for his mother, who had treated him and his brother with such severity, she had not shown herself beyond reproach; while the Prince and the Duke had been ardent Whigs, she had put herself at the head of the Tory party.

However, in the summer of 1789 the Prince was hardly on speaking terms with his family, and he was seriously unpopular with the London crowds. When, soon after the King's recovery, he drove to the Opera, the mob surrounded his coach, forced open the door, and shouted : 'Cry Pitt for ever!' The Prince said sharply: 'Damn Pitt; Fox for ever!' He needed all his courage.

He was no doubt glad, this summer, to visit the Whig stronghold of York.

II

On 24 August, after a visit to the races, the Prince and the Duke of York drove triumphantly to the city; at the boundary, a number of citizens took the horses out of their traces, and drew the carriage to the Deanery. Next day the Prince was presented with the freedom of York, and answered the address 'in a pathetic elegant manner, which added energy to the very beautiful sentiments'. The week passed with a levée, a civic dinner, a dinner with his old preceptor, Dr. Markham, at Bishopthorpe, a ball at the Assembly, a concert, and a visit to Earl Carlisle at Castle

Howard. Whatever his unpopularity in London, the Prince of Wales won the approval of York,

> The elegance and *condescension* with which he behaved upon all occasions, and to all descriptions of people, during his stay in this city, will [wrote a chronicler] secure to him the most *zealous affection* of all its inhabitants. ... But what must endear the ROYAL BROTHERS most of all, to every good mind, was their extensive *benevolence*, and *charity*—for they literally *clothed the naked— fed the hungry—and set the prisoner free!*

They paid 200 guineas for the relief of debtors confined in York Castle, and 20 guineas for clothing female convicts who had been sentenced to transportation. The Prince also paid for the discharge of several debtors in Ousebridge Gaol, and ordered bread to be distributed weekly to the prisoners.

On 2 September, at Wentworth House, Earl Fitzwilliam gave the gala which crowned the visit. Great bonfires blazed in celebration throughout the vast estate; and after dinner the Prince of Wales appeared in the portico, 'and, by means of a speaking trumpet, held intercourse with the delighted multitude' of twenty thousand people. There followed a ball which equalled the brightest festivities at Devonshire House:

> The most high-wrought conceptions [wrote the local historian] must fall short of the singular brilliancy of the scene at first entering, increas'd by the elegant assemblage of ladies and gentlemen—the former in charming light fancy dresses, composed of white and coloured sarsnets, chamberry gauzes, tiffany, or muslin, richly ornamented with silver and gold fringes; the headdresses, chiefly small hats, on the back or side of the head, ornamented with plumes of feathers, and wreaths of flowers, intermixed with brilliants, pearls, &c. His Royal Highness and his suite wore the Windsor uniform (which is blue, superbly embroidered with gold, and red cuffs and collar) ...

The Prince danced a minuet and a number of country dances 'in the most completely elegant style'; and at quarter past two the supper-rooms were thrown open. They

> displayed such a profusion of delicious viands and elegant decorations, as very rarely meets the eye: the tables in each room formed three sides of a square, and rich parterre frames were placed in the centre of each table, some of which had small upright pillars, with medallions on foil pendent, each pillar connected with wreaths of artificial flowers, the bottom of the frames filled with small sweetmeat figures; every table had equally beautiful, but different devices. On each side, at regular, though not far distant spaces, silver branches, with five lights, were placed, and filled up between with rasberries [*sic*], strawberries, plums, nectarines, &c. &c. in fluted oval jelly figures, so transparent as to shew the fruit as perfect as on the trees; *real* wild boar collared, was covered with artificial heads of composition, as large as life; the potted venison was covered with beautiful stags, swans also of the like magnitude, and perfection of form; profusion of the choicest fruits, &c. and every rarity money could purchase, or fancy conceive ...

The Prince of Wales left later that day; he was graciously pleased 'to express uncommon satisfaction at the whole of his Yorkshire Journey'.(*122*)

12

In social life he had always shown a warming vitality and enthusiasm. The Prince who had been acclaimed at York Races was an eager patron of the turf; before he reduced his establishment in 1786, he had twenty-five horses in training at Newmarket, and when he took to racing again in 1788, he won 190 races in three years. He might have remained among the most successful owners of his time, if it had not been for the scandal of 1791. On 20 October that year, the Prince's horse Escape, reckoned to be the best horse on the turf, and ridden by his jockey Sam Chifney, was badly beaten at Newmarket; the following day, when the odds had risen to 5-1 against the horse, it won easily, and the Prince and Chifney were both supposed to have made large sums of money. After the race, one of the stewards told the Prince: 'If you suffer Chifney to ride your horses, no gentleman will start against you.'

Chifney was examined, but nothing was proved against him; the Prince allowed him £200 a year as a sign of confidence. Just before his death, Chifney published a convincing explanation of the horse's conduct in a pamphlet boldly entitled *Genius Genuine*. The whole accusation of dishonesty had been based on imagination and malicious gossip; the Prince took the only dignified action, and gave up racing. His colours were not seen again on a course until the last years of his life.

Racing was not his only sport. He had often hunted with the King, and, as a pupil of Angelo, he commanded a fencing match at the Pavilion, when Jack Edwin, the younger, 'had the honour to exhibit, *fleuret à la main*, in a professional contest with the Chevalier St. George, Monsieur Sainville, and other celebrated foreigners'.(*123*) The Prince who admired the delicate art of the *fleuret* was also a staunch patron of the ring. It is said that he drove a famous bruiser, Tom Spring, through the streets of London; and he knew Tom Cribb, the 'Black Diamond', whose first big fight took seventy-six rounds to win. When the Prince became King, eighteen famous boxers, under the command of Mr. Jackson, Byron's 'Emperor of Pugilism', guarded the doors of Westminster Hall at the Coronation Banquet. Dressed, unconvincingly, as pages, they impressed observers by their size, symmetry and strength; fortunately 'good-humour and forbearance characterised their proceedings'.(*124*)

The patron of pugilists was also the patron of fashion. He led the vogue for taking snuff (he used to buy what was known as Prince's Mixture from Fribourg's in the Haymarket). He possessed, said Captain Gronow, in his *Anec-*

dotes, the finest collection of snuffboxes that were to be had for love or money.(*125*)

I have been at Sr. Joseph Banks's literary saturnalia [reported Horace Walpole in 1791], where was a Parisian watchmaker, who produced the smallest automaton that I suppose was ever created. It was a rich snuffbox, not too large for a woman. On opening the lid, an enamelled bird started up, sat on the rim, turned round, fluttered its wings, and piped in a delightful tone the notes of different birds, particularly the jug jug of the nightingale. It is the prettiest plaything you ever saw—the price tempting—only five hundred pds. That economist the P of W. could not resist it.(*126*)

The Prince of Wales was an arbiter of fashion long before George Brummell took a cornetcy in his regiment, and their friendship was established; and if he dared to wear the latest colour, a brilliant blue-grey called emperor's eye, if he created extravagant vogues for curled hair and large cravats, he himself became every dress, however overdone. He had an encyclopaedic knowledge of uniforms and decorations, and an unfailing eye for incorrect dress (Captain Gronow received a rebuke for appearing in his presence without knee-breeches). He designed shoe buckles and lavishly frogged surtouts for himself, and he would one day delight in devising new uniforms for his army. Such interests did not reveal an effeminate attention to minutiae, a fussy interest in trivia; they were facets of his artistic sense.

One hundred and fifty years earlier, Charles I had knighted Rubens and Vandyck; he had invited Albano and Gentileschi, Honthorst, Vouet and Polenberg to England, writing to Albano with his own hand. Not since the days of Charles I had a prince proved himself to be such a patron of the arts as the Prince of Wales. 'It would always,' he said, 'give him pleasure to patronise whatever appeared so much calculated to promote the public good.'(*127*)

He had given this warm assurance to Caleb Whitefoord when, in 1785, he agreed to become the Patron of the Royal

Society of Arts; and it was curious that, a week later, the Society had postponed 'the further Consideration' of his patronage. The decision came in the week of the Prince's marriage to Mrs. Fitzherbert, and possibly it was affected by some rumour of his private life. But it remains a strange fact that the Prince had no connexion with the Society, though its aspirations must have been his own.(*128*)

In every other way, however, he showed himself a friend to the arts. There were, he knew, only limited honours conferred on English artists: those bestowed by the Royal Academy, and those bestowed by the King. He saw that his own dignity gave him the chance of patronage, and he took his chance with both hands.

He still patronised Cosway: no one dared to offend the cocksure little painter who had the Heir Apparent's approbation. The Prince of Wales appears to have been the only one of George III's fifteen children whose portrait Gainsborough painted after they had left the nursery. He bought *The Blue Boy* (which later passed into the hands of Hoppner); and Gainsborough's poor mad daughter, Mary— who believed that the Prince of Wales was in love with her —presented him, before her death, with her father's portrait of her husband, Mr. Fischer.(*129*)

Reynolds, like Gainsborough, painted Perdita Robinson, and the Prince; it was Reynolds who, in 1790, as President of the Royal Academy, deferred the annual dinner by royal command, so that His Royal Highness might attend it. Twenty-one years later, at another Royal Academy dinner, Sir George Beaumont, the art collector, suggested a posthumous exhibition of Reynolds's pictures; the Prince immediately offered to lend the seven he possessed.

Reynolds was only one of several artists whom he kept at their easels. Among the pictures which George Romney painted in 1789 were two of Mrs. Fitzherbert. 'The Prince of Wales has been at my house,' he told his son on 5 August 1790, 'and admired a new picture of Mrs. Fitzherbert, and told me he would sit to me when he returned from Brighton.'(*130*) There were other commissions in store; the Prince who had watched the future Lady Hamilton striking her famous attitudes asked Romney to record her. On 19 June 1791, much enamoured of his sitter, much flattered by his patron, Romney told his friend William Hayley, the poet: 'The greatest part of the summer I shall be engaged in painting pictures from the divine lady ... I have two pictures to paint of her for the Prince of Wales.'(*131*)

Reynolds and Romney had had their factions; after the death of Reynolds, controversy revived round Hoppner and Lawrence. In 1792 Hoppner's portrait of the Prince (one of five he painted) was shown at the Royal Academy. 'The light of the Prince of Wales's countenance was of itself sufficient to guide the courtly and the beautiful to his easel,' wrote Allan Cunningham. '[But Lawrence], urged upon the Academy by the King and Queen, became a formidable rival to the painter whom it was the Prince's pleasure to befriend.'(*132*) The dissensions in the Royal Family were reflected even in the arts; this conscious division of patronage repeated the chasm between father and son.

There was some mystery about Hoppner's birth in 1759; his mother had been one of the German attendants at the Palace, and the King had sponsored his education. Hoppner let it be understood that he owed something more than his education to the throne. This was probably the ruse of a man who understood the value of publicity: but it received some sort of confirmation when the Prince of Wales filled Hoppner's studio with the world of fashion. If there was a touch of spite in the Prince's patronage, if he himself encouraged the rumours about Hoppner's birth to vex the King, it would not, in the circumstances, have been surprising.

Yet if the tension between the King and his eldest son was publicly reflected in the rivalry between Lawrence and Hoppner, the most blatant evidence of the King's feelings would be found in a canvas by William Beechey. One of the chief attractions at the Royal Academy in 1798 would be Beechey's principal picture: *His Majesty reviewing the Tenth or Prince of Wales's Regiment of Light Dragoons.* The King appeared in the foreground, riding a white horse, and wearing full regimentals, with a cocked hat. Just behind him was the Prince, in the uniform of the 10th, holding up his sword and giving the word of command. The King had several copies made of this picture, and in one at least the figure of the Prince was omitted by his wish: an extraordinary proof of his dislike.(*133*)

The story of the Prince's presence in the original picture was itself unhappily revealing. When the work was nearly finished (according to Beechey's biographer), Beechey said to the Queen: 'Now what I should *like* to do, and what would be the making of the picture, would be to put the Prince of Wales on his black horse behind His Majesty's white one, but I should never dare to do it.' Queen Charlotte answered: 'Oh, do, just dash it in for me to see.' The artist replied that 'it was as much as his life was worth'; but the Queen said that she would take responsibility. The Prince was painted. Soon afterwards, the King came into Beechey's studio. The Queen said that she had sanctioned the Prince's likeness, but the King was 'very wroth, and ordered it to be stripped off the frame and burnt; of course the artist obliged, and thought it was sent away to be burnt, but the Courtier who took it kept it.' Two years later, when the King was reconciled to his son, he asked where the picture was, and inquired: 'Didn't you finish it, Beechey?' He could not remember the incident at all. The courtier who had kept the picture produced it, and the canvas was properly finished with the Prince of Wales in it.(*134*)

Though the visual arts were, perhaps, the arts of the Prince's predilection, he was constantly concerned with the whole art of living:

All herbs of earth are in thy garden seen,
And in thy forests ev'ry glorious tree,
The Indian world has been despoiled clean,
And Africa, to find new beasts for thee:
Gems, armors, marbles, all the proofs of mind,
By which the Romans claim'd the conquer'd world,
And the wise Greeks, in virtue thrice refin'd;
Vast volumes of philosophy unfurl'd

Oft when the bear controuls the silent pole;
These are thy dear delights, and nearest to thy
    soul . . .(*135*)

When the author of *Carmen Britanicum* addressed his ode
to the Prince, in years to come, his effusions would contain
a certain truth.

The Prince who happily read the classics loved the
modern theatre. When, in the summer of 1789, Miss Farren
had enjoyed the highest vogue, it was because 'the Prince
of Wales patronised her; and the effect of his *decided taste*
made her receipts almost, for *a few nights,* emulate those
of Mrs. Siddons herself'.(*136*) As for Mrs. Siddons, who had
'penetrated the circle at Buckingham House', she was often
to perform for him; and her biographer observes that the
Prince's admiration 'was after all of some service' in procuring her second son a post with the East India Company.
This was something she had 'long been making interest
for'.(*137*) The Prince who invited Kemble to dinner led the
festivities when the cornerstone of the new Covent Garden
Theatre was laid.(*138*) 'Without the Sanction of your Royal
Highness,' wrote a pamphleteer in 1795, 'the Theatres, and
every Place of general Amusement would lose their force
of Entertainment, and Pleasure would cease to be.'(*139*)

Among the Prince's pleasures was music. He not only
played the violoncello; he 'possessed an excellent voice,
which had been cultivated by Latour, the Court music-
master, and his Royal Highness organised a private orchestra in Carlton House, to which he lent his assistance'.(*140*)
Wraxall declared that 'he sang an excellent song of which
I have heard him exhibit a proof in a select company after
dinner at Sir John Macpherson's, at Brompton Grove'.(*141*)
The Prince patronised the concerts at the Hanover Square
Rooms, he accepted the dedication of William Parke's oboe
concerto, and he gave him the title of his musician. He
recognised the truly gifted: in December 1791 Joseph
Haydn wrote delightedly to Maria Anna von Genzinger, in
Vienna, that the Prince had invited him to visit the Duke
and Duchess of York at their country seat. On the second

day of the visit, the Duchess had stayed continually at
the composer's side, 'from 10 o'clock in the evening, when
the music began, to 2 o'clock in the morning. Nothing but
Haydn was played. I conducted the symphonies for the
pianoforte', Haydn continued. 'The Prince of Wales sat on
my right side and played with us on his violoncello, quite
tolerably. I had to sing, too. The Prince of Wales is having
my portrait painted just now, and the picture is to hang in
his room.' Haydn was dazzled that Hoppner should paint
his portrait, by royal command; he was delighted with the
Prince of Wales. He was, he wrote, 'the most handsome
man on God's earth; he has an extraordinary love of music
and a lot of feeling, but not much money. *Nota bene*, this
is between ourselves. I am more pleased by his kindness
than by any financial gain'.(*142*)

The question of financial gain proved to be delicate.
Haydn was not paid for his numerous royal appearances, and,
on the advice of his friends, he finally sent a bill to Parliament. It was honoured at once: in April 1796 he acknowledged receipt of £100.(*143*) But Haydn owed a certain debt
to this royal patronage: the Prince of Wales's March is said
to be among the best he wrote; and Haydn's second
London notebook, 1791-2, contains the convivial reminder:
'1 bottle champagne, 1 bottle Burgundy, 1 bottle rum, 10
lemons, 2 oranges, 1½ lbs. of sugar'. These are the ingredients of the Prince of Wales's punch.(*144*)

13

On 6 August 1789, from Strawberry Hill, Horace Walpole
made a succinct observation to Mary Berry. 'Whatever I do
myself, I should not like to have the P. of Wales have two
or *three* wives.'(*145*) Walpole probably spoke for the great
mass of Englishmen. In an age of licence, it seemed ridiculous to play the puritan. But the King was respected because he set a rigid example of fidelity, and his unmarried
son, who was passionate, handsome, young, and the natural

cynosure of all women's eyes, was expected to be immune from continual temptation.

Expectations ran too high; and perhaps Horace Walpole suspected it. On 8 June 1792, Colonel St. Leger, one of the Prince's friends, called on Sir James Harris, and discussed the Prince's private life. He said that the Prince was

> more attached to Mrs. Fitzherbert than ever; that he had been living with Mrs. Crouch; that she (Mrs. Fitzherbert) piqued him by treating him with ridicule, and coquetted on her side. This hurt his vanity, and brought him back; and he is now more under her influence than ever.(*146*)

It was not surprising that the Prince should have been attracted to Mrs. Crouch. The theatrical part of his nature had always responded to theatrical people: to their originality and passion. He himself was, after all, *jeune premier* on the national stage; and he not only consciously played a part in ceremonial, he sometimes lived his private life with a sense of theatre. Mrs. Fitzherbert was not, by her upbringing and her nature, the sort of woman to dramatise situations. She believed in steadiness and commonsense.

Mrs. Crouch, one suspects, had brought new vitality into the Prince's existence. Wraxall declared that she was 'an actress of extraordinary beauty, who to the charms of her person joined an enchanting voice'. She was, presumably, the Mrs. Crouch who performed at concerts of sacred music, and, in 1798, in 'the new grand dramatic romance of *Blue Beard, or Female curiosity*', held Drury Lane with 'a ballad, delightfully sung: *When pensive I thought on my love*'. While the Prince protected Mrs. Crouch, she had an establishment in Berkeley Square; and, not content with £5,000 worth of jewellery, she obtained from him, said Wraxall, 'in one of those moments when weak men can refuse nothing, an engagement under his hand for £10,000'. When the *liaison* was over, and she fell on hard days, she pestered the Prince for payment. The Prince sent a confidential friend, who managed to buy back the promissory note for a thousand guineas, and, since the Prince's inmates were none too discreet, Wraxall heard the whole story at Carlton

House 'in the year 1799, from the very individual who performed the service not a long time after it took place'. Mrs. Crouch, so Wraxall said, later, died 'the martyr of excess'.(*147*)

Mrs. Crouch was not Mrs. Fitzherbert's only cause of grievance; a much more serious rival was Lady Jersey. Frances, Countess Jersey, was the only daughter of Dr. Philip Twysden, the Bishop of Raphoe, in Ireland. She had married George Bussy, fourth Earl of Jersey, in 1770; and she had, it seems, grown weary of fidelity to a husband eighteen years her senior. Lady Jersey was unprincipled, and she was not especially intelligent. But the Prince, who liked mature, well-built women, was physically captivated by a woman nine years older than himself. For months he abandoned Mrs. Fitzherbert, and finally Lady Jersey persuaded him to write a letter of renunciation.

The letter only proved Lady Jersey's native stupidity: the moment the Prince felt that he had left Mrs. Fitzherbert for ever, he could not tolerate finality.

> I understand that the Misunderstanding between the P. and Mrs. F. is made up [Lady Stafford told her son, on 18 July 1791]. After he had been persuaded by a certain Lady to give her up, and to write according to that Idea to Mrs. F., he found he could not live without her, and sent Messengers of Peace in Numbers. But Mrs. F. was for some days sturdy; she could not believe that he could continue to love her, when for Months he had given his time to another, and had behav'd to her with the greatest Cruelty. But they are Friends now, and the mischief-maker is left to find out another, or to go on with you know who. . . .(*148*)

Mrs. Fitzherbert had much to bear; she took back the Prince of Wales, but he could not leave Lady Jersey even now. Since he was weak, and Lady Jersey did not intend to be the abandoned mistress, the ostentatious *liaison* was resumed. Within the next few months, it was the talk of St. James's.

It was said to be Lady Jersey who promoted the Prince's official marriage. 'All well-informed persons,' wrote Lord Holland, in his *Memoirs of the Whig Party,* 'agree that the preference of the Princess of Brunswick was the choice of Lady Jersey and Lady Harcourt.'(*149*)

If Lady Jersey did indeed choose the Prince of Wales's wife, she did so with relentless calculation. Caroline of Brunswick was a Protestant princess, the daughter of the King's favourite sister; the King was almost sure to give his consent. She was also (as Lady Jersey probably knew) a woman who could not be a rival. Whatever else it did, the marriage would end the influence of Mrs. Fitzherbert, and confirm the power of the Prince's current mistress.

Lady Jersey seems to have used her persuasive powers with effect. On 24 August, at Weymouth, the Prince of Wales told his father that he had broken off all connexion with Mrs. Fitzherbert, and that he wished to marry his cousin, the Princess of Brunswick. 'Undoubtedly she is the person who naturally must be most agreeable to me,' the King wrote, that day, to Pitt. 'I expressed my approbation of the idea.'(*150*)

14

On 27 September, from that hive of gossip, Tunbridge Wells, Maria Holroyd, the future Lady Stanley of Alderley, wrote to a Yorkshire friend. 'Is it possible,' she inquired, 'you Doncaster people can be so behindhand in the affairs of the World as not to know the Prince of Wales is really and truly going to espouse his Coz?'(*151*) Oddly enough, the genteel gossip happened to be the truth. Two months later, Sir James Harris, now Lord Malmesbury, was sent to Brunswick to solicit the hand of Princess Caroline for the future King of England.

It was ironic that Malmesbury, of all people, should have been selected for this mission. Nine years ago, at Carlton House, he had urged the Prince of Wales to marry. It

57

would, he had said, please the King and gratify the nation. The Prince had sworn, with vehemence, that he would never marry; and Malmesbury had long known the reason why.(*152*) Whether or not Malmesbury suspected that the Prince had married Mrs. Fitzherbert, he was well aware that he had loved her and was, perhaps, attached to her still. He knew the domestic and financial pressures that were forcing him now into this dynastic *mariage de convenance*. He knew that the Prince was hardly likely to forswear his real devotion, or his infatuation for Lady Jersey, for a cousin he had never seen: for a wife who was virtually imposed on him. Even before Malmesbury set eyes, for the first time, on Princess Caroline, he must have had forebodings of disaster. Unfortunately, he was not required to advise on the suitability of the marriage. He was simply to ask for Princess Caroline's hand.

There could be no question of his failure. Caroline was twenty-six; and had she not received this unbelievably brilliant proposal, she would no doubt have been on the shelf, or married to some petty German potentate. However, by an act of God she happened to be the niece of the King of England, and his eldest son had chosen her. No matter that she was florid, gauche, stocky and overdressed, that 'her head was always too large for her body, and her neck too short'.(*153*) No matter that her teeth were bad, that she was unruly, exhibitionist, utterly without reticence, and actually offensive from lack of washing. No matter that she was a creature of adolescent impulse, carried away by appearances and enthusiasms, 'prone to confide and make missish friendships'.(*154*) It did not matter, either, that she had (in Malmesbury's words) 'no acquired morality, and no strong innate notions of its value and necessity'.(*155*) Caroline of Brunswick was to marry the Prince of Wales.

It was a choice of quite appalling irresponsibility; and what made this marriage of first cousins most appalling was the mental instability on both sides of the family. George III had already suffered months of insanity, and two of Caroline's brothers were imbeciles. Caroline herself, even now, seems to have shown signs of the family weakness. The moment he saw her, Malmesbury must have known that there was little hope for this intermarriage. He must have seen that there were grave prospects for any children born of it.

However, he had no choice at all but to carry out his mission; and, now that the marriage had been decided, no one was more eager for the wedding than the Prince of Wales. On 3 December, a messenger arrived with the Prince's picture, and a letter from him to his envoy, 'urging me *vehemently* to set out with the Princess Caroline *immediately'.(156)* The marriage treaty was signed next day, and Caroline gave Malmesbury a diamond watch for his pains. No doubt he saw time pass with apprehension.

Any of the Prince's brothers (so Lord Holland wrote), or any English traveller in Germany

> would, if asked, have told him that even in that country, where they were not at that period very nice about female delicacy, the character of his intended bride was exceedingly loose. ... Unfavourable reports of the person, and yet more of the manners and character of the destined bride came pouring in from Germany after the articles were signed and it was too late to recede.

Anybody, Lord Liverpool confirmed, some twenty years later, 'might have told him how loose her conduct was'.(157) But nobody's opinion was asked.

Soon after the contract had been sealed, Caroline showed Malmesbury an anonymous letter which had just arrived; it was evidently about Lady Jersey. He thought it was meant to frighten her with the idea that Lady Jersey 'would lead her into an affair of gallantry ... I told her Lady [Jersey] would be more cautious than to risk such an audacious measure; and that, besides, it was death to presume to approach a Princess of Wales, and no man would be daring enough to think of it. ... I said', added Malmesbury, grimly, 'that such was our law; that anybody who presumed to *love* her was guilty of *high treason*, and punished with death, if she was weak enough to listen to him: so also was *she*. This startled her.'(158)

With this mediaeval warning ringing in her ears, Caroline left Brunswick soon after Christmas. The roads were atrocious, the pauses were frequent, and since the Continent was largely involved in the Napoleonic wars, the journey was tortuous and extremely long. However, on Saturday, 5 April 1795, in the royal yacht *Augusta*, Caroline and her suite finally sailed up the Thames, to land at Greenwich.

From the moment she disembarked, Caroline of Brunswick found herself involved in the Royal Family's intrigues. The Prince himself, by some extraordinary whim, did not trouble to meet her; he sent, as his deputy, Caroline's newly appointed lady of the bedchamber. This, by her own contriving and by the unforgivable sanction of the Queen (who had wanted the Prince of Wales to marry her own niece, Princess Louise), was Frances, Countess of Jersey. Escorted by her bridegroom's mistress, and by a detachment of the Prince of Wales's Light Dragoons, Caroline drove off to St. James's Palace. Her cavalcade arrived at about half-past two. Soon afterwards, summoned by Malmesbury, the Prince of Wales arrived to greet his official bride.

Once before he had married, with absolute love and respect. Now, wrote Malmesbury, he could hardly speak. He 'turned round, retired to a distant part of the apartment, and, calling me to him, said "Harris, I am not well; pray get me a glass of brandy." '(*159*)

It is hard not to pity Caroline: she must have known, from that moment, that her marriage was an inevitable catastrophe. Her nervousness made her more gauche than ever. Her bitterness brought out her least attractive qualities, and she was flippant and coarse about Lady Jersey; her frivolity and coarseness only confirmed the Prince of Wales's hatred. The Prince was against her, the Queen was against her, and Lady Jersey was naturally against her. Caroline was foreign, provincial, lonely and ludicrous: she found herself an outcast from the first.

Yet it is difficult not to sympathise with the civilised Prince who was forced to commit himself to this ridiculous *ingénue*: it is hard not to feel for the fastidious, passionate man who was compelled to marry an unclean eccentric. 'The Prince had always been used to women of such perfect cleanliness and sweetness,' wrote Lady Hester Stanhope, the niece of Pitt, 'that it is no wonder that he was disgusted.'(*160*)

Lady Hester was not alone in recalling the sweetness and nobility, the tact and grace of Mrs. Fitzherbert. All those who passed her London house saw that it was lit up in honour of the Prince of Wales's wedding. 'At least,' so Mrs. Fitzherbert wrote, 'I shall have the approbation of my own conscience & heart in knowing I have never said or done anything to hurt him.'(*161*)

Her devotion was returned. Though he toyed with Lady Jersey, though he was driven to marry Caroline of Brunswick, the Prince of Wales had no doubt, now, to whom his love was given. On the eve of his official wedding, by his brother the Duke of Clarence, he sent Mrs. Fitzherbert a brief message: 'William, tell Mrs. Fitzherbert she is the only woman I shall ever love.'(*162*)

On the evening of Wednesday, 8 April, in the Chapel Royal, St. James's Palace, the Prince of Wales married Caroline of Brunswick. The King, her uncle, gave her away with apparent satisfaction. The bride, overcome by her new station, was smiling and nodding to everyone. The bridegroom 'looked like Death and full of confusion, as if he wished to hide himself from the looks of the whole world'.(*163*) When the Archbishop of Canterbury duly inquired if there were lawful impediments to the marriage, he laid down his book and looked earnestly at the Prince of Wales. The Prince was weeping. The Duke of Bedford, one of the two unmarried dukes who attended him, found it hard to stop him falling, for the Prince 'had drunk several glasses of brandy to enable him to go through the ceremony. There is no doubt', said the Duke of Bedford's brother, 'but it was a *compulsory* marriage.'(*164*)

Caroline said that her husband spent the whole of their wedding night drunk on the floor.

'You are now a husband,' wrote a pamphleteer. 'You may soon be a father. ... You are also united to a Princess, of whom all speak with delight and admiration. ... She has a right to demand the sacrifice of former attachments and later partialities. ...'(*165*) Such exhortations, public or private, were certain to be futile. The Prince would not dispense with Lady Jersey, who remained in official attendance during the honeymoon. Though the King commanded Hoppner to paint a portrait of the bride in her wedding dress, though Caroline soon proved to be pregnant, it became increasingly evident that the marriage was a disaster.

After two or three weeks, the Prince and Princess did not live as man and wife. They spent six months, from June to November, at the Pavilion; it was the last place in which the Prince could face the prospect of his permanent misery. In mid July, when he invited visitors to a concert, Caroline's wretchedness was already public.

'She, poor Little Creature,' wrote Miss Holroyd to Ann Firth, 'is, I am afraid, a most unhappy Woman; her lively spirits, which she brought over with her, are all gone, and they say the melancholy and anxiety in her countenance is quite affecting.'(*166*)

To make matters worse, it appeared that the payment of his debts, the condition on which the Prince had agreed to marry, was, after all, to devolve upon himself. Parliament now granted him the handsome sum of £125,000 a year; but since of this total £65,000 and the revenues of the Duchy of Cornwall were to be earmarked for payment of his debts, his situation was little better than it had been before his marriage. He felt he had been duped by Pitt. He was forced to reduce his establishment: and his marriage was hardly made more bearable by such measures.

In fact he could tolerate it no longer. He insulted his wife in every conceivable fashion; he took back the pearl bracelets he had given her as a wedding present, and offered them to Lady Jersey, who wore them, publicly, in Caroline's presence. Queen Charlotte's behaviour was hardly royal: she so detested her daughter-in-law that she openly supported her son and his mistress. Lady Jersey repaid her by spying on the Princess of Wales, and, it is said, intercepting her letters to Brunswick. As for the Duke of Clarence, at a ball at the Castle Inn, Richmond, he gave his opinion to Mrs. Sutton of Molesey. 'My brother has behaved very foolishly. To be sure he has married a very foolish, disagreeable person, but he should [have] made the best of a bad bargain, as my father has done. . . . What do you think, Madam?'(*167*)

On Thursday, 7 January 1796, Caroline gave birth to a daughter. The Prince of Wales had married to clear his debts and produce an heir to the throne. He was clearing his debts; he had now performed the second part of his duty. All he wanted was an immediate and final separation. On 30 April, at Caroline's request, he stated the fact in writing.

Windsor Castle, 30th of April, 1796.

Madam,

As Lord Cholmondeley informs me that you wish I would define in writing the terms upon which we are to live, I shall endeavour to explain myself upon that head, with as much clearness, and with as much propriety, as the nature of the subject will admit. Our inclinations are not in our power, nor should either of us be held answerable to the other, because nature had not made us suitable to each other. Tranquil and comfortable society is, however, in our power; let our intercourse, therefore, be restricted to that, and I will distinctly subscribe to the condition which you required, through Lady Cholmondeley, that even in the event of any accident happening to my daughter, which I trust Providence in its mercy will avert, I shall not infringe the terms of the restriction by proposing, at any period, a connexion of a more particular nature. I shall now finally close this disagreeable correspondence, trusting that as we have completely

explained ourselves to each other, the rest of our lives
will be passed in uninterrupted tranquillity.

I am Madam
With great truth
Very sincerely yours,
GEORGE P. (*168*)

15

When the Princess of Wales received this letter, she happened to be with George Canning, the politician. She asked
him (so he told the Duke of Wellington, years later) how
she should interpret it. 'He decided peremptorily that it
was a letter giving her permission to do as she liked, and
they took advantage of it on the spot. I rather fancy,' added
Mme de Lieven, the wife of the Russian Ambassador, 'that
might have happened even before the letter.'(*169*) It seems
more than probable that Canning was the Princess's lover;
Lady Bessborough, who knew him well, thought the rumour
'in great part true'.(*170*) The Prince of Wales believed it.
Canning himself later asserted that the Princess of Wales
had been his mistress, and in time he resigned his office
rather than join in any proceedings against her.

It would have been understandable for Caroline to have
taken a lover; but it seems quite clear that she threw all
reticence and dignity to the winds. Her mode of life,
wrote Robert Bell, in his Life of Canning, 'surprised and
perplexed everybody. ... She was free, coarse, vulgar,
boisterous; had a gross constitution, used to eat onions and
drink ale, which she called *oil*; and sit on the floor, and
play forfeits and romps; and talk broad, humorous scandal
to her ladies, for the sake of the fun. ... She hardly knew
how to get through her time, ... and was glad of any one
that came to dinner. ... Canning lived in the neighbour-
hood and was constantly invited.'(*171*)

Her only care was to make herself amends for her husband's desertion, and to ensure his humiliation. Mme de

Lieven hinted to Metternich that the husband of an acquaintance was 'suspected, I fancy not without reason, of having had the same relations with her as Mr. Canning.'(*172*) Lady de Clifford, Princess Charlotte's governess, was horrified by Caroline's levity of manner and language; Lord Lucan, to whom the Princess confided her behaviour, answered: 'By heavens, madam, your Royal Highness will be sent a sort of state prisoner to Holyrood House.' Lord Minto, dining with Caroline at her home at Blackheath, noticed that 'Mr. Dundas squeezed the Princess's hand in the tenderest manner possible, called her angel repeatedly, and said he hoped no one but himself would know how much he loved her. What', inquired Lord Minto, 'can the old thing mean?'(*173*) Lord Holland thought the Princess of Wales 'utterly destitute of all female delicacy. ... In short, to speak plainly, if not mad, she was a very worthless woman'.(*174*) The Reverend William Mason, writing to Bishop Hurd, repeated a fairly general opinion: 'I am,' he agreed, 'a perfect convert to your Lordship's Hypothesis of Insanity.'(*175*) Lady Hester Stanhope, who was no prude, expressed herself quite frankly:

Oh! what an impudent woman was that Princess of Wales: she was a downright —.... How the sea-captains used to colour up when she danced about, exposing herself like an opera girl; and then she gartered below the knee: —she was so low, so vulgar! I quarrelled with her at Plymouth, for I was the only person that ever told her the truth; ... and I plainly told her it was a hanging matter, and that she should mind what she was about.(*176*)

Did Caroline perhaps model herself on Catherine the Great? Lady Holland recorded that, soon after their marriage, the Prince had been greatly struck by her interest in a Life of Catherine,

whom she said was a great princess and served for an example '*à toutes princesses*'. He seriously believes that it has passed in her mind to adopt Catherine as a model, and as a proof he declares that she wore usually men's clothes, and received many navy officers in that attire at Plymouth.(*177*)

In the autumn of 1801 Lord Sheffield's sister heard that 'the Prince has told the Chancellor that he had contrived to have a private interview with the Princess and that she is with child'.(*178*) By the autumn of 1804 Lord Colchester reported that her conduct was causing great uneasiness. On the evening of Boxing Day that year, Lady Bessborough, the Duchess of Devonshire's sister, received a visit from the Prince of Wales. 'If he is bad one way, the Princess's levity on the other is inconceivable.... He said tonight he believ'd she was mad.'(*179*) On 14 July 1805, Lord Sheffield declared that some of her servants had been spying on her behaviour. In the early summer of 1806, there burst upon the world that unparalleled and indelicate inquiry known as The Delicate Investigation.(*180*)

The Investigation was, briefly, the result of accusations made against the Princess of Wales by her neighbour at Blackheath, Lady Charlotte Douglas. This handsome, ruthless woman was the wife of a retired major-general, Sir John Douglas; and the couple lived in a *ménage à trois* with Sir John's former colleague, Admiral Sir Sidney Smith, the hero of the Siege of St. Jean d'Acre. Lady Douglas was Sir Sidney's mistress.

In November 1801 Lady Douglas had first met the Princess of Wales; and they had become so intimate that Caroline had been godmother to their second child. At Christmas, 1803, however, when the Douglases were away in Devonshire, Caroline discovered that Lady Douglas had been casting reflections on her conduct. She had asked the Duke of Kent, her brother-in-law, to help her settle the matter; the Duke had sent for Sir Sidney Smith, and Sir Sidney had told him of 'a most scandalous anonymous letter of a nature calculated to set on Sir John and him to cut each other's throats'. Judging by the handwriting and style, Sir Sidney and Sir John were both convinced that the letter was the work of the Princess. The Duke asked Sir Sidney 'to avoid the shameful *éclat* which the publication of such a fact must produce'. He emphasised the effect it would have on the health of the King, and on the relations between the King and the Prince of Wales. A few days later, Sir Sidney assured the Duke that Sir John would, 'under *existing circumstances*, remain *quiet*, if left unmolested; for that he would *not* pledge himself not to bring the subject forward hereafter'.

But Lady Douglas had been discarded by the Princess of Wales, and she was determined on revenge. In the late autumn of 1805, Sir John, who was now attached to the household of the Duke of Sussex, asserted to the Duke that the Princess of Wales had not only committed adultery, but in 1802 at Blackheath had given birth to a child known as William Austin. As Lady Douglas had confidently expected, the Duke reported the matter to his brother, the Prince of Wales. The Prince himself, 'in the greatest agitation', told Lady Bessborough what followed. He had replied that he had heard of it a year before ('which is true', wrote Lady Bessborough, 'for he told it me'),

> but had forborne taking any notice of it from wishing the subject to be dropp'd. The Duke of Sussex answer'd: 'You may do as you please for yourself, tho' it is a little hard upon your Daughter; but at any rate we cannot be so passive and run the chance of being cut out by a stranger.' After much conversation he persuaded the Prince to hear Sir J. and Ly. Douglas's charge.(*181*)

The Prince of Wales had talked to Lord Thurlow, the former Lord Chancellor. 'Sir,' answered Thurlow, 'if you were a common man, she might sleep with the Devil; I should say, let her alone and hold your tongue. But the Prince of Wales has no right to risk his Daughter's Crown and his Brother's claims. The Princess of Wales should be like Caesar's wife, not even suspected. For both your sakes the accusation once made must be examin'd into, but leave it to your Brothers.' The Prince had then given *carte blanche*, and asked to hear no more about it.

An inquiry was duly opened; some of the Princess's

household hinted that she had demeaned herself with Canning, Sir Sidney Smith, Captain Thomas Manby of the Royal Navy, and Thomas Lawrence, the artist. Lord Grenville, the Prime Minister (according to the Prince) had taken the evidence to the King. 'Two years ago this would have surpris'd me,' said the King, 'but not now.' Lord Grenville had asked His Majesty's orders. 'He replied that if it had been one attachment, and even a child, he would have screen'd her if he could have done it with safety to the Crown, but there seem'd so much Levity and profligacy that she was not worth the screening.'(*182*) The King's opinion was shared by others. Samuel Romilly, the Whig politician, declared that the 'Prince could not have acted otherwise than he has done; and if he is to blame, it is for having used too much caution, and delayed too long laying before the Ministers the important facts which had come to his knowledge.'(*183*)

Lady Bessborough, with her ear to the ground, heard the approaching rumours; she recorded them for her former lover, Granville Leveson Gower. On 25 June 1806, she wrote:

> I began telling you, I think, of the Prince and Princess of Wales, and a bad story it is. ... The chief accusations are supposed to have been made by a Lady Douglas from jealousy of Sir Sid. Smith, her lover; the others are a Capn Moresby [*sic*] and—guess—[Canning]! ...(*184*)

Two days later, Lady Bessborough was informed of events by the ultimate authority. The Prince himself arrived,

> [and] said he could no longer delay justifying his conduct to me; that he had forborne for three whole years interfering with the Princess; that if there had been any *common* decency observ'd he would still have tried to screen her, because an unprotected woman in any state was to be pitied, but that I should judge ...(*185*)

He told her of his conversation with the Duke of Sussex, his conversation with Thurlow, the visit to the King, and the setting up of an inquiry. He said that, out of respect for Lady Bessborough (a close friend of Canning's), he had himself scratched Canning's name out of Lady Douglas's statement.(*186*)

On 29 June Lord Boringdon assured Lady Bessborough that he had very little doubt of the truth of the charges.(*187*) Next morning matters came to a head: she received a visit from Canning. 'I was,' she wrote, 'almost afraid of mentioning the Princess of Wales, but he began first. He ask'd me if I had heard him talk'd of. I told him I had; he neither own'd nor denied, but on the whole I am stagger'd, and afraid it is in great part true.'(*188*)

There were still some who protested the innocence of the Princess of Wales. They did so partly from ignorance, partly from chivalry, but, very largely, from dislike of her husband. They were no doubt so intent on recalling his own familiar misconduct that they could only see her as the immaculate victim. 'What does [Walsh Porter] say of his friend the Prince?' Lady Donegal asked Thomas Moore, 'and what is the general opinion of the poor unfortunate Princess? I have not a doubt of her innocence; but I fear that from motives of policy towards the Prince, the story will be hushed up.'(*189*)

Walter Scott, who had attended Caroline's court at Blackheath, hoped that she was innocent of the critical charges brought against her; but he could not persuade himself that the investigation was unwarranted. Lockhart, his son-in-law and biographer, recalled how Scott had regretfully observed 'the careless levity of the Princess's manner ... as likely to bring the purity of heart and mind, for which he gave her credit, into suspicion'. One evening at Blackheath she had taken him, alone, to admire some flowers in a conservatory. She had skipped down the steps; it was dark, and Scott, who was lame, had hesitated before he followed her. The Princess of Wales had turned round, and said, with mock indignation: 'Ah! false and faint-hearted troubadour! You will not trust yourself with me for fear of your neck!'(*190*)

On 14 July 1806, the Royal Commissioners reported to the King on the Delicate Investigation. They were

completely satisfied that William Austin was the son of Sophia
Austin, and was born on 11 July 1802, in the Brownlow
Street Hospital. But while Caroline was acquitted of the
gravest charge against her, 'other particulars of her conduct
had given occasion to very unfavourable interpretations. ...
We think the circumstances to which we now refer, particularly those between her Royal Highness and Captain Manby,
must be credited until they shall receive some decisive con-
tradiction.' It was a statement against the common principle
of English justice. The Princess must be considered guilty
until she could be proved innocent.

How far, in fact, had she been guilty? Captain Manby
seems to be the least likely of her lovers, and nothing was
proved against him. Perhaps she had chosen to implicate
him out of bravado. Nothing had been proved against Sir
Sidney Smith, though Princess Charlotte later suggested
that Edwardina Kent, one of her mother's child protégés,
was her mother's child by Sir Sidney. As for Thomas
Lawrence, one of the Princess's household declared he had
been in great danger 'of losing his head'; and Lawrence's
biographer wrote that after his servant had been examined,
'Lord Eldon, in conversation with Mr. Lawrence, said to
him, "Sir, you are a very fortunate man, indeed. ... You
have the most faithful, clever, and prudent servant, who has
served you cunningly—at the hour of need." '(191) The
implication seems to be that only his servant's wit had
saved Lawrence's misdemeanours from being known. As for
Canning, there was small doubt, in Society, that he had been
the Princess of Wales's lover. 'How strange it seems now,'
wrote Lady Elizabeth Foster in 1807, 'to recollect all that
Canning said to Lady Bessborough of the Princess's encouragement of him, and of the King being hurt at having
a letter telling him of Canning's intimacy with the Princess.'(192)

In March 1819, Caroline herself informed James Brougham
that she had 'humbugged Perceval, Eldon and the whole
lot', and that William Austin was the natural son of Prince
Louis Ferdinand of Prussia, who had always been her first
love. Long after all concerned were dead, George Dawson-

Damer recorded some curious sentences from Mrs. Fitzherbert's conversation.

Princess of Wales married to Prince Louis. Could have
bastardised Princess Charlotte. Compounded with the
mother—Lord Loughborough by George III's commands.
She saw Princess Charlotte who implored her.

A Peer still alive, who had been a lover of the Princess
of Wales, who implored him to destroy the Certificate of
marriage to Princess Louis.(*193*)

16

Whatever her part in contriving the Prince of Wales's marriage, however much she had helped to make it publicly
ridiculous, Lady Jersey had not secured her own position.
In 1798, with the promise that he would always protect
her and her family, the Prince finally left her. Lady Jersey
would never accept her dismissal. Two years later, at the
Duchess of Devonshire's breakfast, she was still observed
'Coasting round' the Prince, who eyed her askance.(*194*) As
late as 1803, one of his household had to signify 'the desire
of the Prince that *she would not speak to him*'.(*195*)

The reason for Lady Jersey's dismissal was not the need
for a new mistress. The Prince of Wales had grown tired
of superficial relationships. Three days after the birth of
his daughter, he had made the will that would move two
Kings of England to tears. He had left all his worldly possessions to 'my true and real Wife', to 'my Maria Fitzherbert,
my Wife, the Wife of my heart and soul'.(*196*) Now his
official marriage was broken, he longed to return to her.

This time, though private emissaries and mutual friends
were sent in pursuit, Mrs. Fitzherbert was not amenable. Her
refusal made him desperate; and, never mild in his emotions, he assured his sisters that he should die if she was
not reconciled to him. The Queen herself wrote to Mrs.

Fitzherbert, 'pressing her to be reconciled to the Prince. ...
A strong step', as Lord Glenbervie said, 'for so moral a
queen to take'.(*197*) Mrs. Fitzherbert also had her ideas of
morality: she could not bring herself to live with the husband of the Princess of Wales.

She gave her promise to rejoin him, and then, in fear,
withdrew it; in vain he wrote her letters of entreaty. At
last, on the night of 11 June 1799, he sent her his final
ultimatum:

> Save me, save me on my knees I conjure you from my-
> self. ... If your answer is conformable which God grant
> it may be to my wishes, by assurance of your being
> again *mine* there is nothing in this world I will not do,
> and in which I will not be guided by you through every
> circumstance in life now and for ever. But if it is the
> reverse, that instant my Father and the rest of my family,
> shall be acquainted with the truth of my situation. As
> God is my judge, and as I hope to receive mercy at his
> hands, this is my last and final determination—on my
> knees have I sworn it, and on my knees do I write it to
> you. Thus my fate now depends solely on you, Life with
> you; or at least a quiet conscience, which will make me
> face everything. I shall have liberated my own heart,
> cleared the character of my only beloved of soul to the
> world, and by voluntarily sacrificing myself proved that
> I have deserved a better fate, and to have been loved by
> you, as I have loved you and shall every day to the last
> moments of my existence.(*198*)

The Prince sent his brother, the Duke of Cumberland, to
deliver this letter into Mrs. Fitzherbert's own hands.

Most women of forty-three, besought by the man they
loved to return to him, would not have taken long to capitu-
late; besought by the Prince of Wales, and by the Queen
of England, they would have been rather readier to submit.
Mrs. Fitzherbert hesitated. If she appeared again, and openly,
with the Prince, she would be proclaiming herself his mistress. If she did not, she might be revealed as his wife,
and bring untold disturbance to him and to the country.

She had always loved the Prince, and she loved him still. But her devotion went against her ideas of morality, her patriotism, and, above all, against her religious principles.

She finally asked a Roman Catholic chaplain, the Reverend Mr. Nassau, of Warwick Street Chapel, to lay the case before the Pope in Rome. If the answer was favourable, she would return to the Prince; if it was not, she would leave the country for ever.

Pius VI died in August, during the appeal, and she waited with resolution. As the century began, the Prince expressed his hope that she might have 'every earthly happiness, and that he might be permitted to contribute his Mite towards that perfect state of blissful enjoyment'.

'The Prince of Wales is supposed to be dying,' noted Lady Holland on 14 February. 'Whatever his illness may be besides, revived love for Mrs. Fitzherbert has aggravated and added to the measure of it. Mde. de Coigny says it's like a *rondeau* in which variations are made *ad libitum,* but the return is to the first air.'(*199*)

In March 1800, Pius VII was elected to the Triple Crown. On 16 June, when he had given his sanction, Mrs. Fitzherbert accepted her happiness. At No. 6, Tilney Street, she gave a wedding breakfast 'to meet the Prince of Wales'.

17

At the turn of the century, the Prince moved happily through the annals of medicine, scholarship and the arts. Late in March 1800, Dr. Edward Jenner, who had recently discovered vaccination, was presented to him at Carlton House. 'His Royal Highness on this, as on every other occasion, received him with marked respect', wrote Jenner's biographer; 'and at future periods showed the interest he felt for the cause of vaccination, by the personal efforts which he was pleased to make for its advancement.'(*200*) Vaccination was the one policy on which the Royal Family agreed; and when the Royal Jennerian Society was estab-

lished to exterminate smallpox, the King became patron and
the Prince of Wales a vice-patron. The Prince expressed 'the
most cordial approbation of the indefatigable perseverance
of Dr. Jenner in perfecting the discovery of vaccination. This
his Royal Highness stated from a full conviction of the
efficacy of the practice, and from a distinct perception of
the incalculable advantages it promised to the world'.(*201*)
He remained Jenner's loyal supporter: in the year of his
coronation, he appointed him physician-extraordinary; and
in 1827 *The Life of Edward Jenner* was dedicated to the
King who, 'on more occasions than one', had expressed his
'unequivocal and generous Royal favour'.(*202*)

In 1796, the year when Jenner had performed his first
successful vaccination, the Prince of Wales had shown his
earliest patronage of literature: he had given two gold
medals, for English composition, and two silver medals, for
elocution, to Winchester College.(*203*) That year, when
Samuel Ireland claimed to have discovered a mass of Shakespeare's papers, the Prince summoned him to bring them;
he questioned him with an acuteness which Ireland 'had
never before witnessed from the learned', and showed a
specialist's acquaintance with Elizabethan documents. The
forgery which the Prince suspected was later confessed. One
thing, he told Sheridan, was clear: there were too many
manuscripts to have been hidden above ground for so
long.(*204*)

Time and again, the Prince appeared as a patron of the
arts. He ordered a set of chairs from Hepplewhite, and it
became the vogue to have heart-back chairs carved boldly
with the Prince of Wales's feathers. He and Mrs. Fitzherbert
inspected the Royal Academy, and appeared in a box at
the Opera; and on 1 December 1804, when the thirteen-
year-old William Betty gave his first performance at Covent
Garden, as Selim, in *Barbarossa*, the Prince of Wales sat in
Lady Melbourne's box, 'an attentive observer of the astonishing performance of the Infant Roscius. In the scene
where he discovers himself,' noted an observer, 'and points
to the scar on his forehead, the Prince took the lead in the
loud and reiterated bursts of applause which followed'.(*205*)

Nothing was talked of but this young actor, wrote Lady
Elizabeth Foster, a few days later. 'In short, he has changed
the life of London; people dine at four, and go to the
Play, and think of nothing but the play. ... Sheridan took
him to Carlton House, and the Prince told me that his manner was perfect; it was simple, graceful, and unaffected.
...'(206)

Carlton House was still the scene of Arabian Nights enter-
tainments: in 1803 the Prince was host to Elfi Bey, chief
of the Mamelukes, and Mahomet Aga, his principal officer,
who tamed the Prince's ungovernable Egyptian horse in a
mere twenty minutes.(207) In 1804, Mr. Creevey, the Whig
politician and diarist, swam into the Prince's ken, and was
invited down to the Pavilion.(208) (The Prince now admired Humphrey Repton's ideas, and economy alone prevented him from improving the Pavilion in Indian style.)
Lady Bessborough was sitting quietly in her travelling dress
at a Brighton inn, when the Prince arrived, and insisted on
taking her, then and there, to a banquet. The invitation
was irresistible; but Lady Bessborough was decidedly put out
by wearing the wrong clothes. 'There was beautiful music
who you would have lik'd,' she told Granville Leveson
Gower, 'but think of poor me sitting quite undress'd in a
formal circle of people I did not know all over Diamonds
and Gold—from eight till past two.'(209) However, she was
not too nonplussed to return next day and examine the
Pavilion with diligence.

I did not think the strange Chinese shapes and columns
could have look'd so well [she informed the same cor-
respondent]. It is like Concetti in Poetry, in outré and
false taste, but for the kind of thing as perfect as it can
be, and the Prince says he had it so because at the time
there was such a cry against French things, &c., that he
was afraid of his furniture being accus'd of jacobinism.

His way of living is pleasant enough, especially if one
might chuse one's society. In the Morning he gives you
horses, Carriages, &c., to go where you please with you;
he comes and sits *rather too long*, but only on a visit.

Everybody meets at dinner, which, *par parenthèse,* is excellent, with the addition of a few invitations in the evening. Three large rooms, very comfortable, are lit up; whist, backgammon, Chess, trace Madame—every sort of game you can think of in two of them, and Music in the third. His band is beautiful. He has also Viotti [the violinist] and a Lady who sings and plays very well.(*210*)

No one could be more conventional than the Prince of Wales, yet no one, at heart, more enjoyed bohemian society. In the summer of 1806 he attended a dinner given by the fashionable Neapolitan Club. At about twelve o'clock, wrote one of the guests,

> we were all surprised to see on the table a dwarf, who ... could not have been more than five and thirty inches in height. He first entered at the bottom of the room ... dressed in a Court suit, with his *chapeau-bras* under his arm, and his sword by his side. After bowing, and running between the decanters and dessert, he made his *obéissance....* The Prince seated him on his knee, where, like a child on the nurse's lap, he sat eating cakes and ices.(*211*)

Among the members present that night were two social planets. One was William Beckford, the eccentric author of *Vathek,* and the builder of Fonthill, the immense Gothick folly in Wiltshire. The other was Beau Brummell.

Many years ago, now, the Prince had met George Bryan Brummell, then an Eton schoolboy, on the terrace at Windsor, and had admired his style and originality. He had given him a cornetcy in his own regiment; and, when Brummell resigned his commission to lead a life of pleasure at 4, Chesterfield Street, the Prince had more than once enjoyed his excellent little dinners. He still appreciated Brummell's elegance: the thought that two glovers were entrusted with each pair of his gloves (one of them making the thumbs, and the other the rest). He was amused to hear (though perhaps, again, the tales were legendary) that Brummell's boots were waxed *au vin de Champagne,* and that the ties

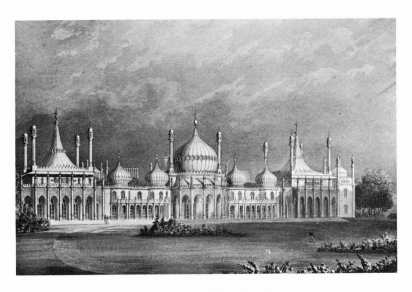

The Royal Pavilion in 1825
From 'The Royal Pavilion at Brighton' by John Nash

The North Front of Carlton House
From an engraving by Reeve, after Woodall

George IV as Prince of Wales
From the portrait by Thomas Gainsborough

of his cravats were designed by the first portrait-painter in London. He and Brummell shared the same tailors, Schweitzer and Davidson, in Cork Street; they opened their snuff-boxes in the identical manner, 'with peculiar grace, and with one hand only—the left'.

But Brummell was to discover, like others, that the Prince of Wales would not tolerate insults to Mrs. Fitzherbert. When, at a ball, the Prince asked him to send for her carriage, Brummell obliged, 'but in doing so, substituted the word *mistress* for the usual one of Mrs., and laid a strong emphasis on the insulting epithet'. Soon afterwards, at a party given by Charles Ellis (later Lord Seaford) at Claremont, the Prince himself turned Brummell from the door. Brummell was one of the very few friends whom he would not forgive.(*212*)

18

In the decade that followed the Prince's marriage, the Princess of Wales was not the only cause of anxiety. Relations between the Prince and his father grew more tense than ever. No doubt they were worsened by the Prince's failure to settle down into domesticity, by his treatment of his wife, his love-affairs, and the constant quarrels over the upbringing of Princess Charlotte. They were also worsened by politics.

In the autumn of 1800, unknown to the King, Pitt and his Cabinet colleagues discussed the advisability of making political concessions to the Irish Catholics. The King was privately informed of what was going on, and he was also privately advised that his Coronation Oath forbade him to agree to any such measures. Early in 1801 he wrote to Pitt, and urged that neither of them should mention the subject again. Pitt offered his resignation. The King read the Coronation Oath to his wife and daughters and added: "If I violate it, I am no longer sovereign of this country, but it falls to the House of Savoy.' A few days later he again went out of his mind.

All the animosities and intrigues of 1788 were once more revived, but after a few weeks the King recovered, dismissed Pitt from office, and invited that monument of incompetence, Henry Addington, the future Viscount Sidmouth, to be Prime Minister. He was guided, he explained to Dr. Hurd (now Bishop of Worcester), by 'my sense of my Coronation Oath, of the Compact on which my family was invited to mount the Throne, and the Act of Union with Scotland ... I have persuaded Mr. Addington to succeed Mr. Pitt, and can assure you his attachment to the Church is as sincere as mine ... I feel I have done my Duty'.(213)

Although the Prince of Wales had had every inducement to act indiscreetly during his father's relapse, his behaviour had caused no particular criticism. 'As Heaven's my witness,' he declared, 'I love my Father to my heart, and never think of his sufferings without tears'. Lady Bessborough said that as he spoke the tears ran down his cheeks.(214) But, just as in 1788, he had been refused all admission to his parents. And 'is it not hard', he asked, 'to be denied the pleasure of attending him, of even seeing the Q. or my Sisters? To be forbid going to my Father's House, and to know that if he continues ill *his* power and *my* birthright will be usurp'd by such a man as *Addington*?'(215) It was hard indeed, for Lady Bessborough declared that she 'never heard the P. at any time mention the K. but with respect and affection'.(216)

However, when hostilities between England and France broke out again in 1803, the Prince of Wales expressed his pent-up feelings. As a youth he had been appointed a colonel in the army, and he had later been made colonel of the 10th Light Dragoons. He had always taken a keen interest in his regiment, and he sometimes went into camp with them (in 1794 his tent had included a bedroom, drawing-room and dining-room, 'all hung with different Chintz Patterns').(217) But though one of his younger brothers was a Field-Marshal, and three of them were Lieutenant-Generals, no other army promotion or appointment had been given to him. It was a settled point in Hanoverian family policy that the heir to the throne should not be given high rank in the army or navy. But now, when Napoleon threatened an invasion of England, the Prince very naturally applied for a military command, hoping that this might 'excite the loyal energies of the nation'.

His appeal was ignored, and in July he wrote to Addington, pointing out the obloquy he would suffer if he was thought to be indifferent to national danger. The King showed his usual intransigence: he replied, through Addington, that the subject should not be mentioned to him again. On 2 August the question was raised by the Prince's friends in Parliament, but no satisfactory answer was given. On 6 August the Prince wrote directly to his father: 'I ask to be allowed to display the best energies of my character; to shed the last drop of my blood in support of your Majesty's person, crown and dignity.'(218) The King applauded his son's spirit, but again expressed the hope that the subject would not be revived. The Prince answered: 'My next brother, the Duke of York, commands the army; the younger branches of my family are either Generals or Lieutenant-Generals; and I, who am the Prince of Wales, am to remain Colonel of Dragoons. There is something so humiliating in the contrast, that those who are at a distance would either doubt the reality, or suppose that to be my fault which is only my misfortune.'(219)

There was a certain amount of popular sympathy with the Prince; and Lady Bessborough, on whom he called at ten o'clock one night, could only commiserate. 'He told us he had had a violent correspondence with the K. He wrote what he thought to be an humble remonstrance, and wishing at least to have the command of a body of volunteers. The K.'s answer was a threat that his own Regiment, the 10th, would be taken away from him. ...'(220) Lady Bessborough listened for four hours to his lamentations, but on 9 September she saw him again, 'still so full of his wrongs that he can talk of nothing else. He says the threat was to take his Regiment away and give it to the D. of Cambridge.

This does seem violent in answer to the letter he read us, which is really very respectful and affectionate, only reminding the K. of a promise he had received from him last war of having some command'.(*221*) The King's behaviour seemed even more extraordinary considering his political apprehensions.

We are here in daily expectation that Buonoparte will attempt his threatened Invasion [he told Bishop Hurd on 30 November]. The chances against his success seem so many that it is wonderful He persists in it. . . . Should his Troops effect a landing I shall certainly put myself at the head of Mine and my other armed subjects to repell them, but as it is impossible to foresee the events of such a conflict should the Enemy approach too near to Windsor I shall think it right the Queen and my Daughters should Cross the Severn and shall send them to your Episcopal Palace at Worcester.(*222*)

However, it seemed that the Prince of Wales was destined to offend his father. In an impulsive moment he published the whole correspondence between them, which infuriated the King even further. For nearly a year they did not meet, and when the King and Queen gave a Drawing-room the Prince announced that he was too ill to attend; he then allowed himself to be seen driving ostentatiously through London. In February 1804 the King was ill yet again, and that April Creevey declared his belief 'that the Regal function will never more be exercised by him';(*223*) on 2 June, observing the daily and nightly attendance of five doctors at Buckingham House, he predicted: 'This must end surely at no distant period—a Regency—and then I hope the game's our own. . . . We [the Whigs] are a great body—the Prince at the head of us. Fox, Grey, &c., are all in great spirits . . .'(*224*)

But once more the King recovered; and, through the Lord Chancellor, he engaged in a delicate negotiation with his son. Princess Charlotte was eight years old, and her formal education had to begin. Until now she had lived at Carlton House, or at Warwick House, which adjoined it, with a governess, and she had been allowed to go to Black-heath to see her mother. The King now proposed that she should come and live at Windsor, and that he and the Queen should be responsible for her education.

As the negotiations dragged on, it became clear that the King intended the child to see much more of her mother. On 12 November he and the Prince met for the first time since their quarrel over the Prince's military command. As soon as the Prince saw that the King wanted to allow the Princess of Wales more influence over the child, he threatened to break off negotiations. 'I am really glad to find he has conducted himself with so much firmness, and at the same time with some decorum', wrote a correspondent to Mr. Creevey.(225)

On Christmas Day, at Carlton House, the poor little Princess played the pianoforte for her father. 'She is very pretty, I hear, and clever,' reported Lady Elizabeth Foster to her son Augustus. 'The King wanted to have her given up to him. The Prince does not consent to that, but appoints as nearly as he can all the persons whom the King would have named about the little Princess. I believe that Miss Trimmer will be sub-preceptress ... What the King's real state is I don't know, but he went to the Play in an admiral's uniform, which he never did before ...'(226)

Early in 1805 it was arranged that Princess Charlotte should live with her father when he was in London, but that she should go to her grandparents when he was away.

It was Mr. Creevey, bursting with gratitude for political favours to come, who recorded the Prince of Wales in the autumn of 1805. Early in September, with his wife and her daughters, he went down to spend the autumn at Brighton. Soon after his arrival, the Prince noticed him on the Steine, and, 'very gracious', came up to speak to him. Creevey presented his step-daughters. A few days later, he was invited to the Pavilion, where the Prince introduced him to Mrs. Fitzherbert, and asked her to call on Mrs. Creevey. Mrs. Fitzherbert called; and, wrote the diarist,

altho' she and Mrs. Creevey had never seen each other
before, an acquaintance began that soon grew into a very
sincere and agreeable friendship, which lasted the remainder of Mrs. Creevey's life. . . .

Immediately after this first visit from Mrs. Fitzherbert,
Mrs. Creevey and her daughters became invited with
myself to the Prince's parties at the Pavilion, and till the
first week in January—a space of about four months—
except a few days when the Prince went to see the King
at Weymouth, and a short time that I was in London in
November, there was not a day we were not at the Pavilion, I dining there always once or twice a week, Mrs.
Creevey frequently dining with me likewise, but in the
evening we were always there.

During these four months the Prince behaved with the
greatest good humour as well as kindness to us all. He
was always merry and full of his jokes, and any one
would have said that he was really a very happy man.
Indeed I have heard him say repeatedly during that time
that he never should be so happy when King, as he was
then.(227)

Creevey gave a warming account of Brighton domesticity: the Prince intent on instructing his band, the foot-
men passing sandwiches and wine at the end of the evening.
Mrs. Fitzherbert, a keen card-player, absorbed in whist or
loo, was not too busy to notice the Prince's behaviour. In
1804, when the Duke of Norfolk paid his annual visit, the
Prince had drunk excessively; this year, when the time of
the visit approached, 'Mrs. Fitzherbert, who was always the
Prince's best friend, was very much afraid of his being again
made ill, and she persuaded the Prince to adopt different
stratagems to avoid drinking with the Duke.'(228) Creevey
dined there on both days, 'and letters were brought in each
day after dinner to the Prince, which he affected to consider of great importance, and so went out to answer
them, while the Duke of Clarence went on drinking with
the Duke of Norfolk'.(229)

It was Mrs. Fitzherbert, on 6 November, who told Mrs.

Creevey the overwhelming news: 'The Prince has this moment recd. an account from the Admiralty of the death of
poor Lord Nelson, which has affected him most extremely.
I think you may wish to know the news, which, upon any
other occasion might be called a glorious victory.'(*230*)

The Prince was griefstricken at Nelson's death. He had
admired him 'as the greatest character England could ever
boast of, and he loved him as a friend'.(*231*) He promised
to do for Lady Hamilton all he could tactfully do or say.
He asked to attend Nelson's funeral as chief mourner, but
he was only allowed to attend it in a private capacity.
(Nelson's affair with Lady Hamilton had 'shocked the King's
morality', and Nelson's reception at Court, after the victory
of Aboukir, had been 'singularly cold and repulsive'.)(*232*)
The Prince also asked that all Nelson's papers in Earl Nelson's possession, and all his letters to the Duke of Clarence,
'should be furnished to form the history of a Life, which
is to be held out as an example of Heroism and professional Talent'.(*233*) The eight volumes of the Life received
'the sanction, and leading assistance', of the Prince of Wales.
and they were duly dedicated to him.

> Those Patriotic Principles [wrote the authors] which
> under your auspices were fostered and encouraged, are
> in the following pages with your sanction recorded, the
> sanction of the Prince of that Country for which NEL-
> SON fought and died; of the Prince by whom he was
> cherished whilst living, and by whom his Memory, after
> death, was honoured in a manner that was congenial with
> the enthusiasm and tenderness of his distinguished
> Character.(*234*)

Nelson's funeral took place at St. Paul's Cathedral on 9
January 1806. Exactly a fortnight later, on 23 January, Pitt
died, and a Parliamentary crisis was at hand. The King had
at last to send for the Whigs. Lord Grenville formed a
coalition Cabinet, the Ministry of All the Talents, in which
Fox held the seals of the Foreign Office, Grey was First Lord
of the Admiralty, Addington (now Lord Sidmouth) was
Privy Seal, and Erskine, the Prince's friend, became Lord

Chancellor. (It was out of compliment to the Prince, and at his request, that Erskine took the title of Baron Erskine of Restormel, from an ancient ruined castle in the Duchy of Cornwall.) (235) Mr. Creevey was appointed Secretary to the Board of Control, a post which, Grey explained, was 'better in point of emolument' than the seat at the Board of Admiralty which had at first been intended for him.

Within five months of the death of Pitt, the brightest of All the Talents was extinguished. On 10 June Fox appeared for the last time in the House of Commons. He was gravely ill, but determined to support the abolition of the slave trade. The bill that gave effect to his resolutions became law the following year. But by that time he was dead. Every bulletin during his last illness was anxiously awaited by both political parties; for all his faults, no public man was ever more loved than Fox for his private qualities. Pitt had commanded confidence and gratitude; Fox inspired profound affection. But dropsy had taken hold of him. He died on 13 September.

The Prince of Wales had a large capacity for giving affection and admiration. He had loved and admired Fox for more than twenty years. He had admired him as a politician and an orator, he had loved him as a brilliant, original companion, a vital, gifted older man who had increased his confidence in himself. Fox had not only symbolised his Whig sympathies, his political independence, he had given him something he greatly needed: mature, dynamic companionship. He would not find it with any other man.

'It is quite impossible,' he wrote to Lady Elizabeth Foster, 'to describe to you all I have gone through of late: such a loss and such a calamity are almost beyond all sufferance.'(236) On 29 September, while he was staying in Yorkshire, he asked to call on his old tutor, Dr. Markham, who had long since become Archbishop of York. When the carriage arrived at Bishopthorpe, the old man of eighty-seven came out to receive the Prince of Wales. The Prince ran up the steps, and knelt to receive his blessing.(237)

A few days later, the King forbade his son to attend Fox's funeral. It was a last revenge for years of political quarrels.

19

Early in December Joseph Farington, the diarist, was assured that the Prince 'cannot live, at least so says an Eminent Medical Man. That He can never recover from the state He is in.—He has now the *strongest tea* made for Him, which stands till it is Cold & It is then *iced* before He drinks it to allay an internal heat'.*(238)* In March 1807 the Prince's tailor, Weston of Bond Street, informed another friend of Farington's 'that the Prince is extremely reduced in his size, so much so that Cloaths which He formerly wore hang like great coats upon Him, and are obliged to be taken in greatly. He also said that the Prince looks very old & wrinkled, very much so considering his age. His Domestics speak of it with much concern fearing for their situations'.*(239)* The Duke of Clarence, always aware of the order of succession, declared that his brother would not live three months.*(240)*

Whatever the self-interest and malice outside its walls, within the Royal Academy the Prince was watched with affection and admiration. On 2 May, when he attended the Royal Academy dinner, 'everybody noticed how very ill He looked'.*(241)* John Julius Angerstein, the art collector, was troubled by his appearance; Farington 'observed He only eat *Fish*, & *Salad* & a little pudding & drank no wine; but He ate some Horse radishes at the end of the dinner.—He had none of the joy and gaiety, & spirit of address which I had at other times seen in him'.*(242)* When the President of the Royal Academy proposed the Prince's health, there was, said Farington, 'much *clapping*, which expressed the general feeling that *He* wanted it'.*(243)*

Hoppner declared that the Prince was 'supposed to have an *Atrophy*'.*(244)* It seems probable that his condition was largely caused by anxiety. There was the shock of Fox's death; there was also the constant horror of Caroline. She had threatened to publish her statement on the domestic situation, and only the change of Government, and the thought of possible favours from a new Ministry, had persuaded her to suppress the book (not, however, before there had been a leakage). She had now been offered a suite at Kensington Palace, and she had been asked to appear at Court. On 5 June, Lady Bessborough duly noted that the Prince and the Princess of Wales 'were both at the Mother's assembly. They did not speak, but coming out close together, both look'd contrary ways, like the print of the spread Eagle'.(245)

Unfortunately, the Prince of Wales was not only turning away from his impossible official wife. He was turning away from the unofficial wife he had long since chosen. Mrs. Fitzherbert was the only woman who had shown him real devotion. She had never demanded material rewards, she had always been lovingly discreet about the certificate of marriage which could have jeopardised the succession. She had forgiven the Prince for his infidelities, and accepted his dynastic marriage with dignity. She had corrected his weaknesses (among them his heavy drinking), she had set him a perpetual example of self-control and high principles. The Prince was the favourite son of his mother; he had always needed a strong, maternal wife. Mrs. Fitzherbert had shown him the strength and constancy he needed in what he called 'the wife of my heart and soul'.

The ultimate cause of their separation could hardly have been more tragic. Mrs. Fitzherbert, unlike certain other women in his life, was maternal by nature; in the summer of 1806, she had confessed to Lady Jerningham that 'She was particularly fond of Children, and Should have Liked to have a dozen of her own'.(246) Perhaps she was incapable of bearing a child. Perhaps, as a good Catholic and the wife of the Prince of Wales, she had borne children whom she was not allowed to acknowledge. The facts may not now be known, for she herself remained nobly discreet, and her confidential papers were destroyed. But her love of children remained; and when she was asked if she would write the story of her life, she simply said that it would break her heart.

For want of children of her own, Mrs. Fitzherbert delighted in a little girl of seven: the daughter of her friend, Lady Horatia Seymour. She had been entrusted with Minny Seymour while Lady Horatia and her husband, Lord Hugh (the brother of Lord Hertford) were abroad; and now that both of them had died, she naturally wanted to keep her. But Lord Hugh's will had been made before the birth of the child, and no guardian had been appointed. His executors objected to Mrs. Fitzherbert, ostensibly on the grounds of her religion, and brought an action in Chancery for the appointment of other guardians. They won the action; Mrs. Fitzherbert appealed to the Lord Chancellor, and lost. She would have appealed to the House of Lords if, on 14 June 1806, Lord Hertford had not announced, as head of the family, that he would be guardian himself. He then appointed her to act for him.

The Prince of Wales had helped to persuade him to take this momentous step. Mrs. Fitzherbert had gained a daughter who would owe her 'more than a daughter's feelings of gratitude & affection'.(247) It was soon observed that, in doing so, she had lost a husband. By November, Robert Plumer Ward, the politician, reported that the Prince had 'taken it into his head' that he was in love with Lady Hertford. Lady Hertford, aged forty-six, had 'taken it into her head to run away to Ireland as the best protection for her modesty.'(248)

It was also the best way to encourage passion. By August 1807, Lady Thomond could tell Farington, over tea, 'that Mrs. Fitzherbert has lost her influence over the P.—He is now devoted to the *Marchioness of Hertford;* to whom while they were in London, He constantly went every day & staid from three o'clock till five.—He now complains that Brighton is too cold for Him, & is going to Cheltenham, which is only 15 miles from Ragley in Warwickshire, the seat of the Marquis'. When Farington objected that the Marchioness was not young, Lady Thomond replied 'that notwithstanding she is an extraordinary [*sic*] fine woman, a *Juno'.*(249)

20

The Prince 'is really distracted and thinks of nothing but la bella e grassa Donna', wrote Lady Bessborough, on 16 October 1807.(250) The Prince, wrote Lady Elizabeth Foster, two days later, 'has given up politics, is good friends with the King, and lives but for Lady Hertford'. And since her native language seemed all at once inadequate to express her boundless surprise, Lady Elizabeth continued: 'C'est vrai je t'assure; à 50 ans près elle a captivé le Prince. Il ne vit, ne respire que pour elle et par elle; la ci-devant amie est inquiète et triste. Je la plains, car c'est une bonne personne qui n'a jamais abusé de son pouvoir.'(251)

Mrs. Fitzherbert deserved every word of praise that she was given. She had never abused her unparalleled power, never lost her dignity. She was still devoted to the Prince; and now, at the age of fifty, twenty-one years after the marriage which neither of them could acknowledge, she was clearly losing him.

On 23 October Lady Bessborough heard from the Prince himself; and what with his letter and the general gossip she wondered if he was going out of his mind. 'I really believe his Father's malady extends to him, only takes another turn,' she confessed to Granville Leveson Gower. 'He writes, day and night almost, and frets himself into a fever, and all to persuade la sua bella *Donnone to live with him—publickly!* A quoi bon, except to make, *if* possible, a greater cry against him?' And then, dispassionately, Lady Bessborough decided:

> I should not be surpriz'd if he and the ci devant [Mrs. Fitzherbert] were to quarrel quite during their meeting at Brighton. She has got irritated, and he bored; for this last there is, alas! no cure—the disease is fatal. Irretrievable quarrels may be made up, injuries forgiven, but weariness!—gradual decay of affection from causes too

slight for complaint, too numerous for removal—when once this begins all is over.(252)

On 26 November Lady Harriet Cavendish recorded that Mrs. Fitzherbert was 'very ill'.(253) Rumour said that the Prince never spent more than three hours in bed, and that he spent most of his waking hours writing to Lady Hertford. On 1 December, from Holland House, that centre of Whig gossip, Henry Brougham, the barrister, wrote to the Earl of Rosslyn: 'The Prince has been *really ill,* and is still in a very unpleasant way, though somewhat better. ... The story of his being so much in love with Lady Hertford is quite true, but certainly is not the sole cause of his lowness. She has treated him pretty cavalierly.'(254) The passion continued, and the puzzle. On the last day of the year, Lord Glenbervie recorded the situation in bewilderment. The Prince, he said, called on Lady Hertford every morning when they were both in town, and often dined *en famille* with her and Lord Hertford. 'What can be the motive of [Lord Hertford's] connivance at an intercourse almost equally inexplicable whether it be commercial, or, as many people suppose, only sentimental?'(255)

The Prince's intercourse (as Lord Glenbervie called it) with Lady Hertford was in some ways his most curious love-affair. It is hard to explain the attractions of Isabella Anne Ingram Shepherd, the second wife of the second Marquis of Hertford. She was elegant and feminine, she had the handsome figure to which the Prince was incurably susceptible, but she was a puritan *grande dame* who did not intend to grant favours, even to the Prince of Wales himself. Dr. Saunders, one of the Prince's physicians, would tell Robert Plumer Ward, in 1811, that 'it was known their attachment was merely platonic'.(256) Lord Stourton insisted that Lady Hertford refused to compromise her public reputation, even at the height of her influence. We are repeatedly assured that the relationship was an intellectual adultery. This makes the desertion of Mrs. Fitzherbert still harder to explain.

However, the Prince was fascinated by 'the Sultana', and (as Lord Holland wrote in his *Memoirs of the Whig Party*), Lady Hertford's character remained 'as timid as her manners were stately, formal and insipid'.(257) She was not only cold by nature, she was cold on principle. The more she withdrew, the more ardent the Prince would be; the higher she set herself, the longer his admiration would last. Lady Hertford was flattered to be admired; she was undoubtedly proud of her strong and increasing influence over him. She was gratified by his perpetual presence; she was delighted to think that she could influence politics. She encouraged the Prince from a love of power.

The Prince was weak, and he liked a woman who sometimes took decisions out of his hands. He needed a dominant Egeria. Lady Hertford was this, but she was more: she was the first woman in his life who offered him an established domestic circle. The Prince who dined *en famille* with the Hertfords was not proclaiming Isabella Hertford's infidelity: he was eagerly joining her family. He had never, since he came to manhood, enjoyed a family life. While the gossips naturally publicised his passion for Lady Hertford, more thoughtful observers may have noticed that her husband was his friend, and her son, Lord Yarmouth (one day to be Marquis of Steyne in *Vanity Fair*) was the Prince's artistic adviser.

Yet whatever the explanation of the Prince's love for Lady Hertford, there was no excuse for his cruelty to Mrs. Fitzherbert. When he paid open attentions to Lady Hertford, in her presence, he showed a sadistic instinct of a weak man. No pension, however generous or regularly paid, could compensate Mrs. Fitzherbert when he refused her a proper place at a Carlton House banquet. He loved her still, in his strange fashion, but he no longer needed her kind of tranquil domesticity. He knew that she would not publish the marriage certificate which they had signed, that she would always show her reticence and dignity. He asked nothing more of her, now.

21

It was unfortunate that the Prince conducted his private
life with so little grace and understanding; for his private
life (which, since it was his, was naturally public) blinded
the greater part of the country to his real and uncommon
merits. Throughout his early years of freedom, his marriage to Mrs. Fitzherbert, his disastrous marriage to Caroline,
his brash affair with Lady Jersey, his reconciliation with Mrs.
Fitzherbert, his obsession with Lady Hertford, he had continued to prove himself the most civilised patron of the
arts.

When he attended the Royal Academy dinner in 1804,
and inspected the pictures with Benjamin West, 'he talked
much', West told Farington, 'abt. advancing the art in this
country, said there shd. have been a Gallery created many
years ago for modern works,—& also for old Masters. He
spoke of the pleasure he derived from works of art. ...'(258)
The remark was not perfunctory. His pleasure was genuine.
Mme Vigée le Brun was the only distinguished French
artist to live in England during the Napoleonic revolution.
She had come to London in April 1802, and settled in
Maddox Street, where she gave a number of *grandes soirées*.
At one of them Mrs. Billington, the soprano (did Mme le
Brun know her history?), and Mme Grassini, the contralto,
sang duets 'with rare perfection', Viotti played the violin,
recorded Mme le Brun, 'and his fine and noble talent enchanted everyone; indeed, the Prince of Wales, who was
present, was gracious enough to tell me: "I usually fly from
soirée to *soirée*, but I shall stay at this one".'(259) The Prince
did not merely pay compliments. Soon after Mme le Brun
reached London, Napoleon broke the Peace of Amiens, and
all French citizens who had not been living in England for
over a year had to leave at once. The Prince of Wales
promised to ask his father to make an exception. He himself brought Mme le Brun written permission to stay, and

it was thanks to him that she visited Brighton, and described it, in her *Souvenirs*, in true Gallic style: 'Brighton . . . is quite a pretty town. It is opposite Dieppe, and from it you can see the coast of France.'(*260*)

But if the Prince's town had small effect on her, the Prince himself was a memorable figure. He seemed older than his forty years, but he was still handsome, and his wig (which recalled the hair of the Apollo Belvedere) suited him wonderfully.

He showed great skill at every sport (recorded Mme le Brun), he spoke French very well, and with the greatest facility. His studied elegance was almost prodigal in its splendour.

It was just before I left that I painted [his] portrait. I painted him three-quarter length and in uniform. Several English painters were furious with me, when they knew that I had begun the portrait, and that the Prince was giving me all the time I needed to finish it; they had long been awaiting this favour in vain. I knew that the Queen was saying that her son was paying court to me, and that he often came to breakfast with me. That was untrue, the Prince of Wales never came to me in the mornings except for sittings.

As soon as the portrait was finished, the Prince gave it to his old love, Mrs. Fitzherbert. She had it set in a movable frame, like a big dressing mirror, so that she could move it as she went from room to room. . . .(*261*)

The portrait which Mrs. Fitzherbert lovingly took as a companion was obviously the work of a woman: the uniform of the 10th Hussars clad a somewhat effeminate figure. But it remains a useful record of the Prince in 1804-1805, and a testimony to his graceful patronage.

For he moved handsomely through the painters' world, and his approbation caused art to flourish. He congratulated Martin Archer Shee on one of his portraits, and Shee long remembered his 'peculiar grace and charm of manner'.(*262*) At the Royal Academy dinner in 1806, he was taken by Angerstein to see *The Village Politicians*, by a

92

young and rising Scots painter called David Wilkie; next
day the 'very extraordinary work' was acclaimed in the
News, and Wilkie and Benjamin Robert Haydon, the historical painter, 'huzzaed, and ... danced round the table,
until we were tired'.(*263*)

The Prince (to the detriment of his finances) remained
an eager builder: a visitor in Brighton in September 1801
found that great alterations had taken place in the past
seven years, and the Prince was now 'adding two large
bulges or bow-window rooms to each end of his house front-
ing the Steine'.(*264*) In July 1804, Porden, the architect,
told Farington he was building stables at Brighton for the
Prince of Wales, 'of a Circular form in imitation of the
famous Corn Market at Paris which was burnt in 1803'.(*265*)
Two years later, the same diarist learned that the Prince
was incurring 'vast expenses' Although Holland's work on
Carlton House had only just been finished, he had ordered
it all to be done again under the direction of Walsh Porter;
Porter had undone all Holland's work and, wrote Farington, 'is substituting a finishing in a most extensive [*sic*] &
motley taste'. The Prince could not restrain his love of
splendour: he had also ordered £70,000 worth of plate
from Rundell's, the jewellers, and among it were articles
which could never be used.(*266*)

The Prince was rightly criticised at times for his extravagance; he was sometimes stupidly criticised for the vagaries
of his private life. In the late summer of 1798, when Mrs.
Siddons was performing, he had frequented the Brighton
theatre 'with great attention and decorum'. However, Mrs.
Siddons (who was there with 'Mr. Sid.') was aware that
the decorum did not extend to the Pavilion; and she had
felt a strong objection to meeting the Prince's mistress. The
Prince caused her some embarrassment when he asked to
meet her at supper. She recorded the incident without
much charity. He had, she told her friend Mrs. Pennington,

issued his sublime commands (which it seems, nothing
but death or deadly sickness will excuse one from obeying)

to have me asked to supper with him, which I, dis-
liking the whole thing, had declin'd; but when I came to
talk it over with Mr. Sid., he thought it best that I
shou'd recant my refusal; and so I went to sup at Mr.
Concannons, where, as I had fear'd, I met Lady Jersey.
However, the evening went off much more easily and
agreeably than I had imagin'd, and as it is not likely to
happen often, perhaps it was better to avoid giving the
offence which I am assur'd I shou'd have incurr'd by a
refusal.(267)

Worldly wisdom had overcome conscience; soon afterwards
Mrs. Piozzi told Mrs. Pennington: 'A letter from a friend
at Brighthelmstone tells how she [Mrs. Siddons] is playing
Mrs. Beverley for the amusement of the Prince of Wales,
Lady Jersey ...'(268) Mrs. Siddons did more than play Mrs.
Beverley. Now that the ice was broken, she forgot her remaining scruples; and Campbell records that she never was
at Brighton, while the Prince was there, without being a
guest at the Pavilion.(269) Early in 1799 her daughter Sally
wrote that she, too, had had 'the honour of dining in company with the Prince of Wales this Winter, and of course
I am of everybody's opinion, that he is a pleasant and highly
bred gentleman'.(270)

The opinion was shared by a young and ambitious Irishman, Tom Moore, who in 1800 received permission to dedicate his translation of Anacreon to the Prince of Wales.
When on 3 August 1800 he was presented to the Prince, he
was instantly under the spell.

He is beyond doubt a man of very fascinating manners
[Moore told his mother]. When I was presented to him,
he said he was very happy to know a *man of my abilities*; and when I thanked him for the honour he did me
in permitting the dedication of Anacreon, he stopped me
and said, the honour was *entirely* his, in being *allowed*
to put his name to a work of such merit. He then said
that he hoped when he returned to town in the winter,
we should have many opportunities of enjoying *each
other's society*; that he was passionately fond of music,

94

and had long heard of my talents in that way. Is not all this very fine?(*271*)

The Prince was always Irish at heart; he warmed to the eager Moore. On 17 March 1801 at 'a little supper after the opera', Moore was introduced to Mrs. Fitzherbert.(272) Ten days later, at a fashionable ball, the Prince greeted him with affability;(273) soon afterwards they met at supper at Lady Harrington's.(274) In an age of rigid class distinction, when every Exclusive shrank from contact with a Nobody, the Prince was an ideal patron of the arts: he showed not only his natural taste and his practical interest, but he was charmingly accessible.

It was only natural that he should take an interest in the Literary Fund. This laudable institution had been established in 1790 by the Reverend David Williams, to give 'temporary Relief to temporary Distress. Annual Income to other Species of Misfortune—& a Collegiate Retreat for a Few of those Literary Benefactors of Mankind, who having out-lived their Connexions, cannot be benefited by Donations and Annuities'. In 1804, when the House Committee expressed some worry about the cost of a house, the Earl of Chichester 'thought his Royal Highness the Prince of Wales, on a proper Representation, might remove the Difficulties'. The Earl (reported Mr. Williams) spoke to the Prince, 'than whom no Prince was ever so qualified to give his Actions certain Attributes of Grace & Kindness'. The Prince charged the revenues of the Duchy of Cornwall with the rent and taxes of a house. This promise of two hundred guineas a year, for the Prince's lifetime, immediately stabilised the society. In 1805 they took a lease of a house in Gerrard Street.

Soon afterwards, a Mr. Thomas Newton (said to be Sir Isaac's last collateral descendant) proposed to bequeath the society his estate; but he wanted to be assured of its permanence as an institution. The Prince gave an assurance that measures would be taken to establish it, and the legacy was duly made. On 13 June 1818 the Fund was incorporated by charter. The Prince allowed it to bear his crest on its arms ('on a Chief Gules the Plume of Feathers Proper'); indeed, he gave his 'full Approbation of the Design, and His particular sense of the compliment conveyed in it'. On his accession to the throne, he became the Patron of the Fund, to which he had given a local habitation and would give, during his lifetime, over £5,000.(275)

While men of letters had cause to remember the Prince with gratitude, musicians welcomed him as an informed and skilful amateur. William Parke, Musician to the Prince of Wales, praised his 'enlightened liberality and good taste'.(276) In Parke's *Musical Memoirs*, the Prince of Wales appeared repeatedly. He entertained Haydn to 'an elegant supper' at Carlton House (he often entertained Haydn, and he persuaded the King, who showed an exclusive interest in Handel, to listen to him). He applauded Parke's performance on the oboe, 'repeatedly exclaiming "Bravi!—the finest tone in the world" '. He patronised a performance of Sacchini's opera, *Alceste*, in aid of the widows and orphans of those who had died in 'the glorious action off Cape St. Vincent'. He patronised subscription concerts (Mrs. Billington, Naldi and Braham) at Willis's Rooms. He attended Crosdill's music parties. Soon after his marriage, Parke records, he 'established a private band, principally Germans, composed of the wind instrument players of his regiment, the Tenth Hussars, they solely attended to perform at Brighton and at Carlton House'. He enjoyed not only Haydn, but Bach, Handel, Mozart and Beethoven, and, among the Italians, Corelli, Paisiello and Cherubini. As the Prince told Moore, he was 'passionately fond of music'.

Fanny Burney's *Memoirs* of her father, the musical historian, underline the Prince's enthusiasm. When, at a concert in Grosvenor Square, Dr. Burney 'came bounce upon the Prince of Wales', the Prince insisted that they sat together; and they talked, recalled the doctor, 'over every piece and performance. . . . I know of no individual, male or female, with whom I talk about music with more sincerity, as well as pleasure, than with this most captivating

Prince.'(277) Again and again Dr. Burney applauds the Prince's love of music:

> Another time, at the opera, the Prince of Wales, perceiving me in the pit, sent for me to his splendid box; and, making me take a snug seat close behind his Royal Highness, entered, with his usual vivacity, into discussions upon the performance; and so re-*jeunied* me with his gaiety and condescension, joined to his extraordinary judgment on musical subjects, that I held forth in return as if I had been but five-and-twenty.(*278*)

At a concert at Lady Salisbury's, in May 1805, Dr. Burney was delighted with the music, which had been 'chiefly selected' by the Prince of Wales. The Prince arrived, and again asked Burney to sit with him; and again, 'our ideas, by his engaging invitation, were reciprocated upon every piece, and its execution'.(279) Lady Melbourne, seeing how happily they talked, invited Dr. Burney to dinner, so that he might meet the Prince once more. 'The Prince, with a smile of unequalled courtesy, said "Aye, do come, Dr. Burney, and bring your son with you". And, turning to Lady Melbourne, he added,—"It is singular that the father should be the best, and almost the only good judge of music in the kingdom; and his son the best scholar." '(*280*)

On 9 July the Burneys duly met the Prince of Wales at a sumptuous dinner at Lady Melbourne's. Dr. Burney was then in his seventy-eighth year:

> I had [he wrote] almost made a solemn vow, early in life, to quit the world without ever drinking a *dry dram;* but the heroic virtue of a long life was overset by his Royal Highness, through the irresistible temptation to hobbing and nobbing with such a partner in a glass of cherry brandy! ...
> The conversation was lively and general the chief part of the evening; but about midnight it turned upon music, on which subject his Royal Highness deigned so wholly to address himself to me, that we kept it up a full half-hour, without any one else offering a word. ...

The subject was then changed to classical lore; and here his Royal Highness, with similar condescension, addressed himself to my son, as to a man of erudition whose ideas, on learned topics, he respected; and a full discussion followed, of several literary matters.(*281*)

When the company went into another room for coffee, 'the Prince took Dr. Burney by the hand, and said: "I am glad we got, at last, to our favourite subject." He then made me sit down by him, close to the keys of a pianoforte; where, in a low voice, but face to face, we talked again upon music.' Dr. Burney, warm with pleasure, asked if he might present a book to the Prince: 'a set of my Commemoration of Handel, which I had had splendidly bound for permitted presentation'. The Prince replied that he was now building a library, and that when it was finished, Dr. Burney's work 'should be the first book placed in his collection'.(*282*)

The Prince's library was in the charge of one of those highly individual clerics who could only have belonged to the eighteenth or early nineteenth centuries. The Reverend James Stanier Clarke was a kind of English *abbé de cour*. His spiritual qualities (if such there were) had made him a naval chaplain and, in 1799, domestic chaplain to the Prince of Wales. In 1812 he received the honorary office of Royal Historiographer. He had, it seems, to pay a price for his advancement: the Prince showed a quite Germanic love of practical jokes, and in 1813 Robert Finch, the diarist, recorded 'an anecdote of the Reverend Stanyer Clarke, and the Prince Regent & the Duke of Clarence putting an ass in his bed at Lord Egremont's.'(*283*) One suspects that it was not the first time that the pompous clergyman had suffered from 'sad undignified amusements'. However, Stanier Clarke survived these profanations of dignity; he had somehow earned a Fellowship of the Royal Society; he had established himself with Lord Egremont in 1804 with the dedication of his edition of Falconer's *The Shipwreck*; and he no doubt entrenched himself still more firmly with the Prince when, in 1809, he dedicated to him *The Life of Admiral Lord Nelson, K.B.*

The Life of Nelson was not the only book of Stanier Clarke's to reflect royal enthusiasm. No one showed a more romantic devotion to the Stuarts than the Prince of Wales, one of the dynasty which had dispossessed them. In 1804, by his command, Sir John Hippisley, the antiquarian, had concluded negotiations with the Abbé James Waters, Procurator General of the English Benedictines in Rome, about the papers of the House of Stuart. These had come into the Abbé's possession as the executor of the Countess of Albany, who had been the wife of the Young Pretender. Before Nelson set out on his last voyage in 1805, Hippisley had asked him to obtain the documents, which had been moved from Rome to Civita Vecchia, and deposited with a British merchant. Alas, a year later, the merchant, a Mr. Bertram, was rumoured to be in prison, 'seized on and confined by the French'. The Prince refused to give up his search. In 1810 he told Hippisley to authorise a Mr. Bonelli to obtain the documents. It was Bonelli

> who at length, though with considerable risk, and through the assistance of the Rev. Mr. Macpherson President of the Scotch College, succeeded in shipping off the Cases for Leghorn, and having there concealed them from the vigilance of the Customs House Officers, they were with great difficulty embarked on a Tunisian vessel bound to Tunis, and thence forwarded to Malta and finally to London, when the whole were placed in the Library at Carlton House.(*284*)

And there the Reverend James Stanier Clarke, LL.B., F.R.S., was commanded to edit the private papers of James II. The 'tedious and protracted' task was fortunately lightened: for, at a late stage in the work, 'when the Editor least expected and most required it', the 'able assistance of Mr. Walter Scott came ... like the cheering radiance of an autumnal evening after days of anxiety and labour'. Queen Charlotte and her eldest son took a continued interest 'in the perusal of the sheets as they came from the press'. In

1816, Longman finally published two solid volumes: *The Life of James the Second, King of England, &c. Collected out of memoirs writ of his own hand.* The preservation and publication of these documents was almost entirely due to the Prince's zeal.(*285*)

It was, perhaps, the zeal of his old preceptor, Dr. Markham, which had made the Prince a classical scholar. One wonders how much the doctor's 'universal' knowledge of the classics, his pure taste and good instruction, his enthusiasm for anecdote and miscellaneous facts were responsible for the Prince's Herculaneum Mission.

It was in 1713 that some Neapolitan labourers, sinking a well, had unearthed a statue in the theatre of Herculaneum. One thousand six hundred and thirty-four years after the eruption of Vesuvius, under twenty-four feet of volcanic matter, the city of Herculaneum was refound. In 1752, 'most wonderfully preserved, under a stupendous mass of volcanick substance', archaeologists uncovered an ancient library of papyri. During the next half-century, eighteen of these blackened rolls were opened and deciphered, and among them was part of a book by Philodemus. The date of the eruption suggested that scholars might recover works by the best writers in antiquity.

However, the work of recovery would be long, exacting and expensive; the Napoleonic wars made it almost impossible for 'the embarrassed sovereign of the two Sicilies', even if he had been so disposed, to subsidise this academic venture. It needed some philanthropic prince with respect for classical literature, for ancient history and scholarship, to patronise the undertaking. In 1800, with the consent of the Neapolitan government, the Prince of Wales undertook to have all the remaining papyri unrolled and copied at his own expense. He sent out the Reverend John Hayter, Fellow of King's College, Cambridge, to direct the work. 'Your ROYAL HIGHNESS,' wrote Hayter, 'will reap the Satisfaction of having made a most princely Attempt in Behalf of Knowledge and Literature, on an Occasion, where their interests might be affected most materially'.(*286*)

Hayter arrived in Palermo in June 1800, when 'the late Lord Nelson, with her Sicilian Majesty, and the late Sir William, together with Lady Hamilton, had just quitted it'.(287) In January 1802 (for there had been unexpected complications) they began to unfold the papyri in the Royal Museum of Portici, near Naples. 'An excellent chymist', Gaetano la Pira, had been recommended to Hayter for the task; and at last, recorded Hayter, 'he was permitted to try vegetable gas. The greatest part of each mass flew, under this trial, into useless atoms. ... The dreadful odour drove us all from the Museum'.(288) However, about two hundred papyri were opened, and nearly a hundred of them were copied before, in 1806, the work was interrupted by the French invasion. The Neapolitan Court migrated to Palermo and Hayter was compelled to abandon the papyri and engravings, and to follow the Court, taking with him only the pencil facsimiles. He occupied the next three years in superintending engravings, and composing a Latin poem, *Herculaneum,* which he humbly addressed to the Prince of Wales.

Sir William Drummond (sometime British Minister to Naples) made it all too clear that Hayter indulged in other activities:

We remarked with regret [wrote Drummond] that month after month you put off the commencement of your task, and we bore with some impatience the eternal repetition of pretexts and excuses, which appeared to us to be far from satisfactory. It was, I believe, about a year after the M.S.S. were restored to you, that what you call your indiscretions began to make so much noise in Palermo. There were many severe reflections thrown upon me for permitting you to remain in my house; but you know that I long resisted the torrent, and perhaps I should have resisted it longer, if you had not contrived to get so fast out of one scrape into another, as to attract the attention of the Police, and even that of the Government. ... The stories of your battles in brothels, &c., made so much noise, and were multiplied so fast, that I found it impossible to apologise for your conduct. In the midst of all the confusion which this conduct created, you suddenly left Palermo, without indicating whither you were going. ... I then determined to take the M.S.S. into my own hands. ... You avowed to me yourself, that your mind was weakened, that you felt yourself incapable of application. ...(*289*)

Hayter had not merely shown his weakness and extravagance; his attempts to restore the texts were of little value. However, in 1809, by order of the Prince of Wales, he returned to England. He brought ninety-four facsimiles of papyri, and the engravings made at Palermo. 'To you yourself alone', he told the Prince in his *Report,* 'these despondent relics of old Greece and Rome could have had recourse for the vindication of their merits, and even for the protection of their existence'.(*290*)

The Herculaneum Mission had not fulfilled the highest expectations of its patron; Hayter's character, international politics, and the primitive methods of science had intervened. But the Prince of Wales had shown himself an enlightened lover of scholarship; and the letter he now addressed to Lord Grenville, the Chancellor of Oxford University, revealed a little of his civilised mind:

My dear Lord,

It is with great satisfaction that I can now inform your Lordship that my endeavours for bringing to light the contents of some of the celebrated Papiri at Portici, have at length met with partial success. ...

... I have every reason to think that there would have been very few of these relics of antient Litterature [*sic*], which would not have reach'd the public eye, from my own exertions and the Zeal of those employ'd, had it not been for the wretched confusion of affairs in that Part of Europe; as it is, ... I can not but esteem the Papers in my possession as singularly interesting.

In order, therefore, my Dear Lord, to complete my principal object in this undertaking, and as far as it is in my power to Satisfy the Public, that did so liberally contribute towards it, I deposit the whole of these Papers in your Lordships care, requesting, that they may be presented by You, in my name, to that most learned and distinguish'd Body, over which You have of late, so worthily been call'd upon to preside.*(291)*

The letter was written on 9 March 1810; on 2 May the University of Oxford conferred the degree of Doctor of Civil Law on the Prince of Wales. It was not a statutory honour paid to royalty. It was a mark of gratitude and respect.

22

The Prince of Wales was now far from being the happy man whom Mr. Creevey had known at the Pavilion. In September 1809, Farington's brother, meeting him on the esplanade at Weymouth, thought that he was much altered in appearance: 'that the lines on his face are more strongly marked, particularly abt. His eyes, that His countenance is sallow, & that He has a shattered look. ...'*(292)* He was intensely disliked by his father, hated by his unbalanced wife, bereft of Fox, and slighted by the Whig politicians; and he remained the object of scurrilous abuse from journalists, cartoonists and pamphleteers. Married to Mrs. Fitzherbert whom, in a way, he continued to love, he was still enslaved by the remorselessly cold Lady Hertford; and late this year, feeling a sudden need for some new, responsive woman, he made advances to Lady Bessborough (who was nearly fifty), protesting eternal love, and promising, she wrote, that 'he would break with Mrs. F. and Ly. H., I should *make my own terms!* ! ... After telling him for two hours that ... I never could or would be on any other terms with him than the acquaintance he had always honoured me with, we came to a tolerably friendly making up'.*(293)* Lady Bessborough, who had had two children by Granville Leveson Gower, had suddenly grown prudish.

The Prince was sometimes awkward in love; but there

were other spheres in which he still displayed his taste and dignity. In April 1810, he gave a dinner at Carlton House to all the Knights of the Garter; and the dinner (so Earl Spencer's daughter told her brother Robert) had been unparalleled in its splendour.

Two hundred lighted candles in the room, a bran new service of plate, the finest cut-glass lustres, bottles and glasses that ever sparkled, the twenty-five blue-ribboned gentry all in full dress and glee, and the Prince doing the honours with due bustle. Altogether it was a glorious piece of—what shall I say? grandeur or nonsense? For somehow it makes one laugh, as if it was a parcel of children playing at great people; so proud of their bits of blue ribbon, and their pretty shining playthings all about them. The Royal host worried and toasted himself till he rather clipped the King's English before it was over. But that's nothing. I love him for having the finest possible pictures of Lord Rodney, Lord Keppel, Lord St. Vincent and, finest of all, that glorious Nelson, hung up as chief ornaments of his great room.(*294*)

The thought of Carlton House was so attractive that, about a fortnight later, through the good offices of Lord Moira, the Spencers received the Prince's leave to see it for themselves. 'He changes the furniture so very often,' Lady Sarah explained, just before they set off, 'that one can scarcely find time to catch a glimpse at each transient arrangement before it is all turned off for some other; the present state of things is unusually fine, they say.'(*295*) It was every bit as fine as she had expected; and next day, as a woman of the world, she wrote to Robert:

I don't know whether you are *worthy* of the beauties of old china vases, gold fringes, damask draperies, cut-glass lustres, and all the other fine things we saw there. I can only tell you the lustre in one of the rooms, of glass and ormulu, looking like a shower of diamonds, cost between *two and three thousand pounds*. I write the number at full length, that you mayn't fancy I have put a cypher too many. However, it is such a peculiarly English manufactory that our heir-apparent is right in encouraging it.(296)

He was anxious to encourage every form of national art. In July Benjamin West, the President of the Royal Academy, told Farington that the Prince

seemed much disposed to make a Collection of the Works of British Artists. The Prince exprd. a desire to Have [Edward] Bird of Bristol's picture 'Village Choristers' which was exhibited this year—West applied to Bird to know the price. Bird wrote 250 guineas. West took the picture to the Prince who *paid Him* for it, and desired Him to give a Commission to Wilkie to paint a companion to it; leaving the subject & the price to Himself.(297)

Nor were the Prince's interests exclusively English. In August he showed West a large collection of drawings by foreign artists, representing the armies of various countries, 'and their operations, with views of places'. The Prince, added West, ungratefully, had now become enormously large, with a figure like that of Henry VIII.(298)

Ungainly, civilised and unhappy, the Prince of Wales now stood on the verge of power. On 2 November his youngest sister, Princess Amelia, died at the age of twenty-seven.

She was said to be the King's favourite child, and the shock of her death overwhelmed him. More than once his mind had gone, but he had come back to his senses. This time he was stricken for ever. 'The Gentleman at the end of the Mall', as Mr. Creevey called him, lapsed into permanent insanity.

23

The disorder had been so sudden that the Prime Minister could not obtain the King's signature for the further prorogation of Parliament. The Houses therefore met, and adjourned from time to time in hopes of his recovery. His recovery seemed to be increasingly remote. By 23 November Walter Scott could only 'trust in God' that the doctors might save him, for where party politics ran high, a regency could only be 'a lamentable business'.*(299)* On 18 December, Lady Sarah Spencer wrote to her brother with less verve than usual:

> There is a sort of a rumpus going on in domestic politics, which is much too dull to explain, but which is occasioned by the King's illness, and *may* end in the Prince of Wales being Regent. Parliament ... has appointed a Committee of Peers to question the King's physicians. Papa, Sunday morning, on reading the newspapers, was surprised at finding himself one of this Committee, obliged to order his chaise and set out for town instantly, amid a chorus of grumbling from all his widowed family.*(300)*

On 31 December, Spencer Perceval moved in the House of Commons that the Regency should be offered to the Prince of Wales, subject to certain restrictions. These restrictions were to last for a year, and for six weeks of the following session of Parliament.

The Prince's friends indulged high hopes of office. Erskine, like the rest of the Whigs, strenuously opposed the suggested restrictions on the Regent's powers; and doubtless he looked from time to time at the uncut topaz seal-ring which the Prince had given him. The Prince had asked him not to have the topaz cut at present, as he meant to give him an earl's coronet to engrave upon it.*(301)*

The restricted Regency Bill was passed, on the plan of that of 1788. The King's condition remained uncertain; and 'by what I hear today', Miss Berry told Charles Stewart, the British Minister at Lisbon, on 2 January, 'I expect that just as the Prince is ready to step into his new title, the King will be ready to govern us just as he has done before.'*(302)* The following week the rumour was confirmed by Elizabeth Foster, now the Duchess of Devonshire. 'The King is now said to be recovering, and ... there is an end of the Regency. ... I am told that the 1st of Feb. is the time fixed for the Regency if it does take place.'(*303*)

It did take place. On Wednesday 6 February 1811, before the Privy Council, the Prince of Wales was sworn in as Prince Regent of the United Kingdom.

George IV as Prince of Wales
From the portrait by Sir Joshua Reynolds

Mrs. Fitzherbert and the Prince of Wales
From the miniatures by Richard Cosway

PART TWO

Prince Regent

24

ON 12 February, the Prince Regent announced his decision to continue his father's government in office; while his powers were restricted, he made it his rule to act as the King would have done.

On 26 February he held the first levée of the Regency: 'great crowds', reported Miss Berry, 'splendid liveries, and hussars of all colours'.(*1*) The days of Kew and of Buckingham House, of the palace of piety, seemed far away. Strangers were overwhelmed by the splendour of Carlton House: Robert Plumer Ward, the politician, thought it finer that anything in England, and not inferior to Versailles or St. Cloud. Count Münster, the Hanoverian Minister, said that 'the palace at Petersburg beat everything in vastness, but was not equal to this in elegance or richness'.(2) Lysons considered the decoration vulgar in its opulence. 'Not a spot witht. some finery upon it,' recorded Farington, 'gold upon gold—a bad taste. [Robert] Smirke [the architect] had seen the apartments, & sd. they are so overdone with finery, & superfluous as, supposing the owner not to be known, would give an unfavourable idea of the kind of mind He must have'.(*3*) But some observed (was it his new sense of responsibility?) that the Regent himself was more silent than usual. One of his physicians reported that he was very serious, 'and supposed to be engaged with religion, and read daily a chapter or two of the Bible with Lady

Hertford'.(*4*) 'In general,' said Mary Berry, 'he speaks much less, both to men and women, than he did—it is the fashion of the day with him.'(*5*)

Miss Berry spoke with a certain bias: she was a friend of the Princess of Wales, and had more than once been her guest at Kensington Palace. When the Regent acknowledged Miss Berry, at last, at Lady Hertford's, he gave her 'a formal grave bow, with *Kensington* legible on it'.(*6*) Now that he was virtually King, he was more determined than ever to dissociate himself from his wife.

He moved, a portentous figure, through the first weeks of the Regency: from dinner at Lord Cholmondeley's to 'an enormous assembly' at Lady Hertford's, from an entertainment at Lady Derby's to 'a great assembly' at Lady Stafford's. On 27 April he attended one of the functions where he shone most conspicuously: he inspected the annual Academy exhibition, and after dinner he addressed the company. Farington recorded the principal point of his speech:

> When He saw so much which manifested the great improvement in art He felt proud as an Englishman that He might with confidence expect that as this country had risen superior to all others in Arms, in military and naval prowess, so would it in Arts.—Others, He sd. might be more able to judge of the excellence of works of art, but could not exceed him in his love of the arts, or in wishes for their prosperity.(*7*)

Wilberforce, who was no poor judge, declared it the best King's speech he had ever heard; and no Academy dinner, said Farington, had ever gone off in so marked a manner, 'nor did there ever before appear so much cordial warmth for the prosperity of art'.

Soon afterwards, the Regent offered the Royal Academy a bronze lamp 'to illuminate the Great Room at the annual Dinner'; and Mr. Vulliamy of Pall Mall was commissioned to design it. The massive lamp, approved by the Regent and the Academicians, and lit up on lecture nights and at annual dinners, was a handsome reminder of princely patronage.(*8*)

This royal interest in the arts, this general enthusiasm, this firm belief in aesthetic sense and patriotic pride in artistic achievement, were to be characteristic of the Regency. As for intellectual curiosity, it was intense and even fashionable: the Royal Institution (the Regent had recently been elected its President) was 'more the *ton* than anything, and Ladies of all ages', reported Marianne Spencer-Stanhope, 'submit to a squeeze of a hundred people in a morning to hear lectures on the Human Understanding, Experimental Philosophy, Painting, Music or Geology'.(*9*) The Regent who endowed readerships at Oxford in mineralogy and geology(*10*) was handsomely encouraging the tastes of the age.

If his speech at the Royal Academy set the artistic tone of his time, if his patronage of the Royal Institution, his endowments at Oxford, confirmed the general interest in scholarship, his grand entertainment at Carlton House on 19 June proclaimed the social brilliance of the era. Over two hundred guests attended, the men in court dress or uniform, the women in 'elegant variegated dresses', enhanced by 'waving plumage' and sparkling diamonds. Louis XVIII and other Bourbons, now in exile, were present. The Regent, in a scarlet coat, 'most richly and elegantly ornamented in a very novel style with gold lace,' presided over the fête like Apollo. In front of him, at the grand supper table, was a basin of water, with 'an enriched temple' in the centre of it; and from this fountain, down the whole length of the table (two hundred feet), meandered a stream, which was bordered with moss and aquatic flowers, spanned by three or four fantastic bridges, and filled with frolicking gold and silver fish. Tom Moore was enchanted. 'It was *in reality* all that they try to imitate in the gorgeous scenery of the theatre.'(*11*) Shelley burned with radical indignation. 'What think you of the bubbling *brooks* and *mossy banks* at Carlton House,—the *allées vertes*, etc.?' he asked a friend. 'It is said that this entertainment will cost £120,000. Nor will it be the last bauble which the nation must buy to amuse this overgrown bantling of Regency.'(*12*)

For three days after the event, the public were admitted,

by ticket, to inspect the apartments. Mary Russell Mitford refused an invitation, and she had good cause to be thankful. On the last day at least 30,000 people determined to come. A stampede followed, and very few ladies could leave Carlton House 'until furnished with a fresh supply of clothes; they were to be seen all round the gardens, most of them without shoes or gowns; and many almost completely undressed, and their hair hanging about their shoulders'.(*13*)

25

The Carlton House entertainment helped to endear the Regent to the higher ranks of society; and this was fortunate, because he was soon to lose the regard of his old political friends, and to incur the lasting hatred and ridicule of the liberal intellectuals.

In July 1811, a few weeks after the fête, the King was assailed by wilder delusions than ever. The physicians were satisfied that he could never recover, and it was clear that in February 1812 the Regent would enjoy complete sovereign powers. Parliament was prorogued until 22 August, but, as Creevey noted on 12 July, 'the general opinion is that the King will die before that day, and then of course Parliament meets again'. The political world was astir; parliamentary opinion (according to Creevey) was that, if the King died, the ministers in office would be retained, and some of the Regent's personal friends would join them.

The easiest course for the Regent would have been to send for the Whigs, consolidate his popularity with his early friends, and win the affection of the great mass of Englishmen. But there was one important objection to a Whig Government, which unquestionably weighed with him. For twenty years England had been at war with France; and now, in 1811, the first faint signs of victory had appeared. Napoleon's hold on Europe had visibly weakened. A number of Whigs were known to be opposed to the war, and in favour of treating with Napoleon (Creevey, for one, expressed the hope that the list of British casualties in Portugal would make the Regent think of concluding peace). The Regent did not want to change a vigorous, fighting Government for a government which partially favoured surrender. Besides, the Whigs were inspired with ideals which he considered 'liberal and anti-Monarchical';(*14*) they were hardly equipped to enforce the heavy taxation which was necessary to fight the war. The Regent did not want an entirely Whig administration; at the same time he was not enamoured of Spencer Perceval (who had set Caroline against him in open battle, and had voted for a restricted Regency); and he disliked certain members of his Cabinet.

As the moment of decision approached, he set off for Brighton 'to inspect the cloathing and fancy new Regimentals round the Coast'.(*15*) In December, at Oatlands, the country house of the Duke and Duchess of York, he slipped and hurt his ankle as he was showing his daughter how to do the Highland fling. He retired to bed for a fortnight, taking doses of laudanum, and inspiring the wildest stories about his condition. 'We are here,' wrote Scott, from Edinburgh, 'alarmd and stund with unauthenticated rumours concerning the state of the Prince Regent's health. God forbid any one of them be founded in truth.'(*16*) 'The Prince is, I believe, extremely ill,' Lady Bessborough informed Granville Leveson Gower. '[Sir Walter] Farquhar says he suffers such agony of pain all over him that it produces a degree of irritation on his nerves nearly approaching to delirium. What will become of us if, as well as our King, our Regent goes mad?'(*17*) On 22 December the same correspondent reported that the Regent had quarrelled with the Duke of Cumberland, 'from hearing of his saying everywhere that his Brother's illness was *higher* than the foot, and that a blister on the head might be more efficacious than a poultice on the Ankle'.(*18*)

The Regent was not only worried by his state of health, he was disturbed by the coming political crisis. Early in 1812 he asked Perceval to draft a letter for him, suggesting a coalition to the Whig leaders. Perceval supplied a draft. 'It is a great misfortune to Mr. Perceval,' remarked His Royal Highness, 'to write in a style which would disgrace a respectable washerwoman.' He and Sheridan then composed a letter to the Duke of York, who was authorised to show it to Earl Grey.

> In the critical situation of the war in the Peninsula, I shall [wrote the Regent] be most anxious to avoid any measure that can lead my allies to suppose that I mean to depart from the present system. Perseverance alone can achieve the great object in question. ... I have no predilections to indulge, no resentments to gratify, no objects to attain but such as are common to the whole Empire. ... I cannot conclude without expressing the gratification I could feel, if some of those persons with whom the early habits of my public life were formed would strengthen my hands and constitute a part of my Government.(*19*)

No doubt the Regent hoped for a coalition composed of his close friends like Lord Moira and Sheridan, moderate Whigs like Erskine and the Duke of Norfolk, and intelligent men like Wellington's elder brother, Wellesley (an aloof personage whom the Regent described as 'a Spanish Grandee grafted on an Irish potato'). Lord Grey conferred with Lord Grenville, and the two of them despatched a frigid and immediate refusal. The Regent was therefore thrown into the arms of the Tories; he could only keep Perceval's Government in office.

In May 1812 all his plans were changed: Perceval was murdered in the lobby of the House of Commons. Once again the Regent proposed a coalition government, and once again his proposal was rejected. On 8 June Mr. Creevey wrote angrily: 'Well, this is beyond anything. Castlereagh has just told us that ... His Royal Highness has appointed Lord Liverpool Prime Minister.'(*20*)

It did not occur to the Whigs that they themselves might be to blame for their failure to achieve office. They simply saw that the Regent had chosen a Tory administration, and that all their years of attachment to him were wasted. They assumed that Lady Hertford had poisoned his mind against them, and on her and on the Regent they poured out their fury. Lord Holland (the nephew of Charles James Fox) later wrote, with remorse: 'We all incurred the guilt, if not the odium, of charging his Royal Highness with ingratitude and perfidy. We all encouraged every species of satire against him and his mistress.'(21) But such justified remorse lay far in the future. In the meanwhile, Lord Grey rose in the House of Lords to denounce an 'unseen and separate influence which lurked behind the throne, ... an influence of ... odious character, leading to consequences the most pestilent and disgusting'.(22)

Henry Brougham went further than denouncing Lady Hertford. Seven years ago, by royal request, he had been invited to meet the Prince of Wales at Melbourne House. 'I was,' wrote Brougham in his autobiography, 'exceedingly pleased with his society. ... Altogether one should have regarded him as a clever and agreeable member of society had he been a common person, and might even have been struck with him.' (23) This had been in 1805; the following year, at the time of the Delicate Investigation, Brougham had carefully avoided taking sides. However, in 1809 he had been persuaded to go to Kensington and be presented to the Princess of Wales.(24)

He had now been in Parliament for two years, he saw no chance of office: he felt that his chance of fame lay in violent opposition. Henceforth his personal disappointment would entirely guide his political ambitions. He would attack the Regent 'in terms which would not have been too strong to have described the latter days of Tiberius'.(25) And, seeing how the wretched position of the Princess of Wales might be made to discredit the Ministers and injure the Regent himself, he offered her his legal services.

26

In March 1812 the *Morning Post* had published a poem describing the Regent as the 'Exciter of Desire' and an 'Adonis of Loveliness'. Such wild panegyric hardly suited the bulky potentate now approaching his fiftieth birthday. Some days later, the radical *Examiner* translated this adulation into what it called 'the language of truth'. In an article, 'The Prince on St. Patrick's Day', Leigh Hunt concluded

> that this Adonis in Loveliness *was a corpulent gentleman of fifty!* In short, that this delightful, blissful, wise, pleasurable, honourable, virtuous, true *and* immortal PRINCE *was a violator of his word, a libertine over head and ears in debt and disgrace, a despiser of domestic ties, the companion of gamblers and demireps, a man who has just closed half a century without one single claim on the gratitude of his country or the respect of posterity.*(26)

It was, by any standards, astonishing vilification, and it must have been deeply felt by the Regent, who resented personal slights much more than real indignities or illusage. Moreover, it came on the eve of an awkward session in the Commons, when questions were asked about his debts, and the salary of Colonel McMahon, appointed to the new office of Keeper of the Privy Purse. It is only surprising that Leigh Hunt and his brother John, the editor of the *Examiner*, were not brought to trial till the end of the year.

However, on 9 December they appeared in the Court of King's Bench, and were charged before Lord Ellenborough and a special jury 'with intention to traduce and vilify His Royal Highness the Prince of Wales, Regent of the United Kingdom'. They were defended by Brougham. 'I fired for two hours very close and hard into the Prince,' he wrote, 'on all points, public and private—and in such a way that they *could* not find any opening to break in upon.'(27)

Brougham established himself as an advocate 'in the sedition line'. But the Hunts were found guilty. Lord Ellenborough fined them £500 each, and sentenced them to two
years' imprisonment. He sentenced one brother to be imprisoned in Surrey, and the other in Middlesex.

The sentence roused indignation in the world of literature and the arts. Haydon, the historical painter, often went
to breakfast with John at Coldbath Fields, and 'spent many
evenings very happily in his prison'. He had nothing but
admiration for the 'poor noble-hearted friend locked up for
an impudent ebullition of his brother's on a debauched
Prince, who at that time amply deserved it'.(28) As for
Leigh's cell in Horsemonger Lane, it became a place of pilgrimage, and, as he sat writing *Rimini*, he was visited by
Shelley (who had proposed a subscription for 'the brave and
enlightened man').(29) Cyrus Redding, the journalist, who
called, missed Byron and Moore, by only about half-an-hour,
on the same errand'.(30) Hunt, in his own words, had been
imprisoned 'for not thinking the Prince Regent slender and
laudable'.(31) But he had expressed the general mood to
such effect that, after the trial, 10,000 copies of the
Examiner were sold within an hour; and a report of the trial
was printed, unknown to Hunt himself, and placarded on
the walls before he could even announce that a correct
account was coming out.

The effects of Leigh Hunt's imprisonment were to be
far-reaching in literature. When, on 2 February 1815, he was
at last released, Keats composed the sonnet *Written on the
Day that Mr. Leigh Hunt left Prison*. And so, 'for showing
truth to flatter'd state', Hunt cemented the alliance which,
for a time, was disastrous to the literary prospects of Keats.

27

The month which had seen the appearance of Hunt's
libel on the Regent, had also seen the publication of one
of Byron's most important works. On 1 March 1812 *Childe*

Harold's Pilgrimage had made its author the lion of London society. In June he had been invited to a ball which the Regent himself had attended.

As Byron had not been to Court, etiquette demanded that he should not appear in the royal presence, and he duly retired to another room. The Regent learnt that he was there, and summoned him at once. Byron was conquered.

> There, too, he saw (whate'er he may be now)
>   A Prince, the Prince of Princes at the time,
> With fascination in his very bow,
>   And full of promise, as the spring of prime.
> Though Royalty was written on his brow,
>   He had *then* the grace, too, rare in every clime,
> Of being, without alloy of fop or beau,
>   A finished Gentleman from top to toe.(*32*)

Byron would in time pay the Regent his grudging tribute in *Don Juan*; meanwhile he hurried to his publisher, John Murray, and described the conversation to him in detail.(*33*)

It was a fortunate conversation, for it had been very largely about Walter Scott; and since the attack on Scott in *English Bards and Scotch Reviewers,* there had naturally been a breach between the author of *Marmion* and the 'young whelp of a Lord Byron'. Both Murray and Byron saw the Regent's comments as a means of healing the breach; and on 27 June, Murray wrote to Scott. He could not, he said, refrain from mentioning

> a conversation which Lord Byron had with His Royal Highness the Prince Regent, and of which you formed the leading subject. ... For more than half an hour they conversed on poetry and poets, with which the Prince displayed an intimacy and critical taste which at once surprised and delighted Lord Byron. But the Prince's great delight was Walter Scott, whose name and writings he dwelt upon and recurred to incessantly. He preferred him far beyond any other poet of the time, repeated several passages with fervour, and criticised them faithfully. He

spoke chiefly of the 'Lay of the Last Minstrel', which he expressed himself as admiring most of the three poems. He quoted Homer, and even some of the obscurer Greek poets, and appeared, as Lord Byron supposes, to have read more poetry than any prince in Europe. He paid, of course, many compliments to Lord Byron, but the greatest was 'that he ought to be offended with Lord Byron, for that he had thought it impossible for any poet to equal Walter Scott, and that he had made him find himself mistaken'. Lord Byron called upon me merely to let off the raptures of the Prince respecting you, thinking, as he said, that if I were likely to have occasion to write to you, it might not be ungrateful for you to hear of his praises.(*34*)

It was not ungrateful: indeed Scott found it 'very handsome & gratifying'.(*35*) On 6 July, Byron himself sent Scott an account of the conversation.

And now let me talk to you of the Prince Regent. He ordered me to be presented to him at a ball; and after some sayings peculiarly pleasing from royal lips, as to my own attempts, he talked to me of you and your immortalities: he preferred you to every bard past and present, and asked which of your works pleased me most. It was a difficult question. I answered I thought the *Lay*. He said his own opinion was nearly similar. In speaking of the others, I told him that I thought you more particularly the poet of *Princes*, as *they* never appeared more fascinating than in *Marmion* and the *Lady of the Lake*. He was pleased to coincide, and to dwell on the description of your Jameses as no less royal than poetical. He spoke alternately of Homer and yourself, and seemed well acquainted with both; so that ... you were in very good company. I defy Murray to have exaggerated his Royal Highness's opinion of your powers, nor can I pretend to enumerate all he said on the subject; but it may give you pleasure to hear that it was conveyed in language which would only suffer by my attempting to transcribe it, and with a tone and taste which gave me a very high idea of his abilities and accomplishments, which I had hitherto considered as confined to *manners,* certainly superior to those of any living *gentleman. . . .(36)*

On 16 July, from Abbotsford, Scott replied with becoming modesty:

My Lord,

I am much indebted to your Lordship for your kind and friendly letter: and much gratified by the Prince Regent's good opinion of my literary attempts. I know so little of courts and princes, that any success I may have had in hitting off the Stuarts is, I am afraid, owing to a little old Jacobite leaven which I sucked in with the numerous traditionary tales that amused my infancy. It is a fortunate thing for the Prince himself that he has a literary turn, since nothing can so effectually relieve the ennui of state, and the anxieties of power.(37)

The 'literary turn' of the Regent had not only healed the breach between Scott and Byron; it had established a firm friendship between them. Byron himself wrote gaily to Lord Holland that he might one day be Poet Laureate: 'I have now great hope, in the event of Mr. Pye's decease, of "warbling truth at court" ...'(38) He was not so flippant as he tried to suggest: soon afterwards, a visitor found him in court dress, with his fine black hair in powder, preparing to attend the Regent's levée.

It is tempting to speculate how different Byron's life and poetry might have been if he had indeed become Poet Laureate: if he had tried to fit the conventional world. However, the levée was postponed;(39) and, as far as is known, Byron never spoke to the Regent again. He found it hard to imagine himself writing odes at Court. 'My politics being as perverse as my rhymes, I had, in fact,' he wrote, 'no business there.'(40) He had indeed no business there. In March 1812, when *Childe Harold* appeared, the *Morning Chronicle* had published two discreetly anonymous stanzas to Princess Charlotte:

To a Lady Weeping
Weep, daughter of a royal line,
A sire's disgrace, a realm's decay;
Ah, happy! if each tear of thine
Could wash a father's fault away!

Weep—for thy tears are virtue's tears—
Auspicious to these suffering isles;
And be each drop in future years
Repaid thee by thy people's smiles.*(41)*

In 1814, thanks to Byron's political perversity, the stanzas were republished over his name.

The publication created an uproar. The Press, he noted, went into hysterics, and his publisher was in a fright. The Regent himself had attributed the lines to Tom Moore; when he learned that Byron had written them, he chose 'to be *affected* "in sorrow rather than anger". ... I feel a little compunctious', said Byron, 'as to the Regent's regret'.*(42)*

No doubt the Regent did regret that such comments should be made by the poet with whom he had talked so happily, less than two years earlier. However, he had had good reason to suspect Tom Moore of writing the lines. For many years, Moore had set his hopes of advancement on his friendship with the Regent's friend, Lord Moira. 'It has been,' he wrote, 'a sort of *Will-o'-the-Wisp* to me all my life'.*(43)* In March 1812, when Moira had suddenly fallen from royal favour, Moore had seen his leading light extinguished. When the Whigs had failed to get into office, there was no more point in playing safe, and Moore decided: 'though I shall have but few to talk *to* me, I will try to make many talk *of* me.'*(44)* In March 1813, he wrote the dedication of *Intercepted Letters, or the Twopenny Post-Bag.*

This sharp little book of political squibs was tossed off with more Irish humour than prudence. It was published anonymously, but its authorship was a pretty open secret. Moore's gibes at the corpulent Regent and the ageing Lady Hertford were as brutal as anything that Leigh Hunt had written. Out of his *Post-Bag* tottered a flaccid caricature of a royal figure, ridiculous and inconstant in love, laughable in appearance, and, as Regent, beneath consideration:

Some monarchs take roundabout ways into note,
But His short cut to fame is—the cut of his coat!
Philip's Son thought the World was too small for his soul,
While our R-G-T's finds room in a lac'd button-hole! (*45*)

Moore reported in June that his book had done him 'infinite service'. Whether he owed it to his talent, his courage, or the general dislike of the Regent, nothing, he said, that he ever wrote had gained him 'so much *pleasant* fame'.(*46*)

It had gained him notoriety; but it had ruined his prospects. He had put himself beyond the pale.

28

It sometimes seemed as if the distinguished writers of the age were so blinded by the Regent's disastrous marriage, by some mistaken loyalty to his wife, that they could not recognise his merits. They simply saw him as a libertine who had left his wife, a prince whose life was spent in continual dissipation. Shelley dismissed the Regent as 'that crowned coward and villain'.(*47*) 'That infernal wretch the Prince of Wales,' he wrote in 1812, 'demands more money, the Princesses must have more. Mr. McMahon must have more. And for what? For supplying the Augean stable of the Prince with filth which no second Hercules can cleanse'.(*48*) The words came curiously from Shelley, who believed in free love, and was no doubt a cause of his first wife's suicide.

If, in this spring and summer of 1812, he had watched the Regent closely, Shelley would have seen an amateur musician giving a handsome concert at Carlton House; he would have seen a lover of the theatre bringing a large party to the private theatricals at Lady Hardwicke's in St. James's Square. The Regent had once expressed the hope 'that this Country may be as distinguished for its excellence in Art, as it is for its other eminent advantages'.(*49*) Shelley might have seen him, now, ratifying the Royal Academy papers, and expressing the hope that his bronze lamp was suitable for the Academy's Great Room.(*50*) If Shelley had been present at the levée on 8 April, he would have seen that science, too, was actively encouraged. That day, unsolicited, the Regent chose to knight Humphry Davy, the chemist. 'This distinction has not often been bestowed on scientific men,' wrote the new Sir Humphry to his brother: 'but I am proud of it, as the greatest of human genius's bore it; and it is at least a proof that the court has not overlooked my humble efforts.'(*51*) The knighthood did as much credit to the giver as to the receiver. As Davy observed, in his notebooks: 'The works of scientific men are like the atoms of gold, of sapphire and diamonds, that exist in a mountain. ... When sovereigns are at the expense of digging out these riches, they are repaid by seeing them gems in their crowns.'(*52*) He invented the safety lamp three years later.

These years were in many ways the most glorious years of the Regency. In December 1812, southern Spain was cleared of the French by Wellington, and the *Grande Armée* was in full retreat. In April 1813, Wellington's final advance through Spain had begun. And yet, that month, when the coffin of Charles I was opened at Windsor, in the Regent's presence, Mrs. Barbauld heard that the King's severed head delivered a warning to the august observer. It was a long speech, full of advice, which ended, like the Ghost in *Hamlet*, with 'Remember me'.(*53*)

The Regent was now more unpopular than ever because he had forbidden his wife to see her daughter more than once a fortnight. The royal domestic troubles had again become wretchedly public. The Princess addressed a letter of remonstrance to her husband; she received a formal acknowledgement from the Prime Minister. On Brougham's advice, she then published her letter in the *Morning Chronicle*. Another royal commission was set up, and supported the Regent's decree. Brougham, incessantly stirring up trouble, wrote womanish, gossipy letters to Mr. Creevey, announcing that the Regent had been hissed on his way to Court, 'and hooted loudly. All this is good'.(*54*) In this correspondence on 'the affairs of the Prinnies', Brougham showed ruthless dishonesty, an implacable determination to exploit the monarchy for the sake of his own career. 'Much indeed is it to be lamented,' wrote a correspondent to Robert Finch, the traveller and diarist, 'that the Ps. of W. should lend herself to be the weak tool of a wicked Junto [*sic*]'.(*55*)

Brougham's letters must be read as political propaganda. They should be set beside Elizabeth, Duchess of Devonshire's comment, in April 1813:

> The singular thing in all this business is that there does not seem to be anybody who has a doubt of the Pss having had attachments and even intrigues. I have never heard anybody for this last 7 or 10 years, I think, express any doubt as to the Princess's imprudence of conduct, indelicacy of manner and conversation, and criminal attachments.(*56*)

There were others in 1813 who saw the Regent in a more kindly light. Lady Elizabeth Feilding attended a fête 'in that Mahomet's Paradise, Carlton House. I do not know,' she told her sister, 'whether we all looked like *Houris*, but I for one was certainly in the 77th heaven.'(*57*) On 4 March the Regent attended a concert of Ancient Music. On 8 May, before the British Institution opened its Reynolds exhibition, the first exhibition devoted to a non-contemporary artist, he attended the inaugural dinner.(*58*) John Constable thought 'his manner was agreeable and I saw him shake hands with many in an easy familiar manner—he seemed to admire the pictures and particularly some portraits'. (Lady Thomond, Sir Joshua's niece, sent his best self-portrait to the Regent, 'doing what I know, living, would have gratify'd him most'.)(*59*) That month, at a 'grand night' at Mrs. Hope's, among 'all of beauty, rank, and

fashion that London can assemble', Maria Edgeworth noted
the Regent standing 'one-third of the night, holding con-
verse with Lady Elizabeth Monk, she leaning gracefully on
a bronze ornament in the centre of the room'.(60) He
listened attentively to his Organ Performer in Ordinary,
Charles Wesley, nephew of the great preacher.(61) He
delighted in original friends: Joseph Jekyll, M.P. for Calne,
and soon to be Master in Chancery (the Prince had long ago
made him his Solicitor-General); Sir John Leicester, later
Baron de Tabley, patron of English painters; and John
Julius Angerstein. Angerstein, who was now nearly eighty,
was of Russian extraction. He had come to London at the
age of fifteen, and, in time, become an underwriter at
Lloyds; he had created for himself 'one of the most extensive mercantile connexions extant'. His wealth (he would
leave half a million pounds) allowed him to be a philanthropist and a patron of art; and, 'fraught with the spirit of the
Medicis', and driven by his Russian temperament, he had
much in common with the Regent.

But the great object of curiosity in London in this summer
of 1813 was Madame de Staël. The turbulent author of *De
la littérature*, she had dared to compare her own age with
the decadent pre-Christian Roman Empire. She had thus incurred the displeasure of Napoleon. The only Continental
power who had resisted him as steadfastly as England, she
had now been exiled for the third time from France. She
arrived from Stockholm with her daughter, her elder son,
and Rocca, her handsome young lover, to excite the envy
of her own sex and enjoy the honours due to her talents.
Soon after her arrival, she signed a contract with John
Murray, who bought the manuscript of *De l'Allemagne* for
1,500 guineas (the book was published in October, and sold
out in three days). She was the literary lion of the season;
she was sought by all Society, and not least by the Regent,
who wanted to invite her to his fête. Since etiquette demanded that she should have been presented, he went to
Lady Heathcote's assembly to meet her. Mme de Staël was
large, coarse and homely, with a total want of grace and
beauty; but he appreciated women of intellect. He sat

beside her, so she said, for three-quarters of an hour, and was 'on ne peut pas être plus aimable'.(62) Henceforward she took every opportunity of 'saying flattering things of the Prince',(63) and Lord Glenbervie reported that 'Lord Hampden, if I heard him right—but he cannot articulate and I am deaf—told me on Sunday that the Prince had given the same account of her'.(64) It seems that Mme de Staël later earned his displeasure, by excusing herself from his breakfast party. But any ill-feeling soon disappeared: with a true sense of distinction, he himself called on her at the house she had taken in George Street, and, wrote Lord Glenbervie, 'remained two hours with her'.(65) She was to stay in England until the fall of Napoleon, nearly a year later.

Other offenders were not, alas, pardoned, and among them was Beau Brummell, who had long ago fallen from grace and favour. In July, the Regent attended the Dandy Ball at the Argyle Rooms, given by Lord Alvanley, Brummell and others. He cut Brummell dead; and Brummell, knowing how to hurt, inquired very audibly: 'Alvanley, who's your fat friend?' One day after this, the Beau found himself exactly opposite the door of the picture gallery in Pall Mall, as the Regent's low, dark-red carriage stopped outside. He raised his hat to the sentries, as if their presenting arms had been for him, and turned his back to the carriage. The Regent gave him an angry look, but said nothing. There was a final encounter between them. One evening, when the Regent left the opera rather before the end, as he always did, and was waiting for his carriage, Brummell found himself pushed back 'and all but driven against the Regent, who distinctly saw him, but who, of course, would not move'. One of the royal suite tapped Brummell on the shoulder, and Brummell turned round to discover the Regent standing only a foot away. 'His countenance did not change in the slightest degree, nor did his head move; they looked straight into each other's eyes; the Prince evidently amazed and annoyed. Brummell, however, did not quail, or show the least embarrassment. He receded quite quietly and backed slowly step by step, till the crowd closed behind them, never once taking his eyes off those of the Prince.'(*66*)

Some three years later, on 16 May 1816, Brummell himself left the opera early, stepped into a chaise, and met his own carriage a little way out of town. Next day, he crossed to France, and left England for ever. He had escaped his tradesmen and his enemies. The following week 'the genuine property of A MAN OF FASHION' was auctioned; and, with the sliding cheval dressing-glass, the Brussels carpet, the Sèvres china, the chocolate cups, the nine wine-coolers, and the capital old port (sold at £4 a dozen), there went a handsome snuff-box. Inside it, the auctioneer found a piece of paper, inscribed, in Brummell's hand: 'This snuff-box was intended for the Prince Regent, if he had conducted himself with more propriety towards me.'(*67*)

29

In the summer of 1813, on the death of Pye, the post of Poet Laureate fell vacant; and the world of intriguers and poets was astir. The Reverend James Stanier Clarke, the Regent's librarian, who was never lacking in assurance, decided to support a candidate. He had sent presentation copies of his own books to Scott, and Scott had acknowledged them in flattering terms; and though Clarke had never met the author of *Marmion*, he now liked to consider him an acquaintance. On 18 August, full of his own small importance, Clarke 'delivered' to the Regent his 'earnest wish and anxious desire' that Scott should have the post. The Regent, so Clarke wrote to Scott, 'replied "that you had already been written to, and that if you wished it everything would be settled as I could desire" '. Mr. Clarke then offered Scott his congratulations.(*68*)

Unfortunately they were premature. When Scott, at Abbotsford, received the formal offer of the Poet Laureateship from the Marquis of Hertford, he did not accept it by return of post. As a husband and father, he was tempted by the thought of the salary (he imagined it might be £400 a year); but, as 'a point of poetical honour', he felt inclined to refuse the office. He thought it 'a ridiculous one somehow or other ... I should make a bad courtier', he told the Duke of Buccleuch, '& an ode-maker is described by Pope as a poet out of his way or out of his senses'. Scott did not want to give offence 'where no one would willingly offend', nor did he want to lose a chance of smoothing the future for his sons. He warily delayed his reply until the Duke had advised him.(69) The Duke advised him within the week. 'I should be mortified to see you hold a situation which ... is stamped ridiculous.'(70)

On 4 September Scott dispatched an unctuous refusal to Lord Hertford, and a courtly letter to Stanier Clarke: 'I shall always consider it as the proudest incident of my life that his Royal Highness the Prince Regent whose taste in literature is so highly distinguished should have thought of naming me to the situation of Poet Laureate.'(71) To a less eminent friend he explained that he had not cared to commit poetical suicide. He contrived to keep his independence, and, as he expressed it, 'every sentiment of loyalty'.(72)

He had also borne another candidate in mind: a candidate who had for years been angling for a sinecure (Royal Historiographer for England, or Steward to Greenwich Hospital for the Derwentwater estates) to improve his straitened means. This was the poet and historian Robert Southey.

Robert Southey had also seen himself as Poet Laureate. He had heard the news of Pye's death, a few days before his departure from Keswick for London; 'and at the time,' he told a friend, 'I thought it so probable that the not-very-desirable succession might be offered me as to bestow a little serious thought on the subject.'(73) By the time he reached London, he found the succession desirable enough to call without delay at the Admiralty. John Wilson Croker, Secretary to the Admiralty (and contributor to the *Quarterly Review*) was his warm supporter. Southey wanted to know how the matter stood.

Croker's version of the story differed a good deal from Clarke's.

He had [reported Southey] spoken to the Prince; and the Prince observing that I had written some good things in favour of the Spaniards, said the office should be given me. ... Presently Croker meets Lord Liverpool, and tells him what had passed; Lord Liverpool expressed his sorrow that he had not known it a day sooner, for he and the Marquis of Hertford had consulted together upon whom the vacant honour could most properly be bestowed. Scott was the greatest poet of the day, and to Scott therefore they had written to offer it. The Prince was displeased, at this; though he said he ought to have been consulted, it was his pleasure that I should have it, and have it I should. Upon this Croker represented that he was Scott's friend as well as mine, that Scott and I were upon friendly terms; and for the sake of all three he requested that the business might rest where it was.(74)

Did Lord Liverpool and the Marquis of Hertford fail to consult the Regent? Did the Regent really support Scott to Clarke, and Southey to Croker? Was Croker telling a white lie to soothe Southey's vanity? It is hard to tell; but apparently the doubt made the succession eminently desirable to Southey. He 'more than half suspected' that Scott would decline the offer, and, before the suspicion was verified, his own mind was made up. There came a graceful letter from Scott: 'I have declined the appointment. ... Will you forgive me, my dear friend, if I own I had you in my recollection?'(75) Southey, eating oysters at Streatham, wrote to Croker at once, sending him an ultimatum. He could not, he said, write poems to order like a schoolboy; but 'if it were understood that upon great public events I might either write or be silent as the spirit moved, I should now accept the office as an honourable distinction'.(76)

Mr. Croker replied, very justly, 'that it was not for us to make terms with the Prince Regent. "Go you," said he, "and write your Ode for the New Year. You can never have a better subject than the present state of the war affords you." '

Southey found a better subject. A few weeks afterwards, the Muse descended; and he addressed some lines to his wife:

> I have something to tell you, which you will not
> be sorry at,
> 'Tis that I am sworn in to the office of Laureat ...
> Keep this, I pray you, as a precious gem,
> For this is the Laureat's first poem.(77)

No doubt Mrs. Southey forgave her husband the style for the sake of the content.

Twenty-four years later, writing the preface to the third volume of his poetical works, Southey gave a different version of events. He protested coyly that 'no wish for the Laureateship had passed across my mind, nor had I ever dreamt that it would be proposed to me'. However, he was delighted enough to swear his oath of allegiance on 4 November 1813; and next day he thanked Scott for the heavensent sinecure of some £90 a year. His letter revealed all the self-esteem of the second-class; and his words to Scott hold an irony, today, that he did not suspect. 'We shall both be remembered hereafter,' he wrote, 'and ill betide him who shall institute a comparison between us. There has been no race: We have both got to the top of the hill by different paths, and meet there not as rivals but as friends.'(78)

Scott, for all his hypocrisy, and his eye for self-advancement, came well out of the affair. He sent Southey his generous congratulations. As for the tierce of Spanish Canary wine, which had once been part of the Laureate's salary, he wrote: 'I know no man so well entitled to Xeres sack as yourself, though many bards would make a better figure at drinking it.'(79)

30

On 5 September 1813, James Wyatt, Surveyor-General, and Comptroller of the Board of Works, and the favourite architect of George III, was killed in a carriage accident near Marlborough. It is said that when his youngest son, Philip, announced his father's death to the Regent, the Regent wept, and said 'that he had just found a man to his taste, and was thus unhappily deprived of him'.(*80*)

Since Wyatt had been killed at the age of sixty-five, it must be admitted that the Regent had taken time to discover him. He had, it was true, supported his candidature for the post of Surveyor-General in 1796; but Wyatt had lost much royal esteem through his inefficiency, and it was not until 1812 that the Regent had employed him for anything more than structural repairs. That year he had asked him to fit up a second library at Carlton House. In August 1813 he had ordered him to survey Marlborough House, next to the Pavilion, which he had just acquired from the Duke of Marlborough. Wyatt had prepared an estimate for its adaptation; now death had deprived him of the only chance which the Regent had given him.(*81*)

There was no doubt that the Regent's favourite architect was John Nash. Twenty years earlier, Nash had won a prize for his plan for Regent's Park. Ever since (wrote Sir Samuel Romilly, the reformer and politician) he had been in favour with the Regent; he now incurred pretty general dislike among architects and others for his overweening self-esteem. 'Nash the architect in London, ... is,' wrote Robert Finch, 'a great coxcomb. He is about 60 years of age. He is very fond of women, although he is married, & attempted even Mrs. Parker, his wife's sister. He lives in Dover Street in London, has a charming place in the Isle of Wight, and drives four horses.'(*82*)

Nash's contemporaries were mystified about the source of his wealth; and it has been implied that the Regent had good reason for generosity. Either before or after her marriage, so it is suggested, Mrs. Nash had been the Regent's mistress. 'The personal friendship between the Prince and his architect seems to have been strengthened,' writes Nash's biographer, 'by the other relationship. The Nashs' drawing-room in later years was full of royal portraits, and some exquisite chairs, inlaid with brass, came from the Regent. And there were other, more personal gifts. A puritan hand consigned them to destruction not so very long ago, and the Regent's pearls popped and fizzled in the flames; only a ring escaped.'(83)

Whatever the personal reasons that strengthened his claims, Nash was now the royal architect. When, in 1812, the Treasury ordered that a cottage in Windsor Great Park should be remodelled for the Regent, it was Nash, as the Woods and Forests architect, who designed the alterations and enlargements. It was he who planned the surrounding plantations, and designed the entrance-front with its gables and its Gothic door; it was he who devised the 'little thatched bonnets' on the roof of the garden-front, and the small rustic verandah where the honeysuckle hung in swathes. It was Nash who designed the conservatory 'formed of cast-iron trellised pilasters' with a green-painted 'trellised temple' in the centre.

In 1812 he had been concerned with the Regent's Canal; now, in 1813, he had started work on the street that would in time be known as Regent Street. He was thought to have 'great interest' in Wyatt's vacant post; and, sure enough, by royal command, so it was said, he became Deputy Surveyor-General. The Office of Works was finally organised with a political head, and Nash, John Soane and Robert Smirke were appointed as 'Attached Architects'; they were given retaining fees of £500 a year, and allowed to practise. It gradually became clear that Nash was taking more than his share of work. As the Regent's favourite, he altered Carlton House, and designed a superb *enfilade* of rooms from Hopper's conservatory on the west to a new Gothic dining-room on the east. There was a Corinthian dining-room, a Corinthian ante-room, a Gothic library, and a Golden

Drawing-room, also Corinthian. Through these royal and splendid rooms many royal and splendid visitors would pass.

31

On 2 April 1814 the French Senate decreed the fall of the Bonaparte dynasty: four days later, Napoleon abdicated unconditionally. On 20 April he went to Elba. Early on Easter morning the Comte de Blacas woke Louis XVIII at Hartwell, in Buckinghamshire, with an urgent dispatch from the Prince Regent: after twenty-five years of exile, the Bourbons were restored to the throne of France.

'There are to be immense rejoicings on Monday,' Thomas Sheridan (the dramatist's son) informed Samuel Whitbread soon afterwards. 'White cockades and tremendous illuminations. Carlton House is to blaze with fleurs de lys &c.'*(84)* It is quite probable that the Regent had intrigued for the restoration of Louis l'Inévitable, or (as he was known in France) le Préfet d'Angleterre. Certainly he proclaimed the Bourbon restoration in style. On 20 April, in person, he brought the new King of France out of exile, and escorted him into London.

Byron would not stir from his rooms in Albany to see the procession pass a few yards away. 'At this present writing,' he informed Moore, 'Louis the Gouty is wheeling in triumph into Piccadilly. ... I had an offer of seats to see them pass; but ... the Most Christian King "hath no attractions for me".'*(85)* Miss Williams Wynn, Lord Grenville's niece, was less cynical, and watched the scene from Lord Dudley's balcony; though 'I cannot say', she wrote, 'that I quite liked to see the British Guards decorated with the white cockade'.*(86)* Fanny Burney, now Mme d'Arblay, went to Grillon's Hotel, in Albemarle Street, where Louis the Gouty was to hold a levée. An imposing chair awaited him, and 'an avenue had instantly been cleared from the door to the chair, and the King moved along it slowly, slowly, slowly, rather dragging his large and weak limbs than walking; but his face was truly engaging; benignity was in every feature'.(*87*) It was small wonder that he was benign. The Regent invested him with the Order of the Garter, and himself buckled the Garter round his leg (it was, he said later, like clasping someone's waist). The King responded by taking off his own insignia of the Order of the Saint Esprit, and bestowing them upon the Regent.

On 24 April, at Dover, on the royal yacht, Louis XVIII embarked for France. He was escorted by eight ships of the Royal Navy, under the command of the Duke of Clarence in the *Jason*. The future of France seemed to be assured. 'Hallelujah,' wrote the Duke of Cumberland to his brother, the Prince Regent, 'that things are as they are.'(*88*)

32

If April was a momentous month, June was to be tumultuous. On 2 June the Princess of Wales appeared in a box at Covent Garden. *God Save the King* was played, and at the words 'confound their politics', the audience burst into applause. A man (hired, perhaps, for the occasion) called for three cheers for the Princess of Wales, and 'three cheers more for an oppressed Princess who should go to Court'. Next day, C. B. Wollaston reported to his step-sister, Mary Frampton, that he had seen the Regent in the park: 'or rather I should say the Horse Guards which *concealed* his carriage'. Everything was silent, except for the clatter of the escort, but in the streets, and near the Palace, Wollaston understood, the Regent had been hooted and shouted at.

It was a remarkable show of disaffection, for the Napoleonic Wars were officially over, and the park guns had just been firing to mark the signing of the Definitive Treaty. But to some people even the thought of peace paled beside the thought of the Regent's treatment of his wife. He had now made himself so detested, wrote Wollaston, that he would probably be insulted despite all the coming galas and rejoicings.(*89*)

The private fears of Wollaston hardly accorded with the public sentiments of Southey. The Poet Laureate was composing his *Carmen Aulica* on the supreme state visit of the century: the arrival of the Allied Sovereigns in England. He began, very naturally, with an Ode to the Regent:

> Enjoy thy triumph now,
> Prince of the mighty Isle!
> Enjoy the rich reward, so rightly due,
> When rescued nations, with one heart and voice,
> Thy counsels bless and thee . . .(*90*)

On 7 June an illuminated London received Alexander I of All the Russias, and Frederick William III, King of Prussia. Alexander, somewhat strangely, took up residence at the Imperial Hotel, Piccadilly: Frederick William stayed at Clarence House, where, it was said, he rejected the fine beds, and insisted on 'his own camp equipage'.(*91*) Alexander determined to be popular, and—at least on his arrival —he 'acted his part decently in society'. Frederick William 'appeared what he was—a plain soldier and mere corporal, and he was overshadowed by his own dragoon, General Blücher, whose coarse and jovial manners, together ·with his veteran appearance, rendered him a prodigious favourite with the multitude'.(*92*) William Cobbett, the radical journalist, declared that though Blücher was old, and had his mouth 'well guarded with whiskers', he expressed his fear 'lest his lips should be carried away by the kisses of the *Ladies of England!*'(*93*)

While the multitude was applauding, and Blücher was expressing his apprehension, the Regent showed his sense of occasion. He recognised that the visit must receive commemoration: that the art of portrait-painting in England in 1814 must prove itself to future generations. He commissioned Thomas Lawrence to paint the portraits of Alexander and Frederick William, of Blücher, and of Count Platoff, whose twenty regiments of Cossacks had devastated the *Grande Armée* on the retreat from Moscow. Now, for the first time, he expressed his own intention of sitting to Lawrence.(*94*) Henceforward he was Lawrence's best patron.

The Regent was not discovering a gifted, unknown artist. Thomas Lawrence was forty-five; and, since the death of Hoppner in 1810, he had been without a rival in portrait-painting. In 1811 Mr. Croker had 'taken the freedom' of telling the Regent that Lawrence was the only man to paint him. 'I have never,' Croker wrote to Lawrence, 'from the earliest hour I have ever judged of a picture, held any other language than of your superiority & latterly of your supremacy in your art.'(95)

On the surface, it might seem surprising that the Regent had neglected Lawrence for so long. The reason for this neglect was not lack of taste; and, despite his patronage of Hoppner, it had never been an exclusive preference for Hoppner's work. Perhaps, when Lawrence showed his portrait of the Princess of Wales and her daughter, at the Academy in 1802, he had already spoilt his chances at Carlton House. For the portrait, in his biographer's words, had 'opened a fine connexion for Mr. Lawrence, and it led to an intimacy between him and her Royal Highness'.(96) He had been cited in the Delicate Investigation.

However, if there had been any personal reason for neglecting him, the Regent chose to forget it in the summer of 1814; and no portrait-painter could have caught the epic atmosphere with more felicity. Lawrence's manner and appearance, said a sitter, 'had a tinge of the time'; on canvas, he showed appreciation of its grace, panache, and grandeur. He began his task at once, and as the allied sovereigns and their suites were absorbed in visiting the institutions of the country, 'it required', wrote his biographer, 'the utmost vigilance and importunity ... to obtain even short and irregular sittings'.(97)

The potentates visited a respectable number of English institutions: one of the first was Covent Garden, where the Princess of Wales, banned from official functions, had determined to create a furore. 'I am out of all patience,' snapped Robert Finch in his diary, 'at the conduct of the Princess of Wales. She was forbidden to go to Court; and she has the audacity to show herself, at the Play ... on purpose to excite a popular ferment. She was greeted with acclamations, and the mistaken audience call'd for God save the King, our good King, the protector of outrag'd innocence, &c.'(*98*) 'Prinny,' wrote Mr. Creevey, stupidly, 'is exactly in the state one would wish; he lives only by protection of his visitors. . . .'(*99*)

However, Caroline's attempt to refer her case to the House of Commons was voted down; and, brazen as she was, she could not make her appearance at Carlton House, when, on 9 June, the Emperor and the King received the Garter; Ascot went off happily, except that the Prince of Orange returned on the outside of a stage-coach, 'and in a highly excited state'.(*100*) The dinners with Lord Liverpool, with the Regent, and Lord Stafford, passed without incident, though, seeing the Regent and Lady Hertford together on a sofa, the Emperor was said to have murmured: 'Voyez ces deux gros, comme ils paroissent heureux!'(*101*) The Dowager Lady Vernon, writing to Mrs. Frampton, could not refrain from deploring the Regent's private affairs. 'The black side of his lanthorn is,' she wrote, 'domestic life.' But Lady Vernon, unlike some, saw both sides of the lantern. She added that 'our Prince Regent is never so happy as in show and state, and there he shines incomparably'.(*102*)

He certainly shone on his visit to Oxford. At eleven o'clock on the morning of 14 June, the royal and imperial procession reached Magdalen Bridge. With nice propriety, the Mayor and Corporation halted at the middle of the bridge, while the Chancellor of the University walked forward to meet the Regent, who wore his robes as a Doctor of Civil Law. Then he was led across, into Oxford; and, in procession, the potentates went to the Divinity School for a speech of welcome. Such orations are often empty conventions; but this one was addressed to the giver of the Herculaneum papers, the founder of two university readerships,(*103*) and it was delivered with conviction.

It is with equal pride and pleasure, that we hail your Royal Highness's arrival at this Seat of Religion and Learning, adorned by so many monuments of Royal munificence, enriched by your Royal Highness with additional treasures of ancient literature, and honoured by still more recent marks of your Royal countenance and protection.

These sentiments we should at all times, and under any circumstances, have been happy to express to your Royal Highness. . . .(*104*)

The royal and imperial visitors toured the public buildings and colleges. At the Clarendon Press they saw a sheet being printed, in four languages, with the verse: 'Thine, O Lord, is the greatness, and the power, and the glory, and the victory, and the majesty.' In the Bodleian Library they inspected the treasures, and received large paper copies of the Oxford edition of Aristotle's *Poetics.* (*105*)

The season was so backward that 'there was the greatest difficulty in procuring one small dish of strawberries'; but that evening, in the Radcliffe Camera, there was 'a sumptuous dinner to 200 persons'. Spectators, admitted into the gallery, watched the sovereigns banqueting, the candles glittering on the gold plate, and old Blücher getting hopelessly tipsy. ('He preferred Strong Beer as his drink when he arrived thirsty,' noted Frederick Barnes, sub Dean of Christ Church, 'and seasoned it with a Glass of Cognac.')(*106*) The Chancellor's niece, Frances Williams Wynn, sized the visitors up pretty sharply. She dismissed the Emperor as 'the dandy Alexander', the Regent as moody; and 'as to the King of Prussia', she wrote, 'he looked as stupid and vulgar as I believe he really is'. But it remained a remarkable evening, with Blücher lost in search of his lodgings, and Alexander of All the Russias wandering down the High Street where the candles glittered welcome in every window.(*107*)

Next morning there assembled, in the Sheldonian Theatre, a Convocation of unexampled majesty. Two reigning potentates received their diplomas as Doctors of Civil Law. They were watched by a third, the Regent, who again condescended to wear his doctoral scarlet; and few English sovereigns had earned it so well.

> Oxford, exult!—behold the period come,
> When conquering kings adorn this classic dome:

Oxford, raise high thy head, and gladly pay
The homage due on this thy festal day ...
For now to thee, great Prince, her vows sincere
Thy Oxford pays, and bids thee welcome here.
Long mayst thou live on peaceful arts to smile,
And long a Brunswick rule fair Albion's Isle. ...(*108*)

The conventional verses, written and spoken by an undergraduate, held for once a modicum of truth. And if Miss Williams Wynn was astonished to hear that none of the foreign royalty understood a word of Latin or Greek, the Regent, one may be sure, appreciated the finer points of the classical orations.

When, on the third day of the visit, he and Blücher dined at Christ Church, he earned a new respect for his grace and scholarship. Charles Stanhope, an undergraduate at The House, told

an anecdote of the Prince whose peculiar grace and elegance shone in its best lustre during the whole visit. Blücher's health being drunk, he returned thanks in German. ... The Prince, perceiving the indecorum of this, at once rose and announced that so excellent a speech should not be lost upon the greater part of the company, who could not be expected to understand German, and that, therefore, in the absence of a better interpreter, he would volunteer for that office himself. ... He then delivered an extremely neat and tactful address of thanks to the University. ...(*109*)

On 17 June Alexander and Frederick William were entertained at Merchant Taylors' Hall. Next day, with the Regent, they dined with the Corporation of London, tried the first turtle of the season, and a baron of beef, and drank fifteen toasts. The procession to Guildhall was watched by that eager provincial novelist, Mary Russell Mitford, who wrote home in a turmoil of excitement:

We got there well and pleasantly, and saw them all most clearly. ...

We had everything that can be imagined excellent as refreshments—ices, cakes, sandwiches, champagne, &c. The procession, of which the chief beauties were the Regent's horses and the splendid military spectacle, was over early enough to allow me to get dressed (I mean only hair dressed, for I wore my crape frock and a spencer) in excellent time to get to the opera. . . .(*110*)

Miss Mitford was not the only literary figure to be fascinated by the royal visit. Tom Moore, still satirical, could not forbear asking Samuel Rogers: 'How does "our fat friend" go on? Among all these fighting chieftains, he seems particularly to distinguish himself in what is called *fighting shy. Is* he or is he *not* hissed wherever he goes?'(*111*) Moore was no doubt gratified to learn from another friend, Mr. Dalton, of the Regent's evident discomfiture:

We have seen [the great visitors] in all places and in all ways. The most striking exhibition which I saw was their first appearance and reception at the Opera. . . . The Regent, who entered along with the Emperor and King of Prussia, and who of course shared in the applause, which was prodigious, turned pale when he saw the artfully timed entrance of the Princess of Wales exactly opposite, at the critical moment when the applause had subsided. I never saw anything so pointed as the manner in which almost the entire audience turned to her and cheered her.

And, knowing the sympathies of his recipient, Dalton saw fit to add:

The Emperor is a very amiable-looking person; the King of Prussia is, I think, much more interesting from his simple and unostentatious demeanour; but the contrast between their natural manner and unaffected dress, and the artificial dignity and manufactured appearance of our Regent, is most striking.(*112*)

Such was the comment made on the Regent: largely inspired by his treatment of his wife. Public opinion is not always just; for the 'poor Body' who earned Whitbread's sympathy had shown herself both unfaithful and unbalanced. She and the Regent had separated eighteen years ago; he could hardly be expected to be reconciled with her now, for appearance' sake. He might have earned the sympathy of thoughtful people when she pestered him in her mad, irrepressible way.

However, even Caroline could not entirely spoil the celebrations. On 20 June peace was proclaimed in London; on 25 June (while Turner sketched the scene) the Fleet was reviewed at Portsmouth. The Emperor of All the Russias issued a proclamation praising 'England, which for twenty years has shaken the colossus of crimes that threatens the universe'. 'Every nation,' wrote Robert Finch, this glorious June, 'speaks of us in the highest terms. We have never betray'd the great and just cause.'(*113*)

Then the princes and potentates departed. The population of London (which, it was said, had been increased by 200,000 by the arrival of the Emperor and King) shrank to its normal size; and Lady Harriet Frampton must have sighed with relief. For the great incursion of visitors had made itself felt in small domestic ways. 'No milk, sometimes,' she had lamented, 'as the cows are all frightened out of the Green Park by the constant huzzas, and many people cannot get their clothes washed, as the washerwomen work for Princes and Kings'.(*114*)

33

The peace and quiet did not last for long. The Regent gave a fête at Carlton House in honour of the Duke of Wellington, Nash built a huge polygonal hall for the occasion, 'and several other rooms in the palace garden', and all the rooms were 'studded with W's' in tribute to a rather embarrassed soldier. On 1 August came the centenary of the House of Hanover; and the Regent determined to celebrate it in style, with temples, towers, pagodas, bridges and drinking booths in the royal parks, and a mock naval battle on the Serpentine.

Satirists buzzed round to make their comments on such extravagance. Puritans condemned such *joie de vivre*. Cyrus Redding, the journalist (the son of a Baptist minister) declared that the proceedings were 'worthy of the Prince's taste, extravagant and puerile as it was'.(*115*)

The chief butt of merriment was the miniature fleet on the Serpentine. One paper declared that a corps of Laplanders, none of them more than three feet six in height, had been dismissed as being eleven inches too tall for the crews. Peter Pindar dismissed the Regent's toy navy in a poem remarkable for its personal offensiveness:

> Thou patron of politer arts—
> To every soul that life imparts,
> To *stay makers* and *wig* contrivers,
> *Tailors* and professions divers! ...
>
> Thou star of elegance and fashion!
> Thou pink of all that's gay and dashing!
> Graceful *em-bon-point* Adonis!
> Prince of modern macaronies!
>
> Long thou'st been the admiration
> Of a wise and thinking nation!
> Oft thou hast surprised us truly,
> Time past gone as well as newly;
>
> But this *last* grand thought astounds us—
> Yes its brilliancy confounds us—
> All thy former prodigies,
> The world must own, *were fools to this*.(*116*)

It seems extraordinary that a sovereign could have been so despised at such a moment of national ascendancy.

> In every tongue, on every shore be heard,
> That Britain to the World is by the World preferr'd ...

So wrote Lord Thurlow in his *Carmen Britanicum*,(*117*) and there was some justification for the cry. No one would withstand the armies which Wellington commanded, the navy which had proved itself, nine years earlier, at Trafalgar. No one challenged the immense and widening British Empire, or doubted its political influence. No one questioned the wealth of Great Britain, or the capacity of Englishmen to write fine poems and design noble cities. The spread of popular education, the interest in penal reform, the eagerness to build churches, and to propagate the gospel at home and abroad: there was much about England to respect. But the Prince Regent earned no respect from the vast mass of his subjects. He was generally hissed in the streets of London. The overwhelming majority of Englishmen would never forgive him for his treatment of his wife and daughter.

34

Popular opinion is often ill-informed and unthinking. It is often irrational. It feeds on rumour and prejudice; and it feeds on them all the more greedily when they are rumour and prejudice about royalty. Few, perhaps, were aware of the Regent's actual marriage to Mrs. Fitzherbert. The Regent's tragedy was the fact that Mrs. Fitzherbert had not been born a Protestant princess. Everyone must have known the terms on which he had been driven into dynastic marriage; and none of his subjects, who showed such vociferous hatred, seems to have considered the prospect of a lifelong, exclusive relationship with an unbalanced nymphomaniac. The situation was enough to encourage the weaknesses and vices in any man.

In June, describing the gala performance at the opera, the Hon. Mrs. Robinson had reported that the visiting sovereigns meant 'to negotiate a reconciliation between the Regent and his wife. They have now certainly been seen under the same roof'. Rumour could hardly have been more ludicrous. That glimpse of the Princess of Wales, 'in a black wig and many diamonds',(*118*) encouraging acclamations from her box, was probably the Regent's last sight of her.

Caroline was brazen; but even she could not allow herself to be ostracised any longer. She had received the King of Prussia's compliments from his steward; she had been banned from the dazzling fête at White's; she had been refused a seat at the thanksgiving service for peace at St. Paul's. Ignored as the legal wife of the Regent, she was also discounted as a mother: she was hardly allowed to see her daughter; and many friends who had been compelled to choose between husband and wife had prudently abandoned her. In 1811, when the Regent broke with her personal and political friends, 'all of that party except Canning, Ward and Granville Leveson, gave up the Princess's acquaintance'; and Brougham recalled a sad dinner at Blackheath 'to which they were all invited, when Canning and Ward alone came, the rest of the chairs being unoccupied'.(*119*)

It was Brougham, the ruthless barrister, the defender of the Hunts, who had then become adviser to the Princess of Wales and her daughter. It was Brougham who now, on 30 July 1814, warned the Princess not to carry out her intention: not, whatever happened, to go abroad:

> Depend upon it, Madam, there are many persons who now begin to see a chance of divorcing your Royal Highness from the Prince. ... As long as you remain in this country I will answer for it that no plot can succeed against you. But if you are living abroad, and surrounded by the base spies and tools who will be always planted about you, ready to invent and swear as they may be directed, who can pretend to say what may happen ... ?(*120*)

The Princess of Wales was stubborn; she had suffered beyond endurance. She had no patience, any longer, with political expediency. It is said that Canning prevailed upon her to go abroad, 'because he saw that sedition had marked her for its own'.(*121*) Certainly, if she possessed any mat-

ernal instinct, it was swept aside: she would not even let
herself be swayed by the misery and pleading of her
daughter. On 8 August, from South Lancing, near Wor-
thing, Lady Charlotte Lindsay, one of her ladies-in-waiting,
announced: 'My dear Mr. Brougham, ... Our baggage is
putting on board the Jason, and this night, or early to-
morrow, we are to embark.' The Princess of Wales was intent on freedom. 'Nothing,' added Lady Charlotte, 'can stop
her. I never saw so fixed a determination.'(122)

Brougham quoted the remark to Earl Grey, next day. The
Princess of Wales was then on board the frigate which, a
few months earlier, had escorted a restored Bourbon king
to France.

35

It was small wonder that Princess Charlotte, the only child
of the marriage, should suffer from the hatred between her
parents. She had been the pawn of each, in turn, in the
ruthless family politics. Her mother had naturally claimed
her, her father quite as naturally protested that Caroline
was not fit to look after her, and the King had determined
to control the upbringing of the child who would no
doubt one day ascend the throne. Charlotte had suffered
from all three. No childhood could have been more disturbed than the childhood of this little girl who so needed
emotional stability. Her governesses and ladies-in-waiting
had been frequently changed; for years she had had no
friends of her own age. She had lived in growing isolation in a harsh adult world.

It was indeed isolation: her mother was allowed to see
her less and less often; Charlotte was virtually imprisoned
in Warwick House, in London, or under her grandmother's
watchful eyes at Windsor. The Regent was always fond of
children. There is no doubt that he loved his daughter. But
he also saw her, understandably, as the symbol of his marriage; she personified a humiliating, lifelong catastrophe. As

he grew older and increasingly unpopular, and as she became a lively and intelligent young woman, he had sometimes resented her youth, and the thought of her popularity.

> Her eyes are completely opened to all the bad pro-
> ceedings and illegal proceedings since my being in this
> country [wrote the Princess of Wales in 1812]. Her father
> hardly speaks to her, and ... she is not in the least
> anxious that they should be upon another footing in
> future; in short ... she has a complete contempt of
> her father's character, which she obtained, not from influ-
> ence, *but from her own sagacity.* ... She abhors *the
> Queen* and *the Duke of Cumberland.* She has no con-
> fidence in any of the princesses, nor in either of the Dukes.
> Miss Elphinstone, as well as Lady Barbara Ashley—two
> young ladies of whose acquaintance the Prince had ap-
> proved two years ago, and who were the only [ones] she
> ever corresponded with—their letters were intercepted
> by the special order of the Regent; and though there was
> no high treason in them, *the correspondence was forbid,
> as well as the waiting,* for which reason my daughter has
> no other intimate friend than her mother. ... She writes
> every day twelve pages, and sometimes more, having no-
> body to whom she could open her heart so freely and so
> trusty [*sic*].(*123*)

It was easy for Brougham to gain the confidence of the
bitter mother and the frustrated daughter; and one day,
in his autobiography, he would explain his conduct. 'I
knew,' he wrote, 'the virulent nature of the Prince's party
both in and out of Parliament, and I was running into the
most entire and irreconcilable hostility to everything that
belonged to Carlton House. ... But I really felt ... that the
conduct of the Prince had been such from the beginning
towards his wife, and his later treatment of both mother
and daughter so outrageous, as made it a duty to take their
part'.(*124*) Brougham was writing for posterity. He naturally wished to present himself as a defender of outraged
womanhood, a patriot who sacrificed his promising future

for the sake of justice. The truth was neither so simple nor so edifying. Disappointed in politics, determined to discredit the Regent (however this might harm the monarchy), Brougham was trading on the royal domestic quarrels; he was exploiting them for the sake of his career. The Princess of Wales and her daughter were excellent political capital; their cause would ensure him fame and popularity. As for the Regent, nobody was likely to take his part.

Brougham therefore reported every detrimental fact to that other disappointed Whig, Earl Grey. Princess Charlotte, so he had written in November 1812,

> is quite furious at *their* treatment of her. I mean Queen, Princesses, Dukes, and her father as much as any. She says she complained of her letters being opened at the post-office *by his orders*, which he denied circumstantially; and that she pressed him until she was obliged to stop, to avoid the unpleasant necessity of convicting him of a plain lie. This is her own story. As for the confinement at Windsor, she entertained a plan of escaping as soon as she was of age (for she conceives she is so next birthday —very falsely in point of law). She also desired my advice on this and other matters, and I am to write a representation as strongly as possible against it.(*125*)

Every malicious statement, every piece of gossip was fuel to Brougham's fire.

> I send you ... a most curious account of our beloved Prince's behaviour to his daughter [this to Earl Grey on 3 January 1813]. He is jealous of her to a degree of insanity, and has been for some time. I believe the Duke of Cumberland and Yarmouth have actually been feeding him with hopes of getting rid of her by divorcing his wife, and this he is fool enough to believe. ... The young Princess is quite aware how much she is in the same boat with her mother, and feels such topics accordingly. ...(*126*)

Grey was as partisan as Brougham. He scanned the papers for useful rumours; he concluded, he said, from the article in the *Morning Chronicle* in answer to the *Courier*, 'that the war was pretty hot between Carlton House and Kensington'.(*127*)

It is possible that the Regent had sometimes thought of his daughter's marriage as a means of removing her from his life. Charlotte had shown a decided interest in the young Duke of Devonshire (the son of Georgiana), but her father had determined that she should marry Prince William of Orange. It is true that the Prince of Orange was 'a dissolute, untidy and stupid young man', and Wellington said that he was inclined to drink. But he had spent two years at Oxford, and served on Wellington's staff in the Peninsula. He was young, he was the heir to the throne of the Netherlands, and he would naturally want his wife to live abroad. The Regent saw the Prince of Orange as a providential candidate.

> The young Princess ... is on perfectly good terms *at present* with her father [Brougham told Earl Grey, on 21 December 1813]. But this is the hot fit, and he is coaxing her; it always succeeds to a certain degree. ... The Princess Charlotte has completely altered her language as to the Prince of Orange, and I am quite clear she will take him if they offer him to her. ... And now that it is all over, I may inform you of a great alarm I had from finding, by the clearest proofs, that she really had a great *penchant* for the Duke of *Devonshire*. This you may rely on; and it is equally certain that *now* she would be furious at the insinuation, as is exceedingly natural in such cases. ... I always thought that the best ... part of her character was the spice of the mother's spirit and temper; but I fear she has a considerable mixture of the father's weakness and fickleness.(*128*)

It was not out of weakness that Princess Charlotte accepted Prince William of Orange; as Brougham reported to Earl Grey, in March 1814, 'she agreed to the match as a mere matter of convenience and *emancipation*, caring for the Prince of Orange literally nothing. The Prince Regent

never named it to her, but brought the Prince of Orange
to her before he went abroad, and then left the room.
The latter popped the question, and she said, "Yes".'(*129*)
But, from whichever parent it came, the Princess had
natural spirit; and, having accepted the Prince of Orange,
she was rational enough to consider the conditions of the
marriage. She saw that there were no preparations for her
and her husband to live in England; she felt that the marriage was a trick to get her out of the country. She was loyally determined to support her mother, and she thought that
they should stay in England, and protect one another. She
summoned the Prince to Warwick House. 'He appeared to
be very unhappy,' reported Lady Charlotte Lindsay to
Brougham, 'but seemed to admit that if Princess Charlotte
adhered to this resolution, the marriage must be off.'(*130*)
Southey's poem on the royal marriage proved to be premature.

When Princess Charlotte told the Regent that she had
broken off her engagement, he dismissed her ladies, whom
he suspected of encouraging her. Charlotte left Carlton
House, and hailed a hackney coach from the Charing Cross
stand, and gave the driver a guinea to take her to her
mother's house in Connaught Place. After consultations between Caroline, Brougham, the Archbishop of Canterbury,
and the Dukes of York and Sussex, she was at last persuaded
to return to Warwick House, but not before the news of her
escapade was public property. 'Why, again, is the Princess
to be treated as a state criminal?' Brougham asked, a few
days later. 'Why are we to have a Queen so brought up?
Out of Turkey is there anything so barbarous?'(*131*)

The Regent was not so barbarous as Brougham chose to
believe. When the interview was over, he spoke to a friend,
at length, of his love for his daughter. He had, no doubt,
treated her harshly because he was afraid that her jilting
of Prince William might spoil her chances of a suitable
marriage. On Christmas Day 1814, when her mother had
gone abroad, Princess Charlotte confirmed certain dis-
quieting rumours that had reached him. She told him that
in spite of the King's injunction not to see her mother

alone, she had in fact often seen her alone and had witnessed many things in her mother's room which she could
not repeat. She told him that when she was driving out at
Windsor, with her governess, she had met Captain Hesse,
of the Light Dragoons. Captain Hesse (said to be the illegitimate son of the Duke of York) had met her regularly for
six weeks and ridden beside her carriage. When his regiment was moved from Windsor, her mother had arranged
frequent meetings between them in her own bedroom. She
had locked them in, and said, as she left them: 'A présent
je vous laisse. Amusez-vous.'(*132*) Through her mother she
had carried on a regular correspondence with Captain
Hesse; and 'God knows', she said, 'what would have become
of me if he had not behaved with so much respect to me'.
She added that she had never been able to understand if
Captain Hesse was her lover or her mother's.

She said that her uncle, the Duke of Brunswick, had
often put her on her guard 'on the subject of my mother's
conduct & told me he was sure that boy [William Austin]
was her child. My mother says', added Princess Charlotte,
'nobody marries, but with the idea of *liberty* of gratifying
one's own inclinations & pleasures & fathering them upon
one's husband'.(*133*)

These 'melancholy and frightful disclosures', as the
Regent called them, helped to bring him and his daughter
together. 'Happily for me,' she told him, in February 1815,
'we are now upon the most comfortable and confidential
terms possible. We have broken through the awkwardness
of talking upon one subject, which is a very delicate and
painful one, and I should grieve if there was anything left
to make us less open with each other.'(*134*) Their affection
for one another had become so strong that no subjects of
conversation were now impossible. When rumours of the
Orange match were renewed, the Regent said he would
never be the first to broach the question. Princess Charlotte
simply repeated her 'strong and fixed aversion' to the marriage, and explained, with tact, that she could not feel
'those sentiments of regard which surely are so necessary in
a matrimonial connexion'. 'You have no reason,' replied

the Regent, 'to apprehend in a union with the Prince of Orange the grievous calamity, which I alas! my dearest child, have experienced from a marriage with a person whose character we have had occasion so recently, so fully and so freely to gather'.(*135*) He emphasised that her mother, with her 'wicked art & deprav'd contrivancies', was bent on besmirching her character in order to bring forward William Austin. 'In such a sad predicament,' he wrote, 'when I am gone you can have no protector but a husband, and that husband can not be a protector unless he shall have a name, a station, and a character in Europe, calculated to repel what may be and what you and I now do clearly see, will be attempted'.(*136*)

The husband and protector had already presented himself to the Regent, as Charlotte's suitor, in the summer of 1814; but now, in 1815, the Regent had other preoccupations.

36

Towards the end of February 1815, Fanny Burney, Madame d'Arblay, was presented in Paris to the Duchesse d'Angoulême. The conversation turned, naturally enough, to the English royal family, and it was evident that the Regent was the Duchess's favourite. The honour he had paid the Bourbons

> in the midst of their misfortunes, and while so much doubt hung against every chance of those misfortunes being ever reversed, did [she said] so much honour to his heart, and proved so solacing to their woes and humiliation, that she could never revert to that public testimony of his esteem and goodwill without the most glowing gratitude.
>
> 'O!' she cried, 'Il a été parfait!'(*137*)

The misfortunes of the Bourbons were not entirely ended. Within a matter of days, their humiliation had returned. On 26 February, dissatisfied at being Emperor of the Isle of Elba, Napoleon embarked for France. By 3 April Robert Finch, the diarist, in Florence, recorded that 'Napoleon the great has enter'd Paris without any resistance, and the family of the Bourbons have fled'.(*138*)

In London, the Regent had little time to think of his daughter's marriage. All last year's celebrations of peace had been premature. On the news of Napoleon's landing in France, he sent a message to both Houses of Parliament, declaring his intention to join the allies. England, Austria, Russia and Prussia bound themselves by treaty not to lay down their arms till Napoleon was finally vanquished. On 5 April Wellington took command of the Allied forces in Belgium.

On the evening of 21 June, an English Member of Parliament, the Hon. H. Bennet, sitting in Brooks's Club, heard Earl Grey and Sir Robert Wilson assure 'a crowded audience that Boney had 200,000 men across the Sambre, and that he must then be at Brussels. Wilson read a letter announcing that the English were defiling out of the town by the Antwerp gate'. The politicians were discomfited. As Wilson was reading the letter, the shouts in the street drew everyone to the window, and, wrote Bennet, 'we saw the chaise and the Eagles'.(*139*) In the chaise was Major the Hon. Henry Percy, one of Wellington's staff. He had travelled straight from the battlefield of Waterloo to announce the victory to the Regent. He found him at Mrs. Boehm's party in St. James's Square. Mrs. Boehm, a rich merchant's wife, 'was much annoyed with the battle of Waterloo, as it spoilt her party'.(*140*) The Regent knighted the officer who laid the insignia of the *Grande Armée* at his feet.

On 8 July, Louis XVIII (Louis Deux-fois-neuf) re-entered Paris. On 15 July, Napoleon, who had abdicated once more, surrendered to Captain Maitland of H.M.S. *Bellerophon*. On 8 August, after asking the Regent in vain for asylum in England, he sailed on the *Northumberland* to St. Helena.

The rejoicings took many forms. The King of Denmark (reported Augustus Foster to his mother, Elizabeth, Duchess of Devonshire), 'sends the Elephant to Wellington and

Blücher and to our Prince Regent. It is a right thing to do, and it is, I suppose, the order Hamlet wore'.(*141*) On 6 July there was a grand performance at the King's Theatre, under the immediate patronage of the Regent, 'in honour of the victory gained over Napoleon on the 18th of June'. As for the Poet Laureate, he duly toiled away at a *Thanksgiving for Victory;* and, in *The Poet's Pilgrimage to Waterloo,* he expressed the general proud and confident patriotism:

Well mayst thou praise the land that gave thee birth,
And bless the Fate which made that country thine;
    For of all ages and all parts of Earth,
To chuse thy time and place did Fate allow
Wise choice would be this England and this Now.(*142*)

37

The Regent who ruled over 'this England and this Now' dispensed his grace and favour with a sense of fitness and grandeur. During the Hundred Days he had knighted Thomas Lawrence, 'and assured him, that he was proud in conferring a mark of his favour on one who had raised the character of British art in the estimation of all Europe'.(*143*) 'No act of our Regent Sovereign,' wrote Robert Smirke, the architect, to the new knight, 'was ever more just; and if he keeps up to that, the country will have cause to be grateful'.(*144*)

Others had cause to be grateful, too. Now that the Battle of Waterloo was becoming an old story, the Louvre had to be stripped of its treasures; the works of art which Napoleon had taken from all over Europe, had to be restored to their rightful owners. The famous bronze horses were sent back to adorn St. Mark's in Venice; but the expense of returning the Apollo Belvedere and other statues to Rome was so heavy that the Pope offered all the sculpture to the Regent. A prince who cared less for art might, paradoxically, have accepted the offer; the Regent replied that however much he would like to own 'some of these inestimable productions, he could not take advantage of the necessity of the owners': he would pay for the statues to be sent to Italy.(*145*)

Whatever he left to be desired in his human relations, the Regent always showed a noble generosity towards art. In December, the Royal Academy asked him to help obtain new casts 'from some of the fine Antiques in Rome, Naples and Florence, by allowing them a free conveyance to London in some of His Majesty's Vessels'.(*146*) Directions were immediately sent to the Admiralty, and to British Consuls throughout Italy, 'to afford all the facilities and assistance in their power'.(*147*)

Among the artists who thronged to Paris to see Napoleon's Louvre was Canova, who had come to claim the Italian works of art. After his visit to Paris, he came to London. He was astonished by the beauty of the streets and squares and bridges, and, not least, by the cleanliness, and the general air of prosperity. The Regent received him charmingly, and presented him with a diamond-encrusted snuffbox, 'containing besides a gift worthy of the donor'.(*148*) He commissioned a group of Mars and Venus, symbolic of War and Peace, a statue of a recumbent nymph, and a group of the Three Graces; and, devoted as ever to the Stuarts, he also asked Canova to design a mausoleum for Cardinal York. Canova, wrote a contemporary,

> was a man of the utmost simplicity, candour, and independence of mind. The manner in which he always extolled the fine taste, sound judgment, and extensive information, that distinguished his present Majesty in matters relative to the arts, can therefore only be ascribed to a love of truth.... He has also been heard to observe, and he had enjoyed frequent intercourse with most, if not all the crowned heads of Europe—'that he knew no Sovereign in whose address were more happily combined, the suavity of the amiable man, and the dignity of the great Monarch'.(*149*)

In the winter after Waterloo the Regent found a surer way to endear himself to posterity. Jane Austen's brother,

Henry, lay ill of 'a dangerous fever' in Hans Place, and his doctor (one of the Regent's physicians) recognised Henry's nurse as the author of *Pride and Prejudice*. Soon afterwards the doctor told Miss Austen that the Regent greatly admired her novels, frequently read them and kept a set 'in every one of his residences'. He had therefore thought it right to inform His Royal Highness that Miss Austen was staying in London.

Next day, by the Regent's orders, Mr. Stanier Clarke arrived to invite Miss Austen to Carlton House. He had, he said, instructions to show her the library and other apartments, and to pay her every attention. He had also been commanded to say that Miss Austen was free to dedicate a novel to the Regent.(*150*)

Sir [wrote Miss Austen on 15 November],
   I must take the liberty of asking you a question.— Among the many flattering attentions which I recd from you at Carlton House on Monday last, was the Information of my being at liberty to dedicate my future work to His Royal Highness the P.R. ... I intreat you to have the goodness to inform me how such a Permission is to be understood, & whether it is incumbent on me to shew my sense of the Honour, by inscribing the Work now in the Press, to H.R.H.—I shd be equally concerned to appear either Presumptuous or Ungrateful.(*151*)

Dear Madam [replied Mr. Clarke next day],
   It is certainly not *incumbent* on you to dedicate your work now in the Press to His Royal Highness; but if you wish to do the Regent that honour now or at any future period, I am happy to send you that permission ...
   Your late Works, Madam, and in particular Mansfield Park reflect the highest honour on your Genius and your Principles; in every new work your mind seems to increase its energy and powers of discrimination. The Regent has read & admired all your publications. ...(*152*)

Dear Sir [Miss Austen instructed her publisher],
As I find that *Emma* is advertised for publication, I think it best to lose no time in settling all that remains to be settled ...
The Title page must be Emma, Dedicated by Permission to H.R.H. The Prince Regent—And it is my particular wish that one set should be completed and sent to H.R.H. two or three days before the Work is generally public. ...(*153*)

On 27 March 1816, from the Pavilion at Brighton, Clarke returned the Regent's thanks 'for the handsome copy you sent him of your last excellent novel'. (Miss Austen quoted the phrase to John Murray. 'Whatever he may think of *my* share of the work,' she added, tartly, 'yours seems to have been quite right.')(*154*) Clarke's letter must have delighted Miss Austen as a piece of unconscious self-portraiture.

Pray, dear Madam [he had written], soon write again and again. Lord St. Helens and many of the nobility, who have been staying here, paid you the just tribute of their praise.
The Prince Regent has just left us for London; and having been pleased to appoint me Chaplain and Private English Secretary to the Prince of Coburg, I remain here with His Serene Highness and a select party until the marriage. Perhaps when you again appear in print you may chuse to dedicate your volumes to Prince Leopold: any historical romance, illustrative of the history of the august House of Coburg, would just now be very interesting.(*155*)

Miss Austen had encountered a character worthy of one of her novels. She answered with an honesty and insight which were no doubt lost on him:

My dear Sir,
I am honoured by the Prince's thanks. ... You are very kind in your hints as to the sort of composition which might recommend me ... But I could no more write a romance than an epic poem. ... No, I must keep to my

own style and go on in my own way; and though I may
never succeed again in that, I am convinced that I should
totally fail in any other.(*156*)

38

The Prince of Coburg, for whom Miss Austen was asked to
change the course of her writing, was soon to be the husband of Princess Charlotte. The third son and eighth child
of a German princeling, Prince Francis of Saxe-Coburg-
Saalfield, he had come to London in the summer of 1814 in
the suite of the Emperor of Russia. He had been selected by
the Emperor's sister, the Grand Duchess Catherine, who had
settled in London and made herself Princess Charlotte's
confidante. The Grand Duchess had seen the unhappy girl
forced into an engagement with the Prince of Orange, and
she had decided that the best hope of making Charlotte
happy and keeping the balance of power in Europe, was to
present her with another suitor: a prince so handsome and
attentive that Charlotte would be conquered, a prince so
insignificant in politics that the great alliances would remain unshaken. It had needed little acumen to choose the
young Apollo with the fair hair and hazel eyes, from the
comic-opera duchy of Saxe-Coburg. Leopold himself was a
prince almost fit for the boards of Drury Lane: when he
came to London, at twenty-three, he was already a
lieutenant-general in the Russian army, with a couple of
decorations, a castle, and a romantic record of service in
the Napoleonic campaigns. He was also pedantic, and
coldly ambitious. He accepted the part that the Grand
Duchess meant him to play. 'Perhaps,' he wrote, as he left
for London, 'I shall end by getting married in England, and
staying there: it would be strange'.(*157*)

It seemed strange indeed; but this penniless careerist,
lodging over a grocer's in Marylebone High Street, and 'so
lodged because He was afraid His money would not hold
out', was presented to the Heiress Apparent in June 1814.

She had not, admittedly, fallen in love with him; but she had since rejected the Prince of Orange, she had been disappointed in her love for Prince Frederick of Prussia, and she had come, at last, to see Leopold of Coburg as a means of emancipation. By 23 January 1815, when all was at an end with the Prince of Prussia, she had 'perfectly decided & made up my own mind to marry, & the person I have decidedly fixed on is Prince Leopold'. It was a completely cool decision. 'At all events,' she had added, 'I know that *worse off*, more unhappy and wretched I *cannot* be than I *am now*, & after all if I end by marrying Prince L., I marry the *best* of all those I *have seen*, & that is some satisfaction.'(*158*)

Once the determination had taken root in Princess Charlotte's mind, she fostered it with the intensity of the desperate and lonely; and, slowly, she had fallen in love, not so much with Leopold, as with the thought of Leopold the liberator. In the spring and summer of 1815 the Regent had been too preoccupied with the Hundred Days to consider the question of her marriage; but in January 1816 Leopold, in Berlin, had received an invitation to England. There was also a note from Lord Castlereagh, the Foreign Secretary, telling him that the Regent intended to give him the Heiress Apparent's hand.

It took Leopold 'only three weeks and three days' to travel from Berlin to London. At three o'clock on the afternoon of Friday, 23 February, he had reached the Marine Pavilion at Brighton. On 19 March Princess Charlotte told Lady Charlotte Lindsay: 'Nothing you can utter in the Prince of Coburg's praise is too much.'(*159*)

'An odd marriage,' decided Elizabeth, Duchess of Devonshire, in Rome, 'for the future Queen of England.'(*160*) And odd, in some ways, it was; but before it took place on 2 May, it was clear that, for Princess Charlotte, a marriage of convenience had become a marriage of love.

I must write one line to you, dearest sister [wrote Lady Liverpool, on 3 May, to Elizabeth, Duchess of Devonshire], to tell you that I was at the Royal marriage yesterday, and not the worse for the exertion. ... May they be happy! I wish it from my very heart! ... When the ceremony was over the Princess knelt to her father for his blessing, which he gave her, and then raised and gave her a good hearty, paternal hug that delighted me.(*161*)

39

The next few months were, in many ways, among the happiest in the Regent's life. The Napoleonic wars were over. His wife was safely abroad, and his daughter was happily married. The government allowed him to satisfy his love of splendour, and he was busy altering his palaces.

At times, it is true, his alterations seemed the mere gratification of a whim: on one occasion, when a room at Carlton House had been superbly decorated, Sir Edmund Nagle observed that the large golden eagles in each corner were the ornaments used so profusely by Napoleon. This was conclusive: the eagles were removed, and very large gilt shells were substituted.

But against such tales of extravagance must be set many facts which reiterate the Regent's care for the arts; and it was fitting that the Royal Academy should pay him a compliment which was probably unique in its history. In April 1816 he asked them to admit a portrait of Prince Leopold into the exhibition. It was after the closing date for submitting pictures. The Academy convened a General Assembly 'to enable the President and Council to deviate from an establish'd Law'. The regulation was suspended, the picture was admitted, and the regulation 'Re-established in its original and permanent force'.(*162*)

The Academy was well aware of his constant practical interest; within two months they were asking him a favour. He had sanctioned the establishment of a Royal Academy school 'for instructing the Students in the practical part of Painting'. It would, they felt, be 'eminently useful' for the students to see the Raphael cartoons from the Royal collection. The Council asked permission 'to have one of them at a time for a few months each in the Royal Academy; and they would further intreat to be honor'd with the loan of Your Royal Highness's fine Rembrandt for the same desireable [sic] purpose'.(163)

Long before the Regent had agreed to lend a cartoon, the Council were considering an unsolicited favour. Charles Long, Joint Paymaster-General of the Forces, had given the President

a List of 26 Casts from marbles in the Pope's Museum which are about to be sent to the Prince Regent and which His Royal Highness is graciously pleased to present to the Royal Academy and ... Mr. Long had further in command from His Royal Highness to intimate to the President that if Casts from any other of the fine Antiques in Rome should be considered desireable [sic] for the School of the Royal Academy, His Royal Highness would, on their being specified, use his influence to obtain them.(164)

The Academy sent a list of casts; on 22 November the President and Council were invited to Carlton House to see the casts 'recently imported from Paris & from Rome, for the purpose of making a selection therefrom for their School of Design'.(165)

While the body of Academicians were asked to Carlton House, Lawrence received a more personal invitation. On 17 August, Sir Benjamin Bloomfield, Chief Equerry to the Regent, had written with a warmth that no doubt delighted him: 'The Prince Regent proposes that you shou[l]d make Him a Visit at the Cottage next week when He will talk over the Composition of the Picture of Lord Anglesey's Children—Believe me that your Presence at Carlton House can never be an Intrusion.'(166) The Regent who welcomed his portrait painter at Carlton House found it no loss of dignity to sit to him in his studio in Russell Square. On one occasion a bevy of ladies were about to settle down to coffee when 'a dreadful knocking was heard at the street door, and Sir Thomas flew to receive his royal guest, leaving us', recalled Miss Croft, who was one of the visitors,

to scamper off as we could. We had just got into the
third room, when we heard the Regent's voice at the painting room door, and ... we made our escape by the back
stairs just before the Regent entered the room we had
quitted. 'Lawrence,' he said, 'it is my fate to disturb your
family, for here is even the coffee pour'd out and not
drunk.' Sir Thomas then explained that we were only a
group of terrified sitters.(*167*)

On another occasion, the Regent arrived to find himself
confronted by a bald woman resplendent in white satin.
Lawrence had much trouble in persuading him 'that the lady
was perfectly indifferent to the state in which he had surprised her': she was, in fact, a lay model clothed as the
Duchess of Gloucester. The Regent and Lawrence made
'united efforts' to put a wig on the 'duchess', but all in
vain.(*168*)

The year 1816 brought many proofs of the Regent's in-
terest in the arts and sciences. It was this year that Lord
Yarmouth (who had long ago bought him Rembrandt's *The
Shipbuilder and his Wife*) acquired for him, at the Henry
Hope sale, *Rembrandt and Saskia about to go out*. It was
this year that the Regent recommended the House of
Commons to value the Elgin Marbles, newly arrived from
Greece, and in June it was duly moved 'that a sum not
exceeding £35,000 be granted to His Majesty for the purchase'.(*169*) In Rome, Canova was finishing his group of
Mars and Venus for the Regent ('the most beautiful thing I
ever saw,' wrote Elizabeth, Duchess of Devonshire, 'and the
best of his works, I do not think')(*170*); he was also 'finishing
for the Prince his Nymph and Amorino, which he means
as an offering'.(*171*) It was this year that the Regent
knighted a frail old man of nearly eighty, too feeble to be
long in company: the astronomer William Herschel, who
had discovered the planet Uranus. And, finally, it was this
year that the Regent established himself as a gourmet, by
acquiring the services of Antonin Carême.

Carême, at the age of thirty-three, was already a master in

the almost uniquely French art of *haute cuisine*. He had survived all the régimes of the past few years. He had learnt his art in Napoleon's kitchens, he had created masterpieces for the Emperor Alexander of Russia, during his stay in Paris. He had ensured the benevolence of delegates at the peace congress at Aix-la-Chapelle. No one could conjure such fantasies out of paste and spun sugar, as Carême. His military trophies and Roman helmets, his Attic ruins, and his lyres and harps, his Chinese cottages and Indian pavilions satisfied the taste for the Romantic, and the most fastidious of palates. *La gelée de fleur d'orange au vin de Champagne; le vol-au-vent glacé garni de cerises....* . The very names of his dishes sang like music. It was partly on the recommendation of Monsieur Lasne, *chef de cuisine* of *Monsieur*, the brother of Louis XVIII, that the Regent's comptroller offered Carême the post of *chef de cuisine*. Carême was delighted at the prospect. 'I was,' he wrote, 'going to reap the fruit of my labours, by serving one of the greatest princes of Europe.' Since he was only to be on duty in alternate weeks, he also thought happily of the time he would devote to his *magnum opus* on the art of nineteenth-century French cooking.

A few days after his arrival at Carlton House, Carême made his début: he contrived twenty *entrées* for a grand dinner which the Regent was giving for the Grand Duke Nicholas of Russia. That afternoon, the comptroller showed him the setting for the banquet:

> The table was laid [recalled Carême], and I was astounded by the richness and elegance of the silver and silver-gilt service which decorated this sumptuous and supremely royal table; and then by this beautiful dining-room which the Prince had had made to receive the august Alexander. The room is Gothic in design, and the details are all in gold on a dull white background; the windows are stained glass. The crystal lustres, the ornaments on the mirrors, the furniture, it all recalled Asiatic taste and luxury. ... I went back sadly to my work. In my heart of hearts I regretted that everything I had just

seen was unique in Europe; I regretted that it did not belong to France.(*172*)

Carême's first banquet had, he recorded, *de la fraîcheur et de l'élégance*, and the Regent sent him congratulations. A few days later, the Court went to Brighton; Carême felt himself transported to imperial Peking. He had, it seems, only two complaints of his service with the Regent. He naturally wanted to leave his seal on his work: to create an entire work of art; and—at least at Brighton—he could not do so. If a banquet was given while he was on duty, he contrived the *entrées* and the sauces; the second *chef de cuisine* prepared the soup, fish and vegetables, while the *chef pâtissier* 'produced what he wanted'. The triumvirate worked in the kitchens with deference to each other, but without co-ordination. In *le Maître d'hôtel français*, a few years later, Carême sadly quoted a menu that he would have liked to present. 'If I had served this dinner at the Prince Regent's table, I know,' he wrote, 'that His Royal Highness would have been delighted ... and French *cuisine* would have shone with new lustre at the English Court'.(*173*)

But it was not disappointments like these which led Carême to abandon a distinguished and rewarding post after a mere eight months. He could not be happy out of France. 'I had left all my heart behind,' he explained, 'in my own dear country, and I decided to leave the English royal household, though I was quite sure I should never find such a delightful and honourable situation again.'(*174*)

Ten years later, King George IV (as the Regent had become) invited him to return as *chef de cuisine*. He offered him a salary of £500, and the promise that should he, the King, die, Carême would be paid £250 a year for the rest of his life. Carême was presiding over the kitchens of Baron Rothschild. He was extremely flattered, but he refused the King of England's offer.(*175*) It is sad that he never again served *aloyau braisé à la George IV* to George IV himself.

40

'At present,' wrote Mrs. Trench to Mrs. Leadbeater, in March 1817, 'we have a starving population, an overwhelming debt, impoverished landholders, bankrupt or needy traders, unemployed farmers and labourers; but we have fine balls at the Regent's . . .'*(176)* Mrs. Trench had little love for the Regent. She was glad to report that he had been sent a mysterious present, a snuffbox set with diamonds, in which were written some verses from *Ezekiel*: 'And thou, profane wicked prince of Israel, whose day is come, when iniquity shall have an end. Thus saith the Lord GOD: Remove the diadem, and take off the crown.'*(177)*

If the Regent had led a dull, domestic life like his father, he might have been forgiven for political indiscretions and for economic conditions. But, as Malmesbury had warned him, years ago, even before his marriage to Mrs. Fitzherbert, he would have no firm hold on the people's affections until he was married, and had children; and his marriage had been so catastrophic that nothing he could do would redeem him. As William Cobbett, the radical journalist, would write, the parting with Caroline was the real cause of the reproach which he had to endure for the rest of his life. In the popular mind, he remained a figure of popular art: a cardboard figure, painted in unrelieved and permanent black. To the great mass of Englishmen, he was an unregenerate villain, a despot of almost oriental extravagance, or, at best, a figure of cruel fun: 'This uncommonly huge mass', as Cobbett defined him, 'this royal man, weighing perhaps a quarter of a ton'.*(178)*

His regency, and his reign to come, would be recognised, by posterity, as the most glorious age in England since the days of Elizabeth I. The British Empire was steadily growing. Not for two centuries had such triumphs of arms, such a flowering of the arts, been seen together; and no Englishman was more aware of the powers and achievements of his country, no Englishman tried harder to foster and reward them, than the Regent who drove to Parliament, in January 1817, through a crowd 'animated by a very bad spirit', and returned to Carlton House through a mob 'amazingly increased both in numbers and violence. Opinions are much divided', wrote Robert Peel, the Secretary for Ireland, 'as to the fact of a shot having been fired from an air gun. The general spirit of the country is worse, I apprehend, than we understand it to be'.(*179*) The Regent's carriage windows were broken, and he said he had felt a stone or bullet pass before his face.

On 18 June, the second anniversary of Waterloo, 'that sunny lovely day', Haydon and his wife watched him open Waterloo Bridge. 'All and everything conspired in the air above, the earth below, and the waters, which flowed under Waterloo Bridge, to make it the most glorious, beautiful, and gratifying spectacle that ever was exhibited.'(*180*) So Maria Stanley told Mrs. Stanley. William Pitt Lennox wrote with acerbity: 'The Prince Regent sheltered under the mantle of the great Wellington, ... and the unpopularity of the heir to the throne seemed forgotten in the enthusiasm.'(*181*) The Regent was acutely conscious of his unpopularity: in September he paid Beechey a hundred guineas 'for altering the large picture of his Majesty on horseback, &c'.(*182*) It was the picture in which, years earlier, the artist had been forced to express George III's detestation of his son.

Despite the political unrest, the unique personal unpopularity, the Regent continued to show his love of the arts. He patronised an exhibition of British pictures at the British Institution. He presented Wellington with Canova's colossal statue of Napoleon. He paid a surprise visit to the Royal Academy. And when it was intimated to him 'that it would be very desireable that the Royal Academy should possess a Cast of the Barberini Faun', Charles Long was commanded 'to communicate to Sigr. Canova his wish that as fine a Cast as could be obtain'd might be sent to him'. On 13 August, Long informed the Academy that 'the Cases

165

containing the Cast ... have lately arrived and are now in the London Docks'.*(183)*

On 6 September, in a letter to the Pope, the Regent himself acknowledged receipt of another nine cases from Italy. They contained a second collection of Stuart papers. No one showed more constant devotion to a dispossessed dynasty than the Regent did the House of Stuart. He had already acquired a mass of papers from the executor of the Countess of Albany. He had sponsored the publication of *The Life of James the Second.* When an unidentified coffin was found in St. George's Chapel, Windsor, the Regent had eagerly consented to have it opened, and to solve a problem in Stuart history. No one had known precisely where Charles I had been interred until 1 April 1813, when the black velvet pall and the lid were removed from the coffin, and the unmistakable features were revealed.*(184)* The Regent who sanctioned the momentous opening of the coffin, and acquired Vandyck's triple portrait of the King, would have been the first to understand why Scott wore a lock of the royal hair in a massive ring, surrounded by the inscription: 'Remember'. He treasured the sword which Charles I had left at Wistow, in Leicestershire, on his way to the Battle of Naseby: his own physician, Sir Henry Halford, who succeeded to the Wistow estate, could hardly have found a more touching relic to offer.*(185)* The Regent admired the King's aesthetic sense, his patronage of the arts (he himself said proudly that England would have Charles I's times again); and, romantic as he was, he was fascinated by the perpetual misfortunes of the dynasty. His earliest memory was of sitting, at Kew, on the lap of a massive man in a snuff-coloured coat: his great-uncle, the Duke of Cumberland, who had defeated the Young Pretender at Culloden.*(186)* He offered (though he forgot to give) a pension to Flora Macdonald, who had saved Charles Edward's life after his escape from the Hebrides in 1746.*(187)* He treasured a legacy from Cardinal York, the Pretender's brother, the last of the Stuarts: the collar of the Garter worn by James II;*(188)* and when, in 1824, the workmen digging the foundations of the new church at St.

Germain came across the coffin of James II, he asked that
it should be removed in state, and buried under the altar
until the new church was finished.(*189*) He planned a
monument to James II at St. Germain: 'which monument
was actually made', wrote a visitor in 1834, 'but they dare
not place it'.(*190*) One of the last acts of his life would be
to ask Scott to head a new commission to examine and edit
the Stuart papers.(*191*)

41

It was in September 1817 that Lady Holland warned Mrs.
Creevey: 'Pss. Charlotte is going on in her *grossesse*, but
there are some strange awkward symptoms.'(*192*) At
Claremont, near Esher, the princely estate which was the
masterpiece of Capability Brown, the preparations were
made for her confinement. The wet-nurse was engaged;
Mrs. Griffiths, the nurse introduced by Sir Richard Croft,
the obstetrician, arrived on 1 October, and observed that
'Her Royal Highness certainly possessed a fine flow of
spirits'. On 11 October Sir Richard himself settled in at
Claremont. On 16 October the Prince Regent visited his
daughter. Three days later, 'the first day I could by reason
expect H.R.H. to be put to Bed', Sir Richard wrote to his
sister Elizabeth. He described the comfortable routine:
breakfast at nine (at eleven for the Princess), the daily exam-
ination, the tranquil dinner. 'The Prince retires with the
Ladies at half past eight, and when we join them at nine, he
is generally singing to her playing, and after Coffee, we
[sit] down to short Whist, sixpenny points, last night I
played with the Duchess of York for my partner, and I
never recollect to have laughed more. ... They leave us
at about half past ten, and he reads to her every night till
twelve, and I think you [will] agree with me, that they are
very reasonable people.'(*193*)

The gaiety was not to last. After 19 October, when the
birth had not taken place, the public grew anxious; and

the papers printed frequent bulletins. On 23 October, however, in her garden chair, with Prince Leopold, and several of their attendants, Princess Charlotte 'proceeded to view the Gothic Temple, which was building in the Park'. The daily excursions continued, and Leopold went happily on his shooting expeditions in the grounds, while on 27 October the Regent 'left on a shooting excursion into Suffolk'. There was no practical reason for him to be at Claremont, and as Croker observed to Peel: 'A father is on such occasions worse than useless.' On 1 November Lawrence called, and Princess Charlotte urged him to bring down her portrait in time for her husband's birthday, 16 December. On 3 November, on the advice of Sir Henry Halford, her physician, Queen Charlotte set out for Bath, to take the waters. She was old, and already gravely ill. Besides, 'the Princess would *not* have the assistance of her Majesty'.(*194*)

Late on 3 November, when it was fifteen days overdue, Princess Charlotte's labour began. On the evening of 5 November she gave birth to a stillborn son. At half past two on the morning of 6 November, she died.

> Daughter of England! for a nation's sighs
> A nation's heart went with thine obsequies! (*195*)

Thomas Campbell's lines caught the anguish of the nation. 'Low our Tree of Hope is laid!' cried Southey. 'What a cruel blow for this poor country death has lately dealt us!' lamented Scott.(*196*) 'The loss of the Dear Princess Charlotte to us is irreparable!' wrote Haydon. 'She was our rallying point, our hope, our sunny land of promise and consolation.'(*197*) 'No description in the papers,' declared Mrs. Trench to Mrs. Leadbeater, 'can exaggerate the public sympathy and the public sorrow. ... The nation would have resigned all the rest of her family to have saved her.'(*198*)

In her answer from Ballitore, in Ireland, Mrs. Leadbeater expressed an equally widespread and disturbing emotion. 'It struck me as surprising,' she wrote, 'that no relative was

watching over a young woman about to bring forth her
first born, and the expected heir to a kingdom ... Yet I
cannot think—I cannot bear to think—there were any
unfair doings.'(*199*) With the nation's shock and grief there
already went angry, bitter enquiries. Why had the Regent
been absent from the death-bed, with Lady Hertford? Why
had Queen Charlotte been away when her grandchild
died? The truth was, as Croker explained to Peel, that
Charlotte had refused her grandmother's presence; but 'the
conduct with regard to His Royal Highness was very extraordinary; notice was *not sent to him* at the beginning of
the labour, and he might have been in London twenty-four
hours sooner if he had been aware that the Princess had
been taken ill'.(*200*) Brougham naturally had no time to
sympathise with the Regent. 'So now,' he added, briskly,
to Grey, 'we are left without heirs to the throne. If our
friend Mme de F. [*sic*] had chosen, she might have been
Queen, at all events mother of a king or queen; but she is
far better as she is. Pray remember me most kindly to
her.'(*201*)

Perhaps, for a moment, the Regent's thoughts turned to
Mrs. Fitzherbert, and to the days of his early happiness. But
he was overwhelmed. Charlotte had been the only issue, the
only justification, of his marriage to Caroline: she alone
had assured him that the crown would descend to his own
line of Kings. And his affections, like his hopes, were torn; in
his erratic fashion, and for all his strictures, for all his
jealousy, he had loved his daughter. At nine o'clock on the
morning she died, he reached Carlton House, changed carriages, and drove to Claremont. He asked to see the bodies
of his daughter and his grandson. 'The most profound
secrecy and silence prevailed in the House'; and, with the
blinds down in his carriage, he drove away. On 11 November, five days before the funeral, the Dowager Lady Ilchester
recorded: 'The Regent has so implored to have the Duchess
of Gloucester with him for a few days at Brighton till all
is over, that the Duke has consented, being much affected
by the manner in which it was asked.'(*202*) On 14 November, Croker told Lord Whitworth: 'All his thoughts and

conversation turn upon the late sad event. He never stirs out of his room, and goes to bed sometimes at eight or nine o'clock, wearied out, and yet not composed enough for rest.'(*203*)

Two days after his daughter died, the Regent commanded Lawrence to bring his portrait of her to Carlton House. He was unaware that she had meant it for Prince Leopold, and he refused to part with it. Lawrence had to go down to Brighton to explain and intercede for it.

The picture was copied for the Regent; and, on 16 December, long before the household had eaten breakfast, Lawrence arrived at Claremont to fulfil his promise and bring the original portrait for Prince Leopold's birthday.

42

When the Princess of Wales embarked for the Continent, in August 1814, she may not have meant to stay away for ever. Her lady-in-waiting, Lady Charlotte Lindsay, had written to Princess Charlotte's friend, Mercer Elphinstone, 'to give all the comfort I can respecting the probability, that the Princess will return to this country again; and the Princess', Lady Charlotte told Brougham, 'has written herself to Princess Charlotte, to assure her of this'.(*204*)

The assurances were of little worth; Caroline's departure was an act of heartless disloyalty to her daughter. At that moment, when the girl was oppressed by all the problems of her broken engagement, when she was deprived of her freedom, miserable, ill, and unsure of her future, she had needed her mother's presence acutely. That Caroline should have chosen that particular moment to leave the country had shown a horrifying lack of maternal instinct; and 'after all', as Charlotte wrote to Mercer Elphinstone, 'if a *mother* has not *feeling* for her child or children, are they to *teach it to her* or can they *expect to be listened to* with any *hopes of success?* . . . She decidedly deserts me'.(*205*)

Caroline had indeed deserted her; but she had soon been guilty of more than desertion. Her freedom went to her unsteady head. After a fortnight at Brunswick, she went on to Cassel and Strasburg, and then to Berne, where she showed a restlessness which belonged 'to the unhappy and unprincipled'. At Geneva, where she stayed for three days, 'the natives were, as she would have expressed it, "all over shock". The suite who travel with her', wrote a spectator, 'declare openly they fear they shall not be able to go on with her; not so much from wrong doings as from ridiculous ones.' Their apprehensions were justified. At a ball that was given in her honour, the same observer 'beheld the poor Princess enter, dressed *en Vénus*, or rather not dressed, further than the waist'. Thus clad, she waltzed throughout the night 'with pertinacious obstinacy. ... If this', wrote the correspondent, 'is a commencement only of what she intends to perform in the South, she will indeed lose herself entirely'. Caroline had always shown signs of unbalance. Now she made herself so ridiculous that it seemed as if, on leaving England, she had gone completely mad.

Indeed, this appears to be the most probable explanation of her conduct. No balanced woman could have behaved as Caroline behaved. As Canning's biographer would observe: 'Her proceedings on the continent were the acts of a mad woman—of one made desperate by the total blight of her affections, the entire misdirection of her life, by the sense of friendlessness and isolation, the mockery of state through which she moved, and by that terrible contempt of opinion which grows upon systematic injustice.'(206)

Brougham had predicted truly: everything she did was immediately reported back to London. In her hatred of her husband, Caroline doubtless revelled in such humiliating publicity. Lord Liverpool wrote and urged her strongly not to go to Naples. No better invitation could be needed. Caroline continued her journey through the Simplon pass, and on 9 October she reached Milan. On 8 November, with her tatterdemalion escort, she finally reached Naples. Lord Liverpool was triumphantly snubbed.

Joachim Murat, the brother-in-law of Napoleon, had prepared a palace for her reception;(207) he led her into his
capital with splendour. The next four months, the closing
months of his reign, were spent in revels; and in the balls
and masquerades, the boar hunts and processions, Murat
himself was the most conspicuous figure. He was, wrote
Dr. Henry Holland, one of the Princess's suite, 'tall and
masculine in person; his features well formed, but expressing little beyond good nature and a rude energy and con-
sciousness of physical power; his black hair flowing in curls
over his shoulders; his hat gorgeous with plumes; his whole
dress carrying an air of masquerade'. He was just the
theatrical figure that Caroline would admire and it is said
that he became her lover. It would have been a liaison
after Caroline's heart. She could hardly humiliate the
Regent more effectively than by giving herself to the brother-
in-law of Napoleon.

In Naples she again appeared at a ball, half-dressed, this
time as the Muse of History. 'The Princess of Wales is playing all sorts of tricks all over Italy,' Lady Melbourne informed Lady Cowper in January. 'They say of her Mon dieu
est-ce lá la vertu opprimée dont nous avons tant entendu
parler?'(208)

Early in March, the Neapolitan revels suddenly ended.
Napoleon had escaped from Elba. Joachim Murat prepared
to march against Austria; and Caroline, angry at his desertion, sailed for Leghorn and Genoa. She took with her, she
told her friend Miss Berry, 'Napoleon's courier, . . . which is
quite a treasure to me, faithful and prudent. I shall keep
him'.

She was indeed to keep him. The relationship was to be
all too faithful, all too imprudent, between the Princess of
Wales and Bartolomeo Bergami.

Bergami was a former quartermaster in the first Italian
regiment of hussars. He had been the confidential messenger
of General Pino. He was an obvious choice as Italian courier
to the Princess of Wales. It is also obvious, from contemporary prints, that the bold, bewhiskered face, not unlike

Frances, Countess of Jersey
After the portrait by John Hoppner

Caroline, Princess of Wales
From the portrait by Sir Thomas Lawrence

Murat's, was that of the coarse, uninhibited soldier for whom such a woman as Caroline might fall.

Caroline had been brought up in the atmosphere of Brunswick, which 'had something in it of the ease and *abandon* of an out-post'. She had been repressed, humiliated and persecuted at the Court of St. James's. She had been deserted by Murat; and now, at her command, she had a virile, swaggering Italian, who was only there to do her will.

'I call'd on the Baroness Ertmann,' wrote Robert Finch, in Milan, on 26 March. 'Talk'd of the Princess of Wales, who did not much like Milan. The Baroness was displeased at the manners of her Royal Highness.'(*209*) If Milan had felt displeasure, Genoa felt consternation. Mme de Boigne, the French Ambassador's daughter, long recalled the sight of Caroline in a pink feathered hat, a very low pink bodice, and a short white skirt which scarcely reached her knees, riding through the streets in a shell-shaped phaeton. The equipage was preceded by a tall, handsome man on horseback, dressed to resemble Joachim Murat; and this living portrait, wrote Mme de Boigne, 'was Bergami, who ... even then, according to the captain of the ship which had brought him from Livorno, assumed the rights of Murat over his royal mistress'.

The Princess who shocked a French observer was still more shocking to an English spectator. On 11 May, Lady Bessborough attended a ball which was given in honour of Lord William Bentinck, the departing English envoy:

I cannot tell you [so she wrote to Granville Leveson Gower] how sorry and asham'd I felt as an Englishwoman. The first thing I saw in the room was a short, very fat, elderly woman, with an extremely red face (owing, I suppose, to the heat) in a Girl's white frock looking dress, but with shoulder, back and neck, quite low (disgustingly so), down to the middle of her stomach; very black hair and eyebrows, which gave her a fierce look, and a wreath of light pink roses on her head. She was

173

dancing ... I was staring at her from the oddity of her appearance, when suddenly she nodded and smil'd at me, and not recollecting her, I was convinc'd she was mad, till William push'd me, saying: 'Do you not see the Princess of Wales nodding to you?' It is so long since I have seen her near before, she is so much fatter and redder, that added to her black hair and eyebrows, extraordinary [sic] deep, I had not the least recollection of her. ... I could not bear the sort of whispering and talking all round about the Principessa d'Inghilterra che era vestita da leggiera, &c. ...(210)

By the early summer, no Englishwoman remained in the Princess's household; and Dr. Holland released himself early from the royal service and made his way home.

And there, all the tales he might have told were already known; and Princess Charlotte, distraught, had made her confession about the Hesse affair to the Regent. The Regent consulted the Privy Council; they advised that when the Princess of Wales returned to England, 'she was *not to be admitted here*'. On 2 May, a few days before the Genoa ball, Princess Charlotte, on her father's orders, copied out his irrevocable decree:

I promise upon my honor never to write from this moment directly or indirectly to [my mother], that all kind of communication shall cease, & that I will abstain from seeing her when she comes to England.(211)

The Princess of Wales had no intention, at present, of coming to England. In August she settled on the shores of Lake Como; on 5 October, in execrable French, she informed Lady Charlotte Lindsay:

Assurez Mr. Brougham que je ne retourne jamais plus en Angleterre excepté quand le Duc ou le Grand-duc serait mort, et que la jeune fille me désire bien ardemment de me revoir! Sans cela, jamais! Ce que je commence à craindre c'est que de tels événements heureux ne pourraient arriver.(212)

While the Duke and the Grand Duke, the Regent and the King, remained alive, Caroline continued her wanderings. She embarked from Genoa, paid a brief visit to Porto Ferrajo, in Elba, and took care to see Napoleon's house (where she was presented with his billiard cue and a book from his library). 'The accounts of the Princess of Wales are worse and worse,' Brougham told Earl Grey on 5 December. 'She embarked on the 17th of November from Palermo, *Courier* and all—Captain Briggs volunteered taking her; and if they have evidence against her, I should think he may bring her home, and not to Palermo. If they have not, the voyage may furnish it.'(*213*) 'I am in despair at what you tell me about a courier,' Princess Charlotte wrote next day to Mercer Elphinstone. 'I had not the slightest or smallest suspicion of the kind. ... Surely, surely, my dear Margerite, there can be *nothing there*, a *low, common servant*, a servant too! & yet you seem to *insinuate* it from the *influence* he has. ...'(*214*)

Bergami's influence became increasingly evident. Late in February, having procured him the dignity of Knight of Malta, Caroline bestowed upon him the sonorous title of Baron de la Francino. At Catania and Augusta she sat twice for her portrait, and posed as the repentant Magdalen, with 'her person very much exposed'. One of these likenesses was given to the Baron. When, in March, at the Regent's suggestion, Princess Charlotte told her future husband, Prince Leopold, about the Hesse affair, 'we did not say much about my mother, as he told me honestly her conduct was so notorious & so much talked of abroad that he was as well informed as everyone else about her'.(*215*) On 8 May (unaware that Charlotte had been married six days earlier) Caroline reached Athens, where she gave two balls. When Robert Finch was in Athens, a year later, he was still regaled with anecdotes. 'We convers'd much about the conduct of the Princess of Wales here,' he noted on 2 March 1817. 'She dress'd almost naked, and danc'd with her servants.'(*216*)

Meanwhile, this summer of 1816, Caroline embarked on a pilgrimage to the Holy Land. On the evening of 12 July, through the astounded multitudes, she entered Jerusalem astride an ass. (The circumstances reminded her chamber-maid of 'the Day of Palms, on which our Saviour made, in the same manner, his entry into Jerusalem'; and 'assuredly', continued the loyal Mlle Demont, 'if anyone can in any way resemble our great Saviour, it is this excellent Princess'.) It was in Jerusalem that the Princess of Wales saw Bergami created a Knight of the Holy Sepulchre. She also instituted an order of her own, the Order of St. Caroline, and she made Bergami its Grand Master.

On 24 September, at last, she returned to the Villa d'Este on Lake Como. Here she created his brother prefect of the palace. She bought Bergami himself the Villa Bergami near Milan, and lived for a time in this villa, which deserved 'rather the name of a common brothel than a palace'. The following summer saw her at the Villa Cassielli, near Pesaro; and here (apart from a few excursions) she finally came to rest.

It was at Pesaro, on the morning of 20 November 1817, that a King's Messenger brought her a letter from a Mr. Robert Gardner. It was not her son-in-law, but his private secretary, who told her of the death of her daughter. 'England, that proud country,' she wrote, 'has lost every-thing in losing my ever beloved Daughter, and I have not only to lament a darling of a Child, but my only truly warm and attached friend—I have not lost her, she is only gone before, and I trust that soon I shall meet her again in a much better world.'(*217*)

43

When Princess Charlotte died, the problem of the succes-sion became an urgent, complex, bitter matter. The Duchess of York was past the age for bearing a child; the Duke of Clarence said he would only marry if the Government made handsome provision for each of his ten natural children, and settled his own debts, which were very great. On 11 December, in Brussels, the Duke of Kent had his astonishing talk with Mr. Creevey, and declared that if the Duke of Clarence had done 'nothing ... as to marrying' before St. George's Day, 23 April, if would become his duty to discard his devoted mistress, Mme St. Laurent, and 'to take some measures upon the subject' himself. The Regent, said the Duke of Kent, would not attempt a divorce. If he did, his own conduct would be exposed to such recrimination that he would be 'unpopular, beyond all measure. ... Besides, the crime of adultery on her part must be proved in an English court of justice, and if found guilty she must be executed for high treason. No: the Regent will never try for a divorce'.(*218*)

The Poet Laureate thought otherwise. The following week, in a letter to Walter Savage Landor, the poet, Southey predicted: 'The amusements of Como may very probably become the amusements of England ere long.'(*219*)

The Regent could hardly be blamed for seeking to divorce the wife whose way of life, for three years and more, had been the talk of Europe. In the autumn of 1817, he had ordered Sir John Leach (soon to be Vice-Chancellor of England) to examine all the details of her conduct, to see whether her guilt was established. In May 1818 Sir John reported that 'upon the whole, considering the public and undisputed fact of the favor and elevation of Barthelemy Bergami ... and assuming that the depositions stated are made by persons of fair character, ... I should be bound to come to the most unfavourable conclusions'. That August, by command of the Regent, Sir John had authorised William Cooke, Lieutenant-Colonel Browne and John Allan Powell 'to proceed forthwith to Milan, and from thence to all other places at your discretion for the purpose of making inquiries into the conduct of Her Royal Highness the Princess of Wales'. The Milan Commission settled down to its distasteful work; a bureau was established for the collection of evidence, a network of spies was organised, the Hanoverian envoy to the Vatican was ordered to lend his diplomatic services, and Caroline's discharged servants were invited to report on their former mistress.

In 1819 there was further talk of a royal divorce, and a correspondent wrote to Creevey: 'It is generally understood that ample materials are come now to warrant one.' Both camps, in fact, had ample material against 'Mrs. P.' In March 1819, James Brougham, the brother of Caroline's legal adviser, had been to the Villa Vittoria near Pesaro, and made a detailed report on the 'General Appearance of Things'.

> Everything [James Brougham wrote] is 'Le Baron' ... Certainly the whole thing tells badly. *His* house and grounds, *his* plates, *his* ordering everything, he even buys her bonnets, this I saw, and all his family quartered upon her! ! !
>
> All she wants is to pass the remainder of her life quietly ... She has not the spirits she used to have, and all the work the P[rince] makes worries her....
>
> She seems very happy here, and you may see how it is with ye Baron. In fact, they are to all appearances man and wife, never was anything so obvious. *His room* is close to hers, and his *bedroom* the only one in that part of ye house. The whole thing is apparent to every one, tho' perhaps there might be difficulty in proving the fact to find her guilty of high treason, yet I should think all the circumstances being stated would completely ruin her in ye opinion of the people of England, that once done, the P. might get a divorce, or at any rate prevent her being Queen. ...(*220*)

The report was addressed to Henry Brougham, whose lack of integrity was at times almost unbelievable. Long after Caroline's misdeeds had become European knowledge, he declared, in his autobiography: 'I can most positively affirm, that if every one of us had been put upon our oaths as jurymen, we should all have declared that there was not the least ground for the charges against her.'(*221*)

44

Within a fortnight of Princess Charlotte's death, in November 1817, Mr. Croker of the Admiralty had informed Robert Peel that jealousies were already felt in the Royal Family; and they would, he predicted, not diminish. 'In short, my dear Peel,' concluded Croker, in despondency, 'I never looked into a blacker political horizon than is now around us.'(222)

The year 1818 brought some savage comments on the royal brothers, their respective states of health, and their prospects of fruitful marriage. Creevey (who had still not forgiven the Regent for his Tory politics) was gratified to learn from Lord Folkestone, on 23 February; 'Prinny has let loose his belly, which now reaches his knees: otherwise he is said to be well. Clarence has been near dying, ... so that your friend the Duke of Kent will be King at last.'(223) As St. George's Day approached (it was now the Regent's official birthday), even Peel, more tolerant of royalty than most, professed himself astonished by the wild behaviour of the Prime Minister. Lord Liverpool had proposed to give increased allowances to the royal dukes to promote their dynastic marriages. How, inquired Peel, could Lord Liverpool expect Parliament to grant an extra £12,000 a year to the Duke of Cumberland? It was now two years since his marriage to Princess Frederica of Mecklenburg-Strelitz, and in the interval his dress and manner had become 'ten times more germanised than they were before ... his beard, whiskers and mustachios making a daily increase of their dominions.'(224) The Duke of Wellington was still more outspoken. When the ubiquitous Mr. Creevey had dined with him at Cambrai on 17 July, they discussed the future of the Regent's brothers. 'My God!' said Wellington, 'there is a greal deal to be said about that. They are the damnedest millstone about the necks of any Government that can be imagined.' (225)

The royal dukes had at least been determined to do their dynastic duty. Four days earlier, on Monday, 13 July, in Queen Charlotte's drawing-room at Kew Palace, the Archbishop of Canterbury and the Bishop of London had solemnised two marriages. The Duke of Clarence, aged fifty-three, had been united to a bride "with hair of a peculiar colour approaching to a lemon tint, weak eyes and a bad complexion': Princess Adelaide of Saxe-Meiningen. The Duke of Kent, aged fifty-two, had become the lawful husband of Victoria Mary Louisa of Leiningen. She was the widowed sister of Prince Leopold; and years later, after her death, a letter from Leopold was found among her papers. It was dated 1818, and it urged the Duke of Kent to marry her.

'You would be entertained with the severity of some of the caricatures respecting these matches,' a correspondent told Robert Finch on 3 August. 'The Q. is in a perfect morbid state, and may have departed *to her own* place before this letter reaches you.'(226)

45

While his brothers inspired caricatures of astonishing severity, the Regent himself was concerned with art. He gave David Wilkie permission to engrave the painting *Blind Man's Buff* which he had commissioned; and Wilkie was now finishing his companion piece, the *Penny Wedding*. Flaxman, the sculptor, was modelling one of his principal works, the Shield of Achilles, and the Regent would pay two thousand guineas for the first cast, in silver gilt.

Not since the days of Hoppner, however, had the Regent shown such favour to an artist as he did now to Sir Thomas Lawrence. Lawrence had painted him, by command, for the Sheldonian Theatre at Oxford; the portrait was to hang between those of the Emperor of Russia and the King of Prussia, to commemorate the Convocation of 1814. A Lawrence portrait of the Regent appeared in this year's

Academy; Lawrence had been commissioned to value the collection of paintings at Carlton House. And, finally, the Regent gave him a truly royal mission: he asked him to go to Aix-la-Chapelle, to finish his portraits of Alexander of Russia and Frederick of Prussia, and to paint the more eminent members of the Peace Congress assembled there.

Lawrence was told to name his own terms; he was so afraid of appearing exorbitant that he walked, for three hours, one evening, up and down Waterloo Bridge, before he could begin to make up his mind. His financial state (he was said to lose at billiards the large sums he earned by painting) made the thought of leaving England somewhat alarming; but when his friend Miss Croft, Sir Richard's sister, suggested that he should ask £1,000 for two months' absence, he called it 'absurd rapacity'. Miss Croft thought otherwise. Next day she persuaded him to consult that unchallenged arbiter, the Duke of Wellington. The Duke, without hesitation, named the same fee.

> Whatever the result, I *am* going to Aix-la-Chapelle [wrote Lawrence to Farington, on 17 September] ... I confide to you the terms on which I go. My usual price 500 guineas for large whole lengths, smaller size in proportion, and £1000 for loss of time, Expence, &c. &c. These were the terms I gave in, and they were accepted ...(227)

Farington expressed his delight. He replied next day: 'The known kind nature of the Prince Regent, and the liberality of his disposition, and His particular regard for you, will ensure you His approbation of any proposal that may be made to Him for your benefit and for the *gratification of the Public*.'(228)

The Regent was certainly liberal. On 22 October Charles Long made a further impressive proposal to Lawrence, who was now at work in France:

> My dear Sir,
>   I am commanded by the Prince Regent to say that it is his Desire that after having completed the Work in

which you are engaged at Aix-la-Chapelle, you should proceed to Rome and that you should there paint for him the Portraits of the Pope and the Cardinal Gonsalvi [sic], and he desires also to defray the Expence of the Journey.

He commands me also to mention for your private Information, that he understands the Collection of Pictures belonging to the Cardinal Fesch now at Rome are to be disposed of, and he wishes while you are there that you would look at them particularly, with the View of acquainting me for HRHs Information what is your opinion of the Value of them—Be kind enough to send me a Line in answer to this Communication. I hope you have met with no difficulties in your present pursuit, and that the Proposition which is now made will not interfere materially with any of your Arrangements....

HRH wishes particularly that it should [not] be known that he has any thoughts of purchasing the Collection of Cardinal Fesch.(229)

Lawrence accepted the new commissions with pride. As for the Fesch collection, he promised to examine it 'with the secrecy and discretion enjoin'd'.(230) It was the Regent who showed himself indiscreet. While Lawrence installed himself at his easel in the Hôtel de Ville at Aix-la-Chapelle, while the allied sovereigns honoured him with sittings, the Regent poured out his plans to Elizabeth, Duchess of Devonshire. On 28 November, from Paris, the Duchess dashed off a letter to Lawrence:

My dear Sir,

When I was in London a fortnight ago, the Prince Regent told me, that he projected asking you to go on to Rome, and that he was very desirous that you should paint the portraits of the Pope and of Cardinal Consalvi the Secretary of State; he wish'd you also to see Cardinal Fesch's collection of pictures, and that if I should be at Rome whilst you was there his R.H. wish'd very much that I should see you and know your opinion about them; I should have great pleasure in being at Rome at the same time that you was there, and shall be most happy to see you there. ... In Cardinal Fesch's collection there is a great mixture I believe, some very good and some quite indifferent—he wants I am told to sell the whole together. ...(*231*)

46

The Regent's confidential talk with the Duchess had taken place a few days before an event which had, for many months, been expected. Queen Charlotte had been ailing at the time of her granddaughter's death; she had been so shocked by the event that her health had rapidly declined, and in May it was known that she was suffering from dropsy. It was in her sick-room at Kew that she had received her sons, the Dukes of Clarence and Kent, on their wedding day. On 17 November, at Kew, in her seventy-fifth year, she died.

However unhappy the Regent's relationship with his father, he had been devoted to his mother, and his devotion had been reciprocated. However severe the Queen may have been during the recurrent political crises, however angrily, at times, she had forbidden him access to his father, or banned him from her presence or Court festivities, she had been proud of him; she had understood his complex nature.

Queen Charlotte's plainness had been a subject for cruel observations; but she had been intelligent, good-humoured and vivacious, and she had shown all the kindness of the unprepossessing, all the patience acquired in living with a difficult husband and bearing him no less than fifteen children. She had been sensible, steady in her affections, proud of her position, and (at least to her eldest son) a companion and a friend.

The Regent's letters to 'my most beloved Madrè', and hers to him, had shown them both at their best. The Regent's *griffonnage*, as he called his writing, had overflowed with affection and vitality as he scribbled her the latest gossip from Brighton, or invited her, when she visited 'the old metropolis', to enjoy the freedom of Carlton House, and give as many parties there as she pleased. He had been full of endearing attentions and, in her letters to him, the Queen had responded to his affection, shared his private jokes and appreciated his allusions. She had written in much the same style as he did, scattering vivid phrases broadcast, using a French turn of speech, a pungent comment, and showing her excellent sense and energy. To her son, the Duke of Cumberland, she spoke of 'yr brother who is all goodness & ever ready to forward the happiness of his family'. Whatever his hatred of his wife, his estrangement from his father, the Regent was 'all goodness' to his brothers and 'the dear sisterhood'; and to his mother he had proved uncommonly understanding.

He was 'extremely affected', wrote Croker, by her death. Angerstein, calling at Carlton House on the last day of the month, learnt that he was as well as could be expected; 'but His Friends,' he told Lawrence, 'all wish Him at the seaside and I hope He will get there in a very few days.'(232)

47

He was there soon afterwards. On 14 December Bloomfield called on Croker, then in Brighton, 'to scold us for not going to the Pavilion at once.' Mr. Croker was soon touring the admirable kitchens, breathless at all the modern contrivances; he dined with the Regent, and in the evening the new music-room was lit up, and the band played, 'both magnificent.' Next day Croker dined there again; and the next day yet again, when the Regent discussed Scott's edition of Swift. There was no other prince with whom one could talk literature so freely. Mr. Croker showed him a copy of a letter written forty years earlier by Mrs. Delany, the widow of Swift's friend. It described a royal visit to Bulstrode, and His Royal Highness was mentioned; the Regent read it with pleasure. Mr. Croker was in fact editing

Mrs. Delany's letters. Encouraged by the Regent's enthusiasm, he showed him all the original correspondence, and the Regent, much entertained with the recollections, declared that every word of them was true. 'You know that H.R.H. has a wonderful memory,' reported Croker to his publisher, 'and particularly for things of that Kind. His certificate of Mrs. Delany's veracity will therefore probably be of some weight with you. . . .'(233)

The Regent's literary tastes were wide. At the end of the year Colburn published *Florence Macarthy: an Irish Tale* by Lady Morgan. That celebrated Irish novelist had cause to rejoice. Her grateful publisher made a gesture unique in the annals of publishing, and presented her with an amethyst parure; and the Countess of Charleville, a hostess celebrated in London and Dublin, sent her a note which must have warmed her heart:

> It gave me pleasure [wrote Lady Charleville], the day I dined with the Regent, to find [your novel] on his table, and to hear him say, when I took it up, 'I hope you like the Eagle and O'Leary; I have never read anything more delightful or more pathetic than Cumhal's catastrophe.'(234)

48

As for Walter Scott, he had managed dexterously to keep in royal favour. He had, for years, been an *habitué* of Blackheath and Kensington; he had sent *Marmion* to the Princess of Wales, and in return she had sent him 'a most elegant silver cup and cover with a compliment.'(235) He had seen her several times in London in 1809. 'Of course I was only a second-rate conjuror,' he told Lady Abercorn, 'but I did my best to amuse her.'(236) In 1811, when the Prince became Regent, Scott had expressed grave doubts of his prudence; and at the thought of his being King, Scott had grown rigidly puritan: 'Alas!' he told Joanna

Baillie, 'a public defiance of morality is but a bad bottom-
ing for a new reign.'(237)

And then came Byron's flattering conversation with the
Regent; and hints reached Scott that the Regent would like
to see him. His loyalties became more complicated. In the
spring of 1813, writing to Lady Abercorn, he expressed
some relief that he found himself in Edinburgh:

> I have had it intimated to me through the Prince's
> librarian that his R.H. desires his library to be open to
> me when I come to town and wishes me to be present,
> with many other words of great praise and civility. I
> should soon lose my sunshine I fancy were I to go to
> Kensington (which I certainly would do if I were asked).
> ... And so four hundred miles' distance has its advan-
> tages.(238)

Two years later, the Princess was abroad, and Scott
found it easier to obey the Regent's wishes. Once he had
eagerly sent *Marmion* to the Princess; now, in 1715, he sent
The Lord of the Isles to her husband. On 19 January,
Stanier Clarke replied in fulsome terms:

> My dear Sir,
>   You are deservedly so great a favourite with the
> Prince Regent, that his librarian is not only directed to
> return you the thanks of his Royal Highness for your
> valuable present, but to inform you that the Prince
> Regent particularly wishes to see you whenever you come
> to London; and desires you will always, when you
> are there, come into his library whenever you
> please. . . .(239)

When Croker announced that Scott would be in town by
the middle of March, the Regent's answer was swift: 'Let
me know when he comes, and I'll get up a snug little dinner
that will suit him.' Scott was presented at the levée: 'a
tall, very simple, but benevolent looking man of middle age,
who spoke broad Scotch.' He was invited to dinner.

Nothing shows the Regent's love of literature more clearly
than his thoughtful friendship for Scott. Determined to give

him the perfect dinner, he consulted Scott's friend, Mr. Adam, who was then in the royal household, on the composition of the party. 'Let us have just a few friends of his own, and the more Scotch the better.' Adam and Croker later assured Scott's biographer that the party was 'the most interesting and agreeable one in their recollection'. Mr. Adam recalled that the Regent had been 'particularly delighted with the poet's anecdotes of the old Scotch judges and lawyers, which his Royal Highness sometimes *capped*'.

Mr. Croker declared that the Regent and Scott were the two most brilliant story-tellers he had known, and he really could not decide which had shone the most. The Regent, he said, 'was enchanted with Scott, as Scott with him; and on all his subsequent visits to London, he was a frequent guest at the royal table.'(*240*)

After his first royal interview, Scott himself decided that the Regent 'was the first gentleman he had seen—certainly the first *English* gentleman of his day;—there was something about him which, independently of the *prestige*, the "divinity", which hedges a King, marked him as standing entirely by himself'.

The authorship of the Waverley Novels was one of the literary mysteries of the age, and many people would have liked to solve it. Some said that the Regent had asked Scott outright if he was the author, and that he had given a solemn denial. Scott refuted the idea. 'I was,' he said, 'never put to the test. He is far too well-bred a man ever to put so ill-bred a question.'(*241*)

In May, before Scott returned to the North, the Regent sent him a gold snuffbox, set with brilliants. It was his tangible tribute to 'genius & merit'.

Scott was determined to exploit such favour. The following year he begged Croker to ask the Regent if he might search for the Scottish regalia.

On the Union of England and Scotland in 1707, the Scottish crown and sceptre and sword of state had been deposited in a strong box in the Crown Room of Edinburgh Castle. It was decreed that they should never be taken out of Scotland. Rumour had suggested that they had since been spirited away. In 1794 a body of Commissioners had un-sealed the room, and seen 'the fatal chest strewd with the dust of an hundred years about six inches thick'. But they did not like to force the lock, and no keys could be found, and the mystery remained unsolved. However, on Scott's insistence, Croker now asked the Regent to authorise a search. The mystery, with its Stuart connexions, caught the Regent's imagination, and on 9 January 1818 Croker wrote happily that the royal consent had been given. Scott might have been expected to show his gratitude for the Regent's understanding. His comment to his friend John Morritt, the classical scholar, revealed his vulgar hypocrisy: 'Our fat friend has remembered a petition which I put up to him ... Our fat friends curiosity ... goes to the point at once.'(242)

On 4 February 1818, Scott and his fellow Commissioners proceeded, with due pomp, to Edinburgh Castle. Solemnly they opened the sealed doors of oak and iron, and broke open the chest which had been locked for one hundred and eleven years. That hazy winter afternoon, at about four o'clock, the sound of cannon from the Castle and a cheer from a regiment drawn up on Castle Hill announced that the crown of the old kings was discovered. Scott assumed his courtly manner: 'My dear Croker,' he wrote that evening, 'I have the pleasure to assure you the Regalia of Scotland were this day found in perfect preservation.... I know nobody entitled to earlier information, save ONE, to whom you can perhaps find the means of communicating the result.'(243)

It was the moment to consolidate a useful royal friend-ship. A draughtsman was employed to make sketches for the Regent 'of these Regalia, which his Royal Highness's goodness has thus restored to light and honour'.(244) Scott's friend, Mr. Thomson, 'who though a clergyman is one of the best of our Scottish artists,' set to work on a painting of the regalia; this was also destined for Carlton House. The Regent was at least sent a likeness of the crown which, as Scott privately informed the Duke of Buccleuch, had never been 'profaned by the touch of a monarch of a foreign dynasty'.(*245*)

It was towards the end of the year, and, apparently, on his own initiative, that the Regent decided to make Scott a baronet. The author of *Ivanhoe* had long seen himself in a feudal setting, and he had designed the mock-Gothic splendours of Abbotsford as a décor for knighthood. He now felt it politic to insist that the title was unimportant to him; but 'it may be very different with respect to my family', he assured the Duke of Buccleuch, 'especially as Walter has declared for the army a line in which *le petit titre vaut toujours quelque chose.'*(*246*)

That it was worth *quelque chose* to Scott was transparent enough. The circumstance which he told the Duke, 'for your Grace's private ear,' was 'whispered to the faithful ear' of Morritt, while Joanna Baillie was soon entrusted with 'a little secret' about 'sublunary honour'. In January 1819 Scott spoke to Lord Melville of the honour which the Regent had resolved to confer 'upon an unworthy follower of literature.... Of course,' he added, 'I shall come up to town in March so soon as the session rises to offer my respectful gratitude.' While he waited for the session to end, Scott published the so-called secret as carefully as he kept the secret of the authorship of the Waverley Novels. He was filled with false modesty, snobbery, and enchantment. 'How do you do my Lady Polwarth?—Thank you Sir Walter—it is right to accustom ones self to dignities by times.' 'Walter Scott is to be a baronet,' recorded Joseph Jekyll, frigidly. 'His *Ivanhoe* is said to deserve it.'(*247*)

49

While Scott rejoiced in the imminence of his accolade, one of the Regent's knights found himself abroad on a royal mission.

When the Prince of Wales (as the Regent then was) had

presented the Herculaneum papyri to the University of Oxford, he had urged that scholars should unroll them with caution. The University had observed his injunctions all too well. A book on the subject had appeared in 1810; the following year a committee had been appointed 'for the custody and management of the MSS.', but their arrangements to publish certain pieces had broken down, owing to the behaviour of Hayter. All the materials in his hands had then been deposited in the Bodleian Library; and the unopened rolls in various museums and libraries in England were left more or less untouched until 1817, when a German by the name of Sickler had undertaken to open them by a process known to himself alone. He was engaged to work on them under the superintendence of a Parliamentary committee, of which Sir Humphry Davy was a member. He had already destroyed seven rolls 'with no other result than an expenditure of £1,200', when the committee ended his activities. In 1818, when Sir Humphry Davy set out to visit the coal-mines of Flanders (to extend the use of his safety-lamp), the Regent had commissioned him to go on to Naples and see what new chemical methods might achieve. Lord Liverpool and Castlereagh had provided the funds for salaries; and Davy had tried to dissolve the bituminous matter between the leaves of the manuscripts.(*248*)

The methods had fully answered his expectations, and his own satisfaction was eagerly confirmed by an Oxford scholar, Peter Elmsley.

> You have probably heard [he assured Robert Finch, on 20 May 1819], that Davy has invented a much better method of opening the Herculanean rolls than any hitherto pursued. His plan is, to send an English chemist and an English scholar to Naples, and he thinks that in about a year, and for about £2,500, all may be done that can be done at all.... I have offered to play the part of the scholar, if the plan is adopted by our government. But I have hardly any expectation that my offer will be accepted.(*249*)

Three months later, Elmsley's offer had been accepted; he

installed himself, with rising hopes, in Naples. But though his enthusiasm was keener and his qualifications were higher than those of Hayter, his problems proved to be all too similar. Late in January 1820 he sadly informed Robert Finch:

> I really am unable to report any progress. Davy is quite indefatigable, but he meets with sad obstacles created by the jealousy of the present set of unrollers and interpreters, who are extremely unwilling to be superseded by us barbarians. They are not so jealous of Sir Humphry as of me. They say that they have eight critical scholars in constant pay and employment, and the deuce is in it if they want the assistance of a ninth from Oxford.... I suspect that the affair will end in smoke....(250)

The Regent's thoughts, in 1819, must often have been in Italy. Sir Thomas Lawrence, fresh from Vienna, where he had been painting the Emperor Francis II and Metternich, arrived in Rome, where Pius VII sat to him, expressed 'his sense of the Prince Regent's attention', and asked for a copy of the Regent's portrait. Cardinal Consalvi, 'his manners but too gracious,' proved to be one of the finest sitters that Lawrence had known.

Lawrence himself turned to his canvases with superb sense of purpose. His 'mission', as he called it, added new authority to his work. In visiting Rome he was realising one of his oldest day-dreams; and he felt that the Regent had sent him there not only to do him honour, but to give him one of the highest pleasures an artist could experience. No court painter could have been more generously encouraged, more eagerly watched, than Lawrence was by the Regent. Bloomfield, increasing his credit on Torlonia, the banker, in the summer, assured him:

> H.R.H. is most highly pleased with the success of your Undertakings, and full of anxiety to see the whole deposited in the Palace.
> You will be glad to hear that His Health is most

remarkable, and His Love for the fine arts unabated....(*251*)

When Lawrence sent home carefully modest accounts of
his progress, Bloomfield reminded him that the Regent, 'in
despite of your diffidence, attaches the highest value to
your Works.'(252) 'The last time I saw the Prince,' wrote
Lord Charles Stewart, the British Ambassador to Austria,
'he talked in wild rapture of all the delight he expected
from your treasures on your return.'(253)

The Regent's love for the fine arts did indeed remain
unabated. Early in the year, the Grand Duke of Tuscany
sent him some fine casts of the group of Niobe. The Regent
asked that they should be unpacked at Carlton House, and
Richard Westmacott, the sculptor, duly arranged them in
the riding house. The Regent examined them with the
eye of a connoisseur, and observed that one of the statues
did not belong to the group.

> I was pleased at the Prince making this remark without
> any observation from me [Westmacott told Lawrence]
> ... I was much pleased with the Prince's remarks, they
> were not only judicious but expressed with a feeling
> and in a language of art that I was not aware he was
> Master of. Mr. Long who was with him asked HRH [*sic*]
> pleasure respecting the Casts when with a grace peculiar
> to himself he desired him to write and present them in
> his Name to the Academy adding in turning to me
> that he could not think of depriving the Academy of such
> valuable materials for Study. I was a little startled by
> HRH asking me where we could place them (and you
> know there is a little difficulty) but I was not displeased
> at the question.(*254*)

The Regent was apt to show an informed interest in the
arts which surprised their regular practitioners. His generosity, which delighted Westmacott, also impressed Joseph
Farington; and, telling Lawrence of the Regent's latest
present, which was to be placed in the council room, he
observed with some justice, that Charles Long appeared 'to

be Minister to the Regent for the department of art'.(255)

It was Long who wrote to the President of the Royal Academy, that June, announcing that the Regent would visit the exhibition, 'and requesting that the Pictures may not be removed till he has seen them.'(256)

PART THREE

King of England

51

'PRAY is the Duke of Kent dead yet? I want to know very much,' Mary Russell Mitford wrote to Sir William Elford. It was 24 January 1820. 'Now, don't fancy it's only on account of crepe and bombazin,' she added, 'though, to be sure, it will add very much to my grief to be obliged to buy a new gown, and I can't do without one. But really one has a respect for the Duke of Kent.'(*1*) What with her loyalty and her thrift, Miss Mitford was understandably anxious. Alas, the Duke had died the previous day.

His death was a shock to everyone. He was only fifty-three. He had been, as Croker said, 'the strongest of the strong; ... and now to die of a cold,' added Croker, 'when half the kingdom had colds with impunity, is very bad luck indeed.'(*2*) The Duke left a widow and a daughter, Princess Victoria, who was eight months old; he had dutifully ensured the future of the monarchy.

Within a week of his death, the succession to the Throne assumed a sudden and increased importance. Just after half-past eight on the evening of Saturday 29 January, in the eighty-second year of his age, 'without any appearance of pain and without a lucid interval,' King George III died, at long last, at Windsor.

Lord, it is past! he cried; the mist, and the weight, and the darkness; ...

195

That long and weary night, that long drear dream of
desertion . . .(*3*)

If he had known a final moment of lucidity, he might indeed have felt the immense relief which Southey made him
express in *A Vision of Judgment*. As for the country over
which he had nominally reigned for some sixty years,
it felt confused with pity, bewilderment and affection. As
Lady Louisa Stuart explained to Miss Louisa Clinton: 'It
will indeed be difficult ever to hear "God Save the King"
without thinking of that excellent man.'(*4*)

On 31 January, Lady Sarah Lyttelton told her brother,
the Hon. Frederick Spencer:

> The poor old, old King, George the Third, who has
> reigned over us, our fathers and grandfathers, from time
> immemorial, is dead! George the Fourth, whom Heaven
> preserve, was proclaimed to-day all over London.(*5*)

King George the Fourth was proclaimed exactly at noon
at Carlton House, inside Henry Holland's Ionic screen.
There was considerable cheering from the troops, but he
himself could only have found it disturbing. He had
pleurisy, and according to the barbarous medical practice
of the time, he was copiously bled. Next day he was naturally 'very unwell. . . . We must get him well soon, however', the Duke of Wellington wrote coolly to Lady Shelley,
'or he also will slip through our fingers.'(*6*) Dorothea Lieven
prayed for the King's recovery with more passion. 'Heavens,
if he should die!' she cried to Metternich. 'Shakespeare's
tragedies would pale before such a catastrophe!'(*7*)

The King's disorder was not entirely physical. He was
no doubt disturbed by his father's death; for despite George
III's wounding and open dislike of his eldest son, George
IV still possessed some filial feelings. Besides, his own accession to the Throne, expected though it was, must have
impressed an extremely emotional man. However, as Croker
reported on 5 February, there was one appalling problem
which delayed the King's recovery. If he was King, then
Caroline was Queen, and she would surely come to claim

her rights. 'The King would be better,' wrote Mr. Croker, 'but that his anxiety about the Queen agitates him terribly.'(8)

That morning the doctors announced, in their bulletin, posted outside Carlton House, that the King was recovering. As he grew better, he became increasingly aware of the horror of his situation. He insisted that the Princess, as he called her, should not be prayed for in the Liturgy (the Liturgy was duly altered by an order in Council). He demanded a divorce; he threatened to dismiss his Ministers if the divorce was not granted. But no new Government would have taken office on condition of giving him his freedom, and he was obliged to accept the terms of his Tory Ministers, and to make 'this great and painful sacrifice of his personal feelings for the sake of public decorum'. The Ministers had read all the evidence of the Queen's behaviour, and they were convinced of her guilt. They agreed privately with the King that if she came back to England they would give him the divorce he wanted. However, they fondly imagined that the Queen would not dare to return and risk a public inquiry into her conduct. The King knew her well enough to think she would.

On the night of 16 February George III was buried at Windsor. Among the last of his subjects to pay their respects had been some boys from Eton, the school to which he had been such a benefactor. The new King had written expressly to their headmaster, Dr. Keate, to ask that they 'might be allowed to see the late King buried, and to see him lying in state after all the other people were excluded'. It was a gesture to impress the new generation, and W. O. Stanley, writing to his sister, declared that the lying-in-state was 'a very fine sight indeed. The room was hung in black all over, and lighted with candles'. In St. George's Chapel, wearing the mourning for King George III which has been worn by Etonians ever since, the Eton boys, 'most preciously squeezed and tired,' waited from six to half-past eleven to watch the funeral procession.(9) As it moved round the edge of the Castle walls, Mr. Croker noted that the dismal and monotonous sound of trumpets from the park below had a very solemn effect.

The new King had been advised by his doctors not to attend the funeral; it would, they said, be 'a dangerous effort of respect and piety'.(*10*) While the trumpets sounded across Windsor Great Park, he sat convalescent at Brighton; and that month Mary Russell Mitford learned that 'the King was as well as ever he had been in his life'. Rumours were finally scotched for Miss Mitford. Sir Matthew Tierney, the Royal doctor, 'could not have said this of a man in whom water was rising, and whose legs were cased every morning in sheet lead, as has been the constant report hereabouts for the last fortnight.'(*11*)

52

The death of George III compelled Mr. Southey to write *A Vision of Judgment*; the task was to keep him at his desk in Keswick for some weeks. 'For if,' he explained, 'I do not finish the poem, which I must of course write before I leave home, my funeral verses would not appear before the coronation.' The Poet Laureate never underestimated his talents. 'If I manage the end,' he added, 'as well as I have done the beginning, I shall be very well satisfied with the composition.'(*12*)

The composition was, on the whole, less memorable than the dedicatory letter which Southey addressed to the King. The reign of George IV had hardly begun; but, as Regent, and as King, he earned the triumphant tributes which the Poet Laureate now paid him:

> We owe much to the House of Brunswick; but to none of that illustrious House more than to Your Majesty.... More has been done than was ever before attempted, for mitigating the evils incident to our stage of society; for imbuing the rising race with those sound principles of religion on which the welfare of states has its only secure foundation; and for opening new regions to the redundant

enterprise and industry of the people. Under Your Majesty's government, the Metropolis is rivalling in beauty, those cities which it has long surpassed in greatness: sciences, arts, and letters are flourishing beyond all former example; and the last triumph of nautical discovery, and of the British flag, which had so often been essayed in vain, has been accomplished. The brightest portion of British history will be that which records the improvements, the works, and the achievements of the Georgian Age.(*13*)

Southey finished *A Vision of Judgment*, and prepared his sanctimonious and pedestrian Ode for St. George's Day. His general satisfaction was only marred when an astute London publisher announced a Life of the King, by a certain Robert Southy, in sixpenny numbers. An anxious Laureate denied the authorship in the *Westmorland Gazette*, and considered taking legal action.

The new King did not only inspire his Laureate with an Ode. His principal painter-in-ordinary—now recognised as the first portrait-painter of Europe—was still busy on the Continent. Lawrence was superbly dashing off the portraits of sovereigns and ministers, prelates and generals, that would adorn the Waterloo Chamber built to receive them at Windsor. He had now almost completed his mission, and he was thinking of home. 'You are about to bask in Kingly favor,' wrote Lord Charles Stewart, from Vienna, on 18 March, 'and shew the Matchless productions of the Modern Titian in all their glory in his own Country and placed at the foot of his Sovereign.'(*14*) Lawrence welcomed the accession of his patron, and hoped that he would now 'suffer less from the outrages of insult and calumny, for the people of England love the monarch of England, and the title of King has its high authority.'(*15*)

On the morning of 30 March, after an absence of more than a year and a half, he landed in England, bringing eight whole-length portraits for the King. He was greeted with the news that Benjamin West had died, and that the Royal

Academy were resolved to elect him President. Within forty-eight hours, he had been elected almost unanimously, and was on his way to Brighton, in the hope of a royal audience. It is doubtful whether any English artist has enjoyed such patronage, such personal interest as Lawrence was constantly shown by George IV. Months ago, Lord Charles Stewart told him, the King had talked 'in wild rapture of all the delight He expected from your Treasures on your return'. Now he received him with a heartwarming sense of occasion. He applauded his work, 'he spoke of the honour which his genius as well as his conduct upon the continent had reflected upon his profession and his country;'(16) and he presented him with a gold medal, bearing the royal profile crowned with laurel, to be worn on a gold chain by Lawrence himself and by all future Presidents of the Royal Academy.

It was, as the Academy told him in their address of thanks, 'a munificent and public testimony of your favour'; and, by the time the address was passed, they had received still more tokens of his interest. In April, he told Mr. Croker to send them 'several cases of Casts recently arrived from Italy'. Almost before the six cases were opened, he gave them a plaster cast 'from one of the Venetian Bronze Horses'. In July he agreed to lend them Raphael's cartoon, *The Miraculous Draught of Fishes*, for the use of the painting school.(17) He could hardly have shown more consistent, practical sympathy.

One of the first portraits to be painted by the new President was that of the King's friend, the author of *Marmion*. Now that the allied powers, their Church and State, had been recorded, George IV wanted portraits of his most distinguished authors and scientists, and the series was to begin with Scott. Lawrence set to work at once, and caught the inspired expression on Scott's face at the proudest moment of his life.

It was indeed a proud moment; for the day that Lawrence was elected President of the Royal Academy, the *London Gazette* announced, at last, that Scott was created a baronet.

He had won his title by his diplomacy as much as by his writing, and now he savoured it to the full. Even before the *Gazette* appeared, he addressed his wife as 'the Lady Scott of Abbotsford—to be'.(*18*) On 9 April he received the accolade. 'No subject,' he recalled, 'was ever more graciously received by a Sovereign, for he scarce would permit me to kneel, shook hands with me repeatedly and said more civil and kind things than I care to repeat.'(*19*)

Lockhart, his son-in-law and biographer, was to repeat them for him. Scott's baronetcy, he wrote, was conferred on him 'by the King personally, and of his own unsolicited motion; and when the Poet kissed his hand, he said to him—"I shall always reflect with pleasure on Sir Walter Scott's having been the first creation of my reign." '(*20*)

The day after Scott received his title, Lady Cowper reported from Brighton that the King's health was 'quite re-established'. She also reported one of the chief causes of the royal recovery. 'The M[archione]ss C[onyngham] sails about here in great Glory very proud of her situation and he says that he never was so in love before in his life, that he's quite ashamed of being so boyish.'(*21*)

53

Elizabeth Conyngham was the daughter of Joseph Denison. The son of humble parents in Yorkshire, he had come to London at seventeen and become a clerk in a counting-house. His first wife had died childless. His second wife, Elizabeth, was the only child of a Mr. Butler, formerly a hatmaker in Southwark. She had borne him a son and two daughters. The Denisons had swiftly risen 'to opulence and title'. Joseph had amassed a fortune by 'unabated industry and rigid frugality'. His son, William Joseph, the banker and Whig Member of Parliament, would die worth over £2,000,000. His daughter Maria married Sir Robert

Lawley, later Lord Wenlock; and Elizabeth married Henry, the third Lord Conyngham (who became the first Marquis Conyngham in 1816).(22)

Lady Conyngham's marriage into this old Anglo-Norman family had given her two sons and two daughters, a handsome castle, Slane, in County Meath, and social status. It had not prevented her, it seems, from falling in love with Lord Ponsonby at the turn of the century, or having (Mme de Lieven said) a 'little flirtation' with the Emperor Nicholas of Russia. She was no doubt overwhelmed that, at fifty-four, an age when women were considered elderly, she had contrived to enthral the King himself.

Lady Conyngham was not intelligent. She had, according to Mme de Lieven, a 'most limited mind. She had no political ideas or opinions'. She had a strong leaning to diamonds and money, 'after this towards love and fashion.'(23) She was considered vulgar. But she was precisely the handsome, maternal figure the King always needed.

The word maternal was not misplaced. Now that his mother had died, the King felt a growing need for a comfortable, warmhearted woman in whom he could confide, with whom he could have a close relationship. This warmth and closeness had always been impossible with Isabella Hertford; she had been incapable of emotional intimacy. The King greatly needed this kind of comfort, and no doubt he felt that Lady Conyngham could give it to him.

He did not want an exacting liaison: during her years of influence, his health would be indifferent, and more than once a cause of anxiety. He suffered frequently from gout; he was often in deep depression. He may not have had much appetite for passion. But, without a wife or daughter, isolated by sovereignty, he needed a companion, and the sense of stable family life. Lady Conyngham may have ministered to his physical needs; she certainly surrounded him (as Lady Hertford had done) with her husband and children. She created the necessary illusion of warm domesticity.

And so, as Mrs. Fitzherbert's power had ended more or less with the Regency, Lady Hertford's ended with the new reign. On the eve of the King's accession, the arch-intriguer,

Mme de Lieven, had sanctimoniously told Metternich: 'I am going to do a really kind thing this morning. I am going to see the ex-favourite. Her fall from favour is official. She was never very nice to me during her reign: now I shall revenge myself by being polite.'(24) Lady Hertford soon returned the call, and talked of nothing but unhappy constancy and love. 'An odd subject for her,' said Mme de Lieven.(25) Jekyll still could not believe that the *esprit faible* of Lady Conyngham could triumph over the *esprit fort* of Lady Hertford. But Lady Hertford's days of power were irrevocably gone. The reign of Lady Conyngham, the Vice Queen, as they called her, had begun.

It had, in fact, begun the previous year. As long ago as Christmas Day, Lady Cowper had reported that 'Ly Conyngham has carried the day completely.... People say she is too foolish to keep him, but she is very handsome, and there is no knowing and any change is for the better'.(26)

Lady Hertford, it appeared, had been the worst person for the King. She was always morose and telling him how people abused him. Perhaps she had hoped that this would reveal her as his one loyal friend; but, if so, she had misjudged human nature. The King had tired of gloom and constant detrimental stories. He wanted gaiety and good-humour. He was also perfectly ready, now, to exchange a woman of sixty (Mme de Lieven said she was sixty-three), for a woman of fifty-four.

Mme de Lieven, who had been the mistress of Metternich, proved censorious at first over the King's affair. '*Mon Prince,*' she told Metternich, on 26 April, 'the King is a dangerous madman. His new passion has turned his head. I have already told you, I think, that the Marchioness of Conyngham ... is a fool and just the kind of malicious fool who might do a great deal of harm.... All sensible people regret Lady Hertford.'(27)

On the last day of the month, Lady Conyngham appeared in Society for the first time since her accession; and Mme de Lieven, performing a quick *volte-face*, decided: 'She is a nice enough woman.'(28) Lady Cowper, attending a levée in May, still felt that Lady Conyngham could not last:

> She is too foolish and vulgar and when she is driven out I really should not wonder if Mrs. F[itzherbert] is to come round again. There are more unlikely things than this have come to pass, and she is handsomer now I think than Ly C who looks so fat and as if she was swelled with drinking Curacoa. . . .

But the King remained blind to Lady Conyngham's strikingly evident faults; and on 1 June, a model of charm and beatitude, Mme de Lieven drove away from Ascot in the carriage with Lady Conyngham and the King. 'I have never,' she declared, 'seen a man more in love.'(29)

Lady Conyngham had not belonged (Mme de Lieven had said, two days ago) 'to the kind of society one invites to dinner.' There was no doubt, now, to whom Dorothea de Lieven should give allegiance. She was dining with Lady Conyngham when, on 5 June, Bloomfield came in to announce a 'pretty piece of news'. The King's prediction had been fulfilled. Queen Caroline had come back to England. 'Had an avalanche from the summit of the Schreckhorn been announced in the drawing-room at St. James's, it could not have produced greater consternation.'(30)

54

The following evening, 6 June 1820, at half-past five, dressed in mourning for George III, 'with a ruff on the model of Queen Elizabeth's,' Caroline drove over Westminster Bridge. She was accompanied by a cheering, running crowd, who so disliked her husband that they were prepared to acclaim this painted hoyden of fifty as an innocent and injured wife.

Half an hour before her arrival, Lord Castlereagh, the Foreign Secretary, had entered the House of Commons with a green bag in his hand, and announced at the bar: 'A

Princess Charlotte and Prince Leopold of Saxe-Coburg
in their box at Covent Garden Theatre
From the engraving by George Dawe

Lady Beauchamp, later Marchioness of Hertford
From the portrait by John Hoppner

message from the King.' The message was read, the bag was laid on the table, and Lord Castlereagh moved that the Commons should consider it next day. The bag contained all the evidence of Caroline's misdeeds, the substantial work of the Milan Commission. The Queen had thrown down the gauntlet, and the Government intended to pick it up.

Years ago, when the vote of censure had been passed on her indiscretions, the Whigs had been Caroline's accusers. Now the Tories stood out against her. The domestic differences between the King and Queen had become a party struggle, and Caroline was the trump card, the Queen in the Whigs' hands.

It would have been easier for the doctors to announce the patent truth that her mental balance had gone. But perhaps they did not dare: perhaps the King and Government felt that the contents of the green bag would bring her more discredit. The summer and autumn of 1820 were thus entirely absorbed by the Queen's affair, which brought the country close to civil war.

'An entire summer missed,' said Mme de Lieven in vexation, 'and all for the mistress of Mr. Bergami.'(*31*) Visiting here, there and everywhere as usual, she recorded how Lady Conyngham rejoiced in Caroline's disastrous challenge, and how Lady Jersey, permanently embittered against her old lover, 'very actively' made proselytes for his wife.

Caroline spent the summer in South Audley Street, in Portman Street, and, finally, at Brandenburgh House, at Hammersmith. From the moment of her arrival, she encouraged contention. In South Audley Street she was besieged by vociferous admirers, shouting her praises, and breaking the windows of neighbouring houses. In Portman Street, she received the Lord Mayor and Common Council of London, and appeared on the balcony, 'wearing a bandeau of laurel leaves, studded with emeralds, and surmounted by a plume of feathers.' At Brandenburgh House she received a stream of devotees, radical and very largely plebeian (trampling down her garden, she said, and damaging her furniture), and bearing illuminated addresses to which she made reply. Half-guinea tickets were given to those who wished to attend, which entitled them to hire dresses for the occasion (Lady Brownlow recorded a red-elbowed potato-seller, resplendent in white satin). The funds for these dresses and hackney coaches almost certainly came from Alderman Wood, a City dignitary whose devotion was 'all party politics'. Never had the British monarchy become such a raree-show as it became in the person of Queen Caroline.

Brougham, discussing the presentation of an address, was reported to have said: 'We shall do very well if we can keep the D.L. sober!' He remained convinced that the Queen had committed adultery during her travels ('she is pure *in-no-sense*,' he said at dinner parties); but he agreed to be her Attorney-General, and defend her when, in August, she was tried by the House of Lords. 'It was,' wrote Lady Brownlow, 'for a woman of whom he thus thought and spoke that Brougham misused his great talents, exciting the minds of the people and causing for a time a feeling of disaffection towards their Sovereign.'(*32*)

There was only one topic of discussion in England that summer, and everyone took sides. 'Are you St. Caroline or "George 4th"?' asked John Clare, the poet, from Helpstone. 'I am as far as my politics reaches "King & Country" no Inovations on Religion & government say I.'(*33*) Mary Russell Mitford declared that she had 'no toleration for an indecorous woman', and that she was 'exceedingly scandalised'.(*34*) Thomas Babington Macaulay, an undergraduate at Trinity College, Cambridge, wrote an ode to the Queen which ended in a burst of wildly misplaced chivalry.(*35*) Coleridge, 'a Queenite', in Highgate, wanted to publish his support of Brougham's 'poor hoaxed and hunted client'; but he was persuaded to suppress it because his mind 'was not sufficiently tranquil', and because it might damage the prospects of his sons.(*36*) Byron, in Ravenna, remembered Caroline's civility in London, and suppressed a stanza in *Don Juan* which seemed to reflect on her character. 'I think the Queen will win,' he told his publisher, John Murray. 'I wish she may: she was always very civil to me.'(*37*)

But some of the old *habitués* of Caroline's court were careful, now, not to show support for her. On 18 June, Sir Thomas Lawrence, invited to dine with Angerstein, arrived to find 'the Queen had just arriv'd there on an unexpected visit—With Mr As concurrence,' he told a friend, 'I return'd instantly; without trusting myself to *any* result that might have attended an Interview. I think you will agree with me that it was prudent to do so.'(*38*) It was certainly prudent. The principal painter-in-ordinary to the King, the new President of the Royal Academy, had had a change of heart since the Delicate Investigation. He was also convinced of the Queen's guilt: he expressed his outrage at 'so flagrant an Example of successful daring Profligacy....'(*39*)

As for Scott, he showed no devotion, now, to the Queen whose 'conjuror' he had been at Blackheath: in fact he thought 'her conduct in Italy was shockingly irregular'.(*40*) In July, in a letter which showed his latent vulgarity, he wrote to his brother, Thomas Scott:

> The Queen is making an awful bustle.... She has courage enough to dare the worst, and a most decided desire to be revenged of *him*, which, by the way, is not to be wondered at. If she had as many followers of high as of low degree (in proportion), and funds to equip them, I should not be surprised to see her fat bottom in a pair of buckskins and at the head of an army—God mend all. The things said of her are beyond all usual profligacy.(*41*)

And then, once again, Scott rejoiced to be at Abbotsford, four hundred miles from the royal domestic problems. He added: 'I think myself monstrously well clear of London and its intrigues, when I look round my green fields.'(*42*)

55

The Coronation was to have taken place on 1 August; on 15 July it was postponed indefinitely, and carpenters began to dismantle the temporary platform and galleries in Westminster Abbey. There was to be a different ceremony in the Palace of Westminster; it was virtually the trial of the Queen of England.

Every peer in the realm, unless debarred by age or ill-health, had been summoned by the Lord Chancellor to attend. Thirty-six years ago, in an interview at Carlton House, Lord Malmesbury had urged the Prince to marry: 'It would, I should think, be most grateful to the nation.' Twenty-seven years ago, Lord Malmesbury had negotiated the marriage, and warned Caroline of Brunswick that a love-affair would be high treason. Now his advice was taken, his warnings were ignored, and all his fears for the marriage had been realised. He must have been almost grateful that he was over seventy, and that his age and infirmity kept him from Westminster.(43)

On Thursday, 17 August, at ten o'clock, this 'very formidable' cause, as Robert Peel described it, was to open. In the House of Lords (which was protected by double rows of strong timber fences, a large body of constables, and detachments of the Foot Guards and Life Guards), the Bill of Pains and Penalties (first announced on 5 July) was read for the second time. It was drawn up 'to deprive Her Majesty Caroline Amelia Elizabeth of the Title, Prerogatives, Rights, Privileges and Pretensions of Queen Consort of this Realm, and to dissolve the Marriage between His Majesty and the said Queen.' The ground for dissolution of the marriage was 'a most unbecoming and degrading intimacy' between the Queen, when Princess of Wales, and Bartolomeo Bergami, 'a foreigner of low station.'

For the rest of August, and the first nine days of September, the House of Lords, and England, buzzed with accounts of the Queen's misconduct. Though the evidence appeared irrevocably to condemn her, she was still a focal point for sympathy. She provided the Whigs with a dangerous political weapon; she provided the enemies of the King with a reason for venting their scorn. She herself remained the King's most inveterate enemy, and said that 'by God she would blow him off his throne'. Years ago, just after their marriage, she had told her husband that Catherine the Great set a fine example for all princesses; he believed that she had thought of adopting Catherine as a model. The comparison now occurred to others: a peer assured Plumer Ward that Caroline was 'as full of revenge as careless of crime, and that if we did not take care might play the part of Catherine II who, by means of the Guards, murdered her husband and usurped the throne'.(44)

No one at all dispassionate could believe that the Queen was innocent of the charges brought against her. Canning implied the likelihood of her misconduct all too clearly when he resigned from the Board of Control rather than support any movement against her. Lord Liverpool persuaded him to withdraw his resignation, but Canning promptly sent it to the King; and the Government was so insecure that he was still asked to remain in office, and excused any part in the proceedings. Small wonder that Lord Liverpool and Castlereagh believed that he had been the Princess of Wales's lover; small wonder that the King declared that 'Mr. Canning had strongly manifested by his conduct, what everybody before believed, almost an open avowal of a criminal intercourse with the P[rincess]'.(45). Caroline would hardly have refrained from further misconduct out of loyalty to her husband.

When the Trial began, Mme de Lieven had professed herself to be horrified: 'Is the Queen really a woman?' she asked Metternich. 'And how can the House of Lords, uniting as it does all that is most dignified and most exalted in the greatest nation in the world, lower itself by listening to such vile trash?'(46) On 6 September, Mme de Lieven touched the heart of the matter. 'Anyway, the Queen is quite mad, and what surprises me is that they don't question the witnesses about that, or at least ask her doctor. If they pronounced her mad they would avoid all this scandal and be nearer the truth besides.'(47)

But, alas, the Bill of Pains and Penalties could not be so sensibly dismissed; and on 3 October, after a break of some three weeks, the House of Lords assembled again, and Brougham opened the case for the defence. 'Her Majesty's Defenders,' observed Sir Thomas Lawrence, frigidly, 'are endeavoring to lead away the public Mind from the damning Evidence of her own Witnesses.'(48) The evidence was certainly damning. Elizabeth, Duchess of Devonshire, now in Naples, forgot her own two natural children and her affair with Cardinal Consalvi, and averted her eyes. 'My dear Sr. Thomas,' she wrote to Lawrence, 'I can't bear to read the English papers. I feel vex'd and ashamed....'(49) 'I shall be glad to hear of the event of the Queen's concern,' Byron wrote to Moore, from Ravenna. 'As to the ultimate effect, the most inevitable one to you and me ... will be that the Miss Moores and Miss Byrons will present us with a great variety of grandchildren by different fathers.'(50) It had hardly been worth suppressing the tendentious stanza in *Don Juan*.

The House of Lords voted on a second reading of the Bill of Pains and Penalties. There was a majority of twenty-eight. On Friday, 10 November, the Bill came up for its third and final reading. It was passed by a majority of nine.

At this, Lord Liverpool rose. Had the third reading, he said, been carried by the same majority as the second, the Government would have felt it their duty to send the Bill to the Commons. 'In the present state of the country, however, and with the division of sentiment so nearly balanced, ... they had come to the determination not to proceed further with it. It was his intention, accordingly, to move that the question "that the bill do now pass", be altered to "this day six months".'

The motion was carried unanimously. The Bill of Pains and Penalties was abandoned, Brougham's fame was solidly established; and the House of Lords, amid the most vehement cheering that had ever been heard in the Palace of Westminster, adjourned until 23 November.

Lord Montagu, writing to Sir Walter Scott, emphasised that the Queen had not been declared innocent by more than three peers in the House. The King was not free, but he had really won his cause.

And the fact was emphasised when, in December, Canning's resignation was at last accepted.

56

The Bill of Pains and Penalties was abandoned, and the country blazed with illuminations. Some lights and candles shone in tribute to the Queen herself; some were simply 'anti-Kingite'. Some were lit with gratitude and infinite relief that the country had been saved from civil war. Certain people felt, and not without reason, that candles should have been lit for the King; and when an attempt was made, in vain, to illuminate in Brighton, Lady Cowper grew indignant: 'What asses people are! The King should reign here if nowhere else after all he has done for Brighton.'(51)

He had indeed created Brighton; and, under Nash's wand, work was still going on at what Dorothea de Lieven called the Kremlin. She deplored the whim which, she estimated, had already cost £700,000; she dismissed the style as a mixture of Moorish, Tartar, Gothic and Chinese. But Mme de Lieven could be relied on to be deprecating. She could not be expected to foresee the permanent prosperity which the King had given the little fishing village; nor did she have the catholicity of taste, the imagination or humour to appreciate architectural fantasy.

She made no mention of another venture on which the King embarked even while the Trial was in progress. In October, Thomas Burgess, the Bishop of St. David's, had suggested the foundation of a Society of Literature, somewhat like the Académie Française. The suggestion, made in a private conversation, was passed on to Sir Benjamin Bloomfield (now the King's Private Secretary), and by him to the King, and on 2 November the Bishop had been summoned to Carlton House. The King discussed the proposal 'with the warmth . . . of the most devoted friend to Literature'. The Bishop was instructed to draw up plans for the Society, and to settle, with Bloomfield, the question of the King's Bounty. Under the patronage of George IV, The Royal Society of Literature was founded, 'to unite and extend the general interests of Literature; to reward Literary Merit by Patronage; to excite Literary Talent by Premiums; and to promote Literary Education by bestowing Exhibitions at the Universities and Public Schools.' The King assigned 1,000 guineas a year from the Privy Purse as pensions to ten Royal Associates, and a premium of 100 guineas for a prize dissertation. He granted the Society some land on which to build its headquarters. Three of his brothers, the Dukes of York, Clarence, and Cambridge were the first Fellows to be enrolled after him, and in 1825 the Society received its Charter of Incorporation from its founder and patron, 'the Friend of Letters'.(52)

The King was indeed the friend of literature: he did more than bestow knighthoods, charters and pensions. He delighted in showing appreciation of men of artistic or intellectual distinction. It was not that he felt it part of his duty: it was that he admired and understood men of creative mind, and men of intellect. He enjoyed their friendship; he was delighted that he could cultivate it.

There is no doubt that they, in turn, respected him for his taste and scholarship, for his practical enthusiasm; and they were immensely flattered by his friendship. But, being human, they were not unaware that friendship with the monarch had its uses; and, sometimes, as one contrasts their public conduct, their courtly manners, with their private comments, one feels that affection and self-interest went hand in hand. Sir Walter Scott was genuinely fond of his sovereign; he was naturally gratified when, early in 1821, he came to Court, and the King treated him 'with great distinction, and shook hands with me before the whole circle'. He was overjoyed to report, a few days later, that the King had commanded him to sit to Lawrence 'for a portrait for his most sacred apartment'.(53) But, writing to his son, Walter Scott, of the 18th Hussars, he could not help remarking: 'I hope my glimpse of Court favour may be useful to your pursuits and views for myself it is all one.'(54) Scott intended to assure the future.

The King who showed such favour to Scott had not forgotten his Poet Laureate: indeed, Mr. Southey was finding that the sinecure he had accepted with huge self-satisfaction was no sinecure at all; and, counting up his official poems, he reckoned that he had written more than any previous Laureate, with the single exception of Ben Jonson. He had hardly finished *A Vision of Judgment,* on the death of George III, before he was commanded to write an ode for the official birthday of George IV. 'Of course,' grumbled Southey, 'my immediate business is to get into harness and work in the mill. Two or three precious days will be spent in producing what will be good for nothing; for as for making any thing good of a birth-day ode, I might as well attempt to manufacture silk purses from sows' ears.'(55)

While Southey laboured, in vexation, at his birthday ode, Sir Humphry Davy, the new President of the Royal Society, was presenting them with the final fruits of a royal mission.

'Do you remember Elmsley at Oxford,' Southey had asked Landor in 1820, '—the fattest undergraduate in your time and mine? He is at Naples, superintending the unrolling [of] the Herculaneum manuscripts, by Davy's process, at the expense of the Prince Regent—I should say, of George IV.'(56) It was Elmsley's arrival which, as Elmsley himself had predicted, finally spoilt the Herculaneum enterprise. As Sir Humphry told the Royal Society:

When . . . the Rev. Peter Elmsley . . . began to examine the fragments unrolled, a jealousy, with regard to his assistance, was immediately manifested, and obstacles . . . were soon opposed to the progress of our inquiries; and these obstacles were so multiplied, and made so vexatious towards the end of February, that we conceived it would be both a waste of the public money, and a compromise of our characters, to proceed....(57)

The Herculaneum manuscripts seemed doomed to suffer from chauvinism and indifference. Some of the Neapolitan editions, said a Victorian scholar, were 'almost unique as examples of pedantic imbecility'.(58) Yet English scholars showed no haste to produce more satisfactory versions. In 1883, the better part of a century since Hayter had hopefully set out for Naples, there still remained the possibility that any one of the papyri in England might 'turn out a prize outweighing in value the whole mass of those hitherto opened'.(59) The enthusiasm and imagination, the taste and generosity of George IV had been poorly rewarded.

57

The year of George IV's coronation seemed to write finis to an age of warfare: on 5 May, Napoleon died in exile on St. Helena. At home, the year brought a spate of notable improvements: gaslight was introduced into nearly every town in Great Britain, steam-boats were established between Dover and Calais, and more of Nash's noble plan for London was realised.

It was an age of well-founded hope, of magnificent confidence. Though its most promising poet, Keats, died as the year began, there remained the constellation of Shelley, Wordsworth, Clare and Coleridge; and in an open *Letter to the Rt. Hon. Lord Byron*, a pamphleteer could write that 'there is nobody but yourself who has any chance of conveying to posterity a true idea of the *spirit* of England in the reign of His Majesty George IV'. Lamb and Hazlitt and de Quincey could still be found in a single magazine. Scott was prodigally turning out the still anonymous Waverley Novels. Kean and Macready were electrifying the theatre.

Lawrence was painting the heroes of the age in epic style, and its women and children with gentle, elegant appreciation; Chantrey matched him, in the art of sculpture. It was an age of genius, and an age of natural and cultivated taste: Nash and Holland and Repton were designing buildings with nobility and, sometimes, a touch of fantasy. Capability Brown was making lawns and waterways and trees conform to his designs, and he was proud and content to design for the future. The industrial revolution had not yet replaced the individual by the mass-produced, or begun to erode artistic standards. It was a fecund, versatile age, and its arts reflected its vigour, taste, diversity and assurance. It was indeed the Age of George the Fourth.

The opening months of the coronation year were bedevilled by Queen Caroline, who did her utmost to cultivate popularity and dissension (in June she began a tour round the minor theatres, 'by way of preparing a stir at the Coronation'). She was assisted by the fact that all the world knew of the King's passion for Lady Conyngham. 'His libertinism,' Miss Mitford had snapped, 'is notorious, undenied, as plain as the sun at noonday. . . . It is undoubtedly a scandal and a horror.'(60)

Lady Conyngham was, indeed, much in evidence; she could hardly have been otherwise, since the King was lonely and demonstrative. She was much criticised in her time, and she has not been *persona grata* with posterity. And yet she sometimes showed a more respectable side of her nature: early in March, Dorothea de Lieven noted that the King had become prodigiously devout, and was 'increasing in piety all the time'. This was due to Lady Conyngham, who was 'a protectress of the Catholics'. Mme de Lieven discovered her surrounded by 'large tomes on theology', and explanations of the oath which the King would have to take at his Coronation. He contended that the oath obliged him to exclude the Catholics from all public offices and civil rights; Lady Conyngham wanted to show him that it did not. 'Evidently,' said Mme de Lieven, 'someone is putting her up to it, and she is the tool of the party. . . .' But perhaps it was to Lady Conyngham's credit that she preached tolerance so earnestly.(*61*)

And so the King himself approached his Coronation: cosseted and cajoled by Lady Conyngham, still pestered by Lady Hertford, disturbed by the Queen, and sadly aware (for the Clarences' infant daughter died in March) of his failure to ensure the succession. He was apprehensive of public opinion: William Pitt Lennox, commanding the escort of the Blues when the King went in state to Drury Lane, reported that the King 'looked jaded', and expected a hostile demonstration. Lennox was told to keep close to the carriage.

The King he shielded was indeed a lamentable figure. He held in his unwieldy body with a broad belt, he hid the lower part of his face in a large black neckcloth, he covered his uniforms with tags and frogging, embroidery and orders. He was trying to conceal his age, his ill-health, his apprehension, his perpetual emotional insecurity. And yet, somehow, he contrived to charm, as he had always done. 'For a man of near sixty,' wrote an observer, 'he contrives to look young by the help of a wig without powder; and his air and manner were as graceful as they used to be.'(*62*)

The grace of George IV still emanates from his correspondence. His letters are instinct with warmth and energy; they are vital, original, individual, the letters of an eager, impulsive man who was much more shrewd than his critics would allow. The intimate letters of George IV have a style as unmistakable as that of his niece, Queen Victoria. They are salted with sharp turns of speech and shot with sudden, illuminating ideas. They are human, royal and surprisingly modern. They are, above all, brilliantly natural: they come as naturally as the leaves to a tree.

And, time and time again, they show a quality quite as endearing as his grace: they reveal his instinctive and disarming kindness. In his position, he could hardly give for return: he gave for merit and, most often, he gave out of goodness of heart. The King possessed that real generosity

which shuns publicity, and is shy of thanks. He had the
tact to give unobtrusively, and to give with grace.

Your Majesty has told me not to say one word. Oh Sir
what words could I say? May I not say that my beloved
Sovereign has made two beings happy, & that those two
beings were even long since devoted to him?*(63)*

One of the most illuminating letters George IV received
was the letter from Wellington's friend, Charles Arbuthnot,
whom he had helped in his financial plight. For this, alone,
much might be forgiven him.

58

It was not to be expected that the creator of Carlton House
and the Pavilion, the superb *metteur en scène,* would allow
himself a sober Coronation. George IV, who had an abid-
ing sense of occasion, did not intend to fail on the supreme
occasion of his life. And if all his artistic instincts, all his
nature, all his waiting led him to demand magnificence, he
was no less guided by his patriotism. If he paused on the
eve of his Coronation to consider his country, he must have
seen England with the same eyes as his biographer:

When we shall have been gathered to the grave
[declared George Croly], and the petty shades and stains
of party shall have disappeared, like the outlines of the
horizon from the face of an ascending sun, History will
contemplate with wonder and thanksgiving, the order that
has been created in the general system—the stately power
by which it has been sustained—the glory which our glory
has kindled.

This is the attestation of posterity. It will see England
standing on the summit of human sovereignty;—the
representative of a beneficent Providence, holding the
most powerful influence ever given to a nation ... [It]
will think of the hand by whose guidance, under Heaven,
she was led resolutely up to universal empire.

It is with feelings established on these solid grounds, that the nation will worthily advance to the altar, where their Sovereign is now to receive his Crown.(64)

Long before the decorations enlivened the London streets, it was clear that this Coronation would be unexampled in its splendour. Early in May, Sir Thomas Lawrence drafted a strangely fervent letter to Clarenceux King of Arms, begging for a place in the procession. There was no precedent which allowed the President of the Royal Academy to take an official part in the ceremony, for there had been no Academy sixty years earlier, when George III had been crowned. Lawrence urgently asserted his claims

as His Majesty's Principal Painter—As President of the Royal Academy, and therefore, *Representative of Art* and —as having been honor'd by a Mission from His Majesty, of more importance, distinction, and (perhaps) difficulty, than was ever assign'd by their Patron Monarchs to the Hands of Vandyke, Rubens, or Titian, in which Mission, by the Monarchs of every Court and their respective Governments, it has been acknowledg'd that without one exception, I have succeeded.

You do me *privately, infinite kindness*—if in the civilisation of past Ages, Art has had distinction, press my Claims, and *publickly, do me Justice*....(65)

This somewhat excessive plea was heard; at George IV's Coronation, two of the King's knights walked side by side: Sir Thomas Lawrence, President of the Royal Academy of Arts, walked with Sir Humphry Davy, President of the Royal Society.

Sir Walter Scott, too, had 'some idea of stepping up to London to see the Coronation'.(66) He was tempted by the thought that steamships could now make the journey from Leith within sixty hours; besides, the occasion was too Gothick to be missed. And, apparently feeling that Scottish letters should be further represented, he secured an invitation for James Hogg, the poet who was known as the Ettrick Shepherd. Hogg was too concerned about his farm to accept. 'He stood balancing the matter,' said Scott, 'whether to go to the Coronation or the Fair of St. Boswell, and the fair carried it.'(67) Charles Lamb, a partisan of the Queen, was hardly tempted to join the multitudes: he summed up his feelings: 'Vivat Regina. Moriatur Rex.'(68)

59

The King whom Elia so warmly wished in his grave, was a better man than his subjects would allow. On the eve of his Coronation, weighed down by domestic and political problems, he found time to receive Count Joseph Boruwlaski.

Years ago, as Prince of Wales, he had shown much kindness to this fiery, graceful, 'extremely complaisant' Polish dwarf who was only twenty-eight inches high. He had asked Boruwlaski to dedicate his memoirs to him. Now the Count, in his eighty-fourth year, had written his memoirs, and he longed to present them in person. The wish was mentioned to Lord Conyngham, who was now Lord Steward of the Household. Charles Mathews, the comedian, was bidden with the Count to Carlton House.

When they were announced, wrote Mrs. Mathews, in her *Life* of her husband.

> the King rose from his chair, and met Boruwlaski at the entrance, raising him up in his arms in a kind of embrace, saying, 'My dear old friend, how delighted I am to see you!' and then placed the little man upon a sofa ... When the Count said something about sitting in the presence of his Sovereign, he was graciously told to 'Remember for the time, that there was no King there!' ...
> The King then asked whether the Count had not brought him a book? The little creature replied: 'Yes, Majesty,' again attempting to kneel while presenting the volume. He was again prevented by his patron, who allowed him to kiss his hand; and turning afterwards to

Lady Conyngham, took from her a little case, containing a beautiful miniature watch and seals, attached to a superb chain; the watch exquisitely embossed with jewels. This, the King held in one hand, while, with the other, he received the book, saying—'My dear friend, I shall read and preserve this as long as I live for *your* sake; and in return, I request you will wear and keep this watch for *mine*.'

The King then asked if Boruwlaski would like to see the Coronation robes; the proposal was doubly tactful, as it allowed the King to ask Mathews, privately, if the dwarf was in material need. For, said the King, 'as he considered he was the Count's oldest friend in this country, he assumed the right to offer whatever might be desirable.' He had also wanted Boruwlaski to visit an old friend, a favourite valet, now on his deathbed.

> The dying man [wrote Mrs. Mathews] told the Count of all the King's goodness to him, and indeed of his uniform benevolence to all that depended upon him; mentioned that his majesty, during the long course of his poor servant's illness, had never omitted to visit his bedside *twice every day*, not for a moment merely, but long enough to soothe and comfort him, and to see that he had every thing necessary and desirable, telling him all particulars of himself that were interesting to an old and attached servant and humble friend.... The dying man [finally told] the Count that he only prayed to live long enough to greet his dear master after his *coronation* ... and that then he was ready to die in peace.

When Boruwlaski returned to the royal presence, he had evidently been weeping. The King seemed affected, too. Then, pointing to his guest's tiny feet, he said: 'My good friend, I must have one of your shoes to place in my cabinet, so pray do not forget to send it to me; *mind*, one that you *have worn*. So, good night! my dear old friend! Good night, and God bless you!'(*69*)

On 18 July, the day before the Coronation, the King sent for Mr. Croker, the Secretary to the Admiralty, whose duties would prevent him from seeing the ceremony. He wanted, he said, to make Croker what amends he could; and, reaching under his pillow (it was ten o'clock in the morning) he pulled out a gold snuff-box, enriched with a fine medallion of himself. He had not forgotten Mrs. Croker or Rosamond, the Crokers' adopted daughter: 'he also sent a gold coronation medal to my wife,' Croker reported, 'and one to *"the darling little girl"*, as he was pleased to call her.'(70)

The King spent that night at the Speaker's house at Westminster, to be near the Abbey. Next morning, as he waited to put on his cumbersome robes, he sent again for Croker, and told him of the Queen's latest venture. Caroline had determined, yet again, to assert her rights. She had come to attend the Coronation. She had been turned away, more than once, from Westminster Abbey, and she had been barred from Westminster Hall, where the Coronation banquet would be held.

She had made a grotesque attempt to create a scene, and she had done herself untold harm. Even Scott, who had once paid court to her at Blackheath, now dismissed her as 'the Bedlam Bitch of a Queen'.(71)

60

And so, assured as he rarely was, of the sympathy of his people, George the Fourth set out for his Coronation. For the last time in history, the King's Herb-woman and her six maids led the procession, strewing the way with herbs. Only once again would Blanc Coursier King of Arms bear the Crown of Hanover to Westminster.

Inside the Abbey the ceremony began. A spectator in an upper pew, gazing down on this scene of unexampled, panoramic richness, thought that it looked 'like a Turkey carpet, continually changing its pattern'.(72) 'The whole thing,' declared Lady Cowper, 'was indeed very handsome,' but the King himself seemed exhausted, 'more like the Victim than the Hero of the Fête. I really pitied him from my heart.' The Coronation, the Queen's repulses, his own indifferent health: there was much to weigh him down that day. 'He was very well received everywhere,' noted the same writer, 'and seemed much gratified.'(73) But if, for a moment, he grew complacent about his popularity, the Archbishop of York allowed him small time for self-congratulation. The Coronation sermon was the most outspoken personal admonition.

It is [declared the primate] the most essential service that a Sovereign can render to a State, to encourage morality and religion ...

It is this condition of a people, this general depravity of morals, which is the last calamity that can befall a State ...

Such a State may for a time be distinguished by every external mark of prosperity—external dominion, accumulated wealth, and successful cultivation of the arts —but its prosperity is not happiness: its magnificence and luxury, however imposing, are a poor and inadequate compensation for the absence of mutual kindness, of temperance and contentment, of the dignity of virtue, and the consolations of religion.

The Ruler then who would be just to his people, whilst he approves himself the faithful and zealous guardian of their civil rights, will preserve their morals from the contagion of vice and irreligion, by 'ruling in the fear of God' ...(74)

The admonition and the Coronation were over, and the King went in procession to Westminster Hall, where, for the last time in history, there would be a Coronation banquet. In some ways it was fitting that this one should be the last: no later banquet could have rivalled it.

Three hundred and twelve persons, besides the royal family, were to sit down to dinner in Westminster Hall.

The mediaeval dream had been realised: the very backs of the chairs were Gothic arches covered in scarlet, and into the Hall (which was floored with blue cloth), at a certain stage in the banquet, the King's Champion would make his traditional entrance on horseback, 'in a complete Suit of Bright Armour, with a Gauntlet in his Hand, his Helmet on his Head, adorned with a Plume of Feathers.' It would be a brilliant and deliberate recollection of the age of chivalry.

Mrs. Trench had been preparing to watch it since the small hours of the morning:

> I opened my eyes on a hairdresser at a quarter before four, was *en route* in a white satin dressing-gown and Court plume at five—at six was seated in the hall, after various difficulties, ... and some danger from the circumstance of my being within a few yards of the gate at the very instant the Guards were called out to oppose the Queen ...
>
> The show was all that Oriental pomp, feudal ceremonial and British wealth could unite. The processions in *The Curse of Kehama* and in *Rimini,* with the painting of *Belshazzar's Feast,* were continually recalled to my memory. The conflict of the *two lights,* from the blaze of artificial day mixing with a splendid sunshine, the position of the King's table, the pomp of the banquet, ... rendered the resemblance so perfect, it seemed as if the feast had been in some degree copied from the picture.(75)

Even those who came prepared to sneer at Old Nick (as some described the King) were converted by the actual scene:

> You may talk disdainfully of the show [wrote Lady Louisa Stanhope to Miss Clinton], and *quiz* the imagined figure of Old Nick or any individual, but you do not know how much there is to attract the *mind* in a great *public* spectacle: how different a feeling it raises from a ball at Carlton House.... And I observe that the young people in particular, going merely with the expectation

of a show, were ever taken by surprise, and found themselves affected in a manner they never dreamt of.... Instead of being inclined to giggle at Old Nick in white satins, they seem to acknowledge that the antique dresses aided the illusion, and transported them back to the days of chivalry. 'It was Kenilworth,' says Louisa Dawson....(76)

Louisa Dawson's opinion was shared by the author of *Kenilworth,* who sent a tedious account to the *Edinburgh Weekly Journal*; and Scott's enthusiasm was endorsed by Lawrence: 'Nothing can be conceived more grand, nothing more gratifying, than the scene in the hall.'(77) But such comments were insipid beside those of Haydon. If any contemporary was fitted to describe this unique and Gothic occasion, it was that turbulent historical painter. It is Haydon who records—in a passage much more glowing, much more inspired than any of his canvases—all the bustle and brilliance, all the Kenilworth romance of George IV's Coronation banquet:

The doors opened, and the flower-girls entered, strewing flowers. The grace of their action, their slow movement, their white dresses, were indescribably touching; their light, milky colour contrasted with the dark shadow of the archway, which, though dark, was full of rich crimson dresses that gave the shadow a tone as of deep blood; the shadow again relieved by a peep of the crowd, shining in sunlight beyond the gates, and between the shoulders of the guard that crossed the platform. The distant trumpets and shouts of the people, the slow march, and at last the appearance of the King himself crowned and under a golden canopy, and the universal burst of the assembly at seeing him, affected everybody. As we were all huzzaing, and the King was smiling, I could not help thinking this would be too much for any human being if a drop of poison were not dropped into the cup ere you tasted it. A man would go mad if mortality did not occasionally hold up the mirror. The Queen was to him the death's head at this stately feast.(78)

Wearing his crown and his robes of state, King George IV left the banquet at twenty minutes to eight, after nearly a day of ceremonies. 'The King's health and strength,' wrote Lady Sarah Lyttelton, from the rural fastnesses of Ryde, 'are astonishing. He certainly consists of iron and cable ropes.'(79) Scott was forced to walk home from Westminster (Lockhart says he was recognised and cheered by the Scots Greys); the Warden of Wadham College, Oxford, commendably acquired some of the great Coronation chandeliers for his Hall;(80) and Mr. Croker revelled in the fireworks, and in the Chinese bridges which, at his suggestion, had been thrown across the lake in St. James's Park.

The King immediately sent for Lawrence, and commanded him to paint a full-length portrait of him, in his Coronation robes, bearing his regalia, and seated in St. Edward's Chair in the Abbey.

61

On 25 July, over 2,000 people, Scott among them, attended the levée. At the drawing-room, a fascinated Jekyll saw His Majesty 'successively and tenderly salute the left cheeks of Ladies Hertford, Conyngham and Jersey'. Monarchy had its moments of embarrassment. And sometimes it seemed that the King could not escape adverse criticism. When he spent money, he was taxed with extravagance. When he failed to spend it, to give 'a Grand Fête or two in honour of the Coronation', Lady Cowper considered that 'it is not handsome towards the foreigners who came here'.(81)

The King was saving his energy for his imminent state visit to Ireland. He embarked at Portsmouth on 31 July. The visit was controversial from the first.

At Drury Lane (the debts of which the King had helped to discharge, two years ago), Robert Elliston had achieved a theatrical miracle. He had re-created the pageant of the Coronation. Determined that every detail should be perfectly reproduced, he had enlisted the help of Court officials. His designers had inspected the royal robes in advance; he himself, superbly regal on and off the stage, had rehearsed his cast of hundreds with the *Morning Herald* in his hand, and he had become so lost in the part of the King that he soon believed he was George IV in person. 'The spectator almost sees the real spectacle, and Elliston contrives to personate the King like a portrait.'(*82*) So wrote Joseph Jekyll, who had known the King for years.

On 30 July, in a moment of reckless anguish, Queen Caroline had chosen to go to Drury Lane, and the spectacle had proved to be her undoing.

At the time of the Coronation, and since (wrote Lady Anne Barnard, who was an old and faithful friend of the King), Caroline had been taking 'nervous medecines & laudanum'. She had done so without medical advice. Now, when she saw the Coronation graphically reconstructed, she felt the first ill effects. She had left her box, and returned to it when *God Save the King* was sung for the second time. 'When over, She got up and curtsied to the Manager, to the pit, Galleries & boxes in a manner so marked—so wild— with a countenance so Haggard, the disease hanging over her at the moment that the person who saw her do so, without loving her, burst into tears to see Royalty and Pride so broken down and Humbled.'(*83*)

It was her final public appearance. As the King cruised down the Channel, on his way to Ireland, it became evident that she was dying. She died on 7 August, from some internal obstruction, aggravated by over-medication. No doubt her death was hastened by a broken heart.

It could hardly have been more dramatic in its suddenness and timing. 'The Queen's death,' wrote one of her doctors, twelve days later,

is a striking Example of the Extreme uncertainty of all human speculations, for who could have guessed that she who but a Month ago was a source of terror and anxiety to all London and actually spoilt the Effect of the Coronation, would be now gone for ever. We have had an anxious and fatiguing time of it. I was up with her seven nights in succession and have scarcely yet recovered [from] the fatigue of it.*(84)*

There was, of course, a burst of public feeling at the event. *The Times* appeared with black columns and edges, and chose piously to mourn 'the greatest, perhaps the best woman of her day'. Lawrence, who, a year ago, had hastened to avoid her,· now closed the schools and library of the Royal Academy until her coffin had left Brandenburgh House. When Caroline's hearse set out from Hammersmith on its way to Harwich (for she had asked to be buried in Brunswick), there were outbursts of popular sympathy, and conflicts between the crowds and the troops.

The sympathy, hysteria and conflict were inevitable; and yet no thinking person could deny that the Queen's death was extremely convenient. An English correspondent, writing to Robert Finch from the distant tranquillity of Leghorn, wrote sensibly: 'As to the Queen (Peace be to her ashes!), I cannot help thinking that her Death is a fortunate thing for the Nation: for the mob are such Fools, that sooner or later, she might have caused some terrible catastrophe.'*(85)* Lady Anne Barnard combined compassion with her Scots good sense. 'Oh what a mercy it is that this country will be freed from an Influence such as hers, tending always to purposes of sedition—poor creature I hope her sins are forgiven her. . . .'*(186)*

The news of the Queen's death was given to the King, on 9 August, on board the *Royal Sovereign* at Holyhead. It would, as Croker said, be absurd to think that he was afflicted by his widowerhood; but he was affected by the news, and retired to his cabin, where he walked about for the greater part of the night.

The young Macaulay, who remained a partisan of the Queen's, demanded 'whether it is proper for any man to mingle in festivities while his wife's body lies unburied'.*(87)* The King made two concessions to bereavement: he would spend his first five days in Ireland in retirement, and he would allow six weeks' Court mourning. But he would not sanction general mourning, and he would not cancel his state visit. He refused to lament the wife whom he had detested for twenty-six years.

62

George the Fourth's state visit to Ireland was a predictable triumph. It was not only the first state visit of his reign, but the first that was ever paid to Ireland by an English sovereign. It was also that of a man who possessed the most endearing virtues of Irishmen. George the Fourth, throughout his life, had a quite extraordinary charm: men and women alike were enthralled by his consummate manners, his original conversation, his ironic humour, his vitality, his ebullient, disarming warmth of feeling. He was Irish in his changing moods of gaiety, depression, anger, fantasy. He was Irish in his impulsiveness, his generosity, and, above all, in his sense of theatre. George the Fourth was not only a king, he could play the part of sovereign better than any monarch since Elizabeth. If Ireland was a theatre, he was the actor for the part. Small wonder if, as Lord Cloncurry said in his recollections, 'a strange madness' seemed to seize the whole of Ireland, and 'there was nothing thought of but processions, and feasting, and loyalty'.(*88*)

The King himself, on board his yacht, was perfectly prepared to love the Irish: indeed, he had always felt a marked predilection for them. Years ago, when the House of Commons had fought to restrict his regency, the Irish Parliament had begged him to be Prince Regent of Ireland. 'I am a most determined Irishman,' he had declared at the time; and he was no less determined now. He remembered his admiration for Burke and Sheridan, his affection for his secretaries, McMahon and Bloomfield, and for Croker (a native of County Galway). Besides, the Conynghams belonged to County Meath, and he would honour them by a visit to Slane Castle.

There was now another, quite un-Irish, reason for the King to love Ireland: after twenty-six years of disastrous marriage, death had done what the House of Lords had failed to do. It had removed his wife. He was free at last. As Lady Anne Barnard wrote to Sir Andrew Barnard, the King's equerry: 'The Hemisphere will be much the clearer [now] that the Bolt hath burst and the storm is over.'(89)

Sir Andrew's answer made it plain that the air had cleared already. During the 'most delightful passage of six hours and a half by the steam boat', he noticed that the King was in great spirits, 'and it being his birthday', he recorded, 'we drank his health in sight of Irish land'.(90) Mr. Croker (in attendance as Secretary to the Admiralty) confirmed accounts of the royal happiness. The King, he wrote, 'was uncommonly well, ... and gayer than it might be proper to tell'. He also 'partook most abundantly of goose pie and whiskey'.(91)

At quarter past four on the afternoon of 12 August, his fifty-ninth birthday, the King set foot, at Howth, on Irish soil. He was wearing a plain blue surtout coat, buttoned close, blue pantaloons, a black stock, and a blue cloth foraging cap, with a gold band. 'He was in excellent spirits, and appeared much browned by the weather.' He shook hands with an old Connaught gentleman by the name of Denis Bowes Daly, he shook hands with a fisherman called Pat Farrell. The *Dublin Mercantile Advertiser* declared that 'he was among his People. It was really like the meeting of old friends'.(92)

There was not one soldier attending him as he drove from Howth to the Viceregal Lodge in Phoenix Park. He had an enthusiastic escort of Irishmen, some on horseback, others in coaches, jingles and outside cars. Before the procession was half way on its road, it had been joined 'by some dozens of farmers and gentlemen on horseback, and nearly two thousand pedestrians'. The procession constantly grew till it reached the Park. When they came to the gates, the King invited them to come to the door; and, before he entered the lodge, he made an impromptu speech:

My Lords and Gentlemen, and my good Yeomanry,

I cannot express to you the gratification I feel ... I am obliged to you all. I am particularly obliged by your escorting me to my *very door*.

I may not be able to express my feelings as I wish. I have travelled far. I have made a rough sea voyage—besides which, particular circumstances have occurred, known to you all, of which it is better at present not to speak. Upon those subjects I leave it to delicate and generous hearts to appreciate my feelings.

This is one of the happiest days of my life. I have long wished to visit you—my heart has always been Irish. From the day it first beat, I have loved Ireland. This day has shown me that I am beloved by my Irish subjects. Rank, station, honours are nothing; but to feel that I live in the hearts of my Irish subjects, is, to me, the most exalted happiness.

I must now once more thank you for your kindness, and bid you farewell. Go and do by me as I shall do by you—drink my health in a bumper. I shall drink all yours —in a bumper of Irish whiskey punch.(*93*)

Queen Caroline had been dismissed rather hurriedly on this, one of the happiest days of his life; but the speech remained a model of charm. What followed was, said one observer, a scene 'perhaps unparalleled in the history of English rule in Ireland'. The King shook hands with everyone who could approach him; he summoned three farmers from Swords to approach him, and would not let them kneel: he electrified the crowd as he shook them warmly by both hands. 'I was a rebel to old King George in '98,' declared an elderly man, 'and by God, I'd die a hundred deaths for his son, because he's a real king, and asks us how we are.'(*94*)

The King's visit appeared, indeed, 'like a blink of sunshine on the island'.(*95*) Not only was the weather quite Italian since he first set foot on Irish soil, but Orangemen and Catholics were acting together like brothers, at this extraordinary meeting of Irishmen. Noblemen might frown at the King's familiarity with labourers, Lord Kingston might observe that the King would spoil the lower classes by giving them such exalted notions of living—but the King had caught the heart of the peasants. He declared that every poor Irishman should have at least a cow, a pig and some fowl, and the forty-shilling freeholder whom he picked out at Howth soon received a milch cow and two pigs, on behalf of His Majesty. Several peasants were presented with pigs, fowls, and clothing; twenty poor children were given shoes and stockings. A deaf and dumb child, who wrote to the King, addressing him as 'Dear George', received ten guineas, and the royal admonition to be a good boy. Such gestures earned the devotion of the Dublin poor. And the upper classes, too, were swept up in the tide of loyalty; 'and I was carried on by the stream so buoyantly', wrote the once-rebellious Lord Cloncurry, 'that I gave a pledge of the sincerity of my own unconditional waiver of all bygones, by inviting his Majesty to honour my house by his presence'.(*96*)

The King lived in retirement, for five days, as a mark of bereavement; but he felt far from bereaved by the loss of his wife. It was hard to persuade him to wear mourning at his private levée, and a crape band round his arm for the rest of the time. On 14 August Queen Caroline's crimson coffin was taken from Hammersmith, on the first riotous, disgraceful stage of its journey home to Brunswick. On 17 August the King emerged, delightedly, from retirement, and made his public entry into Dublin.

Over his regimentals he wore the Order of St. Patrick, and as he stood up in his barouche, and bowed to the multitude in Sackville Street, he repeatedly held up his hat and pointed to the large bunch of shamrock which adorned it. Then he laid his hand on his heart, to show that the national emblem was rooted in his bosom. The procession was brought to a standstill for nearly an hour. The horses of the escorting dragoons were almost unmanageable; they were kept by the fluctuating pressure of the crowd in a state of constant motion, as if they were swimming. The

barouche itself was at times so shaken that the noblemen
who sat facing the King had to hold him up, under the
arms, to keep him erect. The Lord Mayor's toast of 'George,
King of Ireland' seemed, this day, to be heartfelt reality.

> Ere the Daughter of Brunswick is cold in her grave,
>   And her ashes still float to their home o'er the tide,
> Lo! GEORGE the triumphant speeds over the wave,
>   To the long cherish'd Isle which he loved like his
>   bride ...

> But he comes! the Messiah of royalty comes!
>   Like a goodly Leviathan roll'd from the waves!
> Then receive him as best such an advent becomes,
>   With a legion of cooks, and an army of slaves!

> He comes in the promise and bloom of three-score,
>   To perform in the pageant the sovereign's part—
> But long live the Shamrock which shadows him o'er!
>   Could the Green in his *hat* be transferr'd to his *heart*!

> Could that long-wither'd spot but be verdant again,
>   And a new spring of noble affections arise—
> Then might Freedom forgive thee this dance in thy chain,
>   And this shout of thy slavery which saddens the
>   skies ...(97)

Byron, in *The Irish Avatar,* savagely contrasted the desola-
tion of Ireland with the tinsel of royal pageantry; he could
not forgive the Irish for servility to a sovereign whom he
now despised as a despot. He sent his lines to Moore with
the comment: 'It is heartbreaking to see such things ...'(98)
Moore noted in his diary: 'Received Lord Byron's tremendous verses ... Richly deserved by my servile countrymen,
but not, on this occasion, by the King, who, as far as he was
concerned, acted well and wisely.'(99)

Moore deplored the servility of the populace, the inconsistency of politicians like Daniel O'Connell. But, as an
Irishman, he understood that his countrymen had been made

delirious by the contrast between rebellion and acceptance, oppression and good-will.

Meanwhile the King took possession of Dublin Castle. At the first and second Drawing-rooms, 'the fresh beauty of the Irish ladies, with their graceful and symmetrical forms and their soft and silvery voices, fairly won his heart'. On 23 August the Corporation of Dublin gave him a banquet in a room built for the occasion, representing the interior circular court of a Moorish palace open to the sky. Irish harpers strummed their lays, the King 'helped several guests at table to the inviting ingredients', the Lord Mayor grew excited and eloquent, the loyal toast was drunk with acclamations, and Mr. Croker declared that the finest incident of the evening was that after the cheers had subsided 'the distant cheering of the people in the streets burst in, . . . and gave an air of reality to the whole pageant'.(*100*)

Next day (the day of Caroline's midnight burial at Brunswick), the King attended an open-air *déjeuner* given at Leinster House by the Dublin Society. He went carefully round the museum, and then hurried away (too soon, thought Croker), perhaps because he was anxious to get to Slane. There, for three days, in the Conynghams' castle, he forgot the rain and the cares of royalty; he was once again, as he liked to be, in the midst of his family. Lady Conyngham ministered to his needs, the domestic life continued round him, he danced a jig at the ball which was given in his honour; he attended matins at Slane Church. By the time Croker arrived for dinner, that Sunday, to meet the Conynghams, the Bloomfields and the Attorney- and Solicitor-General, the King was radiating happiness. 'The pleasantest dinner I almost ever was at,' recorded Croker, who was not the least critical of men. 'The King in excellent tone and spirits, and the Attorney and Solicitor delighted with him. He pleasantly asked Saurin's legal opinion whether he might not stay where he was, and send Lord Talbot as Lord-Lieutenant to England.'(*101*)

Unfortunately there were still some functions which demanded his presence. Next day he attended the Trinity

College dinner in Dublin; the library had been turned into the reception room, and the theatre into the dining room, and both had been fitted up with great splendour and taste. The King, added Croker (who happened to be a graduate of Trinity), 'seemed much pleased', and the dinner went off very well. None the less, there had been a certain strain on the occasion, when 'some Sir Noodle', as Tom Moore expressed it, rose to praise the poetical talent of Ireland. After the gibes of *The Twopenny Post-Bag*, no one dared to mention Moore by name, and 'those cowardly scholars of Dublin College ... drank, as the utmost they could venture, "*Maturin* and the *rising* Poets of Erin".'(*102*)

The royal visit had been an entire, unprecedented triumph. The residence of a Court and the landed gentry in Dublin had given an immense impulse to trade. The King had asked 'that all his subjects should approach him in Irish manufacture', and the woollen trade had prospered, and the merino factory at Kilkenny had been busy preparing cloth for the King, his ministers, his officers and household. No gentleman, as the Dublin correspondent of *The Times* had said, would now 'appear in any cloth but that emanating from the Irish loom. If this be persevered in it will do more to promote Irish manufacture than all the speeches and fine promises that could be made in a century'.(*103*)

The King himself had averred his belief that poverty and disaffection would disappear in the presence of a resident gentry, and his advice to the landlords to live among their tenants had made a strong impression on the farmers; he had shown himself, in his words and in his benefactions, the poor tenant's friend. He was, as an Irishman observed, 'the first English Sovereign who opened the portal of kindness to the Irish people'; he had, by his Irish nature, melted the barriers of dissension. When, on 3 September, he took his departure from Dunleary (which was that day renamed Kingstown in his honour), the citizens of Dublin declared that

Your Majesty has banished every bad passion, and united six millions of a grateful people in a bond of brotherly love to one another, and of affectionate attachment to your Majesty's person and throne.

We confidently predict that the victory which your Majesty has thus obtained over the dissensions and prejudices of ages will be deemed the most important ever achieved by any British king.(*104*)

Daniel O'Connell ('pre-eminent in blarney and inconsistency', said Moore) earned a vicious stanza in Byron's *The Irish Avatar* by presenting the King with a laurel crown. The King received it with much grace, and said 'may God Almighty bless you all until we meet again'.

The view at this moment was magnificent. The hills were covered with people sending out what the Dublin *Morning Post* described as 'fringes of animation'. The beach was thronged for miles with spectators, the Royal squadron stood, beflagged and at anchor, in the bay, the cannon thundered and the bands played 'Patrick's Day'. The King was rowed out to his yacht (several spectators followed his barge until they were up to their necks in water); he stood on deck until darkness fell, waving his hat to the multitude on shore.

And so, as the twilight melted into the bosom of the night, and the stars came out heralding the stately moon, the passengers of the Royal squadron might have heard the hearty though distant farewell of a people whom George the Fourth, of all his race, seemed to have best understood.(*105*)

It is said that the King never fulfilled his promises to Ireland: that his age (he was fifty-nine) and political opposition prevented him. Certainly, when he gave his assent to the Catholic Emancipation Bill, he would do so much against his will. His visit to Ireland, despite his hopes and promises, was the only visit he made there; and it was remembered, wrote a critic, 'only as having incited Byron to compose *The Irish Avatar*, and by the erection of an unmeaning granite pillar at Kingstown'.(*106*)

Yet perhaps this comment was inadequate as well as ungracious. The value of the visit was much better suggested by a certain Mr. Bielby, writing to Robert Finch:

> Our most gracious [some MSS. read this word *graceless*] Sovereign *takes* prodigiously in *Ireland*—the Irish are absolutely out of their Wits with Joy; so that he is very likely to be new christened *Paddy* the 1st— Seriously, I think it is one of the wisest and most politic Acts of his Life; for his frank and noble manners are admirably adapted not only 'ad captandum vulgus' but all Classes and Degrees of Persons; and they have already voted to build him a royal Palace in *Dublin*....(*107*)

The palace in Dublin was never built; but the letter still suggests how Irish history might have been changed by more attention and affection. And, as Scott wrote to Maria Edgeworth: 'If there was no better result to the King's journey than that single temporary union of feelings and interests it cannot have been made in vain.'(*108*)

63

In the same letter to Miss Edgeworth, Scott declared his relief that the King had not paid an immediate visit to Scotland. After the joy which the Irish displayed, the more reserved Scottish manners would certainly have shown to disadvantage. 'But the German sour-crout and some of the not unwholesome bitters of London will,' Scott continued, 'sharpen his appetite for such fare as we can afford him. I should like to see old Holyrood in splendour for once.'(*109*) Miss Edgeworth had shrewdly suggested 'that Kennilworth [*sic*] put this royal progress & the CORONATION into the King's head', that some of his sayings had been imitations of remarks by Scott's Queen Elizabeth. Scott was flattered and thoughtful. Why should *Kenilworth* not inspire a visit north of the border?

In the meanwhile, in search of 'German sour-crout', the

King set out for his Kingdom of Hanover. Since Dover had acclaimed Queen Caroline the previous summer, he refused to set foot in the town. On 20 September, he embarked at Gravesend. He spent a night at Cliff House, Ramsgate, as the guest of Sir William Curtis, the banker, a former Lord Mayor of London and Member of Parliament. Then he sailed from Ramsgate to Calais.

The place 'was not a little shaken from its monotonous routine by that occurrence. Fishing-boats were laid up, and the fishermen set "all alive-O"—the authorities furbished up their old uniforms'(*110*) and the Duc d'Angoulême, sent by Louis XVIII to welcome the King of England to France, greeted him at Dessin's Hotel. It was, ironically, the hotel which had sent Queen Caroline refreshments when she had sailed home to face the Bill of Pains and Penalties. Now there was another sad figure to greet the King at Calais. As George IV acknowledged the applause of the bareheaded crowd, he saw Beau Brummell.

Brummell, now in rooms at Calais, was still wretched at his fall from favour. When his valet, Sélègne (an excellent cook), went to Dessin's that evening to make punch for the King, Brummell felt compelled to show his affection and contrition. Sélègne took with him, by his master's orders, 'some excellent maraschino, a liqueur to which he remembered the King was extremely partial'. The King was again reminded of Brummell: that evening, when he found himself out of snuff, the British Consul presented the box he had borrowed from the Beau. As the King took the first pinch, he asked: 'Why, Sir, where did you get your snuff? There is only one person I know who can mix snuff in this way.' 'It is some of Mr. Brummell's, Your Majesty,' answered the Consul. The King made no reply.

Brummell had inscribed his name in the book at Dessin's, he had observed the etiquette due to his sovereign; he had made two gestures of affectionate submission. He could do no more without a royal command.

George IV remained inflexible. Next day, as he seated himself in his carriage, he observed: 'I leave Calais, and have not seen Brummell.' He would be reminded of him, some time later, when Brummell was forced to sell his Sèvres china to an English auctioneer. The King paid two hundred guineas for a tea-set. But when, at last, the Beau obtained the sinecure of British Consul at Caen, he would do so by the grace of the Duke of York, and King George IV would be dead.(*111*)

In September 1821, as the King drove across the Continent, he included among his suite a counsellor of high and growing significance. He had often been a friend to members of his household—his family, as he was pleased to call them; but it is doubtful if he ever felt for any of them the respect and devotion which he felt for this grave and steadfast doctor. 'I can scarcely believe my own history,' wrote Sir William Knighton to his wife. 'It is more like a romance than anything else.'(*112*)

William Knighton had been born at Beer Ferris, in Devonshire, forty-six years earlier. His education had been modest: he had gone to school at Newton Bushel, before he was placed with his uncle, a surgeon and apothecary at Tavistock. But Knighton had always been a friend to the arts; he had striven to improve his mind, and, even as a surgeon's apprentice, he was writing poetry. In his nineteenth year, he had come to London; he established such a reputation in medicine that the Marquis Wellesley had taken him on an embassy to Spain. Wellesley had recommended him to the Prince of Wales, and in 1810 he had been appointed one of the Prince's physicians. In 1812 the Regent had created him a baronet, and in 1817 he had made him auditor of the Duchy of Cornwall, and Secretary and Keeper of his Privy Seal and Council Seal. Knighton had given up part of his profession. He had helped to marshal the facts to support the Bill of Pains and Penalties. He had grown still closer to the King, still more essential to him; and when, a month ago, off Holyhead, on his way to Ireland, the King had heard the news of the Queen's death, it had been to Knighton that he wrote:

Continue, I conjure you, from time to time, and constantly if you can, to let me hear from you, be it only that 'all is well'; for even this is a security and comfort to me that you cannot imagine: it is utterly impossible for me to tell you how uncomfortable and how miserable I always feel when I have not you immediately at my elbow.(*113*)

The King was not a strong-minded man; he was glad of an adviser who was loyal, steady, wise and, if necessary, downright. He needed an ever-present counsellor who would treat him with respect but speak to him, at times, with determination. Knighton was fourteen years younger than the King; but his profession had given him good training. He had the quiet authority of a doctor. He was a responsible man, with an understanding of human nature. He had a sound understanding of his Sovereign.

It is also clear, from the letters he sent home to his wife, even from his complaints and criticisms, that he felt a deep affection for him. 'My king, God bless him! never gives me a moment,' he wrote from Brussels, on 28 September. 'The pen is never out of my hand by day, and it is his wish that I sleep in his dressing-room at night; so that he has access to me at all hours....'(*114*) Knighton was the perfect adviser: steady and understanding, discreet and authoritative. He also considered that he belonged to the King.

The visit to Brussels was delightfully gay. When the King and Queen of the Netherlands gave a dinner for George IV at the palace of Laeken, the company were bewildered to find that 'both the King and Queen, without any apparent cause, were at every moment breaking out in violent convulsions of laughter'. The Duke of Wellington, who knew the King's histrionic powers, suspected the reason: the King was mimicking an old stadtholder whose idiosyncrasies had been a standing joke at Carlton House. Such was his mimicry that the King and Queen 'could not maintain their composure during the whole of the day'.(*115*)

Wellington gaily told the story to Thomas Raikes, eleven years later; he still felt the King's fascination. 'He was indeed,' said the Duke, 'the most extraordinary compound of talent, wit, buffoonery, obstinacy, and good feeling—in short a medley of the most opposite qualities, with a great preponderance of good—that I ever saw in any character in my life.'(*116*) And to the admiration of Knighton and Wellington was added that of Lady Anne Barnard, who had known the King for thirty-six years. In this autumn of 1821, she thanked Sir Andrew Barnard, his equerry, for sending her 'such frequent accounts of two personages I love very much, the King himself & the King's friend. I have been delighted,' she wrote, 'through your progress to observe that *He* has been carried through all sorts of dangers and difficulties by a certain Gas which is better than any the steam engine affords, the fire of an ardent mind a good constitution and a now happy heart....'(*117*) Sir Andrew himself was much attached to the King. 'I feel proud & gratified,' he had declared, 'at being one of his servants—I trust ... that the whole people of England will appreciate his great and good qualities in the same manner that those do who have had the happiness of seeing them more closely.'(*118*)

On 1 October 1821 the King and his party reached the momentous village of Waterloo; the King went into the little church, examined all the tablets on the walls, and visited the willow tree under which Lord Anglesey's shattered leg was buried. In torrential rain, accompanied by Wellington, he 'examined every part of the various positions occupied by the army in that dreadful battle'. At Dusseldorf, where he arrived on the evening of 3 October, the whole garrison marched out by torchlight to serenade him; and the style in which they played *God Save the King* was enough, wrote Knighton, 'to electrify one'. As they neared Osnaburg, in the King's own dominions, the roads grew so bad that the horses had to be changed every five miles; but the primitive discomforts of travel were alleviated by the welcome of the Hanoverians, who had not seen a King of Hanover for sixty-three years. Arches of evergreens and flowers spanned the village roads down which the royal carriages bumped and lumbered. Osnaburg was illuminated, and its citizens 'almost mad with joy'. On the evening of 7 October, to a salute of a hundred and one guns, they entered Hanover itself. The King's open carriage was drawn by eight milk-white horses, and surrounded by the pride of the kingdom; he underwent the fatigue of a second coronation, as King of Hanover, he reviewed his army, received civic deputations, and joined in a grand hunting party at Diester. The King of Ireland had worn the shamrock, and danced an Irish jig; the King of Hanover spoke German, and wore the Royal Hanoverian Guelphic Order (which he had founded six years earlier). Once again he established himself as a patriot king.

He was also quick to use his favourite prerogative of mercy. Soon after his arrival, an almost destitute woman, the mother of eight children, came to beg clemency for her husband, who was serving a five-year prison sentence. The King's Hanoverian chamberlain turned her from the palace; but Knighton saw her, and found that her husband's crime could be pardoned, 'and this was done by the King with his pen instantly.' 'The dearest King,' as Knighton called him, 'the beloved King,' was readily moved to mercy. Nor was he afraid to be a man of sensibility. When the University of Göttingen presented him with an address, the ceremony was so impressive that he openly wept. Those who disliked him dismissed such emotion as maudlin, facile, and even contrived. It was more probably the natural feeling of a vulnerable man.

64

On 8 November the King arrived in London from Hanover, 'in perfect health', Sir Thomas Lawrence reported to Angerstein, 'and the better for being thinner'.(*119*)

He returned from the acclamations of Hanover to a kingdom which treated the Royal authority and the King himself 'with a striking degree of levity. . . . No reformers,' wrote Mr. Croker, 'if they knew the whole secret, would wish to reduce the monarch lower in real and effective state and power than his Ministers place him.'*(120)* His Majesty's Ministers could hardly help deploring his private life: they remembered the Queen's affair with distaste, they had objected to the political power of Lady Hertford, and they now resented the interference of Lady Conyngham. Some people even seemed to resent the King's taste of popularity. When Tom Moore, at the outset of the Hanoverian visit, observed: 'The wind is fair for the King to-day,' his companion answered: "Damn it, everything's fair for him.' Lord Blessington, giving supper to Moore during the royal tour, quoted some witticisms about the King: among them the disloyal toast: 'May the King come home in *spirits*'. Byron wrote ominously to Moore that if the King married again, 'let him not want an Epithalamium —suppose a joint concern of you and me ...!'*(121)*

Byron's suggestion fell on deaf ears. Since the Irish visit, Moore, at least, had been converted to monarchy. When the *Morning Chronicle* published some political epigrams he wrote to his compatriot, Mr. Croker, 'begging him to set them right as to any suspicion they may have of me'. He had not published any political verse worth mentioning for some years; 'and with respect to the King, if I occupied my-self about him at all, it would be to praise him with all my heart for his wise and liberal conduct in Ireland'.*(122)* Croker replied that slight as this compliment to the King might be, he read it with pleasure, 'and should hail a *rapprochement* between us on that point with real gratification'.*(123)*

The King was soon on his way to Brighton where, so Jekyll forecast, he would probably make a long stay as usual. His Ministers always grumbled when he went to the Pavilion: they resented the difficulties it imposed on correspondence, and the journeys they were forced to make to Sussex. Robert Peel had to go to Brighton when, on 28 November, he accepted his seals as Home Secretary.

The King's relationship with Peel brought out the virtues in both men. It proved Peel's tact, his civilised tastes, and, at times, his clemency. It emphasised the King's lifelong interest in the arts, and his most endearing humanity.

The criminal law in the 1820s was a law of Draconian severity. One of George IV's earliest acts as King had been to abolish the legal use of torture in Hanover; and he was well aware that in England executions were frequent and brutal, and that often the young were hanged for trivial offences. ('In England,' a visitor would write, in 1827, 'children are independent at eight and hanged at twelve.')(*124*) But even death must at times have seemed better than transportation, which meant exile in savage conditions on the far side of the world. It was Peel's task, as Home Secretary, to advise the King on the royal prerogative of mercy; and this prerogative was one that the King always hoped to exercise. In April 1822 he asked Peel 'to make every possible inquiry into the case of the boy Henry Newbury, aged thirteen, and to commute his sentence from transportation, in consideration of his youth, to confinement in the House of Correction'.(*125*) The sentence was commuted; but in May the thought of a mass execution caused the King oppressive anxiety:

> The King quite approves of Mr. Peel's humane recommendations respecting Davis; but what is to be done concerning his accomplice, Desmond, who is of the same age? Is there any opening for the other poor young man Ward? The King would be truly glad if such could be found.
>
> The King wishes to express to Mr. Peel his warm approbation for his active humanity.(*126*)

The active humanity belonged to the King. Within three hours he was writing an urgent postscript:

> The King has received Mr. Peel's note, and he must say, after the deepest reflection, that the executions of to-morrow, from their unusual numbers, weigh most heavily and painfully on his mind.
>
> The King was in hopes that the poor youth Desmond might have been saved ...
>
> The King therefore desires that Mr. Peel will select for

mercy two besides Ward, so that four, for the same crime, may only suffer in the place of eight, and the King trusts in God that this extension of his royal clemency will answer every purpose of justice.(*127*)

The King's clemency proved to be greater than that of his Ministers. Peel summoned the aid of the Cabinet, and overruled the royal commands. Desmond was transported for life, but Ward was hanged next day.

A year later, the King begged Peel to spare a youth who had been condemned for uttering forged notes. Peel answered that he had consulted the Lord Chancellor, who strongly felt that the law must take its course. The King expressed great regret that they could not recommend mercy, 'a word more consoling to [his] mind than language can express'; but it seems that on this occasion Lady Conyngham had asked him to intercede, and Peel had determined to show disapproval of her interference. He had, said his biographer, 'resolved, if the King persisted, to send a respite, and resign his office'.(*128*)

Meanwhile, in the winter of 1821, when Peel became Home Secretary, even Mme de Lieven could only accuse Lady Conyngham of accepting pearls and diamonds. 'Is it really possible,' she asked, 'to be in love with a woman who accepts diamonds and pearls?'(*129*) One sometimes suspects that Mme de Lieven was a little jealous of Lady Conyngham. When on 1 January 1822 the King ushered in the new year with a concert, she was not averse to being seen beside him on a sofa in the music-room of the Pavilion. She was back again at the end of January, complaining of an inflamed eye, and the heat of the Pavilion and the lamps, and recording the fascination and repulsion of this Kubla Khan palace. 'I do not believe that, since the days of Heliogabalus, there have been such magnificence and luxury,' she told Metternich. 'There is something effeminate in it which is disgusting. One spends the evening half-lying on cushions; the lights are dazzling; there are perfumes, music, liqueurs—"Devil take me, I think I must have got into bad company." You can guess who said that.'(*130*) It was Wellington, who had dined there for the first time.

The King himself was far from happy in his Heliogabalus palace. He was tortured by gout; his nerves were so on edge that the sight of a crooked candle caused a storm of abuse. He had also just dismissed a confidential servant of fourteen years' standing, and expelled Sir Benjamin Bloomfield from his 'family'. The handsome military figure no longer appeared in 'the magic lantern', the small glass-walled sitting-room in the Pavilion to which only the household favourites were admitted.

Bloomfield had first come to royal notice as a young artillery officer, stationed at Brighton, who was proficient on the violoncello. He had been asked to the Pavilion, and charmed the Prince of Wales by his musical skill and, no doubt, by his Irish vitality. In 1808 he had joined the 'family' as a Gentleman Attendant, four years later he had become Chief Equerry (a function which he combined with that of Member of Parliament for Plymouth). In the year of Waterloo he was knighted, the following year he was Auditor of the Duchy of Cornwall, and in 1817, on the death of McMahon, Bloomfield had become the Keeper of the Privy Purse. He had then been appointed Private Secretary.

The existence of this influential and, at the time, irregular office had caused dissatisfaction in the Government and uneasiness in the country at large; but while a placid, responsible man might have continued to hold it, Bloomfield had made it increasingly clear that he was not fit for the task. Now that the Regent had become King, he was less inclined than ever to have a secretary who harassed him by his temper and offended him by his familiarity. In January 1822 the King wrote to Lord Liverpool:

As the Government is now, I hope, fixed on a settled and firm basis, I am desirous that we should have no impediment or interruption to our permanent tranquillity.... With this view it has occurred to me ... that perhaps it might be desirable to get rid of the office of Private Secretary. This, however, cannot be done without making an extended provision for Sir Benj. Bloomfield, because I think it is desirable that he should quit the Privy Purse also, for by thus retiring entirely from my family, it would be the means of saving both myself and the Govt. much inconvenience, arising from the natural consequence of mistaken power and patronage.(*131*)

It was a delicate decision. The King asked the Government to take it on themselves, and to provide 'most amply' for Sir Benjamin; and, naturally generous, he decided that Bloomfield should be offered the Governorship of Ceylon, the Order of the Bath and the first available Irish peerage.

Bloomfield accepted the Red Ribbon, but refused Ceylon and demanded to have a British peerage. The more difficulties he created, the more relief the King must have felt that he had dismissed him from his service.

I wish you to state [he told Lord Liverpool in March], that when the inordinate power of the late office of Private Secretary is retrospectively look'd at, I am bound to say, that the Government have acted wisely ... when they recommended its abolition; but I must however be plain, & therefore have no hesitation in saying, that my ready acquiescence in the measure was entirely influenced, by the embarrassment & painful distress I suffer'd, in consequence of Sir Benjamin Bloomfield's unhappy & oppressive temper; and likewise the change that had been gradually taking place for the last two years, in his general demeanor.

Having made this explanation, tell him if you please, that I have no resentment whatever, that I shall do his good qualities ample justice. . . .(*132*)

The following year, Bloomfield was appointed Envoy Extraordinary to the Court of Sweden. Like Canning's appointment, this March, as Governor-General of India, the honour had the appearance of tactful exile.

But political stability and personal irritation were not

the only reasons for Bloomfield's fall. Lord Liverpool appears to have known, quite as well as the King, the ultimate cause of this domestic change.

> Lord Liverpool and Lord Londonderry [wrote the Prime Minister on 5 March] beg leave most humbly to represent to your Majesty, that they consider it to be of the utmost importance (whatever domestick arrangement your Majesty may be desirous of hereafter making respecting Sir William Knighton) that nothing should be done in this way, at the present moment....(*133*)

The 'present moment' to which Lord Liverpool tactfully referred, lasted only a few months longer. Before the year was out, Sir William had been appointed Keeper of the King's Privy Purse, and in September he ceased to practise as a physician. On 26 October the King directed him 'to undertake the entire management of my affairs'.(*134*)

65

While the King remained in Brighton, irascible and melancholy, his subjects were admiring his likeness in London. Joanna Baillie went by invitation from Lawrence to inspect his picture of the King in Garter robes; it had been commissioned by the Pope, no doubt in exchange for the portrait of the Pontiff which Lawrence had painted. 'A very admirable, splendid gallery piece,' Miss Baillie announced to Scott; 'and yours is the best likeness of you that I have ever seen.... It is very honorable for the King himself that he has desired to have such a picture. I shall think the better of him for it as long as I live.'(*135*) One can only think the better of him for his wish to commemorate his friend: to pay this double tribute to the arts.

On 11 February Lawrence sent the papal portrait of the King to Portsmouth; it was to be embarked on the frigate *Euryalus,* with Mr. Hamilton, the new Minister to Naples. The journey proved to be an odyssey. In mid August,

Charles Eastlake, the artist, wrote to Lawrence from Rome that the portrait had not yet arrived. 'Where it now is I know not,' he confessed in some anxiety, 'but the Euryalus is no longer at Naples and I think I heard she was gone to Corfu—Canova thinks the delay is owing to the Admiral wishing to present your work in person.'(*136*) Did the portrait remain on the frigate for another three months, drifting round the Ionian Sea, awaiting the admiral's pleasure? The delay is difficult to explain. But it was not till November that Lawrence's friend, Pietro Carnuccini, told him, with unfeigned relief:

> I can not help informing you, that at last your beauti-
> ful Picture of his Majesty's Portrait is arrived at Rome.
> ... This morning ... we placed it in the Chamber
> opposite to the door of the Pope's bed room. The Light
> was beautiful, it was about ten, and the weather delight-
> ful: His Holyness came out of his bed chamber, was
> quite pleased [*sic*] with your performance, and sat for
> a very long time before it. My Brother told His Holyness,
> and the munificent Cardinal, that it was a happy thing
> for Rome to posess [*sic*] your masterpiece, as a Pattern
> like that, is quite wanting for the young artists in
> Rome....(*137*)

The King's fertile influence on the arts might be seen in many places. After his visit to Ireland, a large public sub-scription had been raised to erect some monument to the event. Michael Banim, the novelist, urged his compatriots to erect a building for the newly-established Hibernian Academy; in April 1822 Lawrence agreed to recommend such an application of the funds. Art had its permanent centre in Dublin.

The Prospero touch of the King was seen, magnificently, in his capital. Southey, coming to London for the first time since the hectic summer of 1820, found it 'so altered as to have almost the appearance of a new city. Nothing that I have seen elsewhere', he told Landor, 'can bear comparison with the line of houses from Regent's Park to Carlton House. A stranger might imagine that our shopkeepers were like the merchants of Tyre, and lived in palaces'.(*138*)

In Edinburgh, Constable, the publisher, sent Scott a letter from Dr. Kitchener, who was busy arranging a selection of national songs. 'I wish very much,' wrote Kitchener, 'to have as the first song a sort of *new God Save the King,— i.e.* a Song to be called "God Save Great George the Fourth" which I intend to set to Music, myself.... The Song, for as good a King as ever graced Great Britain's throne, should be written by the best Poet Great Britain boasts, need I say that I mean Sir Walter Scott?'(*139*) The problem of finding rhymes to 'Fourth' proved too much even for Scott; but in his reply to Constable there remain the lines he heartily attempted:

> Winds bear the accents forth
> East west and south and north
> Long live King George the fourth
> God save the King,(*140*)

Meanwhile, the King's private life pursued the uneven tenor of its way. He moved from Brighton to London, and held a levée on 11 April; he returned to Brighton, and slammed the door in Lord Liverpool's face for refusing a prebend to one of the Conyngham tutors. His anxiety to please Lady Conyngham continued; and Lady Conyngham saw fit to have 'an attack of prudishness', and would not go near him. The prudishness, reported by Mme de Lieven on 27 April, had passed by 12 May. Lady Conyngham, noted Lady Cowper, 'has behaved rather kinder to him lately, and been often to see him, *un peu de froideur* now and then is not perhaps amiss, par[ticularl]y as he has no resource at hand. He talks soon of removing to the Cottage'.(*141*) 'A King sighing for a Cottage sounds like a moral reflection,' she added, drily, a few days afterwards. 'Here it is not *exactly* that.'(*142*) However, by 2 June any coldness had disappeared, and Mme de Lieven had gently told Lord Londonderry (the former Lord Castlereagh), the Foreign Secretary, that Lady Conyngham could not be opposed. On

6 June, Lady Cowper, returning from a visit to the Cottage, or, as they called it now, the Royal Lodge, Windsor, reported that the King had spent a day driving Lady Conyngham in a little pony-chaise; he was in good spirits and very good humour, and 'any thing *so tender* as he was the first day I never saw before'.(*143*)

The King, when he was in good spirits, was heartwarming company. Charles Mathews, the comedian, was commanded to Carlton House this summer, to give some of his famous imitations. The King shrewdly criticised his Curran, and applauded his Kemble. 'Your Kemble is excellent ... I used to fancy my own imitation of him was very true. I had a great regard for Kemble; he was my very great friend. I'll suffer no one to speak a word against Kemble.' A few days later, Mathews was offered a hundred guineas from the privy purse 'in token of the pleasure his Majesty has derived from Mr. Mathews' superior excellency in ... his profession'.(*144*)

The King was a better judge than most of such imitations. Not long ago he had reduced the King and Queen of the Netherlands to helpless laughter by his mimicry of an old stadtholder. Now Croker, dining off roast wild boar at the Pavilion, was treated to an impersonation of an old and mumbling French duke. 'I never heard anything so perfect,' wrote Croker, 'in the way of imitation of voice, matter, and manner.'(*145*) The King could be grave as well as gay: he then praised Richard Tickell, the pamphleteer and dramatist, and lamented that he had not known him, and been able to save him from suicide. '(Tickell had killed himself in 1793, jumping from the parapet outside his room at Hampton Court.) The King quoted some of Tickell's work, 'and went off into a dissertation on *taste* and *genius*'. After coffee, he sang Italian trios 'at the forte piano', with the two Misses Liddell. The band was in the long gallery, and there, on a sofa, sat old Michael Kelly, the tenor, who had been the first Basilio in Mozart's *Figaro* in Vienna; the King found time to go out and speak to him.

His interest in people was manifest; his interests in literature were wide. Next day, at dinner, Croker confessed that he had edited Lady Hervey's letters, and had published a few anecdotes which he had heard from the King. The King

> said that if I had consulted him and let him into my secret, he would have afforded me still more. He was, he said, a great *reservoir* of anecdote, for he had lived not only with all the eminent persons of the last fifty years, but he had had an early acquaintance with several eminent persons of the preceding half century....(*146*)

This was to be a musical evening, and after dinner the King never left the pianoforte. He sang in *Glorious Apollo, Mighty Conqueror, Lord Mornington's Waterfall* (which was encored), *Non nobis, Domine,* and several other glees and catches. 'His voice, a bass, is good,' wrote Croker, diplomatically, 'and he does not sing so much from the notes as from recollection. He is, therefore, a musician, far from good, but he gave, I think, the force, gaiety and spirit of the glees in a superior style to the professional men.' Then Michael Kelly was wheeled in, 'in a gouty chair, and sang the solo of *Sleep you or wake you,* with all the force of a broken voice; in it, however, there were the remains of better than the other men could now produce'. Lady Conyngham did not conceal her boredom with all this music.(*147*)

66

'If our Fat Friend makes good his word,' wrote Sir Walter Scott to John Morritt, on 18 February 1822, 'there will be plenty of gaieties for Miss Morritt and Gatherings of the Gael and cocking of bonnets.'(*148*) Scott had always found it easy to accept honours and hospitality, and to make coarse jokes about the giver (years ago, when the Regent was fired at, Scott had simply observed that the assault would 'make him a good manageable boy'). But if Ireland had welcomed the King, Scotland could not remain inhospitable;

and Scott had already suggested a state visit to His
Majesty. Early in May, Mr. Thomas Mash, of the Lord
Chamberlain's Office, was ordered to go to Holyrood and
prepare it for a royal visit. Since the King was fascinated
by the House of Stuart, Mr. Mash was instructed 'not to
meddle with the room which was occupied by the Earl of
Darnley, the husband of the unhappy Queen Mary'.

The King planned to visit Scotland the following year,
1823. This year he hoped to go to Vienna. But his Ministers
were increasingly against a Viennese journey. As Wellington
told Lady Cowper at Almack's, it would have the worst
possible effect if the King spent money lavishly on the
Continent, especially as his object was mere amusement.
The Government finally forced the King to abandon Vienna,
and he decided instead to go to Scotland. On 24 June, in
Edinburgh, Sir Walter Scott received official notice that His
Majesty would arrive about 12 August, 'though scarce with
the purpose of going to the moors'.(*149*)

Next day came a second communication to say that the
royal visit was suspended on medical advice. Scott was
on tenterhooks. Four days later the rumour of the royal visit
revived. On 16 July Scott was still in uncertainty; and,
writing to the parson poet, the Reverend George Crabbe,
with the hope of seeing him in Scotland, he added: 'If the
King comes I must be at Edinburgh for a day or two, but
I fancy you will avoid that period of tumult and bustle.'(*150*)
And then, within the week, Crabbe was forgotten, and the
King had decided to come north. On 22 July Scott was
telling the 21st Macleod of Macleod: 'Arms and men are
the best thing we have to show him. Do come and bring
half-a-dozen or half-a-score of Clansmen, so as to look like an
Island Chief as you are.'(*151*)

While, at Dunvegan Castle, Skye, the Macleod of Macleod
prepared to obey Scott's injunction, the novelist himself
undertook most of the organisation of the visit. He alone
had prestige enough to rouse his sober countrymen, in three
weeks, to stage a pageant fit for majesty. He alone knew
enough Scottish history to become the arbiter of tradition.

He was the obvious director for this national performance, this projection of Scottish character. He set to work with Gaelic determination.

He had to arrange everything, it is said, from the order of a procession to the cut of a button. He had to wine and dine and inspire the intractable and indifferent. He had to retrieve Montrose's sword, which he usually kept in the armoury at Abbotsford: it had been sent to London for a new sheath. The correspondence burst like a snowstorm out of Scott's house in Castle Street. Did Lord Melville think the King would like to hear Alexander Ballantyne play the flageolet? Would Peel persuade 'the High Personage who makes us all happy and half crazy' to attend the Edinburgh theatre? If His Majesty agreed to a command performance of Rob Roy.... The stamp of Scott was everywhere. 'No one could well believe,' wrote Lockhart, Scott's son-in-law and biographer, 'the extent to which the Waverley and Rob Roy *animus* was allowed to pervade the whole of this affair.'*(152)*

Byron was moved to write five caustic lines in *Don Juan* on 'this scene of royal itch and loyal scratching'; and a loyal subject in Leith tossed off a song, to be accompanied by the bagpipe;

> ...Cannons tongues and Bagpipes bummin,
> Tell the world that GEORDIE'S comin:
> Geordie's comin wi his woman
> Coninghame an a's comin ...*(153)*

The song remains, understandably, in manuscript. However, the tireless Scott composed *Carle, now the King's come*: an imitation of a Jacobite ditty; and everyone in Edinburgh was no doubt singing it, broadsheet in hand, to the tune of *The Campbells are Comin'*:

> We'll cock our blue bonnets, aha, aha,
> Our Scottish blue bonnets, aha, aha,
> We'll busk on our tartans—the gatherin' blaw,
> King GEORGE the Fourth's comin,' huzza, huzza! *(154)*

The Scotsman, on 3 August, considered the royal visit

more soberly. 'Except in promoting the consumption of beef and wine, silks and mercery, to all appearance it will leave the country exactly as it found it. Still, it is an act of politeness in his Majesty to come and see us, and we have no doubt that he will experience a suitable reception.' This was a dour allusion to the Irish visit of the previous summer, and *The Scotsman* made it perfectly clear. There would be no Dublin delirium in Edinburgh: 'The conduct of the Irish, when the King was at Dublin, ought to be a lesson to us.... We are sure that the sagacity of our countrymen will appreciate what is due to the official station of Majesty—what to private character—what to public conduct;—and that they will so conduct themselves as not to give his Majesty reason to misunderstand their sentiments.' Loyal subjects do not often administer such implicit rebukes to their sovereign.

However, consignments of eagles' feathers and plumes for bonnets duly arrived in Princes Street, not to mention London Welcome Buttons, with the motto: 'You are Welcome, King!'; and the ladies of Edinburgh were invited to buy the Royal Welcome Parasol. *The Scotsman,* level-headed as ever, warned them to practise the difficult art of retiring, unassisted and backwards, from the presence; for long trains might prove embarrassing to those who were unused to them; and 'most painful must be the situation of a young female who is so unfortunate as to make a *faux pas* on such an occasion'.

On 10 August the King embarked at Greenwich for Scotland. He looked very well and in high spirits, reported Lady Cowper, and everyone said it was a beautiful sight.

The King could not have been quite so happy as she suggested. On the previous Friday he had given an audience to Lord Londonderry. He had been shocked by the Foreign Secretary's condition: Londonderry had talked wildly about being the victim of conspiracies, and when the King told him he was mad, Londonderry had begged him not to tell his colleagues. The King had advised him to see a doctor. He had not slept that night.

However, as the *Royal George* sailed up the east coast, towards Leith, the gilt coat-of-arms on its prow gleaming in the sunshine, and the gilt tiller cutting through the North Sea, the King could, for a few hours at least, be divorced from cares. Handsome dishes were brought to the dining-room from the spacious galleys, where 'the cooking process [was] wholly managed by steam'.(*155*) The weather was kind; and ahead of him lay the sort of royal progress at which he excelled.

As the royal yacht approached Leith, the final prepara-tions were made in Edinburgh. Labourers from outlying districts came, equipped with bannocks and whisky, to wait for the royal arrival. A large body of the Campbells marched in, 'fine, manly, and martial, . . . to strengthen the domestic guard of the King'. The last decorations were put in place: the *Mercury* office showed a transparency of the King receiving the keys of the city from Edina, while Mercury waited to convey the glad news to the nation. Thistles, crowns, stars and ciphers were prepared for illumination, and the legend 'Welcome to Auld Reekie'.

At about two o'clock on the afternoon of 14 August, the *Royal George* dropped anchor in Leith Roads. Peel, as Home Secretary, was rowed out to pay his duty. He had just returned on shore when a messenger arrived from Lord Liverpool in London:

> I must beg of you to break the dreadful intelligence of which this messenger is the bearer to the King.
>
> Poor Londonderry is no more: he died by his own hand at nine o'clock this morning [August 12]. There never was a clearer case of insanity.(*156*)

Peel went back at once to the King, 'and broke to him as cautiously as possible this most melancholy intelligence. He seemed,' so Peel told Lord Liverpool, 'almost prepared for it. . . . He spoke of Lord Londonderry in the warmest terms of affection and admiration, and bitterly lamented his loss.'(*157*)

The King had little leisure in which to indulge his grief;

from the moment the yacht dropped anchor till late in the evening, steam-boats were constantly plying round her, filled with cheering crowds. From time to time he was obliged to appear on deck, and bow 'in return for the gratulations'. He was also obliged to receive several visitors from shore; and the first, of course, was Sir Walter Scott, who arrived by barge to welcome His Majesty, and present a silver St. Andrew's Cross from the ladies of Edinburgh. The King vowed to wear it in his hat. He offered Scott a glass of cherry brandy. Scott, forgetting all his gibes at 'our Fat Friend', all his Jacobite sympathies, begged to keep the glass as a memento.

He returned home wet and hurried, with the glass in his back pocket. And at home, by some miracle of inopportunity, he found a guest: the Reverend and venerable George Crabbe.

Scott sat down beside him. As Lockhart wrote: 'His scream and gesture made his wife conclude that he had sat down on a pair of scissors.' The royal brandy glass had been forgotten.

'I dined with Sir W. Scott the day before I left Edinburgh,' wrote Sir Humphry Davy to his brother. '[He] is, in fact, master of the royal revels; and I was very much amused to see the deep interest he took in the tailors, plumassiers, and show dressmakers, who are preparing this grand display of Scotch costume.'(*158*)

It was, indeed, a grand display that they were about to show the King; and Scott's house, which had been like a fairground from seven in the morning until midnight, now 'rang with broadswords & targets & pipes from daybreak to sunset', as three hundred Highlanders used it as their headquarters. The morning after Crabbe's arrival, Scott found him in the parlour, dressed with the utmost clerical neatness, with buckles in his shoes. He stood in the midst of half-a-dozen stalwart Highlanders, exchanging elaborate civilities. The chiefs (who thought him a foreign bishop) were busy speaking Gaelic, while the bewildered Crabbe was excusing his ignorance of French.

Crabbe's Gaelic breakfast could not be prolonged: tha
day the King was to enter Edinburgh. He sat in the stern
of the royal barge till it reached the middle of the harbour;
then he rose, and stood till the barge reached the landing
place. He wore the full-dress uniform of an admiral, with
the St. Andrew's cross and a thistle in his gold-laced hat.
According to one account, he also wore a sprig of heather,
'which harmonised well with the national feeling of his
Scottish subjects'.

Edinburgh melted in his presence. As he entered the city,
his carriage guarded by the Royal Company of Archers and
a prancing detachment of Scots Greys, the crowds noticed
approvingly that his face lit up at 'the magnificence of the
scenery.... In passing along York Place and St. Andrew's
Square, his MAJESTY, as we understand, expressed himself highly gratified with the splendid appearance of the
city ... His MAJESTY, on viewing the buildings on the
Regent Bridge, exclaimed, "How superb", an expression
which was certainly most happily applied'.(*159*) The King
was quite determined to appreciate the Scots; and nothing
warms the heart like appreciation. When he declared:
'They seem to be a nation of gentlemen,' the Scots forgot
all caution: they were delighted by such evident discern-
ment. On 17 August, *The Scotsman*, though hardly tactful,
sounded less severe than usual:

> His Majesty must now be satisfied, from ocular demon-
> stration, that the people of Scotland—of all classes—are
> *truly loyal,* by which we mean, that they are attached
> to the laws, and anxious to pay every rational mark of
> respect to the CHIEF MAGISTRATE OF THE STATE.
> The King was welcomed by the body of his Scottish
> subjects—not with delirious joy, as in Ireland—not with
> anything like sycophancy, or undue servility—but with
> that deference and high regard which a free people may
> evince towards the *Head of the Government.* The de-
> meanour of the people was most creditable to themselves.
> That of his Majesty courteous and apparently grateful.
> ... His Majesty repeatedly took off his hat and bowed

to the spectators. His complexion was rather more sallow than we expected, and his physiognomy, though but slightly touched with the characters of age, seemed to us less youthful than it is generally represented in engravings. . . .

This last remark, it must be added, was not strictly true: the citizens of Edinburgh were entertained by a libellous broadsheet on the English Irish Highlander, representing a flaccid monarch in the tartan; and the same obese figure reappeared in a coloured cartoon, *Landing of the Old Amorous Dandy!!!* Here the Falstaffian sovereign was being greeted by courtesans who were kissing the hem of his kilt. 'I shall na be surprised if he sees me,' observed one to another, 'it will be all over wi' my Lady Cunning-one'; and a third buxom subject interposed: 'Show yoursel' my Lady E-, ye'r Fat, Fair, and Forty, and that's his favourite.'

However, while Lady Conyngham remained south of the border, George IV proved himself to be no Falstaff, but a portly, handsome man, looking and moving every inch a King. He held a levée at Holyrood House, and wore full Highland dress, 'and became the tartan of the Stuarts'. He held a court at Holyrood, 'danced with the young, talked with the old, and won the hearts of all. . . . In uniting dignity with hilarity in his meetings with his subjects,' wrote Lloyd, the King's biographer, 'no monarch ever possessed the art of George IV.' When he agreed to attend the Caledonian Hunt Ball, he insisted on Scots reels and strathspeys in abundance. 'None of your foreign dances,' he is reported to have said. 'I dislike seeing anything in Scotland that is not purely national and characteristic.' The remark was quoted in the press; it was very likely true. The King had a natural desire to please; he also had a strong aesthetic sense.

And he possessed (which is not always a failing in a king) a fine sense of theatre. He saw the part he had to play, and he played it with an assurance that his old friend, Kemble, would have envied. As he rode, in his field-marshal's scarlet, in procession, from Holyrood to Edinburgh Castle, the curtains might have been parting in Drury Lane.

The cannon soon told from the lower batteries that the King of Scotland stood upon the summit of Edina's grey crest.... And though the lowering fog prevented his MAJESTY from enjoying the fine and extensive view, it threw a dark sublimity over the whole, and the broken outlines of cliff, and crag, and turret, came out with the most imposing effect. The KING expressed himself highly delighted; and when some of his attendants regretted that it rained, he said, with a smile, 'Never mind, I can wave my hat'.(*160*)

The whole ceremonial of the procession to Edinburgh Castle had obviously been arranged by Scott to recall 'the Ridding of the Parliament'. Peel had wanted to see it privately, and walked up the High Street with Scott some time before the procession was due. Years later, Peel remembered telling him: 'You will never get through in privacy.' Scott had said: 'They are entirely absorbed in loyalty.' But Peel had proved the better prophet; the lame, white-haired figure of Scott was recognised from end to end of the street, and never, wrote Peel, 'did I see such an instance of national devotion expressed'.(*161*)

Scott was certainly omnipresent. His son and nephew had figured in the procession to Edinburgh Castle. The King duly watched a command performance of *Rob Roy*; and when he attended a Grand Civic Banquet in the Outer Parliament House, it was again the son and nephew of Scott, dressed as pages, in crimson and white, who brought in a basin and ewer of silver for His Majesty to wash his hands. This service, it appears, had its origin in a story which had been told to the King by Scott himself, and His Majesty was highly amused with it.

When the King retired from the banquet, having given two toasts and made three speeches, the Earl of Errol aptly proposed 'Sir Walter Scott, for the trouble he had taken with the King'. Scott, in his quiet, deliberate manner, replied with transparently false modesty. He was, he said, 'totally unconscious of deserving the high honour now paid him'.

However, on 28 August, the eve of the King's departure, Peel was instructed to send Scott a fulsome letter of thanks. 'His Majesty well knows,' wrote Peel, 'how many difficulties have been smoothed, and how much has been effected by your unremitting activity, by your knowledge of your countrymen, and by the just estimation in which they hold you.' Any references to 'our Fat Friend' were conveniently forgotten as the author of *Waverley* composed his answer.

While I am sensible [he replied] that his Majesty's goodness has far overrated any service I may have rendered, ... it is my pride to think that my zeal at least was evident, and his Majesty's approbation of my conduct expressed in such very gracious terms makes me one of the happiest men in these dominions, which his reign makes generally happy. ...(*162*)

The King was to leave on 29 August; on his way he called on the Earl of Hopetoun, who had a magnificent house by the Firth of Forth. There, in the great saloon, he knighted Henry Raeburn, the portrait painter and President of the Scottish Academy, and commanded him to come to London and paint him in Highland dress. The honour took Raeburn almost by surprise—he had only known about it the previous evening—and, doubtless, in his sixty-seventh year, he had not expected to receive it. Raeburn's knighthood 'conferred equal credit on the giver and the receiver. His brother artists,' wrote his biographer, 'considered it as a noble tribute, which threw new lustre on themselves and their profession.'(*163*) It was one of the chief art events of the year; and it was plausibly said that the King had been so struck with Raeburn's handsome presence 'that he would have made him a baronet could he have done so without injustice to the memory of Reynolds'.(*164*)

The following May he appointed Raeburn his first limner and painter in Scotland. Raeburn did not live to enjoy his office. He died two months later; and the Royal Highlander's portrait remained unpainted. It was Raeburn's fellow-countryman, David Wilkie, in 1825, who contemplated 'a splendid painting relative to the King's visit to Holyrood House'.(*165*)

On 29 August 1822 George IV embarked at Leith for London, to follow the route which the steamboats had been plying for the past year.

But if the King had gone, the effects of the Royal visit remained. Scott was now roundly criticised for his ostentatious part in the proceedings:

> It is a pity [wrote a journalist] that the author of *Waverley* should deem it important to figure in every part of a corporation pageant.... Sir Walter, with very bad taste, went on board the Royal yacht uninvited, on the evening of the King's arrival in Leith roads, in stormy and wet weather, and selected the moment his Majesty was receiving the news of Lord Londonderry's death, as the proper opportunity for presenting the King with the Ladies' Silver Cross....
>
> [At the Lord Provost's banquet] Sir Walter was placed at the head of the centre table, and immediately facing the King; it was of all others the place best adapted for any person who wished to attract his Majesty's notice, and the manner of Sir Walter during the dinner was such as to manifest no disinclination to be the object of that distinction; but how vain are human speculations! The King drank repeatedly to the personages round him at the head of the table, but Sir Walter did not immediately catch the Royal eye; he had, however, an expedient left, and he lost no time in trying it—it was a bottle containing some soul-melting beverage which he uncorked and sent to the King. His Majesty then filled a glass to the Baronet, who rose and made two suitable obeisances in acknowledging the honour; and thus he took leave of his sovereign. Sir Walter's friends ought to permit his reputation to rest upon other matters.(*166*)

Scott himself had certainly not lost by the visit; he had

earned wide publicity, the gratitude of the King, and the friendship of Peel. And though Knighton's first impression of him had been unfavourable ('he has no trace in his countenance of such superior genius'), Scott had finally won Knighton's interest. He had done so at a critical moment: Knighton was about to abandon general practice as a physician, and become, in Scott's fine phrase, 'the great Invisible': the confidential adviser, the indispensable servant, as well as the closest friend of the King.

Scott was not slow to ask for favours. He was soon composing a petition for the return of the cannon, Mons Meg, which had been removed from Edinburgh Castle to the Tower of London, after the capitulation of 1745. He was also asking the King to reverse the attainders of 1715 and 1745, and restore the Scottish peerages which had been forfeited in the insurrections. Mons Meg was returned to Edinburgh Castle in 1828, and the peerages were duly restored. The King showed a becoming sense of gratitude.

And when, on 2 September, he landed at Greenwich, and Mr. Croker, of the Admiralty, received him, he began at once to tell him 'all about our friend Scott'. As Mr. Croker told the author of *Waverley*: 'Some silly or malicious person, his Majesty said, had reported that there had been some coolness between you, but, he added, that it was utterly false, and that he was, in every respect, highly pleased and gratified, and, he said, *grateful* for the devoted attention you had paid him.'(*167*)

Scott developed 'an inflammatory complaint' after all his exertion, good living, and anxiety; early in October his legs and arms were still 'spotted like a leopards'. For two months he could not mount a horse. He was behind with *Peveril of the Peak*. But he was still dreaming of the royal visit, which seemed to him now 'like the awakening of Abou Hassan to a dream of sovereignty', something very wild and chivalrous, like a scene from Froissart. The King's loyal subjects, in Edinburgh, were subscribing for an equestrian statue of George IV; but their native caution had returned: the subscription was inadequate, and the horse had to be dispensed with.

The King himself, with the spoils of his visit; an orrery, a sermon, and a knife, fork and spoon which had once belonged to the Young Pretender, the 'unfortunate Chevalier', as he called him, anxiously inquired of Mr. Croker whether Lord Liverpool was in a good humour, 'almost as a boy after holidays asks in what temper Dr. Busby may be'.(*168*)

67

The Prime Minister (who sometimes resembled that famous headmaster of Westminster School) had an exceedingly delicate task to perform: he had to persuade the King to appoint Canning as Lord Londonderry's successor. It was true that, six months earlier, on 27 March, Canning had been appointed Governor-General of India; but the qualifications for this post were more readily found than the combination of toughness and finesse, historical sense and practical ability, demanded for the control of foreign affairs. Canning's chief title to India had been his compromising part in the Queen's affair; and this, of course, was also his chief disqualification for the second highest office in the Government. It would not be easy for the King to work closely with the man who had made, in the King's own words, 'almost an open avowal of a criminal intercourse' with his wife.

Lord Liverpool recognised that the task of winning the King's consent needed more than ordinary diplomacy. The King must be persuaded by a Minister whom he trusted and respected: a Minister for whom he felt affection. It was only a few months since Lord Liverpool had had the door slammed in his face at the Pavilion, because he had offended the Conynghams; he felt uninclined to attempt a delicate personal negotiation. Some people had thought that Peel might be a candidate for the post of Foreign Secretary. Lord Liverpool enlisted Peel to persuade the King to name Canning. On 8 September, within a week of the King's return from Scotland, Lord Liverpool received the King's agreement to the admission of Canning into his service. 'I am,' he told Peel, 'most anxious to give you the earliest information of the King's decision, as I think it due to you on every account, and not the less for your handsome and disinterested conduct throughout the whole business.'(*169*)

The King's letter to Canning was not, perhaps, the most tactful he had written. He could not resist an allusion to the past: 'The King,' he explained, 'is aware that the brightest ornament of his crown is the power of extending grace and favour to a subject who may have incurred his displeasure.'(*170*) Canning could hardly acknowledge such grace and favour with humility. But then, as Lord Liverpool observed, the letter to Canning had been written 'with as much delicacy as, considering the King's strong personal feelings, could reasonably be expected'.(*171*) The King himself deserved some credit for the appointment of Canning as Foreign Secretary on 17 September.

He deserved credit, too, for less spectacular actions: for sanctioning the re-publication of 'a regular series of the ancient historians of the kingdom'. It was he himself who suggested a national military archive: accounts of all the battles in which British troops had been engaged, histories of all the regiments, records of famous soldiers, and paintings of the captured colours and trophies. The Poet Laureate—the Crown Poet, as a Dutch admirer called him —was warmed by a private communication from Knighton:

> I am commanded by the King to convey to you the estimation in which His Majesty holds your distinguished talents, and the usefulness and importance of your literary labours. I am further commanded to add, that His Majesty receives with great satisfaction the first volume of your valuable work on the late Peninsular War.

At the head of the letter were the words: 'Entirely approved. G.R.'(*172*) It was rewarding to write for such a sovereign.

It was delightfully rewarding to paint for him; and while

the officious Southey never entered his inner circle, Lawrence was clearly counted among the King's friends. If any recollection remained of his part in the Delicate Investigation, it was now far back in the King's mind; he was more than gracious to his painter. It is true that he was sometimes vexed by his dilatory manner; but he admired his skill, respected his judgment, and appreciated his charm of manner, his easy, fluent conversation. It was Lawrence who discussed with him the subject for a picture by David Wilkie, when His Majesty 'so distinctly' rejected that of John Knox. It was Lawrence who, as President of the Royal Academy, had received a warning from Knighton on 14 July that the King would visit the Exhibition next morning, soon after ten, 'and it is His Majesty's Pleasure, that *You* should be in readiness at Somerset House, at that Hour, to receive Him'.(*173*) Now, on 14 October, from Windsor, Knighton sent Lawrence word that the King wanted him to paint Sir William Curtis for his gallery of friends; he intended to give Sir William a portrait of himself. That night, from his home in Hanover Square, Knighton sent a second note, which suggests the warm relationship between the King and his principal painter-in-ordinary:

Dear Sir Thomas
   The King desires to have the pleasure of seeing You on Saturday Morning, at Breakfast—Under these circumstances, You will perhaps obligingly permit me to sit to You on Friday morning, and ... on Saturday morning I shall have great Satisfaction in taking You to Windsor in my Carriage....(*174*)

Posterity may guess one topic discussed over breakfast at Windsor; a few days later, Lawrence told the Council of the Royal Academy that the King had presented them with 'ten Casts of Statues from the Antique, brought from Berlin, called the family of Lycomedes, and that he had had the honor of personally offering thanks to His Majesty'.(*175*)

68

The New Year, 1823, opened sadly enough. Mme de Lieven, visiting the Pavilion early in January, found that the King had greatly aged in the past three months. He was limping noticeably; on 4 February he was still too unwell to open Parliament, and it had to be opened by commission. His ill-health was a gift to his critics. Soon afterwards, he read a statement in the *Sunday Times*, said to be made on authority, that his disorder might be hereditary madness.

The King, out of health and much out of spirits, was shaken by such malicious insinuation; he had been hurt long enough by the gibes and caricatures of the Press. He wrote to Peel:

> The King desires, if the law can possibly reach this infamous attack, that the Attorney-General should lose no time in attending to it.
>
> The King is obliged to observe that some steps should be taken with respect to Sunday papers. Why not treble the duty upon all Sunday newspapers? The King reads everything of this kind, and feels it a duty to do so; hence the King can judge of the mischief resulting from this abused liberty of the press.
>
> These observations are equally applicable to obscene prints in the form of caricatures. There is scarcely a shop in London that deals in such trash in which the King is not exposed in some indecent, ridiculous manner. This is now become a constant practice, and it is high time that it should be put a stop to.(*176*)

Peel raised the subject in Cabinet; but the law officers of the Crown advised against a prosecution. They foresaw, all too clearly, the possible inclinations of a London jury. The King had to take the libel in silence, though any common citizen would no doubt have won the case.

It was not only journalists and caricaturists who attacked

the King: he was also attacked in Parliament. A few weeks later, thanking Peel for his management of the King's Property Bill, he wrote with understandable resentment: 'It is not surprising that the King should feel indignation at the attempt made to misrepresent everything that relates to himself, whenever the opportunity occurs, by a certain set in the House of Commons.'(*177*)

It is hard not to feel some sympathy for him. While he was libelled and ridiculed in public, he was also treated with indifference by Lady Conyngham. Glancing round her drawing-room (which was 'like a fairy's boudoir'), she burst out to Mme de Lieven: 'What a pity, now, if all this were to end!' She was fonder of pearls and diamonds and elegant furniture than she ever was of the King. By April he was once again in a wretched state of health, crippled by gout, and hobbling round on crutches. In mid May he had a relapse: he had erysipelas on the foot, and a high temperature, 'Poor King, what a sad life he leads!' cried Mme de Lieven. 'How I should mourn him if he were to die!'(*178*) 'I am in horror,' wrote one of Creevey's correspondents, 'at the thought of the King's dying.'(*179*) Lady Conyngham was practical rather than horror-stricken; and Mme de Lieven observed 'many arrangements being made in the Marchioness's household, that look as if she were taking precautions'.(*180*)

The King himself was well aware that Lady Conyngham was pushing her family (her husband was Lord Steward of the Household; her son, the Earl of Mount Charles, was First Groom of the Bedchamber and Master of the Robes); he must have known, in his heart of hearts, that she was not in love with him. But he had grown accustomed to her, he was reassured by the domestic habit of her presence. He chose to ignore her silly, superficial nature, just as he bore with the criticisms of the public. He remained forgiving and generous to both.

69

In January he resolved to present his father's library, more than 65,000 volumes, to the nation. The Trustees of the British Museum welcomed the collection, and asked Parliament for funds to build a library 'worthy of the taste and dignity' of Great Britain. The King's generosity was matched by that of Parliament. The House of Commons voted £40,000 to begin the work. Robert Smirke drew up a plan, and the foundation of the King's Library was laid within the year. In due course 'this truly noble Collection was removed into the Museum, where it remains a splendid monument to the Munificence of GEORGE THE FOURTH'.(*181*)

The generosity was not entirely appreciated. 'At the same time I admire the munificent gift his Majesty has made,' wrote Samuel Woodburn, the art collector, to Lawrence, 'I cannot but regret a reservation was not made for objects of yet greater importance. Was the Museum to make a sale of the Duplicates of the rare and valuable Books now in their hands the produce would be sufficient to begin a National Gallery of pictures....'(*182*)

Woodburn showed inadequate appreciation of the King's Library; but he was wise to urge the foundation of a National Gallery. Many owners of fine pictures had been impoverished by the long Napoleonic wars; many buyers of different nationalities were now competing keenly in the Continental market. England was rich, she was ruled by a fervent amateur of the arts; and, in the new and noble London that was swiftly rising, there was no place to house the national treasures. Woodburn, who was living in Rome, had already offered to help buy pictures abroad for the Gallery, when it should be founded; now, in January 1823, he wrote to Lawrence more insistently:

> I can with great sincerity declare that my ambition would be completely satisfied was I to see the commence-

ment of a Grand National Gallery in London.... My national spirits is chagrined when I see the Russians offering for and purchasing fine things which ought to adorn the present Capital of the Globe. I think I am not mistaken when I suppose that was you to mention to his Majesty the absolute necessity there is in this enlightened period of our Capital being the most powerful attraction his Majesty would not be unwilling to forward the Arts by a Step which the late King ... from the want of fine old paintings did not establish.(*183*)

Woodburn was preaching to someone who had long since been converted. Lawrence, too, considered a National Gallery essential to English dignity and greatness; but, more aware than Woodburn of the labyrinthine ways of officialdom, he could only see the Gallery, at present, 'through a very long vista of approach'.

The National Gallery did not, in fact, lie far in the future; in the meanwhile, any Londoner could see a hundred signs that the arts were flourishing. The Houses of Parliament were being enlarged and enriched to the designs of Soane. There was to be a new royal entrance to the House of Lords: the *Scala Regia*, or *King's Staircase*, the Royal Gallery, and the Lords' Library. The new entrance and *Scala Regia* were said to have been suggested by the King, who found the old entrance 'mean and insignificant, altogether unworthy of ... a British Monarch'.(*184*)

It was well that Soane should leave his mark on the Houses of Parliament; for 'that fellow Nash', as a vexed contemporary called him, was now, without any doubt, proclaimed to be the Regent's architect. Once he had built a huge rotunda in the gardens of Carlton House, in which the Regent might entertain Wellington. Now his work was spreading over London. He had built Regent Street, he was working on All Souls' Church, and on Regent's Park with its nine terraces; and, just before the Coronation, Soane had received a hard blow to his pride: the King had asked for all the plans of Buckingham House to be sent to Nash.

In the Royal Academy that year, Soane had shown a bird's-eye view of his own design for a new royal palace. According to the Office of Works—of which he was an attached architect—Buckingham House was in his department. There was no doubt that if it was to be altered or rebuilt, he should have undertaken the task. But he made his protests in vain. The Surveyor-General answered that he could not go against the King's wish.

Perhaps some uneasiness on Nash's part helped to explain the ill-advised way in which he went to work. Buckingham Palace—as it would be called—was begun without any proper consideration or plans, and it was to involve him in censure from the Treasury and from Parliament. He himself would admit his dissatisfaction with his building. The most lamentable part of the whole affair would be the destruction of old Buckingham House, which contained some fine early Adam work executed for Queen Charlotte.

Soane (who had dedicated a book to George III), protested against the destruction of an historic house; he wanted to build a new palace on Constitution Hill. But the King was determined to live on the site of Buckingham House: 'there are early associations which endear me to the spot'. When, in 1827, he examined one of Soane's designs, the ageing architect felt the King's condescension deeply: it was, he said, the only opportunity he had had of showing his designs to the Sovereign, since His Majesty was Prince of Wales. Humiliating though it was, he asked outright for a sign of royal favour. Charles Long, now Lord Farnborough, replied that some honour might well be given to 'the architects who are building palaces for the King, whenever in the course of next year His Majesty takes possession of them. I should hope also the same honour may be conferred upon you'. Soane was, in fact, expected to wait his chance of a knighthood with Wyatville, at Windsor, and Nash, in London. Such treatment was both irrational and unjust.

Soane continued, desperately, to angle for honour: in

1829 he sent the King his latest volume of architectural designs; he contributed £1,000 towards the statue on the Duke of York's column. But he would not receive his knighthood until he was seventy-eight. It would be George IV's successor who knighted him.(*185*)

As Lord Farnborough had implied, the King's interest in building was not confined to London. Now that the Pavilion was finished at long last, he turned his attention to Windsor Castle. It was the wreck of a mediaeval stronghold, a gaunt, uncomfortable building, overcast by associations with the old, mad George III. In 1823 the King decided to remodel it; and the taste, the sense of dignity and, not least, the romanticism of George IV would transform the 'rambling crudity' of Windsor into the very prototype of a castle. If Brighton showed his pleasure in oriental fantasy, Windsor showed his deep English sympathies: it would not merely be the most royal of the royal palaces, it would, as he intended, be a proper symbol of English sovereignty.

Windsor Castle was only the most majestic of the King's artistic enterprises. The year which saw the idea of the Windsor transformation, saw numerous other artistic undertakings. When Charles Eastlake, the artist, wrote to Lawrence in January about a new institution for English artists in Rome, he suggested that the plan might not be 'devoid of interest to the Throne'.(*186*) Lawrence approached the Great Invisible, who had long been a friend to the arts, and managed the King's finances with much skill; in April the King offered £200 from his privy purse 'for the professional use of the English Students at Rome'.(*187*)

We one and all [came the answer to Lawrence] feel raised by this Royal Attention—w[h]ether we consider it as giving a 'local habitation and a name' to our Infant Institution—or as [a] fine Compliment to our noble pursuit.

We pray you Sir—to present to His Majesty our most grateful thanks—and expressions of attachment for His

most gracious notice of *us* and our views—when we are
so far away from our Native country.(*188*)

It was appropriate, and eminently touching, that the letter
came from Joseph Severn who, three years earlier, had gone
to Rome with Keats.

The King was the natural patron of artists: the one to
whom they turned instinctively. When Haydon found himself, this year, imprisoned for debt, Miss Mitford promptly
suggested: 'Pray try the King; I have great confidence in
his kindly nature.' It was, however, clear that the King
used his own discretion in patronage. On the death of
Raeburn, Sir Walter Scott, with his usual self-esteem, suggested a candidate for the post of His Majesty's Limner
in Scotland. One detects a judicious note of rebuke in the
Home Secretary's reply: 'Had I received your letter before
I wrote to the King, I doubt whether it would have convinced me of the propriety of appointing an amateur.'(*189*)
The King very suitably appointed David Wilkie, but it
is a measure of his manners that he had a graceful letter
sent to Scott, informing him of Wilkie's appointment. It
was soon announced that Wilkie would perform the task
which his predecessor had left undone, and paint his
Sovereign in Highland dress.

Turner, too, might have left some fine, romantic commemoration of the royal visit to Scotland; but though he
had made a point of seeing all the ceremonies, the result
was only a series of sketches and two unfinished paintings
of the King at the civic dinner, and the King at St. Giles'
Cathedral. Turner's record of the reign of George IV was
not as spectacular as it might have been. In the latter part
of this year, he was working on a large painting of the Battle
of Trafalgar, which had been commissioned by the King.
The *Examiner* said that this was part of an ambitious
scheme: there were to be three Grand Galleries at St.
James's Palace, to be named after George II, George III
and George IV; they were to house a series of pictures of
battles by land and sea, and portraits of the most distinguished commanders of all three reigns. The grandiose,

patriotic scheme would have been characteristic of George IV; but, unhappily, it was not realised. When Turner's picture was hung, the Government were dissatisfied with it; and it was later presented to the Naval Hospital at Greenwich.(*190*)

Cambridge, like Greenwich, was to show a new sign of royal favour. The King's interest in scholarship was magnificently emphasised when, on 12 August, his birthday, by his command, the Speaker of the House of Commons laid the first stone of the new quadrangle—to be called The King's Court—at Trinity College (the King himself had subscribed £1,000 towards it). The royal enthusiasms were wide, and they were widely felt. The Lord Chamberlain was made well aware of the King's active interest in dramatic art: this autumn he was asked to explain why he could not extend the licence for the Haymarket Theatre. Long ago, as Prince of Wales, the King had promised to be a founder-subscriber if the Comédie-Française sent a permanent company to London. Now the Lord Chamberlain felt obliged to assure him that, personally, he would be delighted if a French theatre was licensed in London, but he felt that the institution would cause anti-French riots.

The King's touch was felt in literature when, this year, a Latin work under Milton's name, *De Doctrina Christiana*, was discovered in the State Paper Office. It was translated, edited, illustrated, and handsomely published by royal command. In June, at the first meeting of the Royal Society of Literature, the President recalled that

to His Majesty's love of learning, and desire to promote the Literature of His Country, the Society owes its existence ...

That a Society of Literature should have been so long wanting in a country eminent for its works of History, Poetry, and Philology, cannot but excite surprise; but it is not surprising that it should have originated from a Sovereign, the most distinguished for his classical knowledge and taste, since the reign of Queen Elizabeth.(*191*)

The first ten Royal Associates of the Society included Coleridge, T. R. Malthus (the author of *An Essay on Population*), and Sir William Ouseley, the orientalist. And since literature was not then an exclusive occupation, the Fellows of the Society soon included Chantrey, the sculptor, Matthew Wyatt, the architect, and Sir Thomas Lawrence. On 10 December, addressing the students of the Royal Academy, Lawrence himself showed noble confidence and a proper sense of royal achievement:

> The present auspicious circumstances indicate an approaching aera, that may teach us to look with less regret on the splendour of the past—A People more informed on the subject of the Fine Arts; a Legislature alive to the importance of encouraging them; a Government adopting measures to secure for them the noblest examples; and a gracious monarch to command its efforts! at all times the munificent Patron of this establishment, and whose reign has not been more the glory of his people, than their advancement and happiness are his reward.(*192*)

While Lawrence was addressing the students of the Royal Academy, an eminent Italian composer and his wife were making their slow and tortuous way to England. On 7 December the Rossinis had left Paris on their way to London: a journey which, incredibly, seems to have taken six days. It was now seven years since the first production of *Il Barbiere di Siviglia*, and Rossini's fame was established; but even so he must have been gratified when, soon after his arrival, Count Lieven called on him at 90 Regent Street, to say that the King would like to be the first person to see him.

The invitation may have owed a little to the fact that Rossini had met the ubiquitous Mme de Lieven in Verona; but it owed more to the King's familiar 'passion for music'. Rossini, it is said, acknowledged this signal attention in proper terms. He had had a rough passage across the Channel, and he was suffering from the combined effects of exhaustion and a bad cold. He explained that the state of his health forbade him to profit forthwith from the King's invitation, 'but he promised to inform his Majesty as soon as he got better, and in the meanwhile to receive no visitors'. He kept his promise of isolation: when his nerves did not confine him to bed, he took a pet parrot and sat on the top of the colonnade, which then adorned Nash's noble Regent Street, watching the stream of carriages below. On 29 December Count Lieven drove him to Brighton.

The King, who was 'playing at cards with a lady', received him cordially. He asked him to take a hand at *écarté*, but Rossini modestly declined, saying that he would rather not have so powerful an opponent. After a brief conversation, 'which seems to have left a very agreeable impression upon Rossini', the King invited him to hear his band; and, taking him by the arm, he led him into the music room. Rossini, he said, would now hear some music which might not be to his liking. 'But I have only chosen the first piece,' added the King. 'After that the band will play whatever you wish.' The first piece must have been more or less to Rossini's taste, for it was the overture to his own opera *La Gazza Ladra*.

Rossini had already discovered which were the King's favourite pieces. He now asked for them, and pointed out 'their characteristic beauties'. And, since it was to be an evening of graceful gestures and reciprocated compliments, Rossini finally told his host that he had never heard *God Save the King*, except on the piano, and that he would like to hear it performed by his excellent band. The King was evidently gratified.

'We had Rossini last night,' wrote Harriet, Countess Granville, to Lady Morpeth. 'He must have been much pleased with his reception; the King was quite enraptured at having him. The singing is delicious, such varied powers of expressing whatever he pleases. He is a fat, sallow squab of a man, but with large languishing eyes, and *des traits* which justify his thinking himself, as they say he does, something very irresistible.'

During the evening, it is said, the King presented Rossini 'to all the principal personages of the Court'. His manners were not appreciated as highly as his music. 'The courtiers and the rest of the society were indignant at his familiarity,' Countess Granville told the Duke of Devonshire. 'Being fat and lazy, and consequently averse to standing, he took a chair and sat by the King, who, however, gave him the kindest reception, and, less *petit* than his suite, understood the man, and treated him as his enthusiasm for music disposed him to do.'

As a result of the King's introductions, a committee of lady patronesses organised two concerts for the composer's benefit at Almack's. All the most famous singers in London offered him their services, and refused remuneration. The King gave a Grand Music Party, at which, said the *Morning Post,*

> Rossini was seated at the pianoforte and accompanied himself in two songs, one of which, an *Aria Buffa,* he gave with true comic spirit and humour; the other, Desdemona's beautiful Romance, from his own *Othello,* he sang most divinely, with exquisite pathos and expression of voice and countenance: his voice is a good clear tenor. His Majesty honoured him several times with marks of his royal approbation.(*193*)

Two apocryphal stories remain: it is said that Rossini once accompanied 'the vocal efforts' of George IV himself; the King—a bass—got into the wrong key, but Rossini continued to play as though nothing untoward had happened. 'It was my duty,' he explained, 'to accompany your Majesty. I am ready to follow you wherever you may go.' The other story is less graceful: at a grand concert at St. James's Palace, the King said, 'Now Rossini, we will have one piece more, and that shall be the *finale*'. 'I think, Sir,' replied Rossini, 'we have had music enough for one night.' And he made his bow.(*194*)

Whatever the truth of these stories, it is a fact that Rossini and his wife stayed in London until the end of July 1824; and, as a final mark of esteem, the King asked the Duke of Wellington to give an evening party so that he might hear Rossini once more before bidding him fare-well. A few years later, when Weber was on his way to London for the production of *Oberon*, he asked Rossini for letters of introduction. Rossini gave him a letter to George IV, and the two composers ended a feud of long standing.

Rossini used to say that Alexander I of Russia, and George IV of England, were the two most amiable crowned heads he had met; and he declared that 'of the charm of George IV's personal appearance and demeanour it was scarcely possible to form an idea'.(*195*)

70

There were always those in the world of the arts who re-mained petulant and unsatisfied. One of the most pathetic was Haydon, the historical painter; his diary and corres-pondence show a fire, conviction and pictorial brilliance which were often lacking from his canvases. This convic-tion and fire were, ironically, inspired by the belief that he was misunderstood. The friend of Keats and Wordsworth, Hazlitt and Lamb, he devoted his life to a form of art which, he felt, received no patronage. He espoused the cause of historical painting; and, as time went on, his devotion to his cause grew fanatical. He was obsessed with the belief that the world refused to listen to his gospel, to see the truth.

Haydon's obsession verged towards insanity; he also felt a sense of persecution. He had been imprisoned for debt: 'I who have talents to be an honour to my Sovereign & have been a glory to my Country.'(*196*) He had made the grave mistake of attacking the Royal Academy, and he felt that this would bar him from conventional success, and prevent him from gaining royal favour. 'My character has been so blackened to His Majesty,' he wrote, early in 1824, 'that I will venture to say if my name is mentioned he thinks of

me only as a Radical & Revolutionist.'(*197*) The thought of
Wilkie's new appointment as the King's Limner in Scotland
made Haydon bitter with frustration. Wilkie, he said, had
already offended the King 'by some awkwardness & want of
presence of mind'; Wilkie's painting of the King at Holyrood lacked both grace and taste, and Wilkie had put the
King into jackboots because he could not do justice to his
legs. The thought of his own unrewarded cause enraged
him. When he suggested a royal commission to encourage
historical painting, John Lambton, the politician, answered
that the King was too old to take an interest, and that
any commission must be set up later. 'Yes, sir,' said Haydon,
'if genius could be raised like lettuces, it would be right to
wait.'(*198*)

Lambton's purpose was no doubt to discourage an embarrassing fanatic; for the King, at sixty-one, was by no
means too old to take a lively interest in the arts. He was
'perfectly delighted' that Parliament had allowed him
£300,000 for the restoration of Windsor; it had put him
in an excellent temper with his Ministers. And when Colonel
Stephenson, of the Board of Works, had dared to interfere
with his orders, it had taken all Peel's uncommon tact to
smooth the matter over.

It was this year that Jeffry Wyatt began the transformation of Windsor Castle; and when the King laid the
foundation-stone of Wyatt's accepted design, he let him
change his name to Wyatville. The change was a Gothic
affectation, but it was not a 'meaningless augmentation';
Wyatville had no doubt wanted to assert his professional
independence of his famous uncle, James.

Whatever his foibles and vanities, he established himself
—as surely as Nash—as the architect of George IV. He
demolished twelve houses in the Castle precincts, rebuilt
the Chester and Brunswick Towers, repaired the Devil's
Tower, and designed the George IV Gateway (the King
allowed him to include it, with the motto 'Windsor', on
his coat-of-arms). He designed the York and Lancaster
Towers, the new terrace, and the orangery. He made the

Round Tower some thirty feet higher, and the additional height gave it an extraordinary new grandeur. He converted the old Brick Court and Horn Court into the state staircase and the Waterloo Gallery. He not only transformed the Castle itself: he built lodges, a boat-house, a hermitage, and the ruins at Virginia Water, which were chiefly composed of fragments from Tripoli.

While his architect was restoring Windsor, the King himself sat to Wilkie for the Holyrood picture. 'What an opportunity,' cried Haydon, 'to pour into his ear sound views of art, and high notions of public encouragement!'(*199*) The King approved of Wilkie's painting, and reminded him to include the 'ancient figure' of Scott. He was endearingly loyal to the author of *Peveril of the Peak*; the year had opened with a royal present for Scott's library: the first edition of Montfaucon's *L'Antiquité expliquée*, in fifteen folio volumes, richly bound in scarlet morocco.(*200*) It was a thoughtful present for the novelist whose highest skill was to recreate the past.

The King's enthusiasms were as diverse as they were constant. He took every opportunity to show his interest in famous Englishmen: this year he gave £500 towards a monument to James Watt. And since he, too, desired to be artistically remembered, he asked Chantrey to model a new effigy for the coinage, basing it on the recent bust which everyone agreed was an excellent likeness. Chantrey and William Wyon, the engraver, produced one of the handsomest designs ever found on the English currency.

In the year when the new coins were designed, Mme de Lieven told Metternich that English finances were magnificent. There had not, she said, for thirty years been such prosperity. England was not merely prosperous, she was vigorously creative. On 15 March, the first pile of London Bridge was sunk; on 24 March the House of Commons was asked to sanction a suspension bridge below London Bridge, another at Hammersmith, and a tunnel under the Thames, at Rotherhithe. A year ago, Lawrence had declared that the National Gallery must be seen 'through a very long vista of approach'. Now, on 22 March, the Government acquired, 'for the use of the public', the noble collection of pictures which had belonged to the King's close friend, the late John Julius Angerstein; and to these 38 paintings (which cost £57,000) were added sixteen, the gift of Sir George Beaumont, the connoisseur and patron of art. Lawrence was asked to be one of the five superintendents of the new National Gallery (which for some years would be Angerstein's house in Pall Mall). It was the perfect moment to establish the National Gallery: on the day on which the Government bought the Angerstein Collection, Lord Burghersh, in Florence, wrote to Sir Charles Long: 'I send you a letter I have recd. from the Conte Marescalchi of Bologna together with the Catalogue of his pictures.... He is in hopes they may be wanted for the National Gallery.... Let me have an answer as to whether you thought them likely to suit either His Majesty or the Govt.'(201)

Art was flourishing in other ways: in April the Society of British Artists opened its first exhibition in Suffolk Street. The foundation stone of the Royal Hibernian Academy was laid in Dublin; Lawrence had recommended its Charter of Incorporation, and it was to him that Thomas Mulvany wrote, on 30 April, telling him of the celebration dinner: 'Such an evening I have never before spent—nor shall I ever forget it, the health of His Majesty George the 4th, the father of his people and the patron of the arts was received with a degree of enthusiasm which you may easily imagine Irish men capable of.'(202) Enthusiasm was in the air: in London another Irishman, Moore, had his first glimpse of Regent's Park, and professed himself 'enchanted'; and from Bloomsbury Square, in April, Thomas Leverton Donaldson, the architect, sent Robert Finch a breathless account of the intellectual climate:

My dear Sir,
... Were you in England you would be surprised at a new species of Literature or rather Literary Medium.... A host of weekly Pamphlets have now sprung up.... There are two journals treating on Mechanics recording useful discoveries & some practical hints & introducing

the vulgar to the mysteries of science in a plain unaffected style. The Medical World has a clever little work entitled The Lancet which also contains much useful matter. Divinity has also its hebdomadal register in a work entitled the Pulpit which with Cobbetts register closes the list of the 2 penny productions. All these ... diffuse knowledge at a cheap rate, create an appetite for reading & convey intelligence ... to classes whose instruction has been hitherto little attended to.... We are going on very well in England in a political sense & so rich that the great Capitalists know not how to employ their money —Project after Project Bubble after Bubble rises has its day & then sinks to Nothing.... They have already begun upon London Bridge which is to consist of 5 elliptic Arches.... Scientific Men profiting by the excess of Money in the Market are devising schemes which tend at the same time to public utility & individual profit & by this means we have some very useful projects in Contemplation. There is one of a suspension Bridge near the Tower which will allow vessels of 200 tons to pass up the River without striking their Masts....(203)

It was a time for every kind of project and discovery. Sir Humphry Davy sailed to Copenhagen and back in His Majesty's steamship *Comet*, to test the efficiency of the galvanic protectors. Captain Parry, on the *Hecla*, set sail for a voyage of discovery to the Arctic. An anonymous donation was left to the Middlesex Hospital, to establish a cancer ward; and, at Guy's Hospital, the operation of removing the thigh from the hip-joint was performed for the first time by Astley Cooper.

71

Astley Cooper's record of George IV is among the most vivid, acute and touching records to come down to us. When, in 1820, he was first summoned to Windsor, the King observed: 'I have seen you in your little chariot.' 'I was much surprised,' wrote Cooper, 'for I did not think he knew so unimportant a person as myself.' At fifty-two, Astley Cooper was far from being unimportant. He was a Fellow of the Royal Society, and Professor of Comparative Anatomy to the Royal College of Surgeons; he had a handsome, massive presence, an air of kindliness and rock-like confidence, and such a reputation as a surgeon that the King had summoned him, although he held no royal appointment, to examine a tumour on his head. Cooper had thought it best to delay the operation; but early in 1821, Bloomfield had taken him down to Brighton, where the King had come into his room at one o'clock in the morning, and commanded him to operate at once. Cooper had sensibly refused. 'Your life,' he said, 'is too important to have so serious a thing done in a corner.' He had performed the operation in London soon afterwards.

A fortnight later, the King had suddenly said to him: 'Lord Liverpool has promised to make you a baronet, but I will not suffer it, I shall do it myself.' Cooper asked that the title should be entailed on his adopted nephew. The King agreed. A few days after the Coronation, the baronetcy was gazetted to 'Astley Paston Cooper, Esq., Surgeon to his Majesty's person'. Six months afterwards, the King sent Sir Astley an *épergne* of his own design 'which cost five hundred guineas, and,' wrote Cooper, 'we continued the best friends. . . . I used frequently to go to the Cottage at Windsor, sometimes called on him at Brighton, &c.'

Sir Astley's work had given him an insight into character. It had led him to study men with dispassionate, if sometimes affectionate interest. He was not a courtier; and his memoranda of George IV, which were not written for publication, were the honest opinions of a trained observer: a man without political bias, a man whose views were not distorted by disapproval of the King's private life.

The abilities of George the Fourth were, wrote Sir Astley Cooper,

of the first order. He would have made the first physician or surgeon of his time, the first lawyer, the first speaker in the House of Commons or Lords, though, perhaps, not the best divine . . .

The King was indolent, and, therefore, disposed to yield, to avoid trouble; nervous, and therefore anxious to throw every onus from his own shoulders. He was the most perfect gentleman in his manners and address—possessing the finest person, with the most dignified and gracious condescension, yet excessively proud; familiar himself, but shocked at it in others; violent in his temper, yet naturally kind in his disposition . . .

George the Fourth had an extraordinary memory—he recollected all that he had read, or seen—and had the faculty of quickly comprehending everything. If he saw a steam-engine, he would describe not only its principles of action, but enter minutely into its construction.

He could recount anecdotes of everybody, and could quote the beauties of almost all the works, in prose or verse, of English literature. He also prided himself on his knowledge of Latin, being, in fact, an excellent classic, and frequently quoted Horace. He was a good historian, being fully conversant with the history not only of his own country, but of all Europe. I once said, 'Sire, are you familiar with the fate of Henrietta Maria, after the death of Charles the First? It is to be found, I believe, in Pennant.' 'Oh,' he said, 'read De Grammont; there you will find all about her, together with the history of those times, well described, and minutely given.' . . .

George the Fourth's judgment was good as regarded others, and as respected his country. If I had wanted to decide upon what I ought to do, nobody would have given me better advice; but he very likely would have practised just the contrary himself, for with respect to himself he was too often guided by prejudice . . .(204)

George the Fourth, who always drew men of distinction to him, endeared himself to this shrewd and awe-inspiring doctor. He appears in Sir Astley's memoranda: a gifted, original, massive, exuberant figure, taking 'enormous doses

of opiates' (a hundred drops of laudanum), losing twenty
to twenty-five ounces of blood, eating cold chicken at eleven,
before he rose for a more substantial meal, and regaling his
surgeon with his collection of anecdotes, 'embellishing all
his stories to render them more amusing'. One sees him,
with an enormous appetite for life, waking at five or six
in the morning, and reading till nine or ten, devouring all
the new books of every description: novels, pamphlets,
travels and plays. He mimics Lord Liverpool the moment
the door shuts behind him ('what an awkward creature that
is!'). He dwells with affection on his visit to Ireland ('the
Scotch were a worldly respectable people, but the Irish are
all heart'). He still recalls the Irishman, in red coat and
buckskin breeches, who followed him everywhere to shake
his hand, 'which he did very often, and at last, when I was
in the boat, coming away, ran into the sea, and waded after
me, and would have been drowned—for he could not swim
—if I had not sent a boat to his assistance.'(205) Frequently,
the King and Sir Astley discuss anatomy. Several times, when
the King hears of something novel being found in the course
of investigation, he has the specimen brought for his inspec-
tion. He knows so much about medicine, and the doses of
certain drugs, that Sir Astley is 'always obliged to be unusually careful when writing a prescription for the King.
If his Majesty observed any medicine which was new to
him, he immediately asked its object, and was not satisfied
until he knew all its properties. He was also fond of
inquiring into the uses and objects of the various instruments employed in surgery'.(206)

In the early days of Sir Astley's attendance, Mr. Weiss,
the maker of surgical instruments, invented a saddle for
army surgeons, containing instruments, medicines and band-
ages. Sir Astley mentioned it to the King, who asked to see
the saddle and its inventor. Mr. Weiss was astonished to
find the King so well acquainted with every instrument in
the saddle.

'But, Weiss,' his Majesty said, 'you have forgotten
something most necessary, that is, a large sponge: it might

be put into a bag in front of the saddle. And now as I have improved upon the saddle I shall expect to become a partner'. I answered [said Weiss] 'that I could not have a better, and should be proud of the honour'. His Majesty said, 'I have no doubt of that, but I fancy you would draw bills very fast upon me;' and turning to Sir Astley, he added, 'Do you think I can trust Weiss?' Sir Astley replied, 'I am sure you may trust him, and I will endorse the bills'.(207)

There was one awkward interview with the King, when Sir Astley, summoned in haste, had entered the royal presence with blood on his hands and shirt. 'God bless me ... but I was not aware of it—the King, Sir, is very particular,—he was lying on a couch under a canopy, with a red turban on his head, and looked displeased—and now I see the reason of it.'(208) That look of displeasure must have been one of the few in their relationship. No doubt the King was delighted when, in 1827, Sir Astley became the President of the Royal College of Surgeons. In 1828, as soon as the post of Sergeant-Surgeon fell vacant, he became Sergeant-Surgeon to the King.

72

When Sir Astley Cooper listed the careers which the King might have followed, he could not resist observing that His Majesty might not have made the best divine. The 'palace of piety' at Kew was certain to produce a prince with *joie de vivre*, a man to whom the immediate and tangible delights of this world were more important than the theoretical joys of the next. The passionate Hanoverian lacked the asceticism, the selfless, pastoral dedication that the true cleric needs. And yet it is not impossible to see George IV as a prince of the church: he would have preached with style and feeling, he would have performed its ceremonies with admirable dignity. He knew the meaning of charity;

he delighted to practise what he described as 'active humanity'.

'A little charitable impulse', as he called it, led him to inquire into the circumstances of O'Keeffe, the actor, whom he had met at parties in his youth; O'Keeffe, now eighty, and stone-blind, was given enough money to close his life in comfort. Michael Kelly, the singer, was patronised by the King from his first appearance in 1787, and always received £100 from him on his benefit night. The King gave thousands of pounds for the relief of the distressed Spital-fields weavers.

To the Church itself he was generous. He gave £1,000 to St. David's College, Lampeter, which was founded for the education of young Welshmen, destined for ordination, who could not afford a university. 'The King,' he wrote, 'can not express, in terms of *sufficient commendation*, this most laudable effort of the Bishop of St. David's. Whenever the Money is wanted, the King has order'd his Privy Purse to transmit one thousand pounds in aid of the Bishop's benevolent intentions.'(*209*) His benefaction was made with warmth of heart, and it contributed largely to the success of the venture; he later endowed the college with three operative benefices, and three sinecure rectories. He sub-scribed to the British and Foreign School Society; and when, in 1813, he was asked to be the Society's patron, he asked advice from the Archbishop of Canterbury. The Primate replied that if the Society's scheme of education were to be applied to the working classes, Christianity would 'hardly be safe among us'.(*210*) The Regent continued his subscrip-tion, but refused to be patron.

It might not, perhaps, be true, as one contemporary said, that he always distributed Church patronage with a 'pure and laudable regard to the interests of Christi-anity'.(*211*) He determined to appoint Charles Sumner (tutor to the Conyngham children) to a vacant canonry at Windsor; Lord Liverpool's refusal to do so strained rela-tions between them, but eventually the King appointed his old librarian, Stanier Clarke. However, when Lord Liver-pool suggested a candidate for the see of Gloucester, and was rash enough to mention his social background, His Majesty replied succinctly that

> from his great learning, orthodox principles, and general good conduct, the King considers him a most fit person; this is much more satisfactory to the King's feelings for making him a Bishop than political motives, or his having been tutor to a Duke.(*212*)

For, in general, as Regent and King, George IV supported the Church of England with a strong sense of duty. He subscribed to the National Society for the Education of Children of the Poor in the Principles of the Established Church. When the Primate asked to make public collections for the Society for the Propagation of the Gospel, he found the Regent 'always ready to give the best encouragement'. George III had expressed the wish that every child in Britain might be able to read the Book of God; and during the reign of his successor 'immense efforts' were made to carry his wish into effect. A preacher at Southampton, after the death of George IV, recalled

> that during the reign of our late Monarch, hundreds of thousands of copies of the sacred Scriptures have been distributed by the subjects of the British Crown; not in Britain merely, but in almost every part of the globe, where the race of man is to be found. And not only so—but many hundreds of Missionaries have gone forth from our distinguished country, to exterminate the evils which afflict mankind.(*213*)

In 1826 an assistant curate at Bath could observe that 'all men may worship God in the beauty of holiness in his temple, and have just reason to pray from their hearts, for the peace of our Jerusalem and her king . . .'; after the King had died, a rabbi would praise the 'illustrious and upright Monarch, under whom we, as Hebrews, have had every religious indulgence'.(*214*) If the King showed determination not to emancipate the Catholics, his determination was widely shared by his subjects, and it owed much to the thought that he was Defender of the Faith. The title might have been bestowed on Henry VIII by the Pope himself, but George IV had sworn to defend the established Church in England. He saw emancipation as a grave dereliction of duty.

Thomas Raikes, in his reminiscences, confirmed that the King did not lack 'a proper sense of religious feeling'. When an old housekeeper died at Windsor, after nearly half a century of service, the King sent for his chaplain

> and urged him to improve the feeling excited in the household by the occurrence into a religious admonition: he concluded by saying that he wished him to preach an appropriate sermon in the chapel on the following Sunday and requested that he would take the following text: 'Be ye also ready.' The sermon was preached accordingly.(215)

When Lady Hertford read the Bible with him daily, when Lady Conyngham quoted Scripture to him at the time of Catholic emancipation, they were not addressing themselves to an irreligious Sovereign. When Knighton put a Bible, in large print, in the King's bedroom, he knew that the King would read it well. He knew that the King, who appreciated the prose style of prayers, who needed to express emotion, had, deep in him, some understanding of Christian virtues and principles, a certain will to trust in God and to make his peace with Him.

73

In 1825, in his *Spirit of the Age*, Hazlitt made some astringent observations on his contemporaries: on their love of paradox and novelty, their 'dastard submission to prejudice and to the fashion of the day'. He lamented that the age was an age of talkers, not of doers, that the world was growing old. 'We are,' he wrote, 'so far advanced in the Arts and Sciences, that we live in retrospect, and doat on past achievements. The accumulation of knowledge has been so great, that we are lost in wonder at the height it has

reached, instead of attempting to climb or add to it.'(216)
It was true that the age loved novelty, yet its love of
novelty was not an exclusive affection for trivia, for the
decorative arts, for the lighter forms of literature, or for the
most preposterous fashions in dress. The age was supremely
successful at being elegant and frivolous, but the love of
novelty which the essayist condemned may also be seen as
eagerness for experience, a healthy interest in experiment. The long Napoleonic wars were over, there was a
general zest for life: for the arts, the sciences, travel,
education, religion. The year which saw the publication of
Hazlitt's caustic essays saw a blood transfusion performed
by Dr. Blundell of Guy's Hospital. It saw the spread of
popular education: lectures had recently begun at the
London Mechanics' Institution, and now London shopkeepers decided to close early, at eight o'clock in winter,
and nine in summer, 'to give their clerks and shopmen a
chance of improving their minds'. Nor was higher education neglected: on 26 May, Henry Brougham showed the
finer side of his character: he introduced a Bill in Parliament to incorporate London University. The Royal
Society of Literature, which the King so benignly fostered,
was growing in numbers and distinction; on 18 May, as a
Royal Associate, Coleridge gave his lecture *On the Prom-
etheus of Æschylus*. There was an exciting sense of expan-
sion, an exhilarating feeling of patronage, a heartening
confidence in taste and experiment; and Donaldson, the
architect, writing again to Robert Finch, conveyed the spirit
of the age most truly:

> The Government seems to be taking great interest in
> the embellishments of the Capital & the progress of the
> fine Arts.... A new Academy is to be built for the schools
> of Art & Halls of the Annual Exhibitions. Great dis-
> crimination is used in the choice of designs for the public
> edifices, Mr. Soane our Professor of Architecture has for
> 3 Nights thrown open his House & gallery to all the
> world.... It was a sort of enchantment. Every Room had
> its appropriate light, blazed in all the splendor of

numberless lamps or receiving a spare light presented its objects thro the medium of a solemn twilight. Here were Drawings—there pictures—a variety of the most choice casts arrested the attention in another part— but the central point of attraction, the grand wonder of wonders, was the Belzoni Sarcophagus—A large oblong Egyptian coffin which Mr. Soane has purchased for 2 or 3 Thousand Guineas.... The Catholic Question is gaining ground; bets in the city (the true test of public opinion in that quarter) are that if it do not pass this Season it will before two years. A Company is establishing for the purpose of opening a more extensive commercial intercourse with Egypt....(*217*)

It was hard for Hazlitt to maintain that the age was simply lost in wonder at the past. The first stone of Hammersmith Bridge was laid by the Duke of Sussex in May; the first stone of the new London Bridge was laid by the Lord Mayor in June. The foundation stone of the Duke of York's palace, at St. James's, was laid in July, and six weeks later the building was 'in a great state of forwardness'. It was an age of enthusiasm, an age when aesthetic sense was considered a virtue, an age when all enlightened Englishmen agreed that nobility and elegance were essential to architecture. Fine building was an outward sign of patriotism and progress.

I know not whether I have written to you since my success in the Church way [wrote Donaldson to Finch on 19 August]. I have a Church to erect for Kensington. It's style early Gothic—are you horrorstruck? The sum only £10,000 too little by half. Among all the projects now afloat that of street cutting is the most popular. Mr. Nash has published the scheme of a new Street from Charing Cross to the British Museum. The reason for this has been that 2 years ago the Parliament voted 40,000£ pr Annum for 5 years to erections in addition to the British Museum to form a complete Library, Museums of Natural History, Antiquities & Medals. The nobs at the West end, enraged that so many good things should be so far Eastward made a great noise in Parliament—The Government anxious to justify their proposition in Parliament desired Mr. Nash to form an ample and noble access thereto as the West enders complained that they could not get at the Museum at all.... Mr. Nash's plan being imperfect I have published a supplementary plan & since that I have been employed by parties with 2 other individuals to form a project for a new Street from Bloomsbury ... to the Waterloo Bridge thus affording ready access to the Theatres, Covent Garden, & the Strand from the Northern quarters of the Town....(218)

The King himself ('our amiable *dear Sovereign*', wrote Elizabeth, Duchess of Devonshire) was no less concerned with building than his subjects. Lady Cowper, who saw Windsor Castle in Ascot week, thought the alterations done in the best possible taste. The King found Ascot and the race-course an annual holiday; he was in better health and spirits than she had seen him for a long while. His good spirits must have continued, for, two days after she wrote, the House of Commons made a grant for 'repairs' to Buckingham Palace.

The King's taste was not only evident, this year, in building and decoration: he sat to Lawrence for a portrait for the Paris Embassy, he commissioned him to paint his sister, Princess Sophia; and when Lawrence asked permission to exhibit the Princess's likeness, Lord Conyngham replied from Royal Lodge with a note which seems to catch the King's own charm. 'Though His Majesty does not in general approve of Portraits being exhibited—The King commands me to say He cannot resist the pleasure of obliging You.'(219) In May the King gave Lawrence 'a royal professional mission to Paris': a commission to paint the King of France and the Dauphin. Late in August Lawrence set up his easel at St. Cloud, where Charles X 'said he yielded most readily to H.M.'s flattering desire for his Portrait, and he then honor'd me with a sitting of nearly 2 hours....'(220) The King did not merely commission the portrait: he eagerly followed its progress; and when, in September, Charles Long reported that the picture was excellent, 'he seemed much pleased, and askd me particularly', wrote Long to Lawrence, 'when I expected your Return—I know he will be anxious to see the work in which he takes a very great Interest'.(*221*) It was an age when men of taste were eager to encourage men of talent; and Canning, visiting Carlton House in February, took a pleasure in telling Lawrence: 'I saw your Portrait of the King of France yesterday ... It is exquisitely good.'(*222*) The portraits of Charles X and the Dauphin completed the series for the Waterloo Chamber.

The King who was the chief patron of Lawrence was also the endearing friend of Wilkie. This summer, he heard that Wilkie was ill (the doctors were afraid he had 'a paralytic affection'), and Knighton was dispatched at once to see him. The King's tact and shrewdness and generous warmth were never seen more clearly than in Knighton's account of his mission. He was instructed, he recalled, to tell Wilkie of the King's sympathy,

and his anxiety that no thought about the two or three pictures for the Royal Gallery left unfinished, or about anything else in the shape of business or money, should be allowed to disturb him.... The King said to [me], 'Go to Wilkie—he is proud and shy—he may not want money at all, and it would not do to offer him that: say to him, however, that ... I entertain a confident expectation of his recovery.... Tell him I am so sure of this, that he has my permission to consider me as his banker —so long as he continues to travel, and *does not work*. He may draw for what he wants, and repay me when he comes back, at his leisure, in the shape of pictures. I can never have too many Wilkies in my collection.'

Wilkie had no occasion to accept money, then or later. He went to Italy and Spain, and returned to England in June 1828. Soon after he came home, the King summoned him to bring his Italian sketches; he bought *The Pifferari* and *A Roman Princess washing the Pilgrims' Feet.* The following year, Wilkie showed the King his Spanish pictures. The King bought three, and commissioned a fourth.(*223*) His interest had shaped the artist's career.

In the *Spirit of the Age* Hazlitt had deprecated the triumph of Scott. His comments may indicate a certain envy of Scott's favour at Court. He was not content to point out the novelist's love of the Stuarts: he contrasted it acidly, with his professed devotion to the House of Hanover.

> Sir Walter is a professed *clarifier* of the age. . . . Through some odd process of servile logic, it should seem that in restoring the claims of the Stuarts by the courtesy of romance, the House of Brunswick are more firmly seated in point of fact...! In any other point of view, we cannot possibly conceive how Sir Walter imagines 'he has done something to revive the declining spirit of loyalty' by these novels. His loyalty is founded on would-be treason: he props the actual throne by the shadow of rebellion.(*224*)

Scott himself, the object of these diatribes, remained acutely conscious of royal favour, and the importance of being remembered at Court. In February he asked Knighton's leave for 'a very ingenious mechanick' to inspect His Majesty's armoury; in May, he entertained Chantrey, who was in Edinburgh to choose the site for the non-equestrian statue of the King. In October, Archibald Constable, the publisher of *Marmion*, approached Scott with the plan of a weekly miscellany, a venture intended, in Scott's words, 'to bring all the standard works, both in sciences and the liberal arts, within the reach of the lower classes'. Constable braced himself to suggest a dedication to the Sovereign, 'addressing the King as the real friend of knowledge, the enlightened promoter of the progress of intelligence'. Scott negotiated the matter and Constable duly inscribed his work

TO HIS MAJESTY
KING GEORGE IV
The generous Patron
even of the most humble attempts
towards the advantage of his subjects ...

As for Scott's Stuart sympathies, which had so roused Hazlitt, Scott himself discussed them in October, with Tom Moore, who had come to stay at Abbotsford. As they walked together through a glen, he told Moore how he and the King had eagerly discussed the Young Pretender. The only difference between them had been that the King had naturally referred to 'the Pretender', and Scott had rigorously said 'Prince Charles'.(225)

It was difficult to see where Moore's own sympathies lay. He had once been charmed by the King; after the Whig disappointment, he had attacked him in *The Twopenny Post-Bag*. Four years ago, he had assured Croker that if he wrote about the King, 'it would be to praise him with all my heart for his wise and liberal conduct in Ireland'. Now —inspired, perhaps, by his Irish pugnacity—he had again attacked him.

In June, when it was known that he would publish his *Life of Sheridan*, his old friend Lord Moira, now the Marquess of Hastings, had drawn him aside at Prince Leopold's assembly; and, leading him to 'a retired part of the room', he said that he had heard that Moore intended to publish proof of the King's marriage to Mrs. Fitzherbert. Moore (who had heard of the marriage from Brougham) answered that he had no such intentions: he did not know that any proofs existed. He was naturally intrigued by Lord Hastings' diplomacy: it seemed that Carlton House had expressed alarm, and that he had offered to mediate to prevent a publication which they dreaded. 'Does not this look,' asked Moore, 'as if Lord Hastings was aware that such proofs exist?'(226)

When the *Life of Sheridan* appeared, later in the year, the King found in it a quite different cause of displeasure.

Moore declared that the dying Sheridan had lingered in want for weeks, though his situation was known to the Regent, and the Regent was a friend of long standing. It was hard, said Moore, to suppose that the small sum of money said to come from the Regent, 'so scanty and reluctant a benefaction', was 'the sole mark of attention accorded by a gracious Prince and master' to Sheridan's last wants.

On 25 November, Mr. Croker was summoned to dine and sleep at Royal Lodge. The King had meant to show him the autumn plantations, but it snowed too hard for them to stir. Next morning he admitted Croker to his dressing-room. Moore's book was lying on the table, and, reported Croker, 'in allusion to the variety of misstatements made in that work with regard to His Majesty's conduct, he took up the book to point out to me particularly some of these errors.... His Majesty narrated, or I may almost say *dictated* to me for some hours without interruption....'(227) He reminded Croker, perhaps, how he had offered Sheridan asylum in Carlton House to save him from arrest by his creditors; he recalled, perhaps, how Sheridan had written to McMahon that he had freed himself of all debts 'except the debt of gratitude I owe to him [the Regent] which it will be the object of my life honourably & faithfully to discharge'. The King no doubt told Croker how, unasked, he had given Sheridan £4,000 'as soon as he knew that it would be of essential service'; he told him how, 'under unwarrantable pretences', the money had been detained until it could no longer be of use.(228) He had not failed in loyalty or in generosity.

That day, as Croker was listening to the royal account of Sheridan, the Home Secretary, in Whitehall, was addressing a letter to the King. He wrote with all the assurance of being appreciated:

> ... It appears to Mr. Peel that it would be a very appropriate mark of royal favour, as it would no doubt be a powerful stimulus to science, if your Majesty were pleased to permit Mr. Peel to announce to the Royal

Society that your Majesty had commanded two gold medals to be in future annually given as honorary rewards for the best papers sent in to the Council of the Royal Society on scientific subjects to be proposed by them.(229)

Peel had already consulted Lord Liverpool, who had agreed, 'most cordially', that the Treasury would pay for two medals, worth twenty guineas apiece. Two days later, Knighton told Peel that the King approved of the medals, but desired that they should be worth fifty guineas each.(230)

The medals were to be awarded for important discoveries or useful work in any branch of science, 'without any principle of narrow policy or national exclusion'. But 'I trust', said Sir Humphry Davy, in his presidential discourse, 'you will allow the justice of the decision of your Council, which has claimed for our countryman this first testimony of royal benevolence to science'.(231) The first gold medal was awarded in 1826 to John Dalton, for the development of the atomic theory.

This royal benevolence towards the arts and scholarship was sometimes ill repaid. The trouble blown up by the *Life of Sheridan* continued into 1826. Gossip said that the King had ordered his librarian to review Moore in the *Quarterly,* and in April Moore read 'the long-threatened cannonade'.(232)

The review could not have been more authoritative. It had been written by Lockhart, with the assistance of Knighton and Croker (a frequent contributor to the *Quarterly*), and they had read him the King's own notes. 'I am afraid you will think I have treated Moore too roughly,' wrote Lockhart to Scott,

but I could not help it ... *Entre nous,* his treatment of the King was more unpardonable than anybody knows— for Croker took care to put him fully in possession of all the facts of the case long before the book was printed. First and last old Sherry (besides his sinecure) received from the privy purse upwards of £30,000 in *cash.* Croker and Sir W. Knighton both overlooked my paper ere it was published, and I *heard* the notes of George IV read; for once or twice through inadvertence the style of 'His Royal Highness' was dropt and '*I*' took its place. Besides nobody else *could* have written those notes which prove the writer to be a very clever writer indeed....(*233*)

Moore refused to admit defeat. He decided to put two or three paragraphs in the next edition 'disclaiming all idea of imputing a want of generosity, in pecuniary matters, to the illustrious personage concerned in these transactions, but at the same time defending the accuracy of my own statements'.(*234*)

74

The King had other causes of worry in the opening months of 1826. He was too unwell to open Parliament on 2 February, and in March he was suffering badly from gout. Moreover, during the winter, in a London drawing-room, an unpredictable drama had occurred: Lady Conyngham had found herself face to face with Lord Ponsonby.

The second Lord Ponsonby, now fifty-six, and married to Lady Elizabeth Villiers, was uncommonly handsome. He had, it was said, been Lady Conyngham's 'favoured lover' at the turn of the century. Now he had come back, unexpectedly, from Corfu, and he had not lost his attraction for her. She was 'overcome', noted Mme de Lieven. 'The King heard of it at once and was overcome too—so overcome that he sent for Canning'.(*235*) Circumstances were ironic. It was Canning, as Foreign Secretary, who saved Lady Conyngham for the King. He sent at once for Lord Ponsonby, who had never thought of a diplomatic career, and offered him a post in Brazil.

You will see [Canning told Sir Charles Bagot, the British Ambassador to the Netherlands], that I refer Ld. Ponsonby to you for instructions, which I could not give.

Among other things, it is very difficult for *me* to say, "Be as little in England as possible before your departure". But I wish it said—or at least I wish the thing so to be. There are *pourquois* for it, *qui ne s-expliquent pas.(236)*

Late in February 1826 Lord Ponsonby was sent to Buenos Aires. He was later Ambassador at Constantinople and at Vienna, and became a diplomat of distinction.

However, the sudden glimpse of him did not make Lady Conyngham any happier with the King. Countess Grey reported in February, on the eve of Ponsonby's departure, 'that Lady C. throws herself back on the sofa and never speaks; and the opinion is (which I don't believe) that *she hates Kingy'.(237)* Mme de Lieven reported, in March, that when he was dangerously ill for three days, Lady Conyngham had tried to desert him. The Duke of York had persuaded her to stay. On 14 May the same eager correspondent described a recent *tête-à-tête* with the King; he had talked to her, so she said, for three hours. Mme de Lieven may well have dramatised events to her former lover; but there was no doubt some substance in what she said.

Here [she wrote] is the strange confession which he made to me. His mistress bores him. She is a fool (he might have found that out sooner). He has been in love with me for thirteen years.... 'In a word Heaven made us for one another'.... I took the only course and said that I, too, had always felt that we were close to one another, that our ideas were so much the same that I felt he must be at least my cousin ... I rose; he opened his bedroom door and asked me to look at the portrait facing his bed. It was a sketch of me, done by Lawrence. He told me that he had just bought it, and that he would never part with it. I stopped at the door, curtseyed to the King, and went out. What do you think of this strange scene? ... He is not in love with me at all.(238)

The King, in his affairs of the heart, had always gone to extremes; he had declared each woman, in turn, to be indispensable. He probably recognised Dorothea de Lieven as sharp and hard and managing; he could not, even from Lawrence's portrait—and Lawrence knew how to flatter—have thought her beautiful. But Mme de Lieven knew how to charm, when she felt inclined, and she was not averse to charming the King. She was intelligent, and she knew how to emphasise her own intelligence and the Vice-Queen's stupidity. Mme de Lieven had an intellect, and the King was intellectual. After six years of vapid femininity, he sometimes felt unsatisfied.

He felt all the more unsatisfied as nowadays he spent so much of his life in seclusion. Conscious of vast unpopularity, plagued by ill-health, well aware of his shapeless bulk, he withdrew himself from public gaze. Sometimes his subjects heard of his removal from Windsor to Brighton, from the Cottage to the Castle, but they hardly ever saw him in person. When he held a Drawing-room in London, in May 1824, no one was allowed to wait in the outer rooms to watch him pass. He had stood for nearly two hours to receive his guests, 'but his sitting down in the beau millieu [sic] of the Circle would', wrote Lady Williams Wynn, 'have had far less bad effect than his sulking as he does from the eye of John Bull'.(239) At Windsor, she added, 'when a party are seeing the Castle, they forbid [them] to turn their Eyes to the Window, lest the King should be passing under it. What all this can mean it is impossible to guess, but certainly it must keep up a jealous suspicion in John Bull that all is not right'.(240)

In the depths of his Windsor estate, hidden by dense plantations, the King himself lived a life of clockwork monotony. Lady Shelley, a distant cousin of the poet, described the royal routine in 1826:

The life led at the King's Cottage is as follows: the party consists entirely of C[onyngham]s, and a few of the London fine ladies who call themselves her intimate friends, among them Countess L[ieven] and Esterhazy.

They meet at three o'clock, at which hour five or six
phaetons come to the door, each to receive a lady and
gentleman, who drive about the country until five. At
that hour the whole party dine in a hut on the shore of
Virginia Water.... The party sit at table until between
nine and ten o'clock, then they return to the cottage, dress
presto, and go into the saloon, where they play at écarté
and other games until midnight. It is every day the
same: oh! monotony! ... The King never thinks of anything but building....(*241*)

Creevey deplored the fact that the King and the Duke
of York, who were both over sixty, and both officially single,
should be having palaces built for them. But the King was
not building for himself. This love of building was not
mere extravagance, the folly of a bored monarch, an escape
from the business of government; it was not a mere panacea
for restlessness, or even the satisfaction of the King's
artistic sense. It welled up from far deeper causes: deeper,
it may be, than the King himself would have recognised.
It was as if, leaving no heir to the throne, he had determined
to leave some magnificent, visible legacy to the country:
some lasting, inescapable cause of gratitude.

His interest in the arts continued; and sometimes artists
showed their debt to him. This year John Martin, the
Romantic artist and engraver, dedicated his *Belshazzar's
Feast* to the King; he dedicated to him, too, his *Paradise
Lost*, and the King subscribed for a copy of each of the four
limited editions, published from 1825 to 1827. But,
plagued as he was by gout, the King could not take so active
an interest in the arts as he wished. 'I have been endeavouring to persuade His Majesty to visit the Royal Academy
previous to the opening of the Exhibition.' Charles Long
wrote to Lawrence late in April. 'He complained much of
the great height he had to ascend which he said was very
fatiguing—but as he did not particularly decline it I hope
he will be induc[e]d to pay you a Visit.'(*242*) However, if
the King's gout kept him from the Royal Academy, nothing
prevented him from sharing his own pictures with the

The Marchioness Conyngham
After the portrait by Sir Thomas Lawrence

The King's Cottage, Windsor Park
From an engraving by Melville, 1830

'George IV taking his favorite exercise
near the Sandpit Gate, Windsor Park'
From an engraving by Melville, 1830

public. This summer he lent some of them to the British Institution; and William Bewick, the artist, admired paintings 'of the very first class, by old masters, Titian, Rembrandt, Teniers, Cuyp, Reynolds, &c. &c.'.(243) The King had a particular fondness for Dutch cabinet pictures, and with the help of William Seguier, first keeper of the National Gallery, and curator of the royal picture galleries, he had brought together a fine collection of Flemish works. In Carlton House, at Windsor and Brighton he had also, by now, assembled by far the largest known collection of British works of art, 'and an assemblage of works of art generally such as few sovereigns could boast of, and no private individual could equal'.(244) He still watched over his principal painter with affection; and Lawrence, prevented, it seems, by ill-health, from presenting a picture at Windsor, received an endearing message through Lord Conyngham:

> I must express the Satisfaction with which His Majesty graciously received Your Portrait of the Princess Amelia —Nor [sic] His Majesty's kind expressions in Your favour—His Majesty commands me to send His Majesty's kind regards and feels much concerned at the cause that [prevents] Your being the bearer of so excellent a Portrait.(245)

The King's personal touch was still evident, too, in his relations with Scott. His affection was only strengthened when, early in 1826, Scott was involved in financial disaster. James Ballantyne, his partner in a printing business, found himself liable for £130,000, and Scott assumed the debt. Scott, as Moore expressed it, could 'spin gold from his entrails', and the debt was paid at last from the proceeds of copyrights to his books; but the blow was heavy, and the King was 'quite melancholy all the evening he heard of it. *This* I can well believe,' wrote Scott in his diary, 'for the King, educated as a prince, has nevertheless as true and kind a heart as any subject in his dominions'.(246) In October Scott was summoned to spend a day at the Cottage, and found the King as courteous as ever. No monarch could charm like George IV when he meant to charm; no monarch was so kind. 'The King made me sit beside him,' wrote the novelist, 'and talk a great deal—*too much* perhaps—for he has the art of raising one's spirits and making you forget the retenue which is prudent everywhere, especially at court. But he converses himself with so much ease and elegance, that you lose thought of the princes in admiring the well-bred accomplished gentleman.'(247) And then Scott paid his perceptive tribute to King George IV: a tribute which, confided to his diary, was written in complete sincerity:

> He is in many respects the model of a British monarch —has little inclination to try experiments on government otherwise than through his Ministers—sincerely, I believe, desires the good of his subjects—is kind towards the distressed, and moves and speaks 'every inch a king'. I am sure such a man is fitter for us than one who would long to head armies, or be perpetually intermeddling with *la grande politique.* A sort of reserve, which creeps on him daily, and prevents his going to places of public resort, is a disadvantage, and prevents his being so generally popular as is earnestly to be desired....(248)

Scott stayed overnight at the Cottage; next morning he examined Wyatville's alterations to Windsor Castle. On the whole he approved, for Wyatville seemed to possess much Gothic feeling.

Scott also found time, as might be expected, for 'much confidential chat' with Knighton. A few days later, an earnest letter went to young Charles Scott, at Brasenose College, Oxford. In about six months, wrote Scott, there was every hope of a diplomatic career, 'under auspices which ... can scarce fail to bring you well forwards'. It was, no doubt, with conviction that Scott asked Knighton, in November, to lay his respectful homage 'at the feet of our gracious Master. Whatever I see of other countries and sovereigns makes me', he confessed, 'more attached to my own, where we possess such advantages, if we knew how to prize them' (249)

It was a German visitor who showed appreciation of George IV. On 5 December, Prince Pückler-Muskau, preparing to write his four-volume *Tour in England, Ireland, and France,* was presented to the King at a levée. 'I took occasion,' he wrote, 'to make my compliments to him on the extraordinary embellishment of London since [my former visit], which indeed is to be ascribed in great measure to him.'(*250*)

75

On 4 January 1827, as part of the grand design for improving London, the demolition of Carlton House began. Next day, as if to confirm that the King's youth was long past, the Duke of York, his favourite brother, died of dropsy.

His death, which had been expected for some time, caused genuine regret: not least to the King, who was 'much depressed in health and spirits'.(*251*) It was thought that he might go to Brighton, so as not to hear the tolling bells of Windsor; but he attended the funeral on 20 January. He was, reported the Duke of Rutland, 'most greviously affected,' and 'every minute gun was like a nail driven into his heart; but he had some sleep towards the morning, and was more composed, and I hope that the journey to Brighton, and the change of scene, will divert the intensity of his grief',(*252*) He left for Brighton on 24 January.

ıBefore the King returned to Windsor early in March, one persistent mystery of his reign was, at last, to be solved. The authorship of the Waverley Novels had long been a subject of debate: even Scott's son, Walter, had only been able to surmise that his father was responsible. The secret had, in fact, been known to certain people for a number of years, but they had kept it, rigorously, from each other, and Scott had remained (as Pückler-Muskau said) the Great Unknown. However, in 1826, when James Ballantyne went bankrupt, the secret became the property of so many that

Scott himself could no longer make denials, and he 'only looked for some decent opportunity to lay aside the mask'. In February 1827, he took the chair at a dinner of the Theatrical Fund in Edinburgh; there, at last, he made his public confession. 'And so the murder is out, dear Sir Walter!' cried Lady Louisa Stuart, to whom he had confessed twelve years earlier. 'I have been reading the newspaper account ... and dislike only one ominous expression —"that the rod of Prospero is broken and buried". I hope ... the rod will still work miracles under ground.'(253)

Prospero had not lost his touch: that year the Royal Society of Literature awarded him one of the King's gold medals 'for his Illustrations of the Manners, Antiquities, and History of Scotland, in many works of pre-eminent genius'. The medal was 'a very pretty thing,' said Lockhart, who received it for him, '—the King's head, and the legend *Gualtero Scott—Poetae*'.(254)

The face that was seen in profile on the medal was never far from Sir Walter's mind. In a letter to Lockhart that spring, he wrote blatantly: 'You are aware *strictly inter nos* that my interest lies Windsor ways but the art is to know how the lever should be applied.'(255) A few weeks later, he found a chance to apply the lever. As president of the Bannatyne Club, which concerned itself with the history of Scotland, he sent Knighton its latest publication, 'a most valuable Scottish history, with the hope that the King may not be displeased to see what we are attempting'.(256) Scott took the chance to mention that his son had now graduated at Oxford: it was time for the Great Unknown to remind the Great Invisible that he had promised to show an interest.

Throughout the year, Scott continued to apply the lever at Windsor. In July, when an admirer in New South Wales sent him a couple of emus (which proved, to his horrified surprise, to be six feet high), he tried to transfer the birds to the Royal Menagerie (alas, His Majesty appeared to be provided).(257) When his Life of Napoleon appeared, he 'caused a copy ... to be laid on the table of His Majesty's library'.(258) In November, he applied the lever much more boldly: he asked Knighton directly for advice on his son's career. At last, on 14 December, Scott reported to Morritt that 'our great Master (who has always been my good one), had recommended Charles for the first available vacancy in the Foreign Office.'(259) He became a clerk in February. Scott had known how to work the Windsor machine.

<h1 style="text-align:center">76</h1>

The Windsor machine was being worked busily throughout the year. On 17 February Lord Liverpool had a stroke; he was to live on for nearly two years, but his career was finished. 'Well, ... who is to supply Liverpool's place?' Creevey inquired. 'I think somehow it must be Canning after all, and that then *he'll die of it.*'(260)

The King (so Lady Conyngham reported) would not let anyone mention Lord Liverpool's illness, or his successor; he said he refused to discuss such matters for some time to come. 'Was there ever such a child or Bedlamite?' asked Creevey. 'Or were there ever such a set of lick-spittles as his Ministers to endure such conduct?'(261)

In his days as Prince of Wales, the King had shown convictions in his politics. Admittedly they were largely derived from the wish to be independent, to show his opposition to his father; and they owed something to his personal attachments: his devotion to Lady Melbourne, to the Duchess of Devonshire, to Sheridan, and, above all, to Fox. But, as Prince of Wales, he had not needed to make decisions. As Regent, and now, more than ever, as King, he was obliged to do so, and he found it increasingly difficult and distasteful. He was not a natural politician. He was too impulsive, too emotional, too impatient of manoeuvres and calculations. He was guided too much by his personal dislikes and predilections. He was not a born statesman. He was a patriot, who had always wanted his country's good; but international strategy, the global

panorama of events, escaped his understanding. George IV
had not been endowed with the gifts of an absolute monarch;
and his education had not instilled them into him.

He was well aware himself that he was politically weak,
apt to be influenced by his own prejudice, by designing
statesmen, by unofficial advisers like Knighton, by ambitious
women like Mme de Lieven, and, of course, by Lady
Conyngham. He also knew that he could never gain affection: that whatever he did was certain to offend some
political class. The more he studied the chessboard, the
more impossibly intricate the moves appeared; and so, at
moments of crisis, he found himself in a turmoil of indeci-
sion, and hoped that time would make decisions for him.
There was, as Creevey said, a childish streak in his nature;
and, at such moments, it led him to run away from danger:
to shun responsibility (*'tout s'arrangera,'* he would say),
to play for time, to seek retreat and seclusion. 'The Monarch
stole back to Windsor yesterday,' wrote the implacable
Creevey on 9 March, three weeks, all but a day, after Liverpool's stroke. The King, he added, had been 'fifteen days
at Brighton without leaving his dressing-room, or seeing the
face of a human being—servants, tailors and doctors excepted. What the devil is it to come to?'(262)

Small decisions were easily made. The Duke of Cumberland reported that the King had ordered that the uniform
of the three regiments of Guards and the Blues should be
changed, each officer to have three coats with embroidery
(an expense wildly beyond a subaltern's pay); Lord Hertford ('the gallant Hertford', as Joseph Jekyll called him)
was appointed to proceed on a special embassy to Russia,
and take the new Emperor, Nicholas I, the Order of the
Garter. Only in April, after protracted conversations at
Windsor with Canning, Wellington, Peel, and the Tory
Duke of Rutland (who went, it was said, to protest 'against
Canning being cock of the walk'), was Canning asked to
form a Cabinet.

His appointment as Prime Minister was the signal for
the resignation of Wellington, Peel, and the other Ministers
who had resisted the claims for Roman Catholic emancipa-

tion. Wellington even resigned as Commander-in-Chief of the British Army (a post he had held since the death of the Duke of York), saying that nothing would induce him 'to connect himself with *that man*. . . .' 'Lord Londonderry,' the Earl of Sefton informed Mr. Creevey, 'has resigned the Bedchamber in a letter to the King saying *he* had prevented the Queen being received at Vienna, and that as H.M. had given his confidence to a man who entertained such different opinions *on that subject*, he could no longer serve him. In short, traits of humour are without end.'(*263*)

They were indeed. The new Prime Minister, who had almost certainly been Queen Caroline's lover, had since learned to gratify the Conynghams, and earn Lady Conyngham's influence at Court. Brougham, who had defended the Hunts and Queen Caroline, and reviled the King on political principle for eighteen years, now showed his blatant and deliberate hypocrisy. He chose this moment to approach Knighton on behalf of a new society

> for promoting the diffusion of solid and useful knowledge among all classes. . . . I beg of you [wrote Brougham, on 4 April], to consider whether there would not be a manifest fitness and grace in the King patronising this great and good design. . . . You have no occasion to drop the least hint . . . that I have anything to do with it. But I see no reason why one of the cleverest and quickest, and most accomplished men in the country, merely because he is at the head of it, should not look at our works.(*264*)

Truth sometimes seemed, to Brougham, a simple matter of expediency. Knighton must have reflected dourly on the immorality of politicians.

A German visitor, Prince Pückler-Muskau, must also have had cause to reflect on royal inconstancy. This spring, at Brighton, he spent many evenings with Mrs. Fitzherbert: 'a very dignified and delightful woman, formerly, as it is affirmed, married to the King. She is now,' he noted, 'without influence in that region, but still universally beloved and respected,—d'un excellent ton et sans prétension'.(*265*)

It was Pückler-Muskau, in the summer of 1827, who drew the Windsor landscape with the romantic clarity of a new Ackermann lithograph. Dining nearby, in Ascot week, he noticed in the distance, above the crown of trees, 'the Round Tower of Windsor Castle, with the majestic royal banner floating in the blue air'. Wyatville himself took the Prince on a conducted tour, and explained the details of the new part of the castle: 'a vast work', noted Pückler-Muskau, 'and the only one of its kind in England which is executed not only at a great cost and with technical skill, but with uncommon taste, nay genius'. He took a bourgeois interest in the cost of the enterprise, recording that every pane in the huge Gothic windows cost twelve pounds.(266)

The creator of this castle, waiting for its completion, was living at Royal Lodge. The King whom Creevey ridiculed with thoughtless convention, whom Hazlitt had attacked repeatedly in *The Spirit of the Age,* was still showing a liberal interest in the arts. William Godwin, the author of *Political Justice,* asked Knighton's help in enlisting one of his brothers among the Poor Brothers at the Charterhouse; he was, he wrote, encouraged to do so by 'your intimacy with the generous prince who now fills the throne'. Godwin soon wrote a letter of thanks.(267) No doubt the King had approved this petition from the father-in-law of Shelley. The sovereign who gave his friendship to Scott found time to read Lady Morgan's latest four-volume novel, *The O'Briens and the O'Flahertys,* soon after it appeared. 'The King, I find, was interested in the lighter parts,' Lady Charleville told the author; 'but some of the charges against the Irish government, he said, were too bad, while God knows they were not half bad enough to my mind.'(268) At the anniversary meeting of the Royal Society of Literature, the president congratulated the Fellows on 'the continuance of the truly royal and unexampled munificence of His Majesty's Bounty'.(269) The new library at the British Museum, opened to the public on 22 May, was an impressive sign of the same munificence. At Brighton, Haydon found Chantrey, the sculptor, changed out of recognition by the triumph which owed much to the King. 'His nose at the tip was bottled, large and brown,' wrote the bitter Haydon, 'his cheeks full, his person corpulent, his air indolent, his tone a little pompous. Such were the effects of 8 years' success! He sat and talked, easily, lazily, gazing at the sun with his legs crossed. . . .'(270) The King, a man of natural distinction, drew men of distinction to him, and Lawrence, inviting Scott to the Royal Academy dinner, wrote with conviction that it was 'perhaps the first assemblage of Talent and Rank that this country offers except at the Palace of Majesty itself'.(271) It was a time of magnificent venture: on 1 March the steam vessel *George IV* left Portsmouth on its way to Africa. On 30 April the first stone of London University was laid.

The King round whom all this enterprise revolved, the King who asked no better than to foster and reward every contribution to national greatness, remained secluded, ill and unhappy. 'I can neither walk up nor down stairs, and am obliged to be carried, and in general to be wheeled about everywhere,' he confided to Knighton on 18 June. 'My knees, legs, ankles, and feet swell more formidably and terribly than ever. . . . There is no question it is an increasing and progressive evil (at least so I fear), unless steps be found, and that speedily too, of averting it.'(272)

He must have suspected that, like the Duke of York, he was suffering from dropsy; and, remembering Sir Henry Halford's unremitting attention to his favourite brother, he now gave him an honour not conferred on any other practising physician: a grant of supporters to his coat-of-arms.

On 8 August, within six months of Lord Liverpool's stroke, there came another political crisis. Creevey's prediction was sadly fulfilled: at the height of his powers, at the age of fifty-seven, Canning died. He died, ironically enough, at the Duke of Devonshire's house at Chiswick, where Charles James Fox had died twenty-one years earlier.

It was not the least strange event in the King's career that Canning, who had sent dispatches with 'his most humble & affectionate duty', had grown very fond of his

Sovereign, and that the King had grown very fond of Canning. Whatever his part in events before the Delicate Investigation, whatever his behaviour at the time of the Bill of Pains and Penalties, Canning had long since earned the King's good graces; he had done so by his civilised tastes and his social gifts as much as by his outstanding political talents. He was quick, accomplished, brilliantly intelligent: the kind of man the King appreciated. Five years ago, the King had been more than unwilling to bring him into office as Foreign Secretary. Now he felt his death as a sharp personal loss.

'There are two ways of doing everything,' he had written to him, once, 'and the King is always disposed to take the kindest.'(273) On Canning's death he showed all his grace. 'Which of Canning's friends,' Lord Melrose asked Sir Charles Bagot, 'can feel anything but the warmest gratitude to the King for this beautiful behaviour?'(274) He sent for Viscount Goderich and William Sturges Bourne as the friends whom Canning would have wished him to consult. He pressed high offices on Bourne as Canning's oldest friend in the Cabinet. He ordered the Treasury to give the Commissionership of the Customs to Canning's private secretary. At the end of the year, by his command, Knighton asked Lawrence 'to make a full length Portrait of poor Mr. Canning, from the Picture that You painted for Mrs. Canning'.(275) Mrs. Canning herself was created a viscountess.

Goderich became Prime Minister, though it was clear that he was a caretaker minister of almost incredible weakness. Within ten days of Canning's death, the King had offered Wellington his old post at the Horse Guards, and 'my friend Arthur' was again Commander-in-Chief of the British Army. But there was no question of Wellington's serving in the Cabinet under Goderich; and everything pointed to a political *rapprochement* between the Tory Wellington and the Whig Grey.

While he waited for political power, the Duke discussed the King with surprising ingratitude and bitterness.

The Duke is convinced that no man ever had such a hold upon the King as Canning had [Charles Arbuthnot, the Tory politician, told Peel, in August].

It was evident to the Duke that the King had become a perfect despot. Neither Lady Conyngham nor any one seemed to dare to open their lips, and they were all in the greatest terror of him.

The Duke is certain that Canning and all the present men got their hold upon the King by indulging him in all his expenses and whims. . . .

The consequence of all this is that for the remainder of his life the King will be more difficult than ever to manage.(276)

The King, for his part, was still angry with Wellington, for his behaviour on Canning's appointment. On 28 August, three days after Mr. Arbuthnot wrote to Peel, Lady Cowper recorded:

We are just returned from the King's Lodge. . . . The King is as bitter as ever against the Tories, and has not at all forgiven the Duke of Wellington. . . . The King has a mind to show his power and so forth but I am sure he has no mind to get rid of the present Government, and that he thinks *tout s'arrangera* as he said to somebody. He never ceases in his regrets and praises of C[annin]g and says he never had any Minister he liked half so well. . . .(277)

77

It seems improbable that the King behaved like a despot; but on one point he remained inflexible. Ill, ungainly, and depressed, he sought seclusion more desperately than ever. On 20 August, as Lady Cowper was reporting her visit to Royal Lodge, Prince Pückler-Muskau was roused at an early hour by the Ranger of Windsor Great Park, who wanted to show him the Park before His Majesty was about.

'As soon as he rides out,' explained Pückler-Muskau, 'the private part of the grounds is hermetically sealed to every one, without exception, who does not belong to his own invited company'.(*278*)

In his *Tour in England, Ireland, and France,* with the narrative colour of a novelist, Pückler-Muskau recorded his drive at dawn through the vast, sequestered estate.

The King has had several roads cut, for his own special and peculiar use, through the most interesting parts of his immense park of Windsor. We drove along one of them; and in half an hour reached the royal stables, where the celebrated giraffe is kept. Here, unhappily, we heard that the King's carriages had been ordered, and indeed they stood already harnessed in the yard. There were seven, of various forms, but all with very low wheels, almost as light as children's carriages, and drawn by little poneys; the King's with four, which he drives himself,—the others with two.... Lord H— beheld these equipages with dismay. He was afraid the King might meet us, and feel 'mal à son aise' at the sight of unexpected strangers—for the monarch's tastes are singular enough. It is unpleasant to him to see a strange face, or indeed a human being of any kind whatsoever, within his domain; and the Park is consequently (with the exception of the high road which crosses it,) a perfect solitude. The King's favourite spots are, for further security, thickly surrounded by screens of wood, and plantations are daily laid out to add to the privacy and concealment. In many places, where the lay of the ground would enable you to get a glimpse of the sanctuary within, three stages of fence are planted one behind the other.

Over Windsor Great Park brooded the threat of the King's arrival: his presence seemed almost ominously felt.

We hastened accordingly [continued Pückler-Muskau] to secure a sight of the giraffe, which was led out before us by two Moors who had accompanied her from Africa. ... She uses her long bright-blue tongue like a trunk, in

which way she took from me my umbrella.... Lord H—
hurried off, for fear of the King; and after passing through
a thickly-planted part of the pleasure-ground attached to
the "Cottage", which we only saw from a distance, we
directed our course to Virginia Water, the King's favourite
haunt. It is a large, artificial, but very natural-looking
lake, on which His Majesty almost daily fishes.... A little
frigate lay rocking on the lake, on whose banks were
various little devices—Chinese and Moorish houses executed with taste and not caricatured. The haste with
which we drove along rendered it only possible to see
things in a transient, and for the most part distant
manner....

My venerable host climbed up on the seat of the carriage, and stood there, supported by his wife and me,
to look about whether the King might not be somewhere
in sight; nor was he perfectly tranquil till the gate of the
sanctuary closed upon us.(279)

The previous year, a child of seven had seen it all in
much happier circumstances. Princess Victoria had visited
Royal Lodge with her mother, the Duchess of Kent. She
had found her uncle 'large and gouty but with a wonderful
charm of manner'. He gave her his picture set in diamonds,
which was worn by the Princesses as an order on a blue
ribbon. She was very proud when Lady Conyngham pinned
it on her left shoulder. She was driven to Sandpit Gate,
where the King had a menagerie with wapitis, chamois and
gazelles. Next day she was lifted by royal command into the
King's phaeton ('he said "Pop her in" '), and she was
'greatly pleased, and ... looked with great respect at the
scarlet liveries.... We drove round the nicest part of Virginia Water', she remembered, 'and stopped at the Fishing
Temple. Here there was a large barge and every one went
on board and fished, while a band played in another! '(280)
Mme de Lieven, who had small time for children, was
convinced that the King 'did not like dandling on his sixty-
four-year-old knee this little bit of the future aged 7'.(281)
But it is hard to believe that the child did not commend

herself to her 'dear uncle King'. When he declared that the band should play her favourite tune, she asked at once for *God Save the King*. Queen Victoria already showed her flawless sense of occasion.

78

In January 1828, Brougham resumed his usual tone of cynicism, and sent Creevey news of the King. 'Don't be alarmed, but endeavour to receive with equanimity, and if possible with fortitude, the painful intelligence that your beloved Sovereign has been most dangerously ill, and is still in a very precarious state.' The complaint was said to be due to some trouble with the prostate gland. The King, so Brougham said, was far from rallying as he used to do when he was bled, and his household were 'in much consternation'.(*282*) The King himself ended a letter to Knighton 'in much pain dr. friend'.(*283*)

His health (he also suffered from gout) was hardly improved by the Cabinet crisis this month, which followed the Prime Minister's resignation. Lord Goderich, 'Goody Goderich', as he was usually called, was pleasant and well-meaning, but his weakness of character was legendary, and his tenure of office had been disastrous. Now, after five months in power, he found himself incapable of controlling both Whigs and Tories in the Cabinet. He resigned in tears; the King accepted the resignation, and politely offered him a handkerchief.

The King was then forced to choose between a Whig or a Tory government; he chose the Duke of Wellington and the Tories. He sent for Wellington, who found him ill in bed, dressed in a greasy silk jacket and a greasy turban nightcap. The King's first words were: 'Arthur, the Cabinet is defunct'; he then 'began to describe the manner in which the late Ministers had taken leave of him, on giving in their resignations'. His mimicry was so brilliant that Wellington burst into uncontrollable laughter; fifteen years later he still recalled how the King had 'positively made himself look like' Lord Anglesey; and Croker, hearing his account, declared that he had never seen the King's equal 'for a combination of personal imitation, with the power of exhibiting the mental character'.(284)

The Wellington administration, which began so gaily, did not continue in this happy state. Under the governments of Canning and Goderich, the King had exercised much patronage, and enjoyed a power which he had never known under the authoritarian Liverpool. Wellington was not a pliant man, and he kept to his line of duty. It was soon clear that he and the King would clash on the question of Catholic Emancipation. For thirty years, this highly important issue had been avoided; now it could not be avoided any longer. In July, Daniel O'Connell, who was a Roman Catholic, and therefore barred from sitting in the Commons, was elected Member of Parliament for Clare. Wellington and Peel decided that the time for emancipation had arrived.

The King, as Wellington expressed it, now became 'the most Protestant man in his dominions'.(285) He would not have an open fight with his Ministers, but he determined to thwart them in every way. Wellington said later that if he had not accepted office, he would have spared himself 'loads of misery'. King and Prime Minister took their stands. The King, said Mme de Lieven, found himself so frustrated that he said 'King Arthur must go to the Devil, or King George to Hanover'.(286)

While the question of emancipation gathered steam, there were other causes of dissension. Among them was the recurrent question of the royal prerogative of mercy. The King, thought Peel, was too inclined to be merciful. Hunton, the Quaker, was sentenced to death for forgery: he must, inescapably, go to the gallows. 'No person,' wrote Peel to Wellington, 'ought to be allowed to approach the Lodge in a criminal case. If I had received the King's letter a little earlier, I might have been still more embarrassed, but I would not have given way under any circumstances'.(287) The King was not allowed to be humane in an age of inhumanity.

And his times were not humane: least of all to him. If public opinion had been kinder, he would not have chosen to live in impenetrable seclusion. As it was, the plantations round the Cottage had been carefully designed so that the general public could only see the chimneys of the building. When he rode out, servants were stationed along the tree-lined rides in Windsor Great Park, to prevent the intrusion of strangers. When he went fishing at Virginia Water, or visited the temples he had erected, the same rigid exclusion was enforced.

While the constant sense of unpopularity drove him into retirement, his illness made him more anxious to be hidden. On 2 March, when he was about to return to London (an equerry believed it would be his last visit), Croker noted that he had to be carried to and from his carriage; 'and instead of the open railed gate to the garden of St. James's, ... they have in the last two days substituted a close gate [*sic*] to prevent the people's seeing the operation'.(*288*) The King's ill-health did nothing to create affection or sympathy; three days later, Creevey wrote to Miss Ord, his step-daughter, with venom: 'So you see Prinncy crept into town at last on Monday night in the dark, when nobody could see ... whether he could walk; but as there is a Council at St. James's today we must hear something of him shortly. Lord Rosslyn ... has promised me to keep a sharp look-out on the legs.'(*289*)

A fortnight later, a much less cynical visitor was shown into a back room at St. James's. While Haydon had been in the King's Bench Prison in July 1827, he had witnessed a curious scene: a mock election for the Borough of Tenterden. He had recorded it on canvas. Now the King, through Seguier, had sent for the picture; and, desperate to pay off his creditors, desperate for royal recognition, Haydon brought *The Mock Election* for approval. Three days later, on 21 March 1828, it was added to the Royal collection, and a fervent artist wrote: 'Received of his Majesty, five hundred guineas.' That day, at dinner, so Haydon told Miss Mitford, 'we drank the King's health in the large goblet

I had painted in his picture. God save the King!'(290)
Miss Mitford, in her country cottage at Three Mile Cross,
near Reading, was dizzy with exultation:

A thousand and a thousand congratulations, my dear
friend, to you and your loveliest and sweetest wife! I
have always liked the King, God bless him! He is a
gentleman—and now my loyalty will be warmer than ever.
What has he given for the picture? Where is it to be?
This is fortune—fame, you did not want—but this is
fashion and fortune. Nothing in this world could please
me more.... Are you likely to know the King personally?
If you are, I'm sure you'll take his fancy. How should
you like to be 'Sir Benjamin'? *She* would become the
'Lady', would she not?

God bless you, my dear friends! And God save the
King! (291)

It took all Seguier's good sense to restrain Haydon from
sending the King a letter of gratitude (and emphasising,
no doubt, the duty of patronage). But Haydon abstained
from writing; he turned with fresh spirit to the companion
picture, *Chairing the Member*. Charles Lamb admired the
new work so much, he declared that 'if the former picture
went beyond this I have had a loss, and the King a
bargain'.(292) The Duke of Bedford predicted that the King
would buy the second picture as well.

Chairing the Member was bought for £300 by a Mr.
Francis, in Exeter. But Haydon's days in the King's Bench
Prison had brought him one moment of royal triumph, and
many months of increased confidence. 'Indeed,' he
declared, 'I have received an impulse, which will expire
only with my life'.(293) He sent the King a 'little present
of maps and sketches'. That year he wrote his inquiry into
the decline of historical painting, and suggested that four
pictures, showing the blessings of the monarchy, should
adorn the House of Lords. On Christmas Day he sent a
strong letter to Wellington, and urged that historical painting should be revived by the patronage of state and
sovereign.(294)

Haydon's fanatical persistence could only do him harm; it was probably his deterrent manner, not a lack of talent, that prevented him from decorating the Palace of Westminster. It is sad that he was not allowed to celebrate 'the graceful magnificence of His Majesty'(295) in a few grandiose frescoes in Parliament; but at least he had been royally remembered.

So, this year, was Wilkie, for the King bought two of his pictures; and in November, with Chantrey, he went down to Windsor for two days, apparently to help place the pictures and statues. They spent three hours a day with the King, and Chantrey said the King's kindness to Wilkie was 'beautiful'.(296)

His kindness to Chantrey was something the sculptor often mentioned with pleasure. Francis Legatt Chantrey must at times have been aware of his plebeian origins; his father was a Derbyshire carpenter, and he had started his own career serving in a grocer's shop in Sheffield. But the King, he declared, was a master at putting everyone at ease. 'Now, Mr. Chantrey,' he had said, the first day he had sat for him, 'I insist on your laying aside everything like restraint, both for your own sake and for mine; do here, if you please, just as you would if you were at home.' He himself had shown a gay ease of manner. While Chantrey was preparing the clay, the King had taken off his wig, held it at arm's length, and inquired: 'Now, Mr. Chantrey, which way shall it be, with the wig or without it?' The sculptor had wisely insisted on the wig.(297)

It is said that when he erected his statue of George IV on the Grand Staircase at Windsor, the King affectionately patted him on the shoulder. 'Chantrey,' he said, 'I have reason to be obliged to you, for you have immortalised me.'(298) Whether it was authentic or not, the remark had its justice. Late in 1828 ('as full of conceit as an egg', wrote Haydon),(299) Chantrey went down to Brighton to place the bronze statue of George IV on the Steine. Another bronze statue was erected, after the King's death, at the junction of George Street and Hanover Street, in Edinburgh. A third, equestrian statue—which the King himself had planned to set on the marble arch in front of Buckingham Palace—was finally erected in Trafalgar Square. Chantrey's busts of the King adorned the Goldsmiths' Hall, and the Royal College of Physicians. He immortalised the King in bronze as grandly, and almost as often, as Sir Thomas Lawrence did on canvas.

As for Lawrence, he continued to bask in royal favour. In August he was invited to spend a few days at Windsor, to paint the young Prince George of Cumberland. He was still excited enough by the royal friendship to note the seating arrangement for dinner at Royal Lodge on 8 August. He himself sat opposite the King.(*300*)

He recognised the King's instinctive patronage of art when, this summer, he made his will. He had acquired a collection of drawings by old masters which he knew to be unequalled in Europe; he directed that on his death it should be offered to the King for £18,000 (£2,000 less than its value). If the King refused it, it should be offered to the British Museum. The collection included drawings by Leonardo, Rubens, Vandyck and Poussin. It was not, alas, bought by the King; but the King's death was to follow so closely on the painter's that perhaps the offer was never seriously considered. The collection was, strangely enough, refused by the British Museum, and by Sir Robert Peel; it was auctioned, in time, by a firm of picture-dealers.(*301*)

However, in 1829 this deplorable auction lay years ahead, and Lawrence made his gesture with confidence. In September, Jeffry Wyatville made arrangements to sit for his portrait for the King, and to 'work it in with Windsor'.(*302*) In November, while Chantrey and Wilkie were placing the statues and pictures, Lawrence was urgently commanded to send down the portrait of 'dear Mr. Angerstein', and that of Sir Walter Scott, to be hung before the King went into residence. The King was determined to live among the likenesses of his friends, and Angerstein's son had lent Lawrence his original portrait of the philanthropist and art-collector, so that Lawrence could make a faithful copy. The finished portrait was sent to Windsor with a portrait of Pitt which Angerstein had given to the

King. 'I rather chose that these two should go together.'
Lawrence told Angerstein's son, 'as (what indeed was need-
less) it would remind the King of the generous loyalty of
his spirit, and of his personal regard for his Majesty.'(*303*)
The portraits of Pitt and Eldon were hung on either side
of Scott's. 'Your picture,' Lockhart told Sir Walter, 'has an
honourable place.'(*304*)

Scott had indeed a place of honour in the royal circle:
he dined 'in a very private party' with the King in May,
and found it 'impossible to conceive a more friendly manner
than his Majesty used towards me'. He asked Knighton if
he might dedicate his collected works to the King, and was
assured that this would be 'highly well taken'.(*305*) The
compliment was all too calculated. And it was characteristic of Scott that, five days after the dinner-party, he asked
Knighton, 'the great Invisible', to help Lockhart on the
Quarterly Review. Whether Lockhart continued as editor,
he explained, would largely depend on his obtaining some
confidential hint from time to time 'what he is to do and
what forbear'. Members of the Government suggested
articles of entirely different tendencies, and Lockhart had
no means of knowing 'which with a view to his Majesty's
service he ought to prefer'.(*306*) It sounded like an offer to
sell Lockhart's soul. But no doubt its purpose was to in-
gratiate both Lockhart and Scott himself: three months
later, in a letter to Lockhart, intended for Knighton's eyes,
Scott suggested that his son-in-law should ask Knighton's
advice about a sinecure.(*307*) In a second letter to Lockhart, Scott explained: 'You would perfectly apprehend the
purpose of my last important letter which you must have
observed was written for the eye of the Invisible. I apprehend the best way is to trust to him entirely. . . .'(*308*) Royal
friendship had advantages.

It was this year that the King sanctioned the precursor
of the Great Exhibition, and the first of a series of annual
industrial exhibitions, of National Repositories, was held
in the Royal Mews in Trafalgar Square. The idea had come
a generation too early, and in 1833 it finally failed. But the

King who encouraged industry was, above all, in his later
years, concerned with architecture. He had once built a
fantasy palace on the coast of Sussex, and transformed a
fishing village into a handsome town. He had turned the
disused Carlton House into a model of elegance, and then
demolished it to make way for the sweeping improvements
in London. Now, on 20 March 1828, Mr. Creevey reported
that

> Nash or some of his crew waited upon Wellington the
> other day, stating the King's pleasure to have a part of the
> new palace at Pimlico pulled down and the plan altered;
> to which the Beau replied it was no business of his;
> they might pull down as much as they liked. But as this
> was not the answer that was wanted, he at last said: 'If
> you expect me to put my hand to any additional expense,
> I'll be damned if I will!'—Prinney is said to be furious
> about it.(309)

Next day, in the House of Commons, Mr. Bankes moved
for a Committee to inquire into the expense of public
buildings, and the Government acceded to the motion.
In July, when the Privy Council met to consider the draft
of the King's speech, the King very naturally objected to
the paragraph thanking the Commons for instituting the
Finance Committee. He had to be 'prevailed upon' to say
that he would try to reduce expenditure as far as was consistent with the dignity of his Crown and the interests of
his people.

If the new palace at Pimlico was one source of contention, Windsor Castle was certainly another. Croker, inspecting the new works in March, noted sharply that 'the repairs,
&c.' had already cost £500,000, and he thought they were
only worth one fifth of the sum. The rooms were 'by no
means what they ought to be', and their Louis XIV style
did not accord with the general character of Windsor. Wyatville, thought Croker, had committed 'some gross faults,
such as machicolations over inclined bases'.(310) The gros-
sest fault of all was, no doubt, that the work would cost a
further £700,000.

Six months later, another critical visitor, C. B. Wollaston, was shown over Windsor Castle by Wyatville himself, 'a busy-bustling, vain little man, ... such a person as one might expect to be gratified by the addition of *Ville* to his name'. The Castle was still in a half-prepared state: the few rooms which were finished were papered up, and the chairs and tables were covered. Only corners of the furniture were shown, and nothing, said Wollaston, could conceal the dazzling splendour of the gilding, which seemed much overdone; but Wyatville assured him that it was His Majesty's taste. The whole, so Wollaston explained to his sister, Mary Frampton, 'is no longer "Old Windsor Castle", it is now completely altered, raised, machicolated, and with new Towers added—and so raised, that they are now obliged to raise the Round Tower also'.(*311*)

Two months after Wollaston's visit, when the royal apartments were finished, fires were lighted, carpets laid, and the King's arrival was imminent, Lord Ellenborough, the President of the Board of Control, toured the Castle with Mr. Barbour, the American Minister, 'a very gentleman-like, well-conditioned man'. 'The American,' reported Lord Ellenborough, 'was enchanted'.(*312*) On 9 December, for the first time, the King went into residence. He entered the restored Windsor Castle exactly at four o'clock; at five o'clock his architect delivered the keys to him in a crimson bag, and was knighted Sir Jeffry Wyatville.

That night, in the Lancaster Tower, Sir William Knighton wrote to his youngest daughter:

> As I sleep in this castle to-night for the first time since the restoration of this wonderful pile of buildings, as does his most gracious Majesty George the Fourth, I send you this little memorandum as a curiosity, that when you are grown a woman, and I am dead and gone, you may look upon it as a memento.(*313*)

Just before Christmas, Mme de Lieven paid a visit to Windsor. She declared she had never passed so pleasant a time there. She noticed that the model of a salon in scagliola, a present from the Emperor Nicholas, had been given a place of honour in the Long Gallery; the malachite vase from 'our good Empress' was now the chief ornament of the best drawing-room. The King, she wrote, 'has obviously taken great trouble to place these objects in evidence, in fact it would not have been possible to be more amiable than he was. I am rather troubled, however, by the apparent state of weakness in which his last attack has left him'.(*314*)

Mme de Lieven was not alone in noticing his weakness. Late in September his arm had been so swollen that his valet had been unable to dress him. On 3 November Lockhart had told Scott that the King seemed to have undeniable symptoms of dropsy. His belly, said Lockhart, had disappeared, and his legs were useless, and, a few days earlier, there had even been communication with the Lord Mayor of London about tolling the great bell of St. Paul's.(*315*) The King's health caused statements and counter-statements, rumours and counter-rumours. Within a week of Lockhart's letter, Lord Sefton was telling Creevey: 'The reports about the King's health have no other origin than the mystery kept up about him. You will soon hear of him as well as ever.'(*316*) 'George IV is very well,' wrote Jekyll on 19 November, 'though the newspapers give him a mortal disease once a week.'(*317*) Lady Conyngham told Mme de Lieven late in November that the King had in fact been very unwell and that she was still most uneasy about him. 'He is not happy,' she wrote, 'unless he is ill.'(*318*)

The comment was cynical but sadly revealing. The King was really ill; yet perhaps he was aware that illness sometimes sheltered him from an unsympathetic world, from the routine tasks of his position, from the grand perplexities of government. Illness was at times an escape from responsibility, from the adult need to make decisions. Illness was a form of withdrawal: the one state in which he could hide, and find comfort and attention, like a child.

79

There were, even now, certain immature features in the King's character. He sometimes showed a childish unwillingness to do the tasks he found uncongenial; occasionally he behaved in an irrational, almost superstitious manner. In May 1828, Peel had mentioned to Lord Ellenborough that the King had signed no commissions for more than two years. 'He will not sign parchment,' wrote Ellenborough. 'There can be no reason why the commissions should not be on thick paper; but they say the King would sign them for the first few days and then give it up.'(*319*) In September, Wellington enlarged on Peel's curious statement. He told Croker, the Secretary to the Admiralty, that when the King went to Hanover in 1821, the Regency had signed more than 10,000 papers, and that the King had not signed an army commission since. 'The Duke talked to me,' wrote Croker, 'of the necessity of appointing an officer to affix some kind of signet which should be equivalent to, and supersede, the royal signature.' Such behaviour must have seemed all the stranger to Croker, as the King signed all the Admiralty papers and commissions very regularly.(*320*)

One supremely distasteful task which the King could no longer avoid was to consider Catholic emancipation. He had always been sincerely opposed to emancipation; and since he had taken his Coronation oath 'to maintain the protestant reformed religion as established by law', he also felt he was breaking his solemn vow. He was not an isolated bigot, a stubborn retrograde, sheltering behind a convenient formality. He simply shared the age-old English prejudice against Roman Catholics, the old fear of the insidious power of the Papacy. His emotions and his duty led him, for once, to the same inescapable conclusion: they forbade him to allow the Catholics political opportunity.

Some months ago, Sir Walter Scott had asked Knighton to give Lockhart confidential guidance on the editorial policy of the *Quarterly*: a hint as to which opinion, 'with a view to his Majesty's service', he should prefer. Late in 1828, the Poet Laureate published a paper in the *Quarterly Review* on the Catholic question. It is not surprising to learn that the paper enjoyed royal approval: indeed, the King expressed a wish that it should be separately reprinted for more general circulation. However, Mr. Murray, the publisher, 'having more regard to profit than loyalty', refused to reprint it, 'saying that those who wished to read the article might purchase the number which contained it'.(*321*)

But if Mr. Murray proved to be unhelpful, there was one event which encouraged the King: this was his brother Ernest's return from the Continent. The Duke of Cumberland, declared Lord Ellenborough, 'is a Mephistopheles, and sure, wherever he can, to do any mischief'.(*322*) Early in 1829 Wellington persuaded the King to send Knighton abroad to prevent the Duke from coming to England. Knighton had set off post-haste, but the Duke of Cumberland, Brougham told Grey, 'is fuller of spirits and all mischief than ever, and says he will come if he lives in a coffee-house'. He arrived in London on 14 February.

For the next fortnight the rabidly anti-Catholic Cumberland was perpetually with the King. He had always exercised a strange influence over his eldest brother; and now he reminded him of their father's rigid attitude to Catholicism,(*323*) of the Coronation oath, of the strong arguments against the Bill, until the King was wrought up to a frenzy. Only Wellington could undo the work of Cumberland. On 28 February he reported to the Cabinet the audience he had had of the King. It had lasted five and a quarter hours, and it had been remarkably painful. The King, noted Lord Ellenborough, had been 'in a very agitated state, and had even spoken of abdicating'.(*324*) The Duke said it was the more painful in consequence of the very peremptory language he was obliged to hold to him. However, the King was very kind, and kissed him when he left him.

The victory had been as complete as that of Waterloo.

The Duke had not only kept the King's affection, but the King had ultimately yielded on all points,

> even to the extent of desiring the Duke of Cumberland to leave England. The King declared himself more satisfied with the Bill than with anything he had seen. He had great unwillingness to write *himself* to the household, desiring their attendance in the House of Lords during the Catholic measures, but he had no objection to the Duke of Wellington writing to them in his name.(325)

The Duke of Cumberland had manifest objections. He returned to the attack. On 1 March, just before the Bill was to be introduced in the Commons, Lord Ellenborough heard that the King was 'ill, if not mad. In fact this excitement in which he is may lead to insanity, and nothing but the removal of the Duke of Cumberland from his presence will restore him to peace'.(326)

On 2 March the Duke of Wellington was reported 'much exhausted' after spending three hours with the King.(327) On 4 March, he was again at Windsor, where the King talked for six hours, fortifying himself, continually, with sips of brandy-and-water. The King now objected to every part of the Bill; the Duke entreated him to avoid all reference to the Coronation oath. The King talked 'of postponing the consideration of the Bill till he had seen the Archbishop of Canterbury and the Bishop of London—but he gave up that idea of himself. It seems that he really does not know what his Coronation oath is. He has confused it with the oath of Supremacy'.(328) At last, when all his threats and powers of persuasion proved to be vain, and the Ministers still stood by the Bill, he dismissed them from office.

After the audience, the Conynghams and Knighton found him in a state of collapse. Knighton reminded him, sensibly, that he could not dismiss the Government: the opponents of the Bill were not strong enough to form an administration. There was no alternative to Wellington. Late that night, a messenger brought Wellington the King's decision:

4 March 1829

My dear Friend,

As I find the country would be without an administration, I have decided to yield my opinion to *that* which is considered by the Cabinet to be for the immediate interests of the country. Under these circumstances you have my consent to proceed as you propose with the measure. God knows what pain it causes me to write these words.

G.R.(*329*)

On 10 April 1829 George IV gave his formal assent to the Catholic Emancipation Bill. 'So that matter,' wrote Mme de Lieven, 'has ended in a complete triumph for the Duke of Wellington.'(*330*)

For once the King had been stubborn with reason; but he had found himself in conflict with a liberal, progressive government. He had earned the venom of Cumberland, the taunt of moral cowardice from Southey (though the Laureate made the taunt in private); and he had learned where the true power in the kingdom lay. Perhaps his own comment was contained in the observation accredited to him: 'Arthur is King of England, O'Connell King of Ireland, and myself Canon of Windsor.'(*331*)

80

There was one member of the Government of whom the King could not approve. Lord Ellenborough had naturally incurred his dislike on the third reading of the King's Property Bill. He had questioned the expediency of allowing a childless King to leave certain property away from his successor. This speech not only reminded the King that he had failed to leave a surviving heir; it also angered the Conynghams, against whom it was obviously directed; and the Conynghams, as Lord Ellenborough said, 'never forgive'. From the moment the King presented him with the Privy Seal in January 1828, he had not addressed a word to him; and early in 1829 he gave Lord Ellenborough (then President of the Board of Control) 'rather a marked slight': he invited all the Administration, except himself, to dinner.(*332*)

However, Ellenborough apart, the King was satisfied with his Ministers; he knew that they were strong, and that he was safe in their hands. At times, perhaps, he felt a touch of jealousy that Wellington was so powerful, a touch of resentment at his discipline; but he had a natural respect for him, and a warm affection. The Duke felt occasional respect (he believed the King had 'a wonderful knowledge of character'),(*333*) and there was no doubt that he was fond of him. The Duke, wrote Lord Ellenborough, 'has a very kind heart, and I really believe the King works upon it and takes advantage of it. The Duke cannot bear to see the King in distress. He told me the other day the King was, he believed, attached to him, and would be very sorry to hurt him, but he did not fear him. This seems to be the case'.(*334*)

Wellington had to cajole and command a temperamental sovereign. At one moment the King was in better health, 'and eveything was *couleur de rose;*'(*335*) the next he felt unwell and nervous, and was cold in conversation. One day the King would talk for six hours; another he would keep the Prime Minister waiting, while he changed from the Highland dress in which he was sitting for his portrait. The Chancellor, summoned by the King in May 1829, arrived to hear that he had taken a large dose of laudanum, and would not wake for two or three hours. He would then be 'in a state of excessive irritation', so that his Lordship might as well not see him.(*336*) One persistent cause of aggravation was the Duke of Cumberland, who remained at Windsor: 'all would have been quiet,' said Lady Conyngham, 'if the Duke of Cumberland had not come over, and all would be quiet when he went away.'(*337*) But the Duke of Cumberland stayed on. 'We must do our best for the country, and we shall have it with us,' wrote Lord Ellenborough on 30 June. 'The worst of it is, the King is the most faithless of men, and Cumberland is at work.'(*338*)

The King might vacillate in politics, but he was constantly charming to his friends. In January 1829 Mme de Lieven attended the New Year's festivities and the inauguration of the new Windsor Castle; she was also presented with an excellent engraving of 'a capital portrait of the King': no doubt the engraving of Lawrence's portrait, which Haydon found unbearable and Lawrence himself pronounced universally popular. Jekyll found the King 'very joyous' with his New Year guests and 'much delighted with the little Queen of Portugal'.(*339*) In May he gave a ball, at which she fell down during a dance, and cut her nose with one of her diamonds, 'which made her blubber most unroyally'.(*340*) Lady Cowper, talking to Moore at about this time, 'spoke of the King with great liking; his being so agreeable, and so full of fun and good nature'.(*341*) Early in June he had an evening concert at St. James's Palace: Mlle Sontag and Mme Malibran sang to perfection.

Writers and artists were still expressing gratitude for the benevolence that they had known. In May, Scott sent Knighton the first copy of the popular edition of the Waverley Novels, inscribed, by permission, to the King.(*342*) Haydon, breakfasting with Wilkie, found him showing new confidence. 'The King sitting to him, his being at the levée, and altogether his intercourse at Court have affected him,' wrote Haydon. 'I dare say he will be *Sir* David.'(*343*) In April, when Lawrence was given the freedom of Bristol, he declared that he had received 'the very highest honour (the protection of majesty excepted) that could have rewarded my professional exertions'.(*344*) His acceptance showed gratitude to his sovereign, if little tact towards his native city.

The King who patronised Lawrence was anxious to show approval of Nash; and, indeed, Nash richly deserved it. Richard Rush, the former American Minister, visiting England after a four-year absence, was 'amazed at the increase of London. The Regent's Park,' he wrote,

was now a city; you saw long rows of lofty buildings, in their outward aspect magnificent.... In whatever

direction I went, indications were similar. I say nothing of
Carlton Terrace, for Carlton House was gone, or of the
street, of two miles, from that point to Park Crescent,
surpassing any other in London, or any that I saw in
Europe. . . . I could scarcely, but for the evidence of the
senses, have believed it all.(*345*)

Wellington saw the same improvements with a different
eye. The Duke was not, perhaps, endowed with aesthetic
sense; and he was probably brooding on the controversial
question of building expenses. He also felt, with reason,
that an honour for Nash would not be politic. Nash had
recently been accused, in the House of Commons, of mal-
versation and fraud; a select committee had taken evidence,
and they had cleared him only with reservations. The King
considered that Nash had been 'most infamously used, and
there is but one opinion about it; and therefore,' he wrote
to Wellington, demanding that the baronetcy should be
approved, 'it is not only an act of justice to *him* but *to my
own dignity,* and *this* should *forthwith* be *done'.(346)*
The Duke refused to gazette the honour, because the report
on Nash's conduct had still not been before the House of
Commons. He considered that Nash should wait until
Buckingham Palace was finished.

Nash accumulated many honours. He dined with the King
at the Pavilion (Pugin was to record the occasion); the King
('our dear King,' as Nash would call him) had long ago
sailed to the Isle of Wight to dine with him at East Cowes
Castle. Lawrence painted him as the King's architect, and
Nash urged him to emphasise the royal connexion: 'a bit
of the Pavilion seen through a window, or sticking out of a
portfolio, or the portfolio with a label on it saying Pavilion
at Brighton (as if it contained the drawings) will do'.(*347*)
But the ultimate honour the King wished to give him was
finally denied him: Nash died in 1835, plain Mr. Nash.

'The King was out of humour yesterday,' wrote Lord
Ellenborough on 23 June. 'He wanted to make Nash a
baronet. The Duke refused. The King then went upon his
Speech, which he did not like and had altered.'(*348*) In

September the same diarist reported that the Duke had abandoned the King 'as a bad job.... The King has no constancy', wrote Ellenborough. 'There is no depending upon him from one day to another.'(*349*)

The vacillating monarch was now a pathetic figure. On 12 August, the King's sixty-seventh birthday, Moore described Jekyll's visit to Windsor: the King had never made his appearance till late in the day, 'as the lacing he requires would not be endurable if he underwent it early'.(*350*) On 31 August Peel told Lord Ellenborough that the King was 'very blind'. He had 'lost the sight of one eye'.(*351*) In September Mme de Lieven confirmed that 'the poor King is in danger of becoming blind; he has already lost the sight of one eye, and the other is affected. The operation for cataract will be postponed until blindness is complete; this makes him sad and troubled'.(*352*) On 24 September Lord Aberdeen repeated that 'the King has quite lost the sight of one eye, and the sight of the other is indistinct. It gives him pain, too, and the fear of blindness makes him nervous. The Duke of Cumberland is always about him, mischievous as ever, but pretending not to be hostile'.(*353*) The King himself told Knighton he was 'blind as a beetle'.(*354*)

He was worried, too, in October, by the illness of Lady Conyngham. Lord Conyngham dismissed the complaint as 'a bad bilious fever', but in mid-November Mme de Lieven declared that the illness had affected her nerves, and Sir Henry Halford, the King's physician, called on her every day. 'The King is worried and upset. She thinks that she is dying. She faints constantly, and really I have no idea what is the matter....'(*355*) On 9 December Jekyll recorded that she was still an invalid.(*356*)

Though the King himself drove his phaeton daily, he now spent most of his time in bed. He was called between six and seven, had books and all the newspapers read to him, and then, perhaps, transacted a little work. In November Chantrey gave Lockhart a lively account of the morning council at the Cottage:

himself about the statues; and Wardrop about the stuff-
ing of the Cameleopard on one side of the bed, the D[uke]
of Cumberland and a tailor on the other. The King in a
white cotton nightcap and a rather dirty flannel jacket,
propped up with pillows, and sipping his chocolate
amidst this divan. The Duke of Wellington is announced.
His Majesty gets on forthwith a black velvet cap with a
gold tassel and a grand blue silk douillette, and walks
into the next room to receive him in the character of
George the Fourth. After half an hour ... he came back,
and tumbled into bed again among them, to resume the
discussion on the blue breeches.

The King was dreaming of dressing the Guards, and later
all the infantry, in blue. This, said Lockhart, was 'the D.
of Cumberland's Prussian nonsense'.(357)

The King's occupations were not entirely nonsensical. He
liked to have drama read to him; and, through Sir Thomas
Lawrence, who was painting his portrait, he appointed Miss
Chester as his reader. Elizabeth Chester, who was one of
the handsomest women on the stage, gave solace to the
lover of Perdita Robinson, the admirer of Mrs. Siddons,
the friend of Kemble, the King who had not lost his affection for the theatre. And, though his sight was failing, he
kept his enthusiasm for the visual arts. He had summoned
Chantrey to Windsor again to arrange the bronze statues
from Hampton Court and Kensington Palace in the new
French garden; and he offered him 9,000 guineas for an
equestrian statue of himself, to set on a marble arch in
front of the new Buckingham Palace. The plan was
abandoned, but the statue stands in Trafalgar Square: one
of the many signs that George IV recognised the inspiration
of the carpenter's son from Derbyshire.

On his birthday, 12 August, the King had also fulfilled
an intention which dated from the first year of his reign:
he laid the foundation-stone of the base for the great bronze
equestrian statue of his father. The four-ton granite base
had been designed by Wyatville, and the statue (known as
the Copper Horse) was being sculpted by Westmacott.

George IV
The statue by Sir Francis Chantrey at Brighton

'New Palace, St. James's Park'
From an engraving by Wallis, 1829

Windsor Castle
From an engraving by Sands, c. 1840

'Now, Westmacott,' said the King, 'we depend on you for the remainder. By this day twelvemonth you say it will be finished. I know if you say so, it will be performed.' The statue was finished after the King's death; it was set on the summit of Snow Hill, Windsor Great Park, in the next reign.(*358*)

81

'The weather is dreadfully chilling and intense, with Egyptian darkness attending it.'(*359*) So Lawrence had told his sister, on Christmas Eve. The darkness was now finally to fall. On 6 January he had a long conversation with his friend Miss Croft. He was apprehensive about his health, but he roused himself to paint for an hour, and finished the left sleeve on the King's portrait. Miss Croft asked if he was not tired of painting 'those eternal robes' of the Garter. 'No,' he answered, 'I always find variety in them. If you could compare them, I hope you would find the last was still the best.'(*360*) It was a sadly appropriate wish. Next day, in the full vigour of his powers, at the age of sixty, Lawrence died.

It was some measure of the King's affection for Lawrence that Peel hesitated to send him a cold and formal announcement of his death. His first reaction was to write to Knighton:

> Knowing that his Majesty is not well, I am unwilling to communicate abruptly to him intelligence which I am sure will give pain to his Majesty.
>
> I have this moment heard, from a gentleman of the name of Keightley, that Sir Thomas Lawrence died last night about nine o'clock. I believe that the immediate cause of his death was some affection of the heart....
>
> I undertook to assure Mr. Keightley that I would make the communication to his Majesty of this most distressing event....(*361*)

Knighton was not at Windsor when this letter arrived; perhaps, after all, the King learned the news, abruptly, from an official note. But Peel's apprehensions were justified. 'My dear Sir,' wrote Knighton, on his return to the Castle, 'His Majesty was much grieved at the Melancholy Intelligence, and feels most severely the Loss that has been sustained by the Death of that Unrivalled artist.'(*362*)

An exhibition of Lawrence's work was held, soon afterwards, at the British Institution. It showed how deeply he had been indebted to royal patronage. The first twenty-one portraits had been painted, by the King's order, for Windsor; and another twelve were owned by the King. These thirty-odd paintings commemorated the powers of the post-Napoleonic world, the Allied Sovereigns, their most distinguished generals, and the Bourbon Charles X who, by their grace, was now the King of France. But from the canvases there also looked the faces of John Kemble, in the character of Hamlet, Sir Jeffry Wyatville and Lawrence himself. The exhibition seems a synthesis of the military and political triumphs, the cultural achievements of the time.

Meanwhile, in January 1830, the death of Lawrence released the pent-up emotions of the artistic world. Haydon, seizing the chance to express his own lifelong frustration, declared that Lawrence would not rank high with posterity, and had known scarcely anything of composition; 'and perhaps', added Haydon, 'in the whole circle of art there never was a more lamentable proof of these deficiencies than in his last portrait of the King'.(*363*) The knowledge that a new President must be elected by the Royal Academy was a hurtful reminder of Haydon's misspent energies; and almost before Peel sent the news of the death of Lawrence to the King, the Academy were debating the succession. Martin Archer Shee, the Irish portrait-painter, was soon informed, 'on the authority of a nobleman of very high rank and eminent political station', that the King had observed: 'Shee is their only man now.'(*364*)

It is clear, however, that the King had other intentions. On 20 January Peel informed Lord Farnborough:

The King has an impression that it would be desirable to alter the constitution of the Royal Academy, with the view of placing at its head some distinguished amateur of the arts. He wishes, I understand, to have your opinion on this subject.

Writing confidentially to you, I have no hesitation in declaring that my present opinion is decidedly adverse to this scheme.

The election of a president comes on Sunday next. Surely it would be very ungracious to step in on Sunday with a notice from the King that he contemplated an alteration, the effect of which would be to transfer the nomination to himself. Seeing, too, that the result of the present mode of nomination has been to place in the chair such men as Sir Joshua Reynolds and Sir Thomas Lawrence, I see no public ground on which the King could be advised to alter it.(365)

Lord Farnborough agreed with Peel. And Peel, who understood the King, spoke to him, now, with truth and judicious flattery. 'I told the King,' he reported to Lord Farnborough,

that I had conferred with you on his proposal of himself nominating a nobleman to be President of the Academy; that we thought his Majesty stood so well with the artists of this country, that he was so universally admitted to be the greatest patron that Art ever had in England, that it would not be prudent to risk the excitement of any other feelings. The King at once assented, and said, 'Well, perhaps we had better not meddle with the Royal Academy.' He was particularly good-humoured.(366)

It would have been both unwise and unconstitutional to impose an amateur president on a distinguished professional company; and the King was well advised to refrain from making this absolute gesture. However, one of the offices which had been held by Lawrence was within his powers to bestow, and he appointed Wilkie his painter-in-ordinary. The announcement of Wilkie's appointment

appeared in the *London Gazette* just before the Academy
election. Haydon considered that it destroyed his chances
of the presidency.

The King's open sign of favour to Wilkie may perhaps
have led the Academy to declare their independence;
perhaps they also wanted an innocuous nonentity, a
figurehead who would not give them serious professional
competition. Whatever the reason, Archer Shee was elected
by a large majority.

> Without a movement on my part [he told a friend on
> 26 January]—without an attempt to employ the smallest
> influence in or out of the Academy,—knowing that I have
> neither wealth, nor power—that I have no influence with
> the great, and have never basked in the sunshine of royal
> favour—and in the teeth of a *congé d'élire* which ap-
> peared in the newspapers the day before the election,
> announcing that our friend Wilkie had been appointed
> painter in ordinary to the King—in spite of all this, they
> have made me President.(*367*)

Lawrence had been an artist of extraordinary talent, uncommonly in tune with the epic, elegant, full-blooded age;
he had felt it along his pulses, and he had presented it with
ease and understanding and fire. Shee was little more than
a conventional portrait painter and, as Haydon wrote, he
was 'conscious of no high power in art'. It was almost
symbolic that the King never invested him with the presidential gold medal and chain; it was sent to him by Peel
on the morning of the Royal Academy dinner.(*368*)

82

While the Academicians had been busy electioneering, the
King had been preoccupied by a much more serious
election: Russia and France had agreed to make Leopold
of Saxe-Coburg King of Greece. 'I suppose you have heard,'
wrote Brougham to Grey, 'that Leopold's Greek crown is

of his own getting, chiefly at the Tuileries, and not at all of our giving. The King and rest of the family are all very angry at it.'(*369*) The King was more than angry: he could not endure the thought of a crown for Monsieur Peu-à-Peu, as he called his cold, careerist son-in-law. The Press report that the former husband of Princess Charlotte was to marry a daughter of the Duc d'Orléans was hardly calculated to improve his temper. When Wellington suggested that Leopold would at least be innocuous, and might even be useful, the King asked 'how we could be such fools as to think he would be of any use'.(*370*) However, on 19 January, he 'grumpily acceded' to Leopold's appointment. Leopold was 'very *uppish* upon the subject'.(*371*)

On 21 May, quite suddenly, Leopold declined the throne of Greece. He had a far grander ambition in view. For by then George IV was gravely ill; when he died, only his brother, the elderly Duke of Clarence, would stand between Princess Victoria and the Crown. If Victoria became Queen before the month of May, 1839, there would have to be a regency. Leopold was dazzled by the thought of an English regency, of being the power behind his niece's throne. 'If I had taken command of things in England in 1830,' he was to write, years later, 'many things would have happened differently.'(*372*)

83

George IV had not enjoyed perfect health for years; he had long ago left off stays, and his flaccid bulk betrayed the damage done by overheated rooms and lack of exercise, by prolonged, excessive eating and drinking. He repeatedly suffered from gout and, no doubt, from a strain on his heart. His condition was hardly improved by the bleedings which his doctors often prescribed, and he was in a highly nervous state. On 12 January 1830, when Lord Aberdeen had an audience to discuss the question of the Greek throne, he reported that the King 'was much agitated in dressing himself for the interview. The man who shaved [him] thought he should have cut him twenty times. He had taken 100 drops of laudanum to prepare himself for the interview'.*(373)*

The Press had never been kind to the King; now it was cruel. Early in January, reported Jekyll, the *Herald* 'made great merriment of the poor King's supposed cataract'.*(374)* Captain Gronow noted, in his *Anecdotes*, that the King behaved like a spoilt child,

> and the way he spent his time was frivolous in the extreme. He was very fond of punch, made from a recipe by his maître-d'hôtel Mr. Maddison, and which he drank after dinner; this was the only time he was agreeable, and on these occasions he would sing songs, relate anecdotes of his youth, and play on the violoncello; afterwards going to bed in a 'comfortable' state....*(375)*

At Windsor, the Duke of Cumberland, the most mistrusted of his brothers, still hovered round the King, and tried to influence his politics; the Duchess of Cumberland, it seems, was growing powerful enough to alarm Lady Conyngham. Lady Conyngham (now recovered, and 'so *embellie*', wrote Jekyll, 'that she looks twenty years younger'),*(376)* saw fit to send a warning note to Wellington; 'she is bored to death', recorded Lord Ellenborough, on 13 January, 'and really thinks of removing'.*(377)* The King's illnesses had rarely increased her affection.

Physical pain and political machinations did nothing to lessen the King's interest in the arts. Late in February, at the private view of his exhibition, Haydon was told by Seguier that the King would like to see the pictures at Windsor. Next day, said Haydon, Seguier told the King, on his own initiative, that the pictures could not be brought to him, as the public could not be disappointed. The King replied, gracefully, that Haydon's *Punch* should be sent to him for a week-end, while the exhibition was closed. The picture was sent; it was returned 'with high approbation', but the King did not buy it. Haydon blamed this on Seguier's malice. Once again the shadow of the King's

Bench prison stretched over him. Haydon would always be unlucky in gaining royal patronage. In forty-two years of professional life, he received one commission of 500 guineas from George IV, and one subscription of ten guineas from his successor. Queen Victoria would refuse to appoint him her historical painter; and when, in 1844, he sent Prince Albert his *Essay on Fresco Painting*, the Prince unpardonably returned it to him. George IV would have shown more generosity.(*378*)

For he was generous to the causes he supported, and to artists of every sort who earned his favour. On 14 April, writing to Knighton, Scott showed that he was mindful of royal kindness. He had had 'an awkward fit in spring, somewhat like a paralytic affection', and he asked now to resign the office of a principal Clerk of Session in the Court of Session at Edinburgh.

> Having received so many marks of distinction from his Majesty, I may [he wrote] be permitted to hope his uniform benevolence towards me will dispose him to concern himself in some degree, whether the old *littérateur* whom the King has delighted to honour shall continue to turn the wheel till he die in harness, or shall be allowed a remission from his labours....(*379*)

The King was indeed concerned: Scott was asked to head a new commission to examine and edit the Stuart Papers. The task could hardly have been chosen with more understanding. The offer must have touched his heart, and he accepted gladly. According to Lockhart, he was also offered the rank of Privy Councillor, but refused it on the grounds of his failing health and diminished fortune.(*380*) The King's final marks of friendship for Scott showed the warmth and understanding which he had shown, now, for some fifteen years; and even the kindness of King William and Queen Adelaide, who would lend the dying novelist a frigate in his final search for health and the sun, 'mus[t] not make me forget', so Scott would write, 'what I owe to the memory of George IV who permitted me to call him a personal friend'.(*381*)

84

On 14 April, when Scott wrote to Knighton and asked to resign his office, the King himself, driving in Windsor Great Park, stopped his pony-chair and got out to look at his hounds. As he tried to climb in again, wrote Croker, 'he was seized with a spasmodic difficulty of breathing'.*(382)* He had had such attacks before: in March Sir Henry Halford, his physician, had shown concern about his breathlessness; and only 'by a good contrivance of pillows and a bed chair' had the King slept uninterruptedly for a few hours. But even a herculean constitution (the word was Sir Henry's) could not contend with such troubles indefinitely; Sir Henry Halford knew that the King had a heart disease which must kill him.*(383)* The King's immediate circle were now alarmed.

'I myself,' wrote Croker, 'incline to believe the danger to be more remote than the people in the streets, who are always greedy of bad news, will have it.'*(384)* Croker was optimistic. At half-past six on the evening of 14 April, the Duke of Wellington, just returned from Windsor, reported that the King was 'very unwell.... He was in very good humour', Wellington added to Peel, 'notwithstanding that he had taken above 250 drops of laudanum [*sic*] in the last 36 hours. I did not talk to him about business of any kind. I understand, however, that he is quite prepared to receive and act in conformity with any suggestion that may be made to him respecting the affair of Mr. Comyn'.*(385)*

Comyn, an Irishman, had, it was said, burnt his house to defraud his landlord; he had been found guilty of perjury, forgery and arson, and he had been sentenced to death. The King had written express to the Lord-Lieutenant of Ireland, and ordered a reprieve. Was the royal prerogative used at the instigation of Lady Conyngham? Was it due, as it had often been, to the King's own active humanity? The Home Secretary did not inquire; he did not intend

the King's clemency to sway him. He found the royal prerogative of mercy 'quite intolerable'; he insisted that the
law must take its course. On 15 April Knighton wrote from
Windsor that the King agreed to Comyn's execution.(*386*)
No doubt he was now too dazed with laudanum, and much
too ill, to fight.

The Duke of Wellington, wrote Lord Ellenborough, a
few days later, had described the King as 'a bold man, afraid
of nothing if his Ministers would stand by him, and
certainly neither afraid of pain or of death'.(*387*) The
thought of Comyn facing execution in Ireland had no
doubt reminded him of his own danger. Perhaps, in trying to save him, he had shown his own persistent love of
life.

There was a suspicion among the public that the King
was ill; but, though 'much murmuring was occasioned by
the absence of bulletins', there was, at first, no news from
Windsor. Indeed, Mary Frampton noted in her journal
that 'the secrecy as to everything that was going on at
Windsor Castle was quite impenetrable, and left a wide
field for numerous conjectures of all kinds'.(*388*)

However, as 23 April, the King's official birthday, approached, it became clear that he could not hold a Drawing-
room, and some official statement had to be made. Mary
Frampton suggested that the King himself dictated the
bulletins, and that he and Knighton conspired to keep
everything secret. ('I care very little what is said or thought
of me,' wrote Knighton, in the room next to the King's.
'My duty is to promote the King's comfort and peace of
mind.')(*389*) Whoever issued the statement, now, it gave no
indication of the nature of the King's illness. 'We are all in
the dark as to the disease,' wrote Croker on 26 April. 'Public
opinion is very gloomy about him, and I begin to fear the
thing looks serious. The Duke of Clarence has come to
reside in town. . . .'(*390*)

The Duke of Clarence, pitifully eager for the Crown,
hovered near the seat of government; the Duke of Cumberland, still more grotesque, circled round Windsor. On 27

April Sir Henry Halford told the Prime Minister and the Royal Family that the King had heart disease.*(391)* The King himself behaved with dignity: on 28 April, when Wellington requested an audience, he did not see the King, 'because the King refused to see the Duke of Cumberland, and begged the Duke would not see him unless it is very pressing, that the rebuff to the Duke of Cumberland might be less'.*(392)* Lord Ellenborough, reporting the incident, added, in a coldly practical manner, that some means must be devised to getting signatures for official documents, as the King's state might continue for some months. The King had suffered an attack the previous day, and this morning he had woken 'much relieved, but *with a dropsy*—that is an external dropsy, the water being between the skin'.*(393)* On 30 April Lord Ellenborough noted: 'The Attorney- and Solicitor-General were called in. They evidently thought the King's mind was gone, ... for they proposed a delegation of the Royal authority'.*(394)*

From the end of April the bulletins were regularly shown at St. James's Palace, as they had been in the days of George III. The Lord-in-Waiting, in full dress, stood in one room to answer inquiries, and the Yeomen of the Guard were drawn up in the ante-room, as if for a levée. There was little sign of regret. There were many signs that the King's illness caused inconvenience: Mary Frampton wrote that everyone in London was 'afraid of naming distant days for their balls and parties, lest the expected death of the King should put a stop to all gaiety.... It became almost a fashion in London to go to fine places in old dresses on the pretence of the expected mourning'. The provinces, too, were incommoded. 'In the country the dressmakers and milliners put off their journeys for spring fashions, fearing to embark on large purchases of any sort....'*(395)*

On May Day, Jekyll recorded his apprehension about the imminent new reign. 'How shall we manage,' he asked, 'under Clarence, whom they certainly were constrained to dismiss from the Admiralty on suspicion of craziness?'*(396)* It was a disturbing thought that the next King of England was an elderly, benevolent eccentric, already living in his regal dream. Southey expressed his fears of an increasingly democratic future, 'every successive change ... strengthening that power of public opinion which will lay all our institutions in the dust'.(*397*) Lockhart suggested that Knighton was already ensuring his career: it was, he told his father-in-law, 'generally believed that our friend the Invisible has made sure of his ground at Bushy—that is, is to be Privy Purse under the next reign also....'(*398*) Lockhart's speculations were wrong, but many people were planning for a future which now seemed very near.

While arrangements were coolly made for the reign of William IV, the new royal palace (the Metropolitan Palace, some called it) was rising at the end of the Mall. Buckingham Palace was George IV's last architectural enterprise, his last grand patriotic gesture, his final legacy to the capital which he had largely transformed.

Though he could not boast, like Augustus, that he had found the metropolis of brick, and left it of marble, yet, as one of his biographers would write, 'the astonishing improvements that have been made under his reign, have effected a metamorphosis quite as sudden, and not much less beautiful'.

To some observers, however, his taste lacked an elegant sobriety. In buildings which had been erected or improved under his directions, there was 'a want of the chaste simplicity of the classic models of the art; they are gorgeous rather than grand', wrote a critic, 'and dazzle the eye by their splendour, rather than satisfy the understanding by the harmony of their proportions'.(*399*) James Frampton, inspecting Buckingham Palace in May, criticised the 'immense pillars in Scagliola', some of them in imitation of lapis-lazuli, and the walls of the entrance and staircase; these, he reported, were 'of strawberry and cream-coloured Scagliola, and no such marble is known!' The King had not lost his predilection for splendour, his lifelong taste for Kubla Khan invention. However, the reception rooms reflected his own style more happily: they were grand in proportion, delicate in detail. The palace, concluded Frampton, was 'certainly

very fine', and would look 'most magnificent when full of
company'. The garden was laid out in 'most excellent taste,
and the Marble Arch, at the entrance to the palace, would
be very handsome'.(*400*)

Jekyll saw the palace as an ancient pharaoh's pyramid.
'When the poor Duke of York was so intent on his new
palace,' he wrote on 1 May, 'I looked at it always as his
mausoleum. Another palace now rising reminds me of that
reflection.'(*401*) That same day, Peel told Hobhouse that
the King's disorder was dropsy, and that they must be
prepared for 'a sudden termination of his life'.(*402*)

Sir Henry Halford told Wellington that it was 'a gigantic
struggle'.(*403*) At one moment, thanks to 'great quantities
of ether—quantities much greater than are usually given',
it seemed as if the King was recovering: that 'the miracle
which the physicians had said could alone save him seemed
accomplished'.(*404*) The King, receiving Wellington in
audience, did not express the slightest apprehension—
though the Duke observed that he did so to the women, 'to
try and vex Lady Conyngham'.(*405*) It was a cynical remark;
but then, perhaps, Lady Conyngham deserved the cynicism.
She was probably vexed to think that the cornucopia would
soon be empty. The King may have hoped to provoke some
demonstration of affection, but he could have had few
illusions about her now.

He would have had no illusions about the affections of
his family, if he had known of the urgent, touching letters
they sent to Knighton. Whatever their ambitions for power,
it is clear that the royal dukes felt genuine devotion to their
brother. To Knighton, waiting faithfully in the room next
to the King's, 'promoting the King's comfort and peace of
mind',(*406*) they sent the messages they could not send to
the King himself. To Knighton, whom the King did not
like to be distant from him, they now confided their affection and apprehension. 'I have only,' wrote the Duke of
Clarence, 'to repeat my anxious wishes for that amendment
which gratitude of fifty-nine years' standing calls me to express from the bottom of my heart.'(*407*) The Duke of

Cumberland, who was rarely credited with affection, was horrorstruck by an account from one of his sisters:

> I own to you [he told Knighton] her description of the state in which she found my poor brother went to my very soul, loving him as faithfully as ever one brother did another: for this I can say, I loved him for himself, and never have I had any sordid or interested view in my affection for him, but that of the purest love and attachment....
>
> God preserve him for us all! (*408*)

The Duke of Cambridge was only deterred by his fears of alarming the King from coming home, at once, from Hanover; but if, he told Knighton, 'I had the slightest idea that my going to England would be any comfort to my dear suffering brother, I would travel night and day'.(*409*) The King's sister, Princess Elizabeth, Landgravine of Hesse Homburg, sent Knighton her understanding and sympathy: 'I feel for all those who are attending the King, for all must love him who know him ... I will ... humbly pray God to watch over that life which is of so much consequence to us all.'(*410*)

But what was most affecting (and, to some, most surprising) was Wellington's admiration for the King's courage. In this protracted illness, suffering from the doctors' primitive remedies, watching his physical degeneration, the King behaved with amazing fortitude. 'In constitution and mind he is certainly a wonderful man,' wrote Lord Ellenborough. 'I have no doubt that the feeling that he is always in representation makes him behave in the face of death as a man would on the field of battle.'(*411*) The man who made that discerning comment understood, more than most, the nature of the King.

On 3 May Croker reported that the King had received the Sacrament. He was aware of his situation, and 'contemplates it boldly'. He could no longer lie down; he was always bolstered up in bed, or in a chair; his appetite had gone, and he was 'very torpid, and evidently fading rapidly away'.(*412*) Next day he was 'black in the face', wrote

Lord Ellenborough, 'and the ends of his fingers black. They think he will go off suddenly in one of these attacks'.*(413)* Yet the Royal Household were still laying wagers that he would be at Ascot; and the King himself encouraged speculation by discussing the latest improvements at the Cottage, and insisting that he must have a new dining-room ready by Ascot Week. On 11 May he called for the *Racing Calendar*; they were afraid that he would send for the newspapers, and discover that there were bulletins. But the King did not need to read a bulletin in order to feel despondent: that day they took 'several quarts of water from his feet'.*(414)* Bloomfield, at the Legation in Stockholm, received accounts of the King's state which helped 'to render my lonely life very, very melancholy'.*(415)* In mid May the Duke of Wellington thought the King's appearance had worsened: 'that is, he looked wasted and wasting; but his eye was lively', added Croker, 'his hand cool and healthy, and his mind as clear and active as ever, and even his spirits were good; in fact, he showed strong vitality, and I dare say it will be with him as it was with the Duke of York, he will contest every inch with death'.*(416)*

It seemed unbelievable that the King could withstand, much longer, the combined attacks of illnesses and cures. His legs had been punctured, to draw off the water; now the doctors closed the wounds, for fear of gangrene, and the water was dispersed all over his body. On 15 May his sister, the Duchess of Gloucester, drew an appalling picture for Mme de Lieven: the King had 'become enormous, like a feather bed, while his legs, also swollen, are as hard as stone; his face is drawn and his features pinched, and he has attacks of choking, and in speaking of Leopold, against whom he is furious, he had a seizure which threatened to be fatal. The internal remedies he has taken to arrest the progress of dropsy have upset the functions of the stomach, and for three days he has eaten nothing. . . . Yet only yesterday', wrote Mme de Lieven on 16 May, 'Wellington said to me, "Oh! the King is well—and looks well".'*(417)* On 16 May Peel saw the King, and was 'most agreeably surprised to find him so lively, intelligent, and strong'.(*418*) The King discussed Peel's private affairs with his old astonishing knowledge of detail. On 26 May he still talked of going to Ascot, and told Wellington 'to manage that he might be able to go to Aix-la-Chapelle'.(*419*)

He was, no doubt, happy that his horse, The Colonel, won the Craven Stakes at Epsom on 25 May. But any illusions of Ascot, or of travels on the Continent, grew increasingly hard to maintain. On 27 May the King's Signature Bill was passed, enacting that the Royal Command was to be signified by word of mouth, and documents were to be stamped, not signed. That day, Knighton told his wife: 'The King is particularly affectionate to me. His Majesty is gradually breaking down; but the time required ... to destroy his original fine constitution, no one can calculate upon.'(*420*) At the end of May Sir Henry Halford told the King 'the extent of my fears for his safety'.(*421*) Early in June, noted Croker, the King took leave of Peel, and said they should not see each other again; and when Peel tried to hearten him by mentioning the Cottage, the King said: 'Ah, poor Cottage, I shall never see it again.'(*422*) Peel must have known the truth of the words, for the Ministers were preparing the address for William IV to read to his Council. On 8 June, from Kensington Square, Anne Thompson wrote to Robert Finch, in Rome: 'The King's long illness casts gloom over every thing—indeed we are now hourly waiting to hear of his Death & I have more than once anticipated the sound of St. Paul's Bell—William the IVth will not be very popular.'(*423*)

That night the King talked a great deal to Knighton, 'and was as amusing as ever'.(*424*) Yet he was wisely putting his affairs in order. Lockhart had reported, weeks ago, that when he had first been warned of his danger, he had written a solemn letter to Mrs. Fitzherbert, and authorised her to set herself right with the world, by publishing the letter on his death.(*425*)

Mrs. Fitzherbert had loved the King when she married him at the age of twenty-nine; she was seventy-four, now, and she loved him still. She came from Brighton to London, to be within his call. She could keep her silence no longer.

Sir—After many repeated struggles with myself, from the Apprehension of appearing troublesome or intruding upon Your Majesty, after so many years of continual Silence, my Anxiety respecting Your Majesty has got the better of my Scruples, and I trust your Majesty will believe me most sincere, when I assure you how truly I have grieved to hear of your Sufferings. From the late Account, I trust Your Majesty's health is daily improving, and no one can feel more rejoiced to learn Your Majesty is restored to complete Convalescence, which I pray to God you may long enjoy, accompanied with every degree of happiness you can wish for or desire....(*426*)

When Sir Henry Halford gave the letter to the King, the King 'seized it with eagerness and placed it immediately under his pillow'. Nothing ever so wounded Mrs. Fitzherbert as not receiving one word in reply. She was ill with apprehension, 'too weak to move upon her sofa, so much so that she nearly fainted at making the exertion'.(*427*) But the King himself was now beyond making answer.

For some time, Knighton had drawn his attention to religion; and, unordered, he had put a quarto Bible, in large print, on the King's dressing-table. The King was much pleased with it, and often read it. He was finding comfort in religion; and when his household tried to raise false hopes, he dismissed them firmly: 'No, no! I understand what you think. Call in the Bishop and let him read prayers.' The Bishop of Chichester, kneeling at the bedside, repeated the prayer for the King that was being said throughout the country. When he had finished, the King who had listened with the utmost attention, 'three times repeated "Amen" with the greatest fervour and devotion'. He expressed himself highly gratified with it, and asked the Bishop 'to convey his approbation to the Archbishop of Canterbury.'(*428*) The Bishop of Chichester stayed at the Castle, and saw the King frequently

The King's physical state was critical; yet, in his waking intervals, said Knighton, he was still 'as clear, as communicative, as agreeable, nay as *facetious* in his conversation as he had ever been'.(*429*) He lived in a curious limbo, between lively hope and certainty of death; and he continued, bravely, to balance the possibilities. When a friend of Croker's, probably Lord Farnborough, was received in audience, it seemed like an audience of final leave; but the King, still weighing the chances of life and death, seemed to consider them to be almost equal. He talked successively of his journey to Aix-la-Chapelle, and his funeral procession to St. George's Chapel. Yet, as Croker pointed out, the moment he admitted 'the fatal probability', he must have known that the journey to France was a hopeless alternative. And then, suddenly expressing his need for affection, the King asked 'whether the public took a great interest in his state, and being answered that they did, he seemed much pleased, and expressed his own conviction that it ought to be so, for he "had always endeavoured to do his duty", and had never willingly done harm to anyone'. This led him to talk of the prayer that was being said for him in churches: the prayer that the Bishop had read to him; and, still a lover of good prose, he observed 'it was in good taste'. It was an oddly dispassionate comment; but, as Croker said, it was not uncharacteristic.(*430*)

Some of the feelings noted by Croker were endorsed by Archdeacon Glover, the chaplain to the Duke of Sussex. He reported the King as saying 'that he looked back with sorrow on his early life, but that latterly he endeavoured to benefit his subjects to the best of his power, and that as he had always shown mercy to others, it would be shown to him'.(*431*) None of his circle followed his illness more anxiously than Bloomfield, who now remembered only 'those kindnesses which he heaped on me and my children'. 'My fears are beyond fears,' he told his wife. 'My prayers are unceasing.'(*432*) At Brooks's, the King's subjects took a less spiritual interest, and 'offered to bet that he would not live throughout the week'.(*433*) The King himself was not allowed to neglect his duties. On 16 June Lord Ellenborough noted that Wellington 'got a number of papers stamped—indeed, all the arrears, about 400'.(*434*) The King paid more attention to them than he had ever done while he was well.

Ten days later, just after three o'clock on the morning of 26 June, as Sir Wathen Waller, one of the doctors, was sitting up with him, the King's breathing grew shorter, and he asked for some sal volatile and water. He could not swallow it, and he asked Waller to send for Halford. One of the pages went to find him; and, so Waller told his son, the King

> as usual took my hand in his and I felt him instantly press it harder than usual and he looked at me with an eager eye and exclaimed, 'My dear boy this is Death'.... About an hour after I left the Castle as I had promised the Duke of Clarence, now William the 4th, to do and took Halford officially to announce the event and was the first person that kissed his hand....(*435*)

'My dear Peel,' wrote Wellington, sending him some papers, 'circulate these. Everything shall go on as we before settled.'(*436*)

85

At half-past eight that morning, while Knighton, the King's executor, thought of the indescribable 'weight of care'(*437*) before him, while 'most of the inmates' hastily left the Castle, Lord Ellenborough received a Cabinet box containing the bulletin which announced the King's death. He expressed no regret in his diary, and noted that when, that day, the Privy Councillors assembled, 'there was no grief in the room.... It was like an ordinary levée'.(*438*) Moore declared he had never seen London so excited. 'Crowds everywhere,' he wrote. 'The whole thing reminded me of a passage in an old comedy; "What makes him so merry?" "Don't you see he's in mourning?" ' (*439*) One might suspect

Moore of bias, but a few days later, Mrs. Spencer-Stanhope reported that London 'has been in an extraordinary state, & except that all the shops are partially shut, has more the appearance of rejoicing than mourning... Scarcely anybody is in mourning yet, even the Guards have no crape round their arms'.(*440*) Fanny Kemble, on tour in Scotland, welcomed her three days' holiday from acting, and 'eagerly embraced' the chance of visiting Loch Lomond.(*441*) To some it seemed that George IV was forgotten, even before his funeral had taken place.

And yet there were some who heard the news of his death, that fine June morning, with genuine grief. Jekyll thought sadly of 'my poor King' and the familiar friendship of forty-six years.(*442*) Creevey, in Brooks's, drew a belated sigh for 'poor Prinney'.(*443*) Haydon mourned 'as thoroughbred an Englishman as ever existed.... I have lost in him', he wrote, 'my sincere admirer; and had not his wishes been perpetually thwarted, he would have given me ample and adequate employment'.(*444*) The frustration and egotism were characteristic of Haydon; but it is clear that he felt the death of George IV as a personal loss. So did Scott. 'The whole day of pleasure,' he noted in his diary, 'was damped by the news of the King's death'; and, soon afterwards, in a letter to Wordsworth, he added: 'Here is a new reign which may bring hope to many—but to me only the sad recollection that the late King was very kind and civil to me.'(*445*)

On 20 June, in the House of Lords, the Duke of Wellington paid tribute to the King whom he had known so long and so well.

> His Majesty's manners ... received a polish, his understanding acquired a degree of cultivation, almost unknown in any individual, and he was admitted by all to be the most accomplished man of his age. My Lords, ... no man ever approached him without having evidence of his dignity, his condescension, his ability, and his fitness for the exalted station which he occupied.

And then Wellington spoke as one could speak of few kings:

I appeal to many of your Lordships who have transacted the business of the country which required an
interview with the sovereign, whether his Majesty did
not, upon every occasion, evince a degree of knowledge
and of talent much beyond that which could reasonably
be expected of an individual holding his high station.
My Lords, this is not all the eulogium which His late
Majesty justly deserved. He was a most munificent patron
of the arts in this country, and in the world.(446)

Wellington's theme was repeated and enlarged from
pulpits throughout the country. The Regent had led the
nation through the closing, victorious years of the war
against Napoleon; the King, more than any other man, had
encouraged the arts of peace. At Woolwich parish church,
the Reverend W. B. James looked back to the time

> when universal peace brought repose to our exhausted
> country. What wonders in science, what improvements
> in the arts, what brilliancy in literature, what new fields
> for commerce and enterprise have since that period burst
> forth to elevate our country, and which seemed reserved,
> in an especial manner, for the fostering care of our late
> beloved sovereign to call forth, to appreciate and re-
> ward.(447)

The Reverend S. Barker, preaching at Brundish, in
Suffolk, repeated the encomium. Under the auspices of
George IV, he said,

> the country has advanced in improvements to a degree
> before unknown. Legislation has been revised and simpli-
> fied, science has abounded, and arts have advanced with
> rapid and unprecedented steps. Architecture and decora-
> tion have pervaded our Cities, and embellished the
> Land; and the comforts and elegancies which adorn and
> sweeten life have been encouraged and multiplied. He
> was the constant patron of useful institutions, and largely
> contributed to every establishment for the support and
> alleviation of the miserable and destitute.(448)

The King was praised for his interest in relieving distress, in removing disease: 'everything, in short, that tended to the welfare of the people whom he governed, received his prompt and permanent approval.'(*449*) One of the most touching tributes came from the synagogue in St. Alban's Place, St. James's, where the rabbi, Myer Solomon, praised him for religious tolerance. His late Majesty, he continued,

> was the father of his country, the friend of his people, the great promoter of the arts and sciences, the improver of his country, and the great encourager of inventions for the better preserving the health of his subjects. . . .
>
> The riches of a King are in the possessions and riches of his people. If he governs well, and hath their affections, he hath their purses too, and is always sure of their assistance. . . . His late Majesty in this respect was, I say, immensely rich; instance the public buildings, the growing improvements, the conveniencies and ornaments of our immense metropolis and kingdom at large, the numerous public charities that everywhere abound amongst us, in which his name is to be found the first enrolled; in this consisted the wealth, the property, of his late Majesty, and in this he exceeded all the princes of the age he lived in.(*450*)

Historical sketches of the late King echoed the laudatory sermons:

> His whole study [declared one writer] was how to make his country truly illustrious, by fostering the fine arts; encouraging men of virtue and superior talent; recommending the formation of the most liberal laws, such as the amelioration of the penal code; the emancipation of the Roman Catholics; and numerous other wise and beneficent enactments. [Let us reflect on] the vast improvements that he caused to be made in the Metropolis, intending to make it, what it ought to be—the wonder and admiration of the world.(*451*)

> If Buonaparte [wrote another chronicler] deserved the praise lavished so unsparingly upon him for his improve-

ments of Paris, what praise can be too great for George IV and for his improvements of London? A different city has arisen under his patriotism—a splendid capital, combining the glories of architectural cities with the greatness of London and the domestic civilisation of England. His reign began in the triumph of arms—its conclusion was marked by the triumph of art.(452)

The new President of the Royal Academy asked to attend the funeral of George IV, to show his colleagues' 'grateful respect, and the deep sense they entertain of the loss they have suffer'd'.(453) The Earl Marshal refused the request on the grounds that Benjamin West had not attended the funeral of George III; he added, presumably as consolation, that the President of the Royal Society was also not entitled to attend.(454)

The reign of enlightenment was truly over.

86

From ten till four on Wednesday, 14 July, the day before the funeral, King George IV lay in state in the Great Drawing Room of Windsor Castle. Those of the public who came to pay their last respects walked up the Grand Staircase, which was draped in black, and lined by Gentlemen Pensioners and Yeomen of the Guard. The King's Guard Chamber was hung with black; so, too, was the Presence Chamber leading to the black-hung State Apartment. And there, attended by a Lord of the Bedchamber, two Grooms of the Bedchamber, two Officers of Arms, four Gentlemen Ushers, six Gentlemen Pensioners, and eight Yeomen of the Guard, rested the coffin.

It was covered with a purple pall, on which gleamed '10 Escocheons of the Royal Arms'. On top of it, in dual radiance, glowed the Imperial Crown of the United Kingdom and the Royal Crown of Hanover; overhead hung a purple canopy. The Gentlemen Pensioners, standing rigidly

354

to attention, bore the Royal Standard, the Union Flag, the banners of England, Scotland, Ireland, Hanover and Brunswick.

On Thursday, 15 July, according to the Earl Marshal's instructions, the public were admitted to the room from ten till three.

That evening, at nine o'clock, the funeral procession left the State Apartment on its way to St. George's Chapel. First came the trumpets and kettle-drums, and the drums and fifes of the Foot Guards. Then came the six banners, borne by peers, the crowns of Hanover and the United Kingdom, borne by Blanc Coursier King of Arms (so soon to be obsolete), and by Clarenceux King of Arms. Then came the household dignitaries, then the coffin, its pall supported by six dukes, and four eldest sons of dukes; the canopy was borne by ten peers, eight admirals, and eight generals. The Duke of Wellington bore the Sword of State. And then came the chief mourner. King William IV wore 'a long Purple Cloak, with the Star of the Order of the Garter embroidered thereon', and the collars of the Garter, the Bath, the Thistle, St. Patrick and the Royal Hanoverian Guelphic Order.(455) He was dizzy with delight at being King of England, and 'talked incessantly and loudly to all about him, so that the most frivolous things were overheard'.(456)

The processional route was lined by Grenadier Guards, every fourth man bearing a flambeau to light the summer night. The troops held flambeaux, too, in the Chapel, and Jekyll learned that the smoke eclipsed the spectacle.(457)

And this, perhaps, was just as well. It was a deplorable sight. The Duke of Cumberland was much affected, and descended alone into the vault after the body was lowered.(458) But he was the only person who appears to have mourned the King. 'All Windsor drunk,' reported Jekyll. 'Suppers and champagne for parties who remained there, and everything but grief or regret.'(459)

87

A champagne mood seemed to prevail as the new reign began. William IV, as Mme de Lieven observed to her brother, was eager for attentions, like a parvenu. He took special pains to behave in a way totally opposed to his brother's. The public were, apparently, quite ready to forget his callous behaviour to Mrs. Jordan, his ten illegitimate children, and to accept him as a model of domesticity. 'The mob adores him,' noted Mme de Lieven in July, 'he goes about openly and treats everyone familiarly—that is enough for John Bull. The contrast between his ways and those of the late King is altogether favourable to the present. In fact England is quite a new world, and Wellington said to me quite truly: "This is not a new reign, it is a new dynasty . . ." '(*460*)

The first public act of William IV, on the day of his accession, was to dismiss all George IV's French cooks. As Lord Ellenborough said, happily: 'He will have no foreigners about him.'(*461*) 'His Majesty swears that nothing shall be encouraged but *native talent*,' wrote Mrs. Kemble to her daughter Fanny; Sir George Smart, the leader of the Covent Garden orchestra, was 'to get up a concert at the Duke of Sussex's, where the royal family are all to dine, at which none but English singers are to perform'.(*462*) 'The German Band is all disbanded,' added Lady Williams Wynn to her son, 'which Article alone cost £14,000 per ann. & throughout His Household he has dismissed every Foreigner'.(*463*) George IV had been criticised for changing the uniforms of certain regiments; but no one really bothered when William IV changed the uniforms of the army and the navy.

Wellington was probably glad that the new King spent his time on trifles, for it meant that politics remained under the control of the Prime Minister. True, as Lord Aberdeen observed, King William could not receive the diplomatic corps with the same grace as his brother, and neither, as Lord Aberdeen politely said, could the King 'speak French well'.*(464)* But intellectual worth and social graces hardly mattered. The King bustled round, shook hands with everyone, introduced his dowdy wife, and proved himself pre-eminently uxurious; and, after all, as Mme de Lieven said, 'what a nation most appreciates in its sovereign is domestic virtue'.*(465)*

Within a few days of the late King's funeral, she presented herself at Court; and the difference that met her eyes was astonishing:

> What a totally new spectacle the Court presented, and what a completely different nation are the English of to-day! From grave and depressed they have become possessed of a gaiety, a vivacity, and a movement which makes them scarcely recognisable. The King, for whom the proverb 'Happy as a king' seems certainly to have been invented by anticipation, imparts to all about him this extraordinary animation. He shows by his manners, his good nature, and cordiality, a sense of gratified pleasure which is quite contagious.*(466)*

Lady Charlotte Lindsay, writing to the Countess of Hardwicke, precisely echoed Mme de Lieven: 'Our King at least seems to be pleased with and to please his people, and really to be "as happy as a King", which I had never thought a true proverb till now.'*(467)*

The only fear was one that was pretty widely entertained: would the King's delight become beyond control? Nobody could hope to damp his natural ebullience; but his delight was sometimes unfortunate; when, on the morning of his accession, Wellington had called on him, the King had promptly returned to bed 'saying that he wished particularly to do so, having never yet been in bed with a Queen'.*(468)*

'The new King is very popular,' wrote John Disney to Robert Finch, 'but seems to be rather too much excited by his elevation. Some fear is entertained that he may suffer a similar attack to that of his father.'*(469)* 'If he don't do *too much*, and can keep steady,' repeated Miss Berry to the

Countess of Hardwicke, 'I am persuaded he will continue very popular.'(470)

The more popular William IV became, the more the late King was disparaged. If he was remembered at all, said Mme de Lieven, in the month of the funeral, it was only to criticise his morals. 'It is in the middle and lower classes especially that this side of his character has left a very unfavourable impression which overshadows much that was striking and brilliant in his reign. His glory is forgotten, and his vices exaggerated.'(471) One of William IV's most popular gestures was made early in his reign: the famous Cottage at Windsor was demolished. There would be no more reminders of Lady Conyngham and the Cottage *côterie*. The Pavilion at Brighton was accepted, but in time it suffered its inevitable decline. William IV's successor, Queen Victoria, did not take kindly to it—and she had her own marine residence in the Isle of Wight. A visitor, wandering round Brighton in 1857, contrasted it sadly with the town of 1809:

> How different is Brighton at the present moment, the Pavilion stripped of its gorgeous but fanciful furniture, has now degenerated into a public building—the scene of flower-shows and cheap promenade concerts.
>
> The royal cortège has given way to flys and donkey carriages; and the statue of the Fourth George alone reminds the passer-by of the glories of that mighty magician, who Aladdin like, raised a magnificent town from a small insignificant fishing village.(472)

88

The mighty magician, like his Pavilion, was to be abused; and as his friends and contemporaries died, as the Victorian ideal of bourgeois domesticity took hold, as the English puritan instinct reasserted itself, as the art of living became, somehow, equated with self-indulgence, George IV was sure to decline in favour. Much that Sir Thomas Lawrence painted, decided Fanny Kemble, in her *Record of a Girlhood,*

> partook of the false and bad style which, from the deeper source of degraded morality, spread a taint over all matters of art and taste, under the vicious influence of the 'first gentleman of Europe'. ... Hideous Chinese pagoda pavilions, with grotesque and monstrous decorations, barbarous alike in form and in colour; mean and ugly low-roomed royal palaces, without either magnificence or simplicity; military costumes, in which gold and silver lace were plastered together on the same uniform, testified to the perverted perception of beauty and fitness which presided in the court of George the Fourth. Lawrence's own portrait of him ... comes as near a caricature as a flattered likeness of the original (which was a caricature) dares to do. To have had to paint that was enough to have vulgarised any pencil.(*473*)

Thackeray was morally bound to present George IV as a corseted elderly roué, a bewigged and beribboned model of sloth and sin. Henry Crabb Robinson, the diarist, read Thackeray's lecture in 1860, in the days of the Prince Consort and of Tennyson's *Idylls of the King.* It was only natural that he should accept Thackeray's judgment:

> I read the lecture of Thackeray on the Fourth George ... the voluptuary heartless fop; the dandy of forty. He was the very worthless fellow described; but that is now universally acknowledged. It may be safely said under another sovereign, and it is popular doctrine.(*474*)

Now, perhaps, we may question the value of popular doctrine. We may see George IV as the most gifted King of England since Charles I. 'Well may Prinney say as he does that "he sees distinctly we are going to have Charles 1st's times again".'(*475*) The remark, reported by Creevey, was eloquent. No King since Charles I had been so truly interested in the arts; and George IV showed a width and diversity of patronage, in music, painting and sculpture, the theatre and literature, medicine and science, architecture and scholarship, which no English monarch has equalled.

Carlton House is, alas, his Nonesuch, long ago destroyed; but his Pavilion still proves his sense of fantasy, his romantic exuberance; and round the Pavilion, by his grace, hums the town of Brighton, which he created. Regent's Park, which his favourite architect designed, remains the most inspired example of town-planning in London. Windsor Castle, which he altered with Wyatville, is very largely a monument to his taste; and Buckingham Palace bears his generous mark. The faithful patron of Hoppner and Lawrence, he also knighted Raeburn and sat to Cosway, Gainsborough, Reynolds and Chantrey; he gave commissions to Canova, collected Flemish pictures, and immensely enriched the Royal collection. His laurelled effigy is worn on a gold medallion by the President of the Royal Academy; his medals are awarded by the Royal Society for scientific distinction. He knighted Herschel and Humphry Davy. He made Astley Cooper a baronet, and gave his constant encouragement to Jenner. The friend of Scott, the patron of Jane Austen, he earned the grudging admiration of Byron; he founded the Royal Society of Literature and largely established the Royal Literary Fund; he gave the King's Library to the British Museum. As a classical scholar, he supported the literary mission to Herculaneum. As a lover of the theatre, he gave his friendship to Sheridan and Kemble, and assistance to the son of Mrs. Siddons. As an amateur of music, he earned the admiration of Haydn and Rossini. A man of extraordinary natural distinction, he drew men of distinction to him. He gave a heartwarming impetus to the art of living.

A century after Thackeray's denunciation, we may also feel a certain pity for the man who needed, and never knew, the serenity of domestic life, the prince who was officially united, for twenty-six years, to Caroline of Brunswick. And, even in his private life, we owe him, too, some credit for his constancy. In 1796, in his will, he had asked 'that *my constant companion, the Picture of my beloved wife, my Maria Fitzherbert,* may be interred with me, suspended round my neck by a Ribbon as I used to wear it when I lived, *and placed right upon my Heart'*.(476)

Thirty-four years later, it was buried with him. When Mrs. Fitzherbert was told, she made no observation, but she wept.(477)

NOTES

Asp./G   =   *The Letters of George IV, 1812-1830*, edited by A. Aspinall. (Cambridge University Press, 1938.)

Asp./PoW   =   *Correspondence of George, Prince of Wales, 1770-1812*, edited by A. Aspinall. (Cassell. 1963-)

RA   =   Royal Academy of Arts

RSL   =   Royal Society of Literature

PART ONE

PRINCE OF WALES

1. Delves Broughton/Papendiek, I, 27
2. Ibid, I, 28
3. Huish, I, 14
4. Papendiek, I, 64-5
5. Ibid, I, 50
6. Ibid, I, 50
7. Papendiek, I, 61
8. Ibid, I, 77-8
9. Ibid, I, 94
10. Terry, 106-8
11. Manners, 36
12. Angelo, I, 191
13. Markham, 22
14. Ibid, 41
15. Ibid, 76-7; 11 December 1800
16. Ibid, 43, note
17. Steuart, II, 18-19; 9 April 1777
18. Hurd MSS., 14
19. Ibid, p. 7
20. Ibid, p. 9
21. Ibid, 19, 138. 6 August, 1776
22. Ibid, 14, p. 8b
23. Ibid, 19, 126. Bishop Hurd to the Prince of Wales, 1 January 1780
24. Ibid, 14
25. Ibid.
26. Asp./PoW, I, 34; the King to the Prince of Wales, 14 August, 1780
27. Huish, op. cit., I, 25
28. Quoted by Fulford in *George IV*, 20
29. Papendiek, op. cit., I, 132

30. Hurd MSS., 12, 19. George III to Bishop Hurd, 23 July 1782
31. Huish, I, 45
32. Ibid, I, 47
33. Ibid, I, 46
34. Papendiek, I, 138-9
35. Manners, 68-9
36. Papendiek, I, 138-9
37. Ibid, I, 91
38. Asp./PoW, I, 34; the King to the Prince of Wales, 14 August 1780
39. Richardson, *The Disastrous Marriage*, 14
40. Asp./PoW, I, 56; 10 April 1781
41. Whitley, *Artists*, 183
42. Wheatley/Wraxall, V, 369
43. Ibid, 369 sqq.
44. Ibid.
45. Ibid.
46. Lieut-Col. Gerard Lake to the Prince of Wales, 23 January 1781. Asp./PoW, I, 45
47. Prince of Wales to Prince Frederick, 17 July 1781. Asp./PoW, I, 65 sqq.
48. Ibid.
49. Ibid.
50. Ibid.
51. Ibid.
52. Ibid.
53. Ibid.
54. Ibid.
55. Ibid.
56. Asp./PoW, 1, 44; 20 January 1781
57. Quoted by Richardson, op. cit., 14
58. Parke, I, 63, and *passim*
59. Hilles, 124-5
60. Lloyd, 126-7, 128; Angelo, II, 46-9; Parke, I, 198 sqq.
61. Asp./PoW, I, 134; 7 November 1783
62. Fulford, 35
63. Oliver, 108; 22 March 1782
64. Papendiek, I, 229
65. Landon, 122-4; 20 December 1791
66. Rush, 117
67. Lloyd, 63-4
68. Molloy, II, 461-2; Whitley, op. cit., 230
69. Papendiek, I, 214-16
70. Ibid, I, 245-6
71. Whitley, op. cit, 235
72. Lloyd, 64
73. Baker, 150-1, 235, 273, 140
74. Angelo, II, 88

75. Doran, III, 346
76. Richardson, op. cit., 13
77. Richardson, *My Dearest Uncle*, 102
78. Papendiek, I, 234-5
79. Wraxall, V, 362-3
80. Ibid, V, 363
81. Harris, *Diaries*, II, 124-5
82. Walpole, *Last Journals*, II, 496-7
83. Ibid.
84. Richardson, *The Disastrous Marriage*, 228
85. Ibid, 15.
86. Ibid, 60
87. Asp./PoW, I, 152; the Prince of Wales to the Duchess of Devonshire, 19 July 1784
88. Aspinall, op. cit., I, 155
89. Ibid, 156; letter of 27 August 1784
90. Ibid, 161; letter of 2 September 1784
91. Ibid, 162; letter of 6 September 1784
92. Ibid, 164; report of 27 October 1784
93. Siddons, *Reminiscences*, 12-13
94. Aspinall, op. cit., I, 151; the Prince of Wales to the Duchess of Devonshire, 19 July 1784
95. Harris, op. cit., II, 124-5
96. Ibid, II, 128-30
97. Asp./PoW, I, 151
98. Aspinall, op. cit., I, 151
99. Holland, *Memoirs*, III, 14
100. Richardson, op. cit., 18
101. Ibid.
102. Ibid, 19
103. Williamson, 23
104. Cunningham/Heaton, II, 347-8
105. Boulton, 207/8; Bell, 97-8
106. Bell/Gainsborough, 122-3; but Boulton, 244-5, says that the Prince of Wales tried to set the tide of fashion towards buying the unsold pictures, on the artist's death. He therefore called on Mrs. Gainsborough, and gave 2,000 guineas for two landscapes, which he presented to Mrs. Fitzherbert.
107. Wraxall, op. cit., V, 379
108. D'Arblay, *Diary*, III, 76
109. Ibid, III, 416-17; 2 August 1787
110. Note to Farington, V, 144
111. Powell/Rogers, 28-9
112. Parke, II, 319 sqq.
113. Campbell/Siddons, 129
114. Papendiek, II, 9
115. Ibid, II, 12

116. Ibid, 14-15
117. Ibid, 19
118. Ibid, I, 303
119. Fulford, 44
120. Ibid, 48
121. R. B. Johnson, 97; 30 March 1789
122. *The Tour to York, passim*
123. Angelo, I, 327; Prothero, I, 99
124. S. C. Hall, I, 28-9; Prothero, II, 336-7; Lennox, *Recollections*, I, 106, 109-10
125. Gronow, *Anecdotes*, 226-7
126. Lewis, I, 286; 5 March 1791
127. Royal Society of Arts; Society Minutes, 1785-6, pp. 46-7
128. Ibid, p. 53
129. Bell, 97-8, 100, 118; Boulton, 240, 244-5
130. Romney, 217
131. Cunningham, V, 115-16; Molloy, II, 498; Powell/Rogers, 108-9
132. Cunningham, V, 244-5
133. Roberts, 57-9
134. Ibid, 62-3
135. Thurlow, 24
136. Boaden/Jordan, 168
137. Ibid, 217; Knapp, 224-5
138. Baker, 178, 292
139. *Congratulatory address*, 20-22
140. Lennox, *Reminiscences*, I, 78
141. Wraxall, V, 359
142. Landon, 122-4; 20 December 1791
143. Ibid, note, p. 147
144. Ibid, 270
145. Lewis, I, 179
146. Harris, *Diaries*, II, 452
147. Wraxall, V, 357-9; and Parke, I, 101, 111-12, 260
148. Granville, I, 93.
149. Holland, *Memoirs*, III, 143-4
150. Dobrée, 251-2
151. Adeane, *Girlhood*, 305
152. Harris, *Letters*, II, 128-30 and 452
153. Richardson, op. cit., 27
154. Ibid, 29
155. Ibid.
156. Harris, *Letters*, III, 161
157. Holland, III, 145-7; Stuart, 191
158. Richardson, op. cit., 28
159. Ibid, 32
160. Stanhope, I, 311-12
161. Richardson, op. cit., 33

162. Ibid. loc. cit.
163. Ibid. 34
164. Holland, III, 122-3, note
165. *Two Words of Counsel* . . . , pp. 48-50
166. Adeane, 327; 19 July 1795
167. Bickley, I, 71; 5 September 1796
168. Richardson, op. cit., 37
169. Quennell, *Private Letters*, 98; 22 December 1820
170. Granville, II, 206
171. Bell, 310
172. Richardson, op. cit., 44
173. Ibid, 38-9
174. Holland, III, 121
175. Hurd MSS., 4, Part II, 61-2; 18 June 1796
176. Richardson, op. cit., 39
177. Lady Holland, *Journal*, II, 199; 8 February 1807
178. Bickley, I, 255-6; 4 October 1801
179. Granville, I, 502
180. For a detailed account of The Delicate Investigation, see Richardson, *The Disastrous Marriage*, pp. 38-67
181. Granville, op. cit.
182. Granville, II, 203-4
183. Romilly, II, 148; 19 June 1806
184. Granville, II, 202
185. Ibid, II, 203
186. Ibid, II, 204
187. Ibid, II, 205
188. Ibid, II, 206
189. Russell, VIII, 58
190. Lockhart, II, 100-101
191. Williams, I, 260
192. Stuart, 156; 29 April 1807
193. Richardson, op. cit., 67
194. Ibid, 43
195. Grieg/Farington, II, 120-1; 6 July 1803
196. Richardson, op. cit., 40
197. Bickley, II, 13; 1 February 1808
198. Richardson, op. cit., 41-2
199. Ilchester, II, 49; 14 February 1800
200. Baron, I, 375
201. Ibid, I, 573-4
202. Ibid, I, dedicatory letter
203. Brettell, 3 sqq.
204. Lloyd, 228-31
205. Anon. *Memoirs of Mr. W. H. W. Betty*, 12
206. Foster, 191-2; 5 December 1804
207. Lloyd, 266-7; November 1803.

208. Creevey, I, 46-7, and *passim*
209. Granville, II, 120; 9 October 1805
210. Ibid, II, 120; 10 October 1805
211. Angelo, I, 16; 14 July 1806
212. Jesse, 28, and *passim*
213. George III to Bishop Hurd, 13 February 1801; Hurd MSS. 19, 53. The King felt much respect for the Bishop. Among the Hurd MSS. (19, 21) is a letter he sent him on 20 August 1782, when his youngest son, Prince Alfred, was dying. 'I place my confidence,' wrote the King, 'that the Almighty will never fill my Cup of sorrow fuller than I can bear.'
214. Undated letter; Granville, I, 454
215. Ibid.
216. Ibid.
217. Adeane, op. cit., 298; 12 August 1794
218. Fulford, 62.
219. Ibid.
220. [September] 1803; Granville, I, 429
221. 9 September 1803; Granville, I, 430
222. George III to Bishop Hurd, 30 November 1803; Hurd MSS. 19, 64
223. Creevey, I, 25; 2 April 1804
224. Ibid., I, 28-9
225. Ibid, I, 30; 23 November 1804
226. Foster, 195; letter of 25 December 1804
227. Creevey, I, 48
228. Ibid, 50
229. Ibid, 50
230. Ibid, I, 69-70; 6 November 1805
231. 31 December 1805; Foster 261-2
232. Holland, *Memoirs*, III, 30
233. Clarke and M'Arthur, I, dedicatory letter
234. Ibid.
235. Lovat-Fraser, 89
236. Fulford, 69
237. Markham, 76-7
238. Farington, IV, 54; 4 December 1806
239. Ibid, IV, 98; 11 March 1807
240. Ibid, IV, 130-1; 2 May 1807
241. Ibid.
242. Ibid.
243. Ibid.
244. Ibid.
245. Granville, II, 251
246. Richardson, op. cit., 60
247. Asp./G III, 110; Mary Seymour to the King, 13 July 1825
248. Richardson, *The Disastrous Marriage*, 61
249. Farington, IV, 191; 18 August 1807

250. Granville, II, 294
251. Foster, op. cit., 311; 18 October 1807
252. Granville, II, 297-8
253. Gower, *Hary-O*, 258
254. Brougham, I, 393-4
255. Bickley, II, 5. In his diary for 1813 (MSS. Finch e 6) Robert Finch recorded some comments on the Prince's private life. On 10 December he talked to a Mr. Webster about the Prince of Wales and Lady Jersey. 'Jerningham the poet communicated to Lady Jersey the Prince's dissolution of the connexion with her. She told him "Damn you, I wish you joy of your new trade." The present Lord Jersey is a great gambler. Marchioness of Hertford.' On 19 December, at Brighton, Finch 'dined with a Captain Riboleau, and spent an agreeable evening . . . Mrs. Fitzherbert calls the Princess of Wales only Princess Caroline. In this she does not show her sense. She is going to get up a French play at her house here, at which the Baron and Baroness de Montalembert are to act the principal parts'.
256. Phipps, I, 319-20; 8 January 1811
257. Holland, *Memoirs*, III, 72
258. Farington, II, 233-4 and 234; 28 and 30 April 1804
259. Le Brun, II, 133-4
260. Ibid, II, 150-1
261. Ibid, II, 138-40
262. Shee, I, 256-7
263. Taylor, I, 41-3
264. Bickley, I, 250
265. Farington, II, 270; 20 July 1804
266. Ibid, II, 214; 3 May 1806
267. Knapp, 69; 8 August [September?], 1798
268. Ibid, 68; 14 September [1798]
269. Ibid, 71
270. Ibid, 184; 23 January 1799
271. Russell, I, 107-8; 4 August 1800
272. Ibid, I, 111
273. Ibid, I, 112
274. Ibid, I, 113
275. Royal Literary Fund; Reports, 1923 and 1936, and archives
276. Parke, II, 3
277. D'Arblay, *Memoirs*, III, 357-8
278. Ibid.
279. Ibid, III, 354
280. Ibid.
281. Ibid, III, 354-7
282. Ibid.
283. Finch diary, 30 November 1813; MSS. Finch e 6 (Bodleian Library, Oxford)
284. Clarke; *Life of James II*, Vol. I, Preface, pp. ix sqq.

285. Ibid.
286. Hayter: *The Herculanean and Pompeian Manuscripts*, 20-21
287. Hayter; *Report*, 80 sqq.
288. Ibid, 50-1
289. Letter from W. Drummond to John Hayter, 13 December 1808. MS. Gr. Class, c 10, Bodleian Library, Oxford
290. Hayter: *Report*, 4-5
291. The Prince of Wales to Lord Grenville, 9 March 1810. MS. Gr. Class, c 10, Bodleian Library, Oxford
292. Farington, V, 237; 16 September 1809
293. [December] 1809; Granville, II, 349-50
294. 24 April 1810; Wyndham, 101
295. 10 May 1810; ibid, 103-4
296. 11 May 1810; ibid, 104
297. Farington, VI, 89; 16 July 1810
298. Ibid, VI, 106; 23 August 1810
299. Letter to Joanna Baillie, 23 November 1810; *Letters*, II, 403
300. Wyndham, 117
301. Lovat-Fraser, 97-100
302. Lewis, II, 449
303. Foster, 347; letter of 10 January 1811. On 4 June 1811, George III's 73rd birthday, Henry Stapylton wrote to Robert Finch:

> I fear from all we learn here, this is the most inauspicious Anniversary of the *Day* we have seen, the termination of the King's Disorder, if rightly reported, can be looked to with little hope. Insanity, Dropsy, & 73! Under present Circumstances, it is consolatory to advert to the Conduct of the Regent, who had conducted himself most unexceptionably; placed as he has been in Re dubia. How well, how providentially has it been order'd; that he should have had an Opportunity afforded him of duly appreciating the Services & Merits of both his Father's Advisers, & his own . . . Now he may see with his own Eyes, and not another's: there is doubtless much Talent, and I trust what is still more: Honor and Honesty in the present Cabinet, and God has lately, we must own, prospered their Endeavours for their Country's Weal. (MSS. Finch d 15, Bodleian Library, Oxford.)

PART TWO

PRINCE REGENT

1. 26 February 1811; Lewis, II, 458
2. Phipps, I, 399-400
3. 27 February 1811; Farington, VI, 244
4. Dr. Saunders to Plumer Ward, 8 January 1811; Phipps, I, 319-20

5. Lewis, II, 471
6. Ibid.
7. 27 April 1811; Farington, VI, 264-5
8. Royal Academy Council Minutes, IV, 290-1, 317, 369-71, 380
9. Stirling, I, II; 4 March 1805
10. Mallet, III, 213, 215
11. Russell, I, 254-5
12. Ingpen, 99-100; 20 June 1811
13. L'Estrange, I, 134, 136-7
14. G IV to Cabinet, 1824; Asp./G, III
15. Creevey, I, 146; Granville, II, 413; 2 November 1811
16. Letter to Joanna Baillie, 12 Dec. 1811; Scott, *Letters*, III, 34
17. December [?] 1811; Granville, II, 422
18. Letter to Granville Leveson Gower; Granville, II, 426
19. Fulford, 86
20. Creevey, I, 165
21. Fulford, 90
22. Ibid, 88
23. Brougham, II, 134 sqq.
24. Ibid.
25. Romilly, III, 236; 20 March 1816
26. *The Examiner*, 22 March 1812
27. Quoted by Jackson, III, 18
28. Taylor, I, 208
29. Prothero, II, 205-6
30. Redding, *Fifty Years' Recollections*, I, 274
31. Letter to Archibald Constable; Constable, II, 217
32. *Don Juan*, LXXXIV; Nonesuch edition, p. 409
33. Smiles, 88-90
34. Ibid, 89
35. Letter to Murray, 2 July 1812; *Letters*, III, 135
36. Prothero, II, 134-5
37. Quoted by Lockhart, II, 402-3
38. 25 June 1812: Prothero, 127-9
39. Prothero, II, 134-5
40. Ibid, 135
41. Robert Finch wrote in his diary for 7 February 1814; 'Lord Byron means, I understand, to publish . . . 2 couplets, address'd to the Princess Charlotte of Wales, justifying her in rebellion against her father, which is really shocking." (MSS. Finch e 7. Bodleian Library, Oxford.)
42. 10 February 1814; Prothero, III, 32
43. 6 March 1812; Russell, I, 271
44. Ibid.
45. Appendix to *Twopenny Post-Bag*, p. 107
46. Russell, VIII, 143-4; June 1813
47. 7 May 1812; Ingpen, 308

48. 16 April [?] 1812; Ingpen, 292
49. RA Council Minutes, IV, 349; Council of 25 March 1812
50. Ibid, pp. 369-371; Council of 16 May 1812
51. 10 April 1812; Davy/Davy, I, 434
52. Ibid, II, 70
53. Letter of 15 May 1813 to Miss Carr; W. S. Scott, 77
54. Creevey, I, 178
55. W. Macdonald to R. Finch, 16 March 1813 (MSS. Finch d 11, Bodleian Library, Oxford). In this letter, Macdonald drew a depressing picture of royal dissensions:

> Alas . . . I think England is preparing bloody days of intestine broils— to her royal family will she owe much future misery. Not a day dawns but brings with it some fresh charge against some member of the House of Brunswick. Oh that they would take warning . . . from what has taken place upon the continent, & show common prudence. Much indeed is it to be lamented that the Ps of W. should lend herself to be the weak tool of a wicked Junto. She has doubtless been an ill used woman; but it is no less plain that she is a very silly one. I confess her husband does not seem to have acquired any fresh honours from the agitation of this *Jugnaut* question.

56. 3 April 1813; Stuart, 191-2
57. 10 February 1813; Mundy, 158-60
58. Pope, I, 306, note
59. Leadbeater, II, 252; Mrs. Trench to Mrs. Leadbeater, May 1813
60. May 1813; Edgeworth, 186
61. Asp./G, I, 294
62. Sichel, 171: 29 June 1813
63. Ibid, 165; 25 June 1813
64. Ibid, 171; 29 June 1813
65. 22 July 1813; Sichel, 183
66. Jesse, 86-7, 87-8, 88-9
67. Ibid, 98-101
68. Lockhart, III, 80-1
69. *Letters*, III, 324; 24 August 1813
70. Partington, 285; 28 August 1813
71. *Letters*, III, 344
72. Ibid, III, 341; 3 September 1813
73. Southey, *Life and Correspondence*, IV, 41-2; 20 September 1813
74. Ibid.
75. Scott, *Letters*, III, 335-6; 1 September 1813
76. Southey, L/C, IV, 40; 5 September 1813
77. Ibid, IV, 45; undated letter of 1813
78. Partington, 79-80; 5 November 1813
79. *Letters*, III, 380; 13 November 1813
80. Dale, 99-100
81. Ibid.

82. Finch Diary, 12 January 1817; MSS. Finch d 19 (Bodleian Library, Oxford)
83. Summerson, *John Nash*, 76-8
84. Letter of April 1814; Creevey, I, 190
85. Prothero, III, 70-2
86. Hayward, *Diaries*, 95
87. Mme D'Arblay, *Diary and Letters*, VII, 34
88. Asp./G, II, 440; 2 May 1814
89. Mundy, 203-4
90. Southey, *Works*, 194-8
91. Finch Diary, 14 June 1814; MSS. Finch e 8 (Bodleian Library, Oxford)
92. Vassall, 196-7
93. Cobbett, I, Chapter V, paragraph 277
94. RA: Lawrence Corr., II, 19, note
95. Ibid, IV, $\frac{79;}{1}$ 17 November 1824
96. Williams, I, 226
97. Ibid, I, 341
98. Finch Diary, 9 June 1814; MSS. Finch e 8 (Bodleian Library, Oxford)
99. Creevey, I, 196; 14 June 1814
100. Asp./G, I, 457, note
101. The Prince, in boots, had weighed 17 st. 8 lb. on 5 December 1797; he weighed 11 st. 12½ lb. on 21 January 1805. It seems that he had since put on weight again.
102. Mundy, op. cit. 225
103. Mallet, *History of the University of Oxford*, III, 213 and note, 215
104. Anon. *An Account of the Visit of H.R.H. the Prince Regent . . . to the University of Oxford*
105. Ibid.
106. Letter of 1 September 1814; MS. Top. Oxon. d. 238. Bodleian Library, Oxford. In the same letter, Barnes writes: 'Blücher was at our House, which, you will see by the newspapers, was constantly surrounded by the Mob eager to see him . . . He is a fine old man, very little the worse for wear in appearance, in his 71st year . . . The Prince was vastly well received, and, of course, highly pleased, as it was not certain whether all things would have passed off so agreeably.' In a letter to his father, from Christ Church, 18 June 1814, Barnes writes: 'We found he [Blücher] liked good strong Beer, Rum and Cognac. Almost whenever he came into the House he lay down on his Bed, and took his Pipe, so that Mr. du Pre said—that dear Blücher he lies down just like a pointer Dog.'
107. Hayward, 97-9
108. Anon. *An Account of the Visit . . . to Oxford*
109. Stirling, I, 318
110. 19 June 1814; L'Estrange, I, 278-9
111. Russell, VIII, 180
112. Ibid, II, 19-20; 27 June 1814

113. Finch Diary, 24 June 1814; MSS. Finch e 8. (Bodleian Library, Oxford)
114. Mundy, 224
115. Redding, op. cit., I, 254-5
116. Peter Pindar: *The Regent's Fleet*, stanzas 65, 68, 69, 70
117. Thurlow, 22
118. Malmesbury, *Letters*, II, 418; 12 June 1814
119. Brougham, II, 144-5
120. Ibid, II, 254
121. Cobbett, I, Chapter IV, paragraph 199
122. Brougham, II, 258
123. Ibid, II, 151-3; letter to Lady Charlotte Lindsay, 'just received' on 2 September 1812
124. Ibid, 169
125. Ibid, 171
126. Ibid, 172-3
127. Ibid, 174-5
128. Ibid, 178
129. Ibid, 206-7
130. Ibid, 208-9. On 29 June 1814, Robert Finch had reported in his diary: 'The union between the Prince of Orange and the Princess Charlotte of Wales appears to be completely broken off upon the ground, as it is said, of her Royal Highness refusing to go over to Holland. It may be difficult to know whether this is the real reason.' (MSS. Finch e 8. Bodleian Library, Oxford)
131. Brougham, II, 242; 24 July 1814
132. Fulford, 99
133. Asp./G., I, 519 and 521
134. Fulford, 112
135. Ibid, 113
136. Ibid.
137. D'Arblay, op. cit., VII, 64
138. Finch Diary; MSS. Finch e 14. (Bodleian Library, Oxford.) Robert Finch had taken a close interest in French politics. On 5 May 1814 (MSS. Finch e 7) he had reported Louis XVIII's entry into Paris:

The King look'd well. His countenance wore an appearance of amiable dignity, there was a calm resignation display'd in his countenance and his manner was completely that of the good Monarch of a great nation. He look'd as if he remember'd that he was a King, but forgot not that royalty have many cares, and many sorrows. He bow'd with a graceful ease, and look'd round him without inviting the looks of others. Next to the Monarch sat the Duchess d'Angoulême . . . She wore an air of tender melancholy blended with such amiable sweetness, as must have almost arrested the dagger even of a Robespierre . . . Opposite to her sat the Comte d'Artois, and next to him the venerable Prince of Condé . . . The Duchess was simply and elegantly dress'd in white satin. The King's dress was plain & simply decorated. He had the order of the Garter, as well as of the Holy Ghost.

On 24 July 1814 (MSS. Finch e 6), Finch recorded that his friend Dr. Granville

saw Napoleon in the Isle of Elba, where the people almost worship him. He is carrying on great public works there. He told an English naval Captain that the Bourbons would not reign long, for that France could not be govern'd by Imbecilles. He holds a constant correspondence with Murat, and with his sister. No foreign officers are now with him, and there is only an English brig of war, which cruises off the coast.

On 14 September 1814 (MSS. Finch e 11), Finch noted:

Mr. Baillie, a Naval officer, . . . transported Buonaparte's Baggage to the Isle of Elba, and receiv'd great attentions from him, as well as a present of a ring . . . Mr. Baillie thinks that he was sorry to have murder'd the Duke d'Enghien. He told him that the Duke of Wellington was the first General in Europe. He is making great improvements in the Isle of Elba. He does not understand English, but he wishes to do so, as he told Mr. Baillie. When he speaks, he has a most fascinating manner. He now reads a great deal, and collects books. The iron mines produce him a revenue of twenty thousand pounds per annum.

On 18 September 1814 (MSS. Finch e 11), Robert Finch continued:

Napoleon has a great disgust at being view'd as a sight by people, who visit the Isle of Elba, Mr. and Mrs. Orby Hunter were there with an English Nobleman. Napoleon receiv'd them on the terrace of his garden by moonlight; he only bow'd without speaking . . .

On 8 March 1815 (MSS. Finch e 13), the diarist observed:

Napoléon a absolument debarqué à Antibes avec quinze cents hommes; et un Prince l'a recontré sur la route, auquel il a dit qu'il seroit à Paris le 24 de ce mois.

On 25 March (MSS. Finch e 13), Robert Finch finally wrote:

Mr. Grattan, a young Irishman, din'd with Count Bertrand the very day that Napoleon [landed in France]. After dinner was some time over, the Count retir'd, alledging that he had business. Mr. Grattan staid some time with Mme Bertrand, after which he retired to his inn. After remaining there some time, he heard a bustle in the Port, when, going out, he observ'd seven or eight vessels under weigh, and, taking a boat, he row'd round them, and distinguish'd His Majesty on the deck of his Brig of War, as it was a moonlight night.

139. Creevey, I, 240-1
140. Bagot, II, 4
141. 11 July 1815; Foster, 406
142. Southey, *Works*, 754

143. Cunningham, III, 57
144. 23 April 1815; RA, Lawrence Corr., II, 32
145. Lloyd, 372-3
146. RA Council Minutes, V, 239-41: Council of 14 December 1815
147. Ibid, p. 251-2; Council of 10 January 1816
148. Memes, 375-6
149. Ibid.
150. Austen-Leigh, 146-8
151. 15 November 1815; Chapman, 429
152. 16 November 1815; ibid, 429-30
153. 11 December 1815; ibid, 446
154. 1 April 1816; ibid, 453
155. Ibid, 451
156. 1 April 1816; ibid, 452-3
157. Richardson, *My Dearest Uncle*, 22
158. Aspinall, *Charlotte*, 186; letter of 23 January 1815
159. Brougham, op. cit., II, 316
160. 22 March 1816; Foster, 414
161. Ibid, 415-16
162. RA Council Minutes, V, 272 sqq; Councils of 18, 22 April 1816
163. Ibid, 287-9; Council of 15 June 1816
164. Ibid, 300 sqq.; Council of 2 August 1816
165. Ibid, 318
166. RA, Lawrence Corr., II, 48
167. Layard, 264-5
168. Ibid, 263-4
169. See also Pope, II, 520. Robert Finch, in Athens, wrote on 5 March 1817: 'I find the Earl of Elgin very generally dislik'd here on account of the robbery he has committed, and also on account of his having seriously damag'd the Parthenon by employing rude workmen to take down the metopes.' (MSS. Finch d 19. Bodleian Library, Oxford)
170. 29 December 1816; Foster, 426
171. Ibid.
172. Carême, *Le Maître d'hôtel français*, II, 153, sqq.
173. Ibid, II, 179
174. Ibid, II, 153 sqq.
175. Carême, *L'Art de la Cuisine française au XIXe siècle*, I, ix-x
176. March 1817; Leadbeater, II, 290
177. 15 July 1817; ibid, 299-300
178. Cobbett, Ch. II, para. 60; Ch. IX, para. 192; Ch. VI, para. 332
179. 29 January 1817; Parker, I, 237
180. June 1817; Adeane, *Early Married Life*, 401
181. Lennox, *Fifty Years' Biographical Reminiscences*, II, 58-9
182. Roberts/Beechey, 244-5
183. Royal Academy Council Minutes, V, 408 sqq.
184. Munk, 53 sqq.
185. Ibid. 62-3. The Lawrence Correspondence at the Royal Academy

(III, 25) records some more of the Regent's Stuart mementoes. Elizabeth, Duchess of Devonshire, living in Rome, writes to Lawrence on 5 July 1819: 'I have got the Stuart rings and seals for the P. Regent.'

186. Wraxall, V, 355
187. Ibid, V, 356-7
188. Lloyd, 457-8
189. Asp./G., III, 90, note
190. 23 September 1834; Lady Louisa Stuart to Miss Louisa Clinton. Home, 2nd series, 423-4
191. Lockhart, VII, 212-13
192. Creevey, I, 266
193. RA. Lawrence Corr. II, facing p. 67a; 19 October 1817
194. Richardson, *My Dearest Uncle*, 53; Munk, 152
195. Campbell, *Works*, 276; lines spoken by Mrs. Bartley on the first opening of Drury Lane Theatre after the death of Princess Charlotte
196. November 1817; *Letters*, V, 15
197. 7 November 1817; Pope, II, 137
198. 17 November 1817; Leadbeater, II, 302-3
199. 17 December 1817; Leadbeater, II, 304
200. Richardson, op. cit., 61
201. Brougham, II, 333-4
202. Mundy, 299
203. Croker, I, 105. The Lawrence Correspondence at the Royal Academy includes the following note (II, 68):

Sir William Congreve presents his compliments to Sir Thomas Lawrence and is commanded to request that He will come to Carlton House this morning as early as his convenience will possibly allow, and that He will have the goodness to bring with him the Portrait of the Lamented Princess Charlotte which her disconsolate Parent is *most anxious* to see—Carlton House,
Saturday morning
8th Nov. 1817

204. 8 August 1814; Brougham, II, 195
205. 27 July 1814; Aspinall, *Charlotte*, 137-8
206. Bell Canning, 314
207. Finch Diary, 17 November 1814; MSS. Finch e 12 (Bodleian Library, Oxford)
208. *Vide* Richardson, *The Disastrous Marriage*, 91-116
209. Finch Diary; MSS Finch e 13 (Bodleian Library, Oxford)
210. 12 May 1815; Granville, II, 534-5
211. The Hunter/Baillie correspondence at the Royal College of Surgeons casts an occasional light on the lives of the Princess of Wales and her daughter. In a letter to Dr. Matthew Baillie, written from Blackheath on 3 November 1806, the Princess of Wales reveals her distress after the Delicate Investigation and the death of her father: 'The Princess

of Wales will be very much obliged to Dr. Baily if he will be kind enough to order for her some more of the composing Draughts which he has lately prescribed to her in case of great agitation of spirits to convey them to a quiet state, . . . as she has been lately under some new distress and unforeseen calamities, by which her mental state has dreadfully suffered.' (III, 9). On 6 November 1817, the day of Princess Charlotte's death, Dr. Baillie writes to his wife: 'I came to town to have a conversation with the Prince Regent, who is quite satisfied that no medical error was committed. . . . Sir Richard Croft is very low, but I hope will soon be better.' (VIII, 41)

212. Brougham, II, 294
213. Ibid, 298-9
214. 6 December 1815; Aspinall, *Charlotte*, 217
215. March, 1816; ibid, 237
216. Finch Diary; MSS. Finch d 19 (Bodleian Library, Oxford)
217. The Royal College of Surgeons: Hunter/Baillie Letters, III, 41. The Princess of Wales to Dr. Baillie, 2 December 1817
218. Creevey, I, 268-271
219. 17 December 1817; Southey, *Life and Correspondence*, IV, 287
220. Richardson, *The Disastrous Marriage*, 113-14
221. Brougham, II, 382
222. 15 November 1817; Croker, I, 108
223. Creevey, I, 272
224. 14 April 1818; Parker, I, 263. On 21 February 1814, Robert Finch had reported in his diary: 'The Duke of Cumberland is, it is said, about to marry one of the Mecklenburgh family. It seems that he will not return to this country, having been found guilty of Sodomite practices, as is reported. All the Royal Family are nerveless as to women.' (MSS. Finch e 7. Bodleian Library, Oxford)
225. Creevey, I, 277
226. Francis Lee to Robert Finch, 3 August 1818; MSS. Finch d 10 (Bodleian Library, Oxford)
227. Layard, 133
228. 18 September 1818; ibid, 135
229. RA, Lawrence Correspondence, II, 96
230. Undated draft letter; ibid, 100
231. RA, Lawrence Correspondence, II, 101
232. 1 December 1818; ibid. A week after his mother's death, the Regent was affirming his admiration of his principal painter-in-ordinary. Among Lawrence's letters in the Royal Academy is the following (II, 102):

Carlton House
Nov. 25th 1818

My dr Sir Thomas,
    The Prince Regent is most highly pleased with the opportunities which have been afforded to you for the execution of your arduous

work, upon which point alone His Royal Highness felt anxiety, for the Success of the Measure is already, He is persuaded, beyond doubt—
If you will draw upon Coutts to be charged to my Account, Directions are given for the acceptance of your Draft or Drafts to the amount of £1000
Say candidly if that Sum will meet your Exigencies and believe me
very sincerely yours
B. Bloomfield.
My absence from Town and the State of Affliction into which we have been thrown has delayed this letter, but which [sic] I know you will pardon . . .

233. Undated letter, quote in Smiles, 221
234. Stevenson, 201
235. 3 April, 1808; *Letters*, II, 35
236. 14 September 1809; *Letters*, II, 240
237. 4 August, 1811; ibid, II, 529
238. Ibid, III, 242; 23 March 1813
239. Lockhart, III, 340
240. Ibid, III, 340-1
241. Ibid, III, 344-5
242. 14 January 1818; *Letters*, V, 48-50
243. 4 February 1818; ibid, V, 74
244. 7 February 1818; ibid, V, 74-5
245. 14 January 1818; ibid, V, 52
246. 5 December 1818; ibid, V, 250
247. 17 January 1819; Jekyll, 78
248. The most comprehensive account of the Herculaneum Mission is given in W. Scott's introduction to *Fragmenta Herculanensia*, pp. 1 sqq.
249. MSS. Finch d 5, Bodleian Library, Oxford
250. 25 January 1820; MSS. Finch d 5
251. RA, Lawrence Correspondence, III, 25; 31 July 1819
252. Ibid, III, 27; 6 September 1819
253. Undated letter; Layard, 152
254. RA, Lawrence Correspondence, III, 5; 23 January 1819
255. Ibid, III, 14; 6 April 1819
256. RA, Council Minutes, VI, 73-4; 18 June 1819

PART THREE

KING OF ENGLAND

1. 24 January 1820; L'Estrange, II, 83
2. 24 January 1820; Croker, I, 155
3. *A Vision of Judgment*; Southey, *Works*, 774
4. 11 February 1820; Home, 54
5. Lyttelton, *Correspondence*, 209-10

6. 1 February 1820; Edgcumbe, II, 96
7. 2 February 1820; Quennell, 11
8. Croker, I, 157
9. 17 February 1820; Adeane, 420
10. Munk, op. cit.
11. February 1820; L'Estrange, II, 86
12. Southey: *Life and Correspondence*, V, 18-20, 11 February 1820
13. Southey, *Works*, 766-7
14. RA, Lawrence Correspondence, III, 34
15. 19 February 1820; Williams, II, 234
16. Williams, II, 250-1
17. RA Council Minutes, VI, 159-61: Council of 24 July 1820. Ibid, 133, 140 sqq., 147-8, 152
18. 28 March 1820: *Letters*, VI, 157-8
19. 9 April 1820; ibid, VI, 173
20. Lockhart, IV, 366
21. Lever, 31
22. Lady Conyngham's ancestry is discussed by Sir Osbert Sitwell in *Left Hand, Right Hand!*, 45 sqq.
23. Sudley, 265-6; Temperley, 117-18
24. 6 January 1820; Quennell, 5
25. Ibid, 6-7
26. Lever, 23
27. Quennell, 31-2
28. 1 May 1820; Quennell, 34
29. 2 June; ibid, 36
30. Bell/Canning, 305
31. 25 June 1820; Quennell, 45
32. Richardson, op. cit., 141
33. 1 December 1820; Tibble, 73
34. 5 July 1820; L'Estrange, II, 102-3
35. Trevelyan, I, 118-19
36. Coleridge, *Letters, Conversations and Recollections*, I, 128-9; 25 October 1820
37. Prothero, V, 60-1
38. 19 June 1820; CA, Lawrence Correspondence, III, 48
39. 27 June 1820; ibid, III, 50
40. 27 June 1820; *Letters*, VI, 215
41. 23 July 1820: *Letters*, VI, 235
42. Ibid.
43. Malmesbury, *Letters*, XI, 536
44. 6 July 1820; Phipps, II, 56
45. Richardson, op. cit., 147
46. 23 August 1820; Quennell, 65
47. 6 September 1820; Quennell, 71
48. Letter marked 'Recd. Oct. 21 1820.' RA, Lawrence Correspondence, III, 66

49. 7 October 1820; ibid, III, 65. On 1 July 1820, the Duchess had written to Lawrence (Corr. III, 50): 'I am very uneasy at the state of things in England, I wish and always had wish'd that the Queen had been treated with an attention and consideration that might have tempted her to some propriety of conduct and have avoided all appearance of persecution—the measure of erasing her name from the liturgy seem'd to me to be quite unworthy of the King—but now, these riots, her journey to England and the part wh the populace take in her favour make me think that the King must proceed in the trial wh he has announced or he will have the appearance of being alarmed —and yet God knows what may be the consequence.'
50. Richardson, *The Disastrous Marriage*, 188-9
51. 16 November 1820; Lever, 61
52. Royal Society of Literature Archives
53. *Letters*, VI, 368; 28 February 1821
54. Ibid, VI, 372; 1 March 1821
55. Southey, *Life and Correspondence*, V, 63; 4 March 1821
56. Ibid, V, 21; 20 February 1820
57. Davy/Davy, II, 173-4
58. W. Scott, *Fragmenta Herculanensia;* introduction, 10
59. Ibid, introduction
60. October, 1824; Chorley, I, 95
61. 4 March 1821; Quennell, 124
62. 23 March 1821; Mundy 322
63. Asp/G, III, 47; Charles Arbuthnot to the King, 2 December 1823
64. Croly, *The Coronation*, 54-6
65. 8 May 1821; Layard, 165-6
66. *Letters*, VI, 492
67. Partington, 97, note
68. 17 July 1821; *Letters*, II, 30
69. Mathews, 138-45
70. Croker, I, 195
71. Letters, VI, 503
72. Gerard, 138
73. Lever, 86; 20 July 1821
74. *Sermon*, 11-13
75. Gerard, 137-8
76. 24 July 1821; Lyttelton, *Corr.*, 237; Home, *Letters*, I, 153-4
77. Layard, op. cit.; see also Williams, op. cit.
78. Taylor, II, 24-6
79. 21 July 1821; Lyttelton, Corr., 237
80. Mallet, op. cit., III, 413
81. 31 July 1821: Lever, op. cit., 91
83. Jekyll, 116
83. 8 August 1821; Powell/Barnard, 292-3
84. Dr. Thomson to Mrs. Finch, 19 August 1821; MSS. Finch d 15 (Bodleian Library, Oxford)

85. J. Bielby to Robert Finch, 10 September 1821; MSS. Finch d 2 (Bodleian Library, Oxford)
86. 14 August 1821; Powell/Barnard, 295
87. 31 August 1821; Trevelyan I, 124-5
88. Cloncurry, 277
89. 8 August 1821: Powell/Barnard, 292-3
90. 13 August 1821; ibid, 294
91. Croker, I, 201; 12 August 1821
92. S. Hubert Burke, *Ireland Sixty Years Ago*, gives much information about the Irish visit
93. Quoted by Burke, op. cit.
94. Quoted by Burke, op. cit.
95. Lloyd, 418
96. Cloncurry, 277
97. Suggested by a passage from the *Dublin Evening Post*. Prothero, V, 399
98. Prothero, V, 364
99. Ibid, note
100. Croker, I, 205
101. Ibid, I, 206-7
102. Russell, III, 275
103. 8 August 1821, quoted by Burke, op. cit.
104. Quoted by Burke, op. cit.
105. Ibid.
106. Murray 83
107. 10 September 1821; MSS. Finch d 2 (Bodleian Library, Oxford)
108. October 1821; *Letters*, VII, 25-6
109. Ibid.
110. Jesse, 126
111. Ibid, 127, 129, 137
112. Knighton, I, 156; 25 September 1821
113. Ibid, 144-8; 10 August 1821
114. Ibid, 158
115. October 1832; Stoddard/Raikes, 187-8
116. Ibid.
117. 13 October 1821; Powell/Barnard, 302
118. 27 January 1821; ibid, 284
119. Williams, II, 262; 10 November 1821
120. Croker, I, 212; 16 September 1821
121. 27 September 1821; Prothero, V, 378
122. 14-22 November 1821; Russell, III, 302-3
123. Ibid.
124. Pückler-Muskau, 29 July 1827; IV, 112
125. 13 April 1823; Parker, I, 315
126. Parker, I, 315-16; notes of 21 May 1822
127. Ibid.
128. Ibid, I, 317
129. 23 December 1821; Quennell, 145

130. 27 January 1822; Quennell, 150
131. Asp./G. II, 490
132. Ibid, 494; the King to Liverpool, [21] January 1822; ibid, 514-15; the King to Liverpool, 21 March 1822
133. Ibid, 503-4
134. Ibid, 504, note
135. Partington, 263
136. 15 August 1822; RA, Lawrence Correspondence, IV, 14
137. RA, Lawrence Correspondence, V, 73; letter postmarked November 1822
138. 29 February 1822; Southey, *Life and Correspondence*, V, 115-16
139. Note to Scott, *Letters*, VII, 107
140. 23 March 1822; ibid, VII, 107
141. Lever, 96
142. 17 May 1822; Lever, 98
143. Lever, 98-9
144. Mathews, I, 185-7
145. Croker, I, 243-7
146. Ibid, I, 248-50
147. Ibid.
148. *Letters*, VII, 70
149. Ibid, VII, 193
150. Ibid, VII, 211
151. Ibid, VII, 213
152. Parkes, I, 318; Lockhart, V, 198
153. Manuscript poem in scrapbook *King George IV's Visit to Scotland* (British Museum: 1876 e 24)
154. Broadsheet from above scrapbook
155. Details quoted in *The Scotsman*, 14 August 1822
156. Parker, I, 319
157. Ibid, 319-20. Sir Thomas Lawrence, writing to Elizabeth, Duchess of Devonshire on 12 August, sent her details of the death of Londonderry, and added:
    Singular that on these two journies to Ireland and Scotland, His Majesty should have lost in one, his most harassing Enemy—in the other his ablest Servant—checking the unmix'd Joy of his Reception in both Cases. All Circles and Parties here have lost, if not a Favourite in all, a Man whom all admir'd . . .
    (R.A., Lawrence Correspondence, IV, 13)
158. Davy, II, 156-7; 11 August 1822
159. Unidentified newspaper cutting of 22 August 1822, from scrapbook above
160. Unidentified cutting from scrapbook above
161. Lockhart, V, 202-3
162. Parker, I, 318
163. Andrew, 75-9
164. Ibid.

165. *The Courier*, 11 July 1825
166. Unidentified cutting from scrapbook above
167. Lockhart, V, 217-18
168. Croker, I, 232; 2 September 1822
169. Parker, I, 335
170. Ibid, 336
171. Ibid, 335
172. Archives of The Royal College of Physicians
173. RA, Lawrence Correspondence, IV, 11. The dilatory nature of Lawrence is suggested by a note from Joseph Jekyll, written on 7 January 1817 (or 1818):

> Dear Sr Thomas.
>
> This Day it is exactly a Twelvemonth since I sate last to you—am I totally forgotten?
>
> . . . The Prince Regent likes the Portrait & I must get H.R.H. in the Name & on behalf of his Majesty to command you to proceed. The Court of Chancery would have finished the Picture with ten times more Dispatch . . .
>
> Yrs ever
>
> Joseph Jekyll.

(II, 76)

174. Ibid, 18
175. RA Council Minutes, VI, 305; 26 October 1822
176. Parker, I, 337-8; 11 February 1823
177. Ibid, 338-9; 17 March 1823
178. 15 May 1823; Quennell, 263
179. Creevey, II, 61
180. 21 May 1823; Quennell, 266
181. *Letter from the King to the Earl of Liverpool*, 15 January 1823 (British Museum: c 11 d 9)
182. 19 February 1823; RA, Lawrence Correspondence, IV, 26
183. 8 January 1823; RA, Lawrence Correspondence, IV, 26
184. Brayley, 406
185. *Portrait of Sir John Soane*, 87 and *passim*
186. RA, Lawrence Correspondence, IV, 27; 15 January 1823
187. RA, Lawrence Correspondence, IV, 36; 14 April 1823. Lawrence continues:

> Perhaps you will agree with me, that besides the pleasure of a private acknowledgment from you, some answer of a more general character should be sent to me, that if opportunity occurs may be plac'd before His Majesty, which whilst conveying the just sentiments of Gratitude and Reverence from the English and Artists at Rome may have the subordinate effect of reviving and strengthening the impression of the subject on His Majesty's mind, and disposing his gracious nature to future acts of favor and protection . . .
>
> In any Letter that may be seen by His Majesty no second name should

be introduc'd; but in another pray mention Sir William Knighton's name, who is generally friendly to the Arts.

On 6 May 1823, Eastlake sends Lawrence his draft reply to the King (RA, Lawrence Correspondence, IV, 41):

. . . The gradual establishment of a National Academy for the Fine Arts in England was one of the glories of the last reign, and the beneficial effects of that institution in the development [sic] of native talent have long been experienced; but while the necessity or propriety of visiting the capital of Italy for the purpose of improvement has been ever acknowledged, it was reserved for his present gracious Majesty to give the important sanction of His approbation and encouragement to this method of enlarging the views and purifying the taste of the artist . . .

188. RA, Lawrence Correspondence, IV, 40; 1 May 1823
189. Partington, 247; 15 July 1823
190. The Lawrence Correspondence at the Royal Academy (V, 36) includes a letter from Lord Farnborough (the former Sir Charles Long):

Whitehall Gardens,
May 19th [1827]

My dear Sir Thomas

You are probably aware that His Majesty has given the two Sea pieces which were in the room at St James's Palace to the Hall of Greenwich Hospital—I was anxious if they were to be removed from the Place where they hung that they should be placed in some public Institution.

I cannot help submitting to your Consideration whether before Mr. Turner's picture goes to the Hospital it would not be desirable that he should just look at it and consider whether it would not be very advantageous to the Picture to give the Ships a little more solidity—I leave this however entirely to your Judgment—but as you know I think highly of his Talent I could not help suggesting what appears to me would be a great improvement.

Dear Sir Thomas
Yrs very sincerely
Farnborough

191. Report of first general meeting; RSL archives
192. Lawrence: *Address to Students*, 19-20
192. *Morning Post*, 1 January 1824
194. Information from Mr. Robert Speaight
195. Edwards, 246-9, 262; Toye, 97-9, 114 sqq., 121
196. 25 May 1823; Pope, II, 413
197. 1 February 1824; ibid, II, 459
198. Taylor, II, 70; late February 1824
199. Ibid, II, 76-7; 19 August 1824

200. Lockhart, V, 328; Scott's library catalogue, 223
201. RA, Lawrence Correspondence, IV, 61
202. Mulvany, 90-1
203. 12 April 1824; MSS. Finch d 5 (Bodleian Library, Oxford). Donaldson helped to found the Institute of Architects, and was Emeritus Professor of Architecture at London University, 1841-1864
204. Cooper, II, 347 sqq.
205. Ibid, II, 237-8
206. Ibid.
207. Ibid, II, 354 sqq.
208. Ibid.
209. 17 May 1822; Brettell, appendix
210. Asp./G, I, 340-1, 361-2, 363
211. Lloyd, 467
212. 24 January 1824; Asp./G., III, 58
213. Draper, *Sermon*, 18 July 1830; 6-7
214. Sermon of 29 January 1826, pp. 6-7; Solomon, 13
215. Stoddard/Raikes, 309 sqq.
216. *Spirit of the Age*, 61
217. 7 April 1825; MSS. Finch d 5 (Bodleian Library, Oxford)
218. MSS. Finch d 5 (Bodleian Library, Oxford)
219. RA, Lawrence Correspondence, IV, 93; 4 April 1825
220. Williams, II, 405, 406, 478; Layard, 194, 197
221. RA, Lawrence Correspondence, IV, 114; 28 September 1825
222. RA, Lawrence Correspondence, V, 3; 16 February 1826
223. Bayne, 120-1, 133-4
224. *Spirit of the Age*, 148
225. Russell, IV, 340
226. Ibid, 261 and 292-3
227. Croker, I, 288-9
228. Asp/G, III, 194-7
229. Parker, I, 387
230. Ibid. The formal offer of the medals was made by Peel on 3 December. On 20 December Sir Humphry Davy expressed his 'humble and dutiful thanks' for 'His Majesty's gracious disposition to promote the objects of the Royal Society and the general Interests of Science.' (Royal Society Council Minutes, 15 December 1825, 26 January 1826.) Among the domestic MSS. of The Royal Society (Vol. I) is a draft letter from the Duke of Sussex to Sir William Knighton, 11 May 1832, discussing the subsequent history of the medals. In the Council Minutes for 8 July 1830 is a draft address to King William IV on his accession; the Council lament his brother as 'a Gracious and Munificent Patron, who uniformly evinced the greatest zeal for the interests of Science, and was pleased to testify, in an especial manner, by placing the Annual Royal Medals at the disposal of the Royal Society, His approbation of their efforts to promote those interests, and to enlarge the Boundaries of Human Knowledge.'

231. Presidential Discourse to the Royal Society, 1826. H. Davy, *Collected Works*, VII, 92-3, 98, 99
232. Russell, V, 40-41, 54
233. April 1826: Partington, 146-7
234. 17 April 1826; Russell, VIII, 263-4
235. 8 November 1825; Quennell, 355
236. 2 December 1825; Bagot, II, 305 and note
237. Creevey, II, 96
238. Quennell, 367-8
239. 25 May 1824; Leighton, 315
240. 18 May 1824; ibid, 313
241. Edgcumbe, II, 146
242. RA, Lawrence Correspondence, V, 9; 26 April 1826
243. Landseer, I, 277
244. In the Lawrence Correspondence at the Royal Academy (IV, 28) is a letter from Francis Rosaspina [?] of Bologna, to Sir Thomas Lawrence, 26 January 1823:

> I beg leave of intruding upon you, Sir, with this, in order to condescend at a request of a respectable friend of mine, Count Charles Marescalchi, in whose Gallery are two of the most beautiful & authentick pictures of our famous Coreggios.
>
> The said Count wishes me to let you know, (if it be true what is vociferated here that the King of England intends making a Selection of Pictures from the best Authors) that he would have no objection to allow them to come & adorn his Britanick Majesty's Museum—
>
> I am also informed that Count Marescalchi is disposed to sell them at a reasonable price; in consideration of which I, am more emboldened to take the liberty of offering his pictures to you, Sir, begging of your kindness and sagacity to strive to induce H.M. not to suffer such famous works to pass elsewhere . . .

The Lawrence Correspondence also includes (IV, 61) a letter from Lord Burghersh, in Florence, to Sir Charles Long, 22 March 1824. 'I have been requested by Bartolini to state for the King's information that the Vase of which there was so much conversation in the year 1819 he is now at liberty to dispose of and he asks 400£ for it. The truth is that this is not one third of its real value, but whether the King will choose to possess it, is another question . . .' On 7 December 1820 (III, 69), William Mulready, the artist, writes to Lawrence to acknowledge a draft drawn by Bloomfield on Messrs. Coutts for 200 guineas, 'that sum being the price of my picture of the Wolf and the Lamb purchased by his Majesty.' On 27 October 1838, Knighton tells Lawrence (V, 73) that the King has bought a picture by Mulready for 300 guineas

245. RA, Lawrence Correspondence, V, 23; 2 November 1826
246. 4 March 1826; Lockhart, VI, 254
247. 20 October 1826; Lockhart, VI, 360-1

248. Ibid.
249. 12 November 1826; *Letters*, X, 126-7; quoted by Knighton
250. Pückler-Muskau, III, 163
251. 15 January 1827; Jekyll, 169
252. Duke of Rutland to Lady Shelley: Edgcumbe, II, 151
253. Home/Stuart: *Selections*, 237
254. Council Report, 26 April 1827; RSL Archives. Letter of 6 May 1827; Parkington, 153
255. 26 April 1827; *Letters*, X, 197
256. Ibid, X, 222-3
257. 12 July 1827; *Letters*, X, 255-6. The King had presented his physician, Sir Henry Halford, with two fine emus sent him from abroad. The birds had proved to be very mischievous on Sir Henry's estate at Wistow, 'but this was borne with in consideration of their royal donor.' When the King granted Sir Henry supporters for his coat-of-arms, and Sir Henry chose two emus proper, he showed that he was indeed, 'the friend of the Royal family', see Munk, 169-70
258. *Letters*, X, 268; quoted by Knighton, I, 292
259. Ibid, X, 336-7
260. 19 February 1827; Creevey, II, 106
261. 6 March 1827; ibid, 108
262. 9 March 1927; ibid, 109
263. 13 April 1827; ibid, II, 113
264. 4 April 1827; Knighton, I, 373 sqq.
265. Pückler-Muskau, III, 355-6; see also III, 319-20; IV, 7
266. Ibid., IV, 139-40
267. 11 June 1827; Knighton, I, 382 sqq.; and cf. also ibid, 386-7
268. Stevenson, op. cit. 256
269. 26 April 1827; RSL Archives
270. 20 January 1827; Taylor, II, 144-5
271. 27 April 1827; Partington, 247
272. 18 June 1827; Knighton, I, 375-6
273. Stapleton, I, 169; Canning to Lord Liverpool, 10th October 1824
274. 18 August 1827; Bagot, II, 422-3
275. 15 December 1827; RA, Lawrence Correspondence, V, 52
276. 25 August 1827; Parker, II, 18
277. Lever, 174
278. Pückler-Muskau, IV, 141 sqq.
279. Ibid.
280. *The Letters of Queen Victoria*, ed. Benson and Esher, I, 15-17
281. 8 August 1826; Quennell, 374
282. Creevey, II, 146
283. Asp./G., III, 367; 16 January 1828
284. Croker, I, 430-1; Stoddard/Raikes, 194
285. 5 June 1828; Law, I, 139
286. Robinson, 152
287. 8 December 1828; Parker, II, 42

288. Croker, I, 408
289. Creevey, II, 155
290. Haydon, *Conversation and Table-Talk*, II, 120-1; *Memoir*, II, 184-6
291. L'Estrange, II, 250-1
292. Taylor, II, 202
293. Haydon, *Explanation*, 13
294. Taylor, II, 204-5
295. Haydon, *Enquiry*, 34-5
296. 28 November 1828; Partington, 157
297. Jones, 113-17; *Chantrey and his Bequest*, 11-14
298. Ibid.
299. Taylor, II, 128
300. Royal Academy, Lawrence Correspondence, V, list facing p. 68. In the same volume, p. 66, is a note which suggests Lawrence's close relations with the Cottage coterie:

Friday Noon.
[2 July 1828]

My Dear Sir Thomas
    The [three words illegible] had better be put aside for a couple of Days until the urgency of your Cold has subsided;—But I recommend You to take the two Pills that accompany this Note when you go to Bed to Night.—
    Have a boiled Chicken for your Dinner;—boiled to rags—
Your's ever very
sincerely
W Knighton

301. Williams II, 565-7
302. Royal Academy, Lawrence Correspondence, V, 72; 26 September 1828
303. 25 November 1828; Williams, II, 266
304. 28 November 1828; Partington, 157
305. 11 May 1828; *Journal*, II, 178
306. 16 May 1828; *Letters*, X, 420-2
307. 4 August 1828; ibid, X, 479-81
308. Ibid, 482-3
309. Creevey
310. 30 March 1828; Croker, I, 414-15
311. 12 September 1828; Mundy, 336-8
312. 24 November 1828; Law, I, 263
313. Knighton, II, 43-4
314. 24 December 1828—4 January 1829; Robinson, 169-70
315. 3 November 1828; Partington, 155
316. 7 November 1828; Creevey, II, 186-7
317. Jekyll, 186
318. 27 November 1828; Sudley, 6
319. 7 May 1828; Law, I, 101-2
320. 17 September 1828; Croker, I, 430-1

321. Southey, *Life and Correspondence*, VI, 22, 29
322. 23 July 1828; Law, I, 173-4
323. In a letter to Bishop Hurd on 13 February 1801 (Hurd MSS. 19, 53), George III had written:

> An unfortunate opinion implanted in the mind of Mr. Pitt by persons in no means friend to our happy Church and State Establishments to bring in a Bill enabling Dissenters to hold Offices without taking the Test Act, and repealing the Law of 30 Car. 2do which precludes Papists from sitting in Parliament has made me reluctantly permit him to retire from My Service.

324. Law, I, 368
325. Ibid, I, 366
326. Ibid, I, 370
327. Ibid, I, 374
328. 4 March 1829; Law, I, 376-7
329. Quoted by Fulford, op. cit., 222
330. 2-14 April 1829; Robinson, 193
331. 17-29 March 1829; ibid, 187. One of Peel's comments on the Catholic question is found in a note to Lawrence on 25 February 1829 (RA, Lawrence Correspondence, V, 83):

> . . . I am very callous to the abuse to which you refer—I was so long accustomed to the violence of Roman Catholics—that I am case-hardened against the attacks of their ultra-opponents.

> I very much doubt whether vulgar abuse and scurrility are not in the end an advantage to a public man

332. Law, I, 143-4, 295, and 297
333. Croker, I, 430-1
334. Law, I, 375
335. Ibid, I, 404
336. 11 May 1829; ibid, II, 34-5
337. Ibid, II, 15, 16
338. Ibid, II, 60
339. 8 January 1829; Jekyll, 193
340. Russell, VI, 39-40
341. Ibid, VI, 58
342. 18 May 1829; Scott, *Letters*, XI, 185-6
343. 12 June 1829; Taylor, II, 217
344. 9 April 1829; Williams II, 496
345. Rush: *Memoranda*, 2nd edition, xvi-xvii
346. 14 June 1829; quoted by Summerson, 251
347. 25 December 1824; RA, Lawrence Correspondence, IV, 86. This picture does not appear to be the picture catalogued by Mr. Kenneth Garlick, in his *Sir Thomas Lawrence*, exhibited at the Royal Academy in 1827 and now at Jesus College, Oxford. Mr. Garlick (p. 52) lists only one portrait of the architect by Lawrence, but it seems possible that there were two.

348. Law, II, 55
349. Ibid, II, 100; 24 September 1829
350. Russell, VI, 69-70
351. Law, II, 91
352. 12-24 September 1829; Robinson, 198
353. Law, II, 100
354. Asp./G., III, 467; 26 December 1829
355. 17 November 1829; Sudley, 9
356. Jekyll, 210-11
357. 9 November 1829; Partington, 158-9
358. 'The Copper Colossus of Windsor.' *The Times*, 16 October 1964
359. Williams, II, 533
360. Ibid, II, 546-7
361. 8 January 1830; Knighton, II, 94-5
362. 11 January 1830; RA, Lawrence Correspondence, V, 110
363. 9 January 1830; Taylor, II, 230
364. Archer-Shee, I, 417
365. Parker, II, 142
366. 27 January 1830; ibid, II, 143
367. Archer-Shee, I, 418
368. Ibid, I, 419 and 431
369. 24 January 1830; Brougham, op. cit., III, 20
370. Law, II, 170-2; 15 January 1830
371. Ibid, II, 174; 20 January 1830
372. Richardson, *My Dearest Uncle*, 99
373. 13 January 1830; Law, II, 167-9
374. 8 January 1830; Jekyll, 218
375. Gronow, *Anecdotes*, 311
376. 15 March 1830; Jekyll, 226
377. Law, II
378. Haydon: *Correspondence and Table-Talk*, II, 131-2; Taylor II, 236-7
379. *Letters*, XI, 335-7; quoted by Knighton
380. Lockhart, VII, 212-13
381. 26 October 1831; *Letters*, XII, 35
382. Croker, II, 56, 22 April 1830
383. Parker, II, 145
384. Croker, loc. cit.
385. Law, 224-5; and Parker, II, 147-51
386. Ibid.
387. 21 April 1830; Law, II, 224-5
388. Mundy, 342-3
389. Knighton, II, 120-1; 26 April 1830
390. Croker, II, 56
391. Munk, 182-3
392. Law, II, 229-30
393. Law, II, 231-2
394. Ibid.

395. Mundy, 344
396. Jekyll, 230
397. Southey, *Life and Correspondence* VI, 102-3; 15 May 1830
398. 17 May 1830; 159-60, Partington
399. Lloyd, 472
400. 25-6 May 1830; Mundy, 346-7
401. Jekyll, op. cit., 231
402. Parker, II, 152
403. Law, II, 235; 3 May 1830
404. Law, II, 233-4; 2 May 1830
405. Ibid.
406. Knighton, II, 120
407. 16 April 1830; Knighton, II, 116-17
408. 1 May 1830; ibid, 123
409. 18 May 1830; ibid, 134 sqq.
410. 3 May 1830; ibid, 125 sqq.
411. 9 June 1830; Law, II, 266
412. Croker, II, 57-8
413. Law, II, 238-9
414. 12 May 1830; Law, II, 244-5
415. Bloomfield, II, 301
416. 14 May 1830; Croker, II, 61
417. 16-28 May 1830; Robinson, 220-1
418. Croker, II, 61
419. Law, II, 257-8
420. Knighton, II, 140-1
421. Munk, 183
422. Croker, II, 233
423. MSS. Finch d 15 (Bodleian Library, Oxford)
424. Knighton
425. 17 May 1830; Partington, 159-60
426. Richardson, *The Disastrous Marriage*, 227
427. Ibid.
428. Knighton, II, 141-3
429. 11 June 1830; Croker, II, 64-5
430. Ibid.
431. Stirling, II, 134
432. 10 June 1830; Bloomfield, II, 301-2
433. Stirling, loc. cit.
434. Law, II, 270
435. Richardson, *The Disastrous Marriage*, 239-40
436. Parker, II, 153. The Duke of Wellington told Lord Ellenborough that 'the late King had three disorders which must have proved fatal, and he died of bursting a blood-vessel in the stomach. He had a concretion as large as an orange in his bladder, and his liver was diseased, and his heart was ossified. Water there was not much, and all

proceeding from the interruption of circulation about the heart.'
(29 June 1830. Law, II, 291)

437. Knighton, II, 144
438. Law, II, 276, 279, 280
439. Russell, VI, 123
440. Stirling, op. cit. II, 135-6
441. Kemble, II, 136
442. Jekyll, 236
443. Creevey, II, 211-12
444. Taylor, II, 251
445. Lockhart, VII, 215; and Scott, *Letters*, XI, 373, 2 July 1830
446. Lloyd, 470-1
447. W. B. James, 18-19
448. Barker, 7
449. R. C. Dillon, 14-15
450. Solomon, 13, 17 and 29-30
451. *Historical Sketch*, 3
452. Anon, *An Historical Account . . .*, 58
453. RA Council Minutes, VII, 382 sqq.; 29 July 1830
454. Ibid.
455. *Ceremonial for the Interment of His late Most Sacred Majesty King George the Fourth.* Issued by the Earl Marshal, 12 July 1830
456. 17 July 1830; Jekyll, 242
457. Ibid.
458. Ibid.
459. Ibid, 242-3
460. 8-20 July 1830; Robinson 224-6
461. Law, II, 299
462. Kemble, op. cit., I, 157
463. Wynn/Leighton, 377; 27 July 1830
464. Law, II, 300
465. Op. cit., 225
466. 16-28 July 1830; Robinson, 230
467. 27 July 1830; Lewis, III, 388
468. Mundy, 348
469. 24 July 1830; MSS. Finch d 5 (Bodleian Library, Oxford)
470. Lewis, III, 387
471. Robinson, op. cit. 225
472. Lennox, *Story*, I, 6-9
473. Kemble, II, 54
474. Morley/Robinson, *Books and their Writers*, II, 799; 13 October 1860
475. Creevey, II, 156; 20 March 1828
476. Richardson, *The Disastrous Marriage*, 228
477. Mundy, 13

SELECTED BIBLIOGRAPHY

The following are among the books consulted. Place of publication London, unless otherwise stated.

ADEANE, J. H. (ed.) — *The Girlhood of Maria Josepha Holroyd (Lady Stanley of Alderley)*. Recorded in Letters. (Longmans, Green. 1896.)
The Early Married Life of Maria Josepha, Lady Stanley. (Longmans, Green. 1899.)

ANDREW, W. R. — *Life of Sir Henry Raeburn*. (W. H. Allen. 1886.)

ANGELO, Henry — *Reminiscences*. (Colburn. 1828-30.)

ANON — *An Account of the Visit of H.R.H. the Prince Regent, with their Imperial and Royal Majesties, the Emperor of All the Russias and the King of Prussia, to the Corporation of London, in June 1814*. (*Nichols. 1815.*)
An Account of the Visit of H.R.H. The Prince Regent . . . to the University of Oxford in June MDCCCXIV. (Oxford. Clarendon Press. 1815.)
An Address to the Inhabitants of Dublin on the intended Visit of the King. (Dublin. Milliken. 1821.)
An Historical Account of the Public and Domestic Life and Reign of his Late Majesty George the Fourth. (Harrogate. Blackburn. 1830.)
An Historical Sketch of the Life and Reign of his late Majesty, King George the Fourth. (Smeeton. 1830.)
A Letter to the Prince of Wales, on a second Application to Parliament, to discharge debts wantonly contracted since May 1787. 10th edition, enlarged. To which is added a new postscript. (Owen. 1795.)
Authentic Account of the Visit of H.R.H. the Prince Regent to the University of Oxford. (Oxford. Cooke. 1814.)
Ceremonial for the Interment of His Late Most Sacred Majesty King George the Fourth, of Blessed Memory, in the Royal Chapel of St. George at Windsor, On Thursday Evening the 15th of July 1830. (Issued by the Earl Marshal. Printed by Clarke. 1830.)
Chantrey and his Bequest. (Cassell. 1904.)

ANON—*cont.* *King's Visit to Scotland, The.* (Book of press-cuttings. British Museum reference 1876 e 24.)
Memoirs of H.R.H. the Prince of Wales. 2nd edition. (Hughes. 1808.)
Memoirs of Mr. W. H. W. Betty. (Cousins, n.d.)
Observations on the Public and Private Life of H.R.H. the Prince Regent. (Swan. 1815.)
The Ceremonies to be observed at the Royal Coronation of His Most Excellent Majesty King George the Fourth on Thursday the 19th day of July, MDCCCXXI (Bentley. 1821.)
The Tour to York. A Circumstantial Account of H.R.H. the Prince of Wales's Visit to that City. 1789.

ARMITAGE, Harold *Francis Chantrey.* (Mills & Boon. 1915.)
ARMSTRONG, Walter *Lawrence.* (Methuen. 1913.)
ASPINALL, A. (ed.) *The Correspondence of George, Prince of Wales.* (Cassell. 1963-)
The Letters of King George IV, 1812-1830. (Cambridge University Press. 1938)
Letters of the Princess Charlotte, 1811-1817. (Home and Van Thal. 1949.)

ASSISTANT CURATE AT BATH, An *God Save the King. A sermon preached 29 January, the day appointed to commemorate His Majesty's accession to the Throne of his Ancestors.* (Hatchard. 1826.)

AUSTEN-LEIGH, J. E. *A Memoir of Jane Austen.* (Bentley. 1870.)
BAGOT, Josceline (ed.) *George Canning and his Friends.* (Murray. 1909.)
BAKER, Herschel *John Philip Kemble.* (Cambridge, Mass. Harvard University Press. 1942.)

BALSTON, Thomas *John Martin, 1789-1854.* (Duckworth. 1947)
BARKER, S. *A Sermon, preached in the parish church of Brundish and Tannington, in the County of Suffolk, on the 18th day of July 1830, being the Sunday after the interment of . . . King George the Fourth.* (Woodbridge, Loder. 1830.)

BARON, John *The Life of Edward Jenner, M.D.* (Colburn. 1827.)

BAYNE, William *Sir David Wilkie, R. A.* (The Walter Scott Publishing Co. 1903.)

BEATTIE, William *Life and Letters of Thomas Campbell.* (Moxon. 1849.)

BEERBOHM, Max *Works.* (Heinemann. 1922.)
BELL, N. *Thomas Gainsborough, a record of his life and works.* (Bell. 1897.)

BELL, Robert *The Life of the Rt. Hon. George Canning.* (Chapman & Hall. 1846.)

BICKLEY, Francis (ed.)   *The Diaries of Sylvester Douglas (Lord Glenbervie).* (Constable. 1928.)

BLOOMFIELD, Georgina, Lady (ed.)   *Memoir of Benjamin Lord Bloomfield, G.C.B., G.C.H.* (Chapman & Hall. 1884.)

BOADEN, James   *Memoirs of Mrs. Siddons.* (Gibbings. 1893.)
The Life of Mrs. Jordan. (Bull. 1831.)

BOLTON, Arthur T. (ed.)   *The Portrait of Sir John Soane, R.A. (1753-1837.)* (Sir John Soane's Museum Publication. 1927.)

BOULTON, William B.   *Thomas Gainsborough, His Life, Work, Friends and Sitters.* (Methuen. 1905.)

BOURKE, Algernon (ed.)   *Correspondence of Mr. Joseph Jekyll with his sister-in-law, Lady Gertrude Sloane Stanley, 1818-1838.* (Murray. 1894.)

BRABROOK, Edward W.   *The Royal Society of Literature of the United Kingdom. A Brief Account of its Origin and Progress.* 2nd edition. (Asher. 1897.)

BRAYLEY, Edward Wedlake   *Illustrations of His Majesty's Palace at Brighton; formerly the Pavilion: executed by the command of King George the Fourth . . . To which is prefixed, a history of the Palace, by Edward Wedlake Brayley.* (Nichols. 1838.)
Londiniana. (Hurst, Chance, 1829.)

and BRITTON, John   *The History of the Ancient Palace and Late Houses of Parliament at Westminster.* (Weale. 1836.)

BRETTELL, J.   *George IV, The Patron of Literature.* A Discourse delivered at the anniversary meeting of the Royal Society of Literature, April 26, 1831. By the President. (Rivington. 1831.)

BROADLEY, A. M., and JERROLD, W.   *The Romance of an Elderly Poet.* (Stanley Paul. 1913.)

BROUGHAM, Henry, Lord.   *The Life and Times of Henry Lord Brougham,* written by himself. (Blackwood. 1871.)

BUCKINGHAM and CHANDOS, Duke of   *Memoirs of the Court of George IV. 1820-1830.* From original family documents. (Hurst & Blackett. 1859.)

BURKE, S. Hubert   *Ireland Sixty Years Ago.* (Hodges. 1885.)

CAMERON, H. C.   *Sir Joseph Banks.* (Batchworth Press. 1952.)

CAMPBELL, Thomas   *Complete Poetical Works.* (Oxford University Press. 1907.)
Life of Mrs. Siddons. (Effingham Wilson. 1834.)

CARÊME, A.   *Le Pâtissier royal parisien.* (Paris. Dentu. 1815.)
Le Pâtissier pittoresque. (Paris. Renouard. 1842.)
Le Maître d'Hôtel Français. (Paris. Renouard. 1842.)
L'Art de la Cuisine française au XIXe siècle. (Paris. Renouard. 1847.)

CARÊME, A.—*cont.*   *Catalogue of the Library at Abbotsford.* (Edinburgh. Constable. 1838.)

CHAPMAN, R. W. (ed.)   *Jane Austen's Letters to her sister Cassandra and others.* (Oxford University Press. 1952.)

CHORLEY, Henry (ed.)   *Letters of Mary Russell Mitford. Second series.* (Bentley. 1872.)

CLARKE, James Stanier   *The Life of James the Second.* (Longman, Hurst, &c. 1816.)

and M'ARTHUR, John   *The Life of Admiral Lord Nelson, K.B.* (Cadell & Davies. 1809.)

CLONCURRY, Valentine, Lord   *Personal Recollections.* (Dublin. McGlashan. 1849.)

COBBETT, William   *History of the Regency and Reign of King George the Fourth.* (Cobbett. 1830, 1837.)

COLERIDGE, S. T.   *Letters, Conversations and Recollections.* (Moxon. 1836.)

CONSTABLE, Thomas   *Archibald Constable and his Literary Correspondents.* (Edinburgh. Edmonston & Douglas. 1873.)

COOPER, Bransby Blake   *The Life of Sir Astley Cooper, Bart.* (John Parker. 1843.)

COTTON, William   *A Catalogue of the Portraits painted by Sir Joshua Reynolds.* (Longman. 1857.)

CROLY, George   *The Coronation. Observations on the Public Life of the King.* (Warren. 1821.)

CUNNINGHAM, Allan   *The Lives of the Most Eminent British Painters, Sculptors, and Architects.* (Murray. 1830.)
    The Lives of the Most Eminent British Painters. Revised edition. Annotated and continued to the present time by Mrs. Charles Heaton. (Bell. 1879-1880.)

DALE, Antony   *James Wyatt, Architect. 1748-1813.* (Oxford. Blackwell. 1936.)

D'ARBLAY, Mme   *Diary and Letters.* (Colburn. 1842-6.)
    Memoirs of Dr. Burney. (Moxon. 1832.)

DAVY, John (ed.)   *Fragmentary Remains, Literary and Scientific, of Sir Humphry Davy, Bart.* (Churchill. 1858.)

DAVY, Sir H.   *Miscellaneous Papers and Researches.* (Smith, Elder. 1840.)
    Collected Works. (Smith, Elder. 1840.)

DELVES BROUGHTON, Mrs. V. (ed.)   *Court and Private Life in the time of Queen Charlotte. Being the journals of Mrs. Papendiek.* (Bentley. 1887.)

DILLON, R. C.   *A Sermon preached on . . . the Day of the Funeral of His Late Majesty, George IV. 2nd edition.* (Cochran. 1830.)

DOBRÉE, B. (ed.)   *The Letters of King George III.* (Cassell. 1935.)

DORAN, Dr.   *Annals of the English Stage.* (Nimmo. 1888.)

DRAPER, B. H.   *The Death of the King*. A Sermon. 2nd edition. (Southampton. King. 1830.)

EDGCUMBE, R.   *The Diary of Frances, Lady Shelley, 1818-1873*. (Murray. 1913.)

EDGEWORTH, Maria   *Chosen Letters*. With an introduction by F. V. Barry. (Cape. 1931.)

EDWARDS, H. S.   *The Life of Rossini*. (Hurst & Blackett. 1869.)

FINBERG, A. J.   *The Life of J. M. W. Turner, R.A.* (Oxford. Clarendon Press. 139.)

FOSTER, Vere (ed.)   *The Two Duchesses*. (Blackie. 1898.)

FULFORD, Roger   *George the Fourth*. (Duckworth. 1949.)

GARLICK, Kenneth   *Sir Thomas Lawrence*. (Routledge. 1954.)

GEORGE IV, King   *Letter from the King to the Earl of Liverpool. 1823.* (British Museum reference C 11 d 9.)

GERARD, Frances A.   *Some Fair Hibernians*. (Ward & Downey. 1897.)

GOLDRING, D.   *Regency Portrait Painter*. The Life of Sir Thomas Lawrence, P.R.A. (Macdonald. 1951.)

GOWER, Sir George Leveson (ed.)   *Hary-O. The Letters of Lady Harriet Cavendish, 1796-1809.* (Murray. 1940.)

GOWER, Lord R.   *Sir Thomas Lawrence*. (Goupil. 1900.)

GRANVILLE, Castalia, Countess (ed.)   *Lord Granville Leveson Gower (First Earl Granville.) Private Correspondence, 1781-1821.* (Murray. 1916.)

GRIEG, James (ed.)   *The Farington Diary*. (Hutchinson. 1922-6.)

GRIERSON, H. J. C. (ed.)   *The Letters of Sir Walter Scott*. (Constable. 1932-37.)

GRONOW, R. H.   *Anecdotes of Celebrities of London and Paris*. (Smith, Elder. 1873.)

Recollections and Anecdotes. (Smith, Elder. 1863.)

Reminiscences. (Smith, Elder. 1862.)

HALL, S. C.   *Retrospect of a Long Life*. (Bentley. 1883.)

HANOVERIAN, A.   *A Letter to the House of Peers, on the present bill, depending in Parliament, relative to the Prince of Wales's debts*. 2nd edition. (Lee. 1795.)

HARE, Augustus (ed.)   *The Life and Letters of Maria Edgeworth*. (Arnold. 1894.)

HARRIS, James, First Earl of Malmesbury   *Diaries and Correspondence*. (Bentley. 1844.)

A Series of Letters of the First Earl of Malmesbury to His Family and Friends from 1745 to 1820. (Bentley. 1870.)

HAYDON, B. R.   *Correspondence and Table-Talk*. With a Memoir by his son, Frederic Wordsworth Haydon. (Chatto & Windus. 1876.)

Some Enquiry into the Causes which have obstructed the Advance of Historical Painting, for the last 70 years in England. (Ridgway. 1829.)

HAYTER, John — *The Herculanean and Pompeian Manuscripts. A Letter to the Prince Regent, 1800.* (No date or place of publication given.)
A Report upon the Herculaneum Manuscripts, in a second letter, addressed, by permission, to H.R.H. the Prince Regent. (Phillips. 1811.)

HAYWARD, A. (ed.) — *Diaries of a Lady of Quality from 1797 to 1844.* (Longmans, Green. 1864.)

HAZLITT, William — *Political Essays, with Sketches of Public Characters.* (Hone. 1819.)

HILLES, F. W. (ed.) — *Letters of Sir Joshua Reynolds.* (Cambridge. Cambridge University Press. 1929.)

HOLLAND, Henry Edward, Lord (ed.) — *Memoirs of the Whig Party during My Time.* By Henry Richard, Lord Holland. (Longman. 1852.)

HOLLAND John — *Memorials of Sir F. Chantrey.* (Longman. 1851.)

HOME, James A. (ed.) — *Lady Louisa Stuart. Selections from her manuscripts.* (Edinburgh. David Douglas. 1899.)
Letters of Lady Louisa Stuart to Miss Louisa Clinton. (Edinburgh. David Douglas. 1901.)
Letters of Lady Louisa Stuart to Miss Louisa Clinton. Second series. (Edinburgh. David Douglas. 1903.)

HUISH, Robert — *Memoirs of George the Fourth.* (Kelly. 1831.)

ILCHESTER, Earl of (ed.) — *The Journal of Elizabeth, Lady Holland (1791-1811.)* (Longmans, Green. 1908.)

INGPEN, R. (ed.) — *The Letters of Percy Bysshe Shelley.* (Pitman. 1912.)

JACKSON, G. A. (ed.) — *Brougham and his Early Friends. Letters to James Loch, 1798-1809.* (Darling & Pead. 1908.)

JAMES, W. B. — *National blessings a ground for national gratitude and obedience. A sermon . . . on the occasion of the death of his Late Majesty, George IV.* (Rivington. 1830.)

JENNINGS, Louis J. (ed.) — *Correspondence and Diaries of John Wilson Croker.* (Murray. 1885.)

JESSE, Captain — *The Life of Beau Brummell.* New edition. (Clarke & Beeton. 1854.)

JOHNSON, R. B. — *The Letters of Lady Louisa Stuart.* (John Lane: the Bodley Head. 1926.)

JONES, George — *Sir Francis Chantrey, R.A. Recollections of his life, practice and opinions.* (Moxon. 1849.)

KEMBLE, Frances Anne — *Record of a Girlhood.* (Bentley. 1878.)

KNAPP, O. G. (ed.) — *An Artist's Love Story.* Told in the Letters of Sir Thomas Lawrence, Mrs. Siddons and her Daughters. (Allen. 1904.)

KNIGHTON, Lady — *Memoirs of Sir William Knighton, Bart., G.C.H.* Two volumes. (Bentley. 1838.)

LAMB, Charles — *Letters.* (Dent. 1945.)

LANDON, H. C. Robbins (ed.) — *The Collected Correspondence and London Notebooks of Joseph Haydn.* (Barrie and Rockliff. 1959.)

LANDSEER, Thomas — *Life and Letters of William Bewick, artist.* (Hurst and Blackett. 1871.)

LAW, Edward, Lord Ellenborough — *A Political Diary, 1828-1850.* (Bentley. 1881.)

LAWRENCE, Sir Thomas — *Address to the Students of the Royal Academy . . . 10 December 1823.* (Clowes. 1824.)
The Lawrence Gallery. First Exhibition. A Catalogue. (Richards. 1835.)

LAYARD, G. S. (ed.) — *Correspondence of Charlotte Grenville, Lady Williams Wynn, and her Three Sons.* (Murray. 1920.)

Leadbeater Papers, The (Bell & Daldy. 1862.)

LENNOX, Lord William Pitt — *Fifty Years' Biographical Reminiscences.* (Hurst and Blackett. 1863.)
My Recollections from 1806 to 1873. (Hurst & Blackett. 1874.)
The Story of My Life. (Hurst & Blackett. 1857.)

L'ESTRANGE, A. G. (ed.) — *The Life of Mary Russell Mitford, related in a selection from her letters to her friends.* (Bentley. 1870.)

LEVER, Tresham (ed.) — *The Letters of Lady Palmerston.* (Murray. 1957.)

LEWIS. Lady Theresa (ed.) — *Extracts of the Journals and Correspondence of Miss Berry from the year 1783 to 1852.* (Longmans, Green. 1865.)

LLOYD, H. E. — *George IV. Memoirs of his Life and Reign.* (Treuttel and Würtz. 1830.)

LOCKHART, J. G. — *Memoirs of the Life of Sir Walter Scott, Bart.* (Edinburgh. Cadell. 1837-8.)

LOVAT-FRASER, J. A. — *Erskine.* (Cambridge. Cambridge University Press. 1932.)

MCKAY, William and ROBERTS, W. — *John Hoppner, R.A.* (Colnaghi. 1909.)

MALLET, Charles Edward — *A History of the University of Oxford.* Vol. III. *Modern Oxford.* (Methuen. 1927.)

MANNERS, Lady Victoria, and Williamson, G. C. — *John Zoffany, R.A.* (John Lane. The Bodley Head. 1920.)

MARKHAM, Clements — *A Memoir of Archbishop Markham, 1719-1807.* (Oxford. Clarendon Press. 1906.)

MARSH, W. — *The Coronation. A Sermon preached at St. Peter's, Colchester.* (Colchester. Swinborne & Walter. 1821.)

MATHEWS, Anne — *A Continuation of the Memoirs of Charles Mathews, Comedian.* (Philadelphia. Lea and Blanchard. 1839.)

MAXWELL, Sir H. (ed.) *The Creevey Papers.* (Murray. 1903.)
MEMES, J. S. *Memoirs of Antonio Canova.* (Edinburgh. Constable. 1825.)
MOLLOY, Fitzgerald *Sir Joshua and his Circle.* (Hutchinson. 1906.)
MOORE, Thomas *Intercepted Letters; or, the Twopenny Post-Bag.* To which are added, trifles reprinted. Eighth edition. (Carr. 1813.)
MORGAN, Lady *Italy.* (Colburn. 1821.)
MORLEY, Edith J. (ed.) *Henry Crabb Robinson on Books and their Writers.* (Dent. 1938.)
The Correspondence of Henry Crabb Robinson with the Wordsworth Circle. 1808-1866. (Oxford. Clarendon Press. 1927.)
MULVANY, Thomas J. *Letters . . . to his eldest son; and appendix containing correspondence with Sir Thomas Lawrence.* (No publisher given. British Museum reference 10905 de 1.)
MUNDY, H. G. (ed.) *The Journal of Mary Frampton.* (Sampson Low. 1885.)
MUNK, William *The Life of Sir Henry Halford, Bart.* (Longmans. 1895.)
MURRAY, Patrick Joseph *The Life of John Banim, the Irish Novelist.* (Lay. 1857.)
NICHOLLS, John *Observations on the Situation of His Royal Highness the Prince of Wales.* (Miller. 1795.)
OLD ENGLISHMAN, An *Two Words of Counsel, and one of Comfort. Addressed to H.R.H. the Prince of Wales.* (Mason. 1795.)
OLIVER, J. W. *The Life of William Beckford.* (Oxford University Press. 1932.)
PARKE, W. T. *Musical Memoirs . . . 1784-1830.* (Colburn & Bentley. 1830.)
PARKER, Charles Stuart (ed.) *Sir Robert Peel, from his private papers.* (Murray. 1899.)
PARTINGTON, Wilfred (ed.) *The Private Letter-Books of Sir Walter Scott.* (Hodder & Stoughton. 1930.)
PHIPPS, Edmund *Memoirs of the Political and Literary Life of Robert Plumer Ward, Esq.* (Murray. 1850.)
PINDAR, Peter *The Regent's Fleet; or, John Bull at the Serpentine. A Poem.* (Johnston. 1814.)
The Royal Showman; or, the Regent's Gala. A Poem. (Johnston. 1814.)
PLUMB, J. H. *The First Four Georges.* (Batsford. 1956.)
POPE, Willard Bissell (ed.) *The Diary of Benjamin Robert Haydon.* (Cambridge, Mass. Harvard University Press. 1960.)
POWELL, Anthony (ed.) *Barnard Letters, 1778-1824.* (Duckworth. 1928.)

POWELL, G. H. (ed.)   *Reminiscences and Table-Talk of Samuel Rogers.* (R. Brimley Johnson. 1903.)

PROTHERO, R. E. (ed.)   *The Works of Lord Byron. Lettters and Journals.* (Murray. 1898.)

PÜCKLER-MUSKAU, Prince   *Tour in England, Ireland, and France, in the years 1826, 1827 and 1828.* (Effingham Wilson. 1832.)

QUENNELL, Peter (ed.)   *Byron. Selections from his Poetry, Letters and Journals.* (Nonesuch Press. 1949.)
The Private Letters of Princess Lieven to Prince Metternich. (Murray. 1937.)

QUINCY, Quatremere de   *Canova et ses Ouvrages.* (Paris. Le Clere. 1834.)

REDDING, Cyrus   *Fifty Years' Recollections, Literary and Personal.* (Skeet. 1858.)
Literary Reminiscences and Memoirs of Thomas Campbell. (Skeet. 1860.)

RICHARDSON, Joanna   *The Disastrous Marriage. A Study of George IV and Caroline of Brunswick.* (Cape. 1960.)
My Dearest Uncle. A Life of Leopold, First King of the Belgians. (Cape. 1961.)

RITCHIE, John   *'He Removeth Kings.' A discourse suggested by the demise of King George the Fourth.* (Edinburgh. Whyte. 1830.)

ROBERTS, R. Ellis   *Samuel Rogers and his Circle.* (Methuen. 1910.)

ROBERTS, W.   *Sir William Beechey, R.A.* (Duckworth. 1907.)

ROBINSON, Lionel G. (ed.)   *Letters of Dorothea, Princess Lieven, during her Residence in London, 1812-1834.* (Longmans, Green. 1902.)

ROMILLY, Samuel   *Memoirs.* (Murray. 1840.)

RUSH, Richard   *Memoranda of a Residence at the Court of London.* 2nd edition, revised and enlarged. (Philadelphia. Key & Biddle. 1933.)

RUSSELL, Lord John (ed.)   *Memoirs, Journal, and Correspondence of Thomas Moore.* (Longman. 1853-6.)

SCOTT, Sir W.   *Journal.* From the original manuscript at Abbotsford. (Edinburgh. David Douglas. 1890.)

SCOTT, Walter (ed.)   *Fragmenta Herculanensia.* A descriptive catalogue of the Oxford copies of the Herculanean Rolls. (Oxford. Clarendon Press. 1885.)

SCOTT, Walter Sidney (ed.)   *Letters of Maria Edgeworth and Anna Letitia Barbauld.* (The Golden Cockerel Press. 1953.)

SHEE, Martin Archer   *The Life of Sir Martin Archer Shee.* (Longmans, Green, 1860.)

SICHEL, Walter (ed.)   *The Glenbervie Journals.* (Constable. 1910.)

SIDDONS, Sarah Kemble   *Reminiscences.* Edited by William Van Lennep. (Cambridge, Mass. Widener Library. 1942.)

SITWELL, Osbert   *Left Hand, Right Hand!* (Macmillan. 1945.)

SMILES, Samuel   *A Publisher and his Friends. Memoir and correspondence of John Murray.* (Murray. 1911.)

SMITH, Edward   *The Life of Sir Joseph Banks.* (John Lane, The Bodley Head. 1911.)

SOLOMON, Myer   *A Funeral Sermon on the Death of his late Majesty George IV.* (Wertheimer. 1830.)

SOUTHEY, Rev. C. C. (ed.)   *The Life and Correspondence of the late Robert Southey.* (Longman. 1849.)

SOUTHEY, Robert   *Poetical Works.* (Longman. 1847.)

STANHOPE, Lady Hester   *Memoirs.* (Colburn. 1845.)

STAPLETON, Edward J. (ed.)   *Some Official Correspondence of George Canning.* (Longmans, Green. 1887.)

STAVORDALE, Lord (ed.)   *Further Memoirs of the Whig Party, 1807-1821.* By Henry Richard Vassall, Third Lord Holland. (Murray. 1905.)

STEUART, F. (ed.)   *The Last Journals of Horace Walpole.* (John Lane. The Bodley Head. 1910.)

STEVENSON, Lionel   *The Wild Irish Girl. The Life of Sidney Owenson, Lady Morgan, 1776-1859.* (Chapman & Hall. 1936.)

STIRLING, A. M. W. (ed.)   *The Letter-Bag of Lady Louisa Spencer-Stanhope.* (John Lane: the Bodley Head. 1913.)

STODDARD, R. H. (ed.)   *Personal Reminiscences by O'Keefe, Kelly, and Taylor* (N.Y. Scribner, Armstrong. 1875.)
Personal Reminiscences by Cornelia Knight and Thomas Raikes. (N.Y. Scribner, Armstrong. 1875.)

STROUD, Dorothy   *Henry Holland.* (Art & Technics. 1950.)

STUART, D. M.   *Dearest Bess.* The Life and Times of Lady Elizabeth Foster, afterwards Duchess of Devonshire, from her Unpublished Journals and Correspondence. (Methuen. 1955.)

SUDLEY, Lord (tr. and ed.)   *The Lieven-Palmerston Correspondence, 1828-1856.* (Murray. 1943.)

SUMMERSON, John   *John Nash. Architect to King George IV.* (Allen & Unwin, 1935.)

TAYLOR, Tom   *Life of B. R. Haydon, historical painter.* (Longman. 1853.)

TEMPERLEY, Harold (ed.)   *The Unpublished Diary and Political Sketches of Princess Lieven.* (Cape. 1925.)

TERRY, Charles Sanford   *John Christian Bach.* (O.U.P. 1929.)

THACKERAY, W. M.   *The Four Georges.* (Smith, Elder. 1861.)

THURLOW, Edward Hovell, Lord Thurlow   *Carmen Britanicum.* (White, Cochrane. 1814.)

TIBBLE, J. W. and Anne (ed.)   *The Letters of John Clare.* (Routledge. 1951.)

TOYE, Francis *Rossini*. (Arthur Barker. 1954.)

TREVELYAN, G. O. *The Life and Letters of Lord Macaulay*. (Leipzig. Tauchnitz. 1876.)

VERNON, Edward (Archbishop of York) *A Sermon preached at the Coronation of King George IV*. (Rivington. 1821.)

WHEATLEY, Henry B. (ed.) *The Historical and Posthumous Memoirs of Sir Nathaniel William Wraxall, 1772-1784*. (Bickers. 1884.)

WHITLEY, William T. *Artists and their Friends in England, 1700-1799*. (Medici Society. 1928.)
Art in England, 1821-1837. (Cambridge. Cambridge University Press. 1930.)
Thomas Gainsborough. (Smith, Elder. 1915.)

WILLIAMS, D. E. *The Life and Correspondence of Sir Thomas Lawrence*. (Colburn. 1831.)

WILLIAMSON, G. C. *Richard Cosway, R.A., and his Wife and Pupils*. (Bell. 1897.)

WOOD, Henry Trueman *A History of the Royal Society of Arts*. (Murray. 1913.)

WYNDHAM, Hon. Mrs. H. (ed.) *Correspondence of Sarah Spencer, Lady Lyttelton, 1787-1870*. (Murray. 1912.)

Index